D1571581

ABOUT THE AUTHORS

Eskimos were a familiar sight to Paul Thiry who was born in Nome, Alaska, during the heyday of the Gold Rush. As a child he watched them in the springtime as they beached their laden umiaks on the low sloping beach paralleling Front Street, Nome's main thoroughfare at the time.

These Eskimos came out of curiosity but principally to trade or sell pelts, ivory and other items in exchange for guns, ammunition and the hundred and one things possessed by these newcomers, articles which would make the life of the Eskimo easier. This was a transition period for him, it was a time of cultural exchange as well as a commercial one.

Young Paul well remembered the visiting Eskimos, for in spite of their jovial, friendly attitude there was a wildness about them that was hard to forget or ignore.

With them they brought walrus tusk, cribbage boards, ivory carvings of animals, baskets woven of baleen and grass. All these were of great interest to the people of the community who collected them as souvenirs and remembrances of an awesome experience in life encountered by few in the far off outside world.

All these memories remained with Paul Thiry, when as architect for the Seattle Historical Society, he designed the initial Seattle Museum of History & Industry and saw a collection of Alaskan artifacts on loan from the Smithsonian Institution which he arranged for the opening exhibition of the Museum.

Mrs. Thiry assisted in the preparation of this first exhibit. Her interest was excited by the experience and she and her husband became enthusiastic collectors of Eskimo artifacts, not as anthropologists or ethnologists but because of their admiration of the basic beauty of artifacts designed for use, beautiful in structure, color and texture; art in its most meaningful form.

Together they have gathered and produced the material for this book with the collaboration of Hugh Stratford, photographer.

Paul Thiry is a practicing architect. He graduated from the University of Washington, holds a Diploma from the Ecole des Beaux Arts, Fontainebleau, France and has been honored by a Doctorate in Fine Arts from Saint Martins College.

Mrs. Thiry (Mary Thomas) holds a Bachelor Degree in Philosophy and has for many years been interested in music and the fine arts generally. She and her husband have traveled world over on many occasions.

Hugh N. Stratford was born and reared in Los Angeles, California. He joined the United States Navy in June 1941 and served for six years in the Pacific Theater. During his enlistment in the service Mr. Stratford became interested in photography and after the war enrolled in the Los Angeles Art Center School, from which he graduated in 1953.

Mr. Stratford has been a free lance photographer gaining an outstanding reputation for his architectural, general interest and travel subjects which appear regularly in journals, magazines and periodicals.

Eskimo Artifacts Designed for Use

THE DUST JACKET shows a fragment of Eskimo wearing apparel made of tanned salmon skins sewn together with fine sinew. Bleached white deer hide is appliqued in designs over inserts of brown deer hide; the figures are sewn in black cotton thread. Small cuts have been made in the white surfaces to expose a brown body on each small figure. (Entire piece is reproduced on page 3.)

Eskimo Artifacts

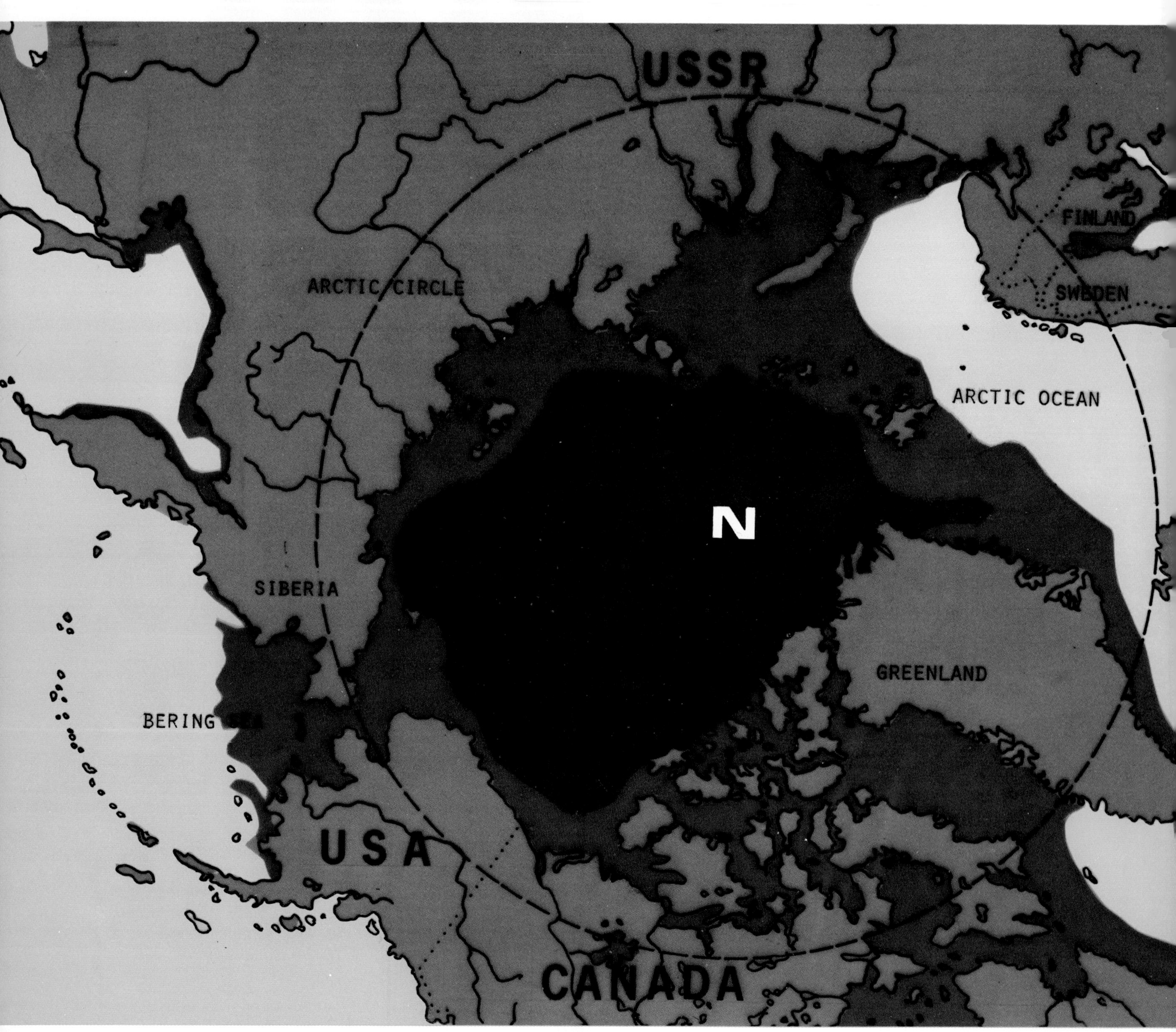

Designed for Use

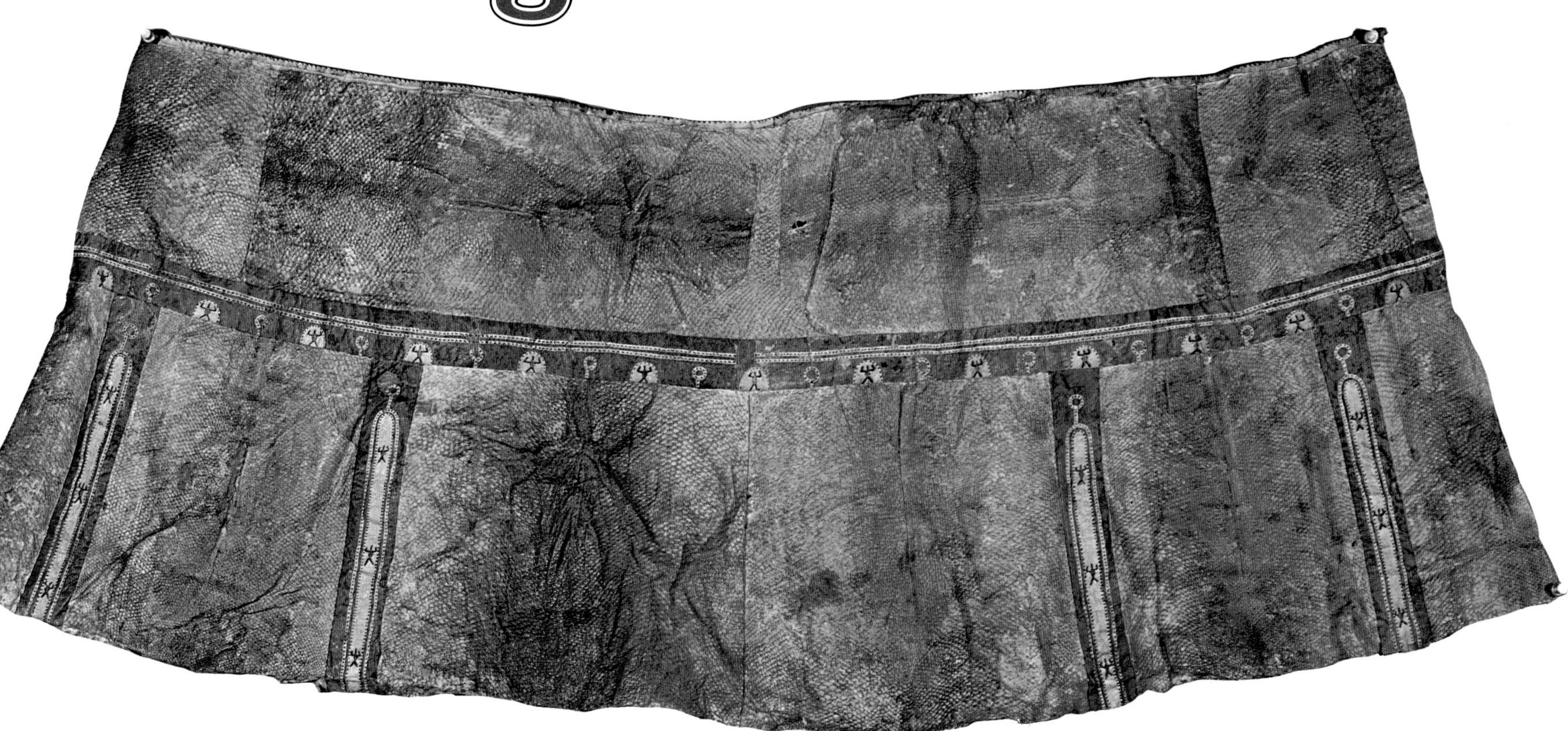

Paul and Mary Thiry

A SALISBURY PRESS BOOK
by

Superior PUBLISHING COMPANY, SEATTLE

Library of Congress Card Number 77-14553

Library of Congress Cataloging in Publication Data

Thiry, Mary.
Eskimo artifacts.

Includes index.

1. Eskimos — Art — Pictorial works.
2. Eskimos — Implements — Pictorial works.
I. Thiry, Paul, 1904-joint author. II. Stratford, Hugh N. III. Title.
E99.E7T45 970'.004'97 77-14553
ISBN 0-87564-016-8

FIRST EDITION

The objects illustrated in this volume are from the Collections of Mr. and Mrs. Paul Thiry of Seattle, Washington, and their sons Paul, Jr., and Pierre. They were photographed and prepared for Publication and Exhibition under the auspices of the Thiry Foundation: An organization established for the extension of knowledge with emphasis on the presentation of the Primitive Arts.

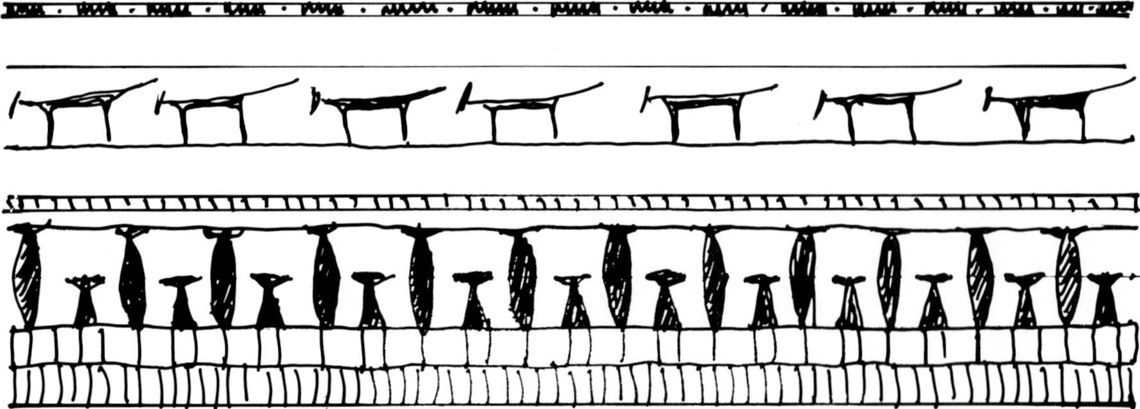

PRINTED IN THE UNITED STATES OF AMERICA

FOREWORD

The contents of this book illustrate the artifacts of the Eskimo, that man who for centuries has inhabited the shores of the Arctic Seas and the frozen hinterlands of the North. For the purpose of our identification the term Eskimo includes the natives of the Aleutian Peninsula and Islands.

The Eskimo, probably the most durable and enduring of all humans, has a history which predates Christianity by several thousand years. His origin is shrouded in mystery and speculation. Maybe he crossed the Bering Straits from Siberia for at one time the Siberian and Alaskan shores were contiguous; maybe he migrated overland from the North American Continent; maybe the first Eskimo came from Northeastern Europe. His Asiatic origin is favored, however, but ethnologically speaking he is Eskimo and has been these many centuries, wandering the vast, barren lands of the Arctic regions, always seeking food from the seas, over the ice caps and floes, or extracting such bounties as the rolling and boundless tundra provides, migrating with the season, moving with the hunting and fishing opportunities which sustain his life.

Now in total night and within periods of twilight or perpetual sunlight, the Eskimo has endured unbelievable hardship and has survived. No man can boast a hardier ancestry, all this unfortunately, before explorers from other lands intruded with different outlooks and possessing armaments and cultural habits of a more sophisticated but less rugged society.

The Eskimo seasoned by his environment and his nomadic existence called for little but life's essentials. Trade and barter were known to him, but he traveled light and as unfettered as possible out of necessity. A system of trade was not an overriding or important ingredient of his survival.

His was a land of seemingly ceaseless gales, of winds, wintered in snow and ice, and summered in dust in one place, but mired in wet lands in another. His was a land of shadowless sun on icepacked surfaces, of uncontrollable glare over seas and frozen wastes. His was a land of majestic hardship, of low undulating hills snow-encrusted during the darkness of winter, moss-covered and infested by mosquito hordes, which blackened the sky during the endless light of the summer sun. His was a land of brutal fogs and mists shrouding the earth and enclosing all creatures within their fold.

Within and without these stretches of ice and tundra, the Eskimo lived and wandered, trailing the once abundant seal and walrus, harpooning the whale, spearing fish and tensioning his bow towards the caribou. His was a survival hunt. He lived as man creature among the hunted. He too was prey to polar bears and wolves. He had to conjure with the wiles of prowling creatures, the white furred fox and others.

Often he faced starvation when Natures bounties were removed from him by blizzards and storms, when the ice holes of Arctic seals were covered by snow and it seemed all life had disappeared into a white nothingness. He experienced joy when springtime came and his world reawakened as if from sleep, game became plentiful and the meadows and the low lying hills blossomed with moss, lichen, grasses and edible berries. With summer came longer periods of daylight and time to reorganize thoughts and to prepare for the continuance of the somewhat predictable seasons and the migrations of caribou and other creatures of vital interest to him. Now was the time to advantage himself of available game, to acquire skins and hides for clothing and other paraphernalia. Now was the time to look to securing shelter against the long cold darkness of winter. Now was a time for community meeting and dancing before parting company to continue the search for sustenance.

Explorers, exploiters, settlers, and tourists have brought a new way of life to the North Country, a life fraught with complexities coupled with spiritual and physical opportunities of other worlds.

The Eskimo is snared in a modern trap where environmental problems appear to be all white or all black, much as the polar solstice which for a period in summer is all day and in winter all night. The Eskimo cannot retain the twilight, for it, like the seasons, passes into a statement of attitude. As necessity and the pressures for survival disappear, so too the Eskimo, who defiantly lived with the spirits of the lower and upper regions and the great trackless wastes changes caste. He can no longer be the Eskimo of his father's breed for he is subject to ever developing change.

There is no reason to speculate for indeed the Eskimo of history will soon be gone to a spirit land where surely "all men are brothers" and where the caribou and the salmon abound. Only his artifacts provide his earthly testimony.

6

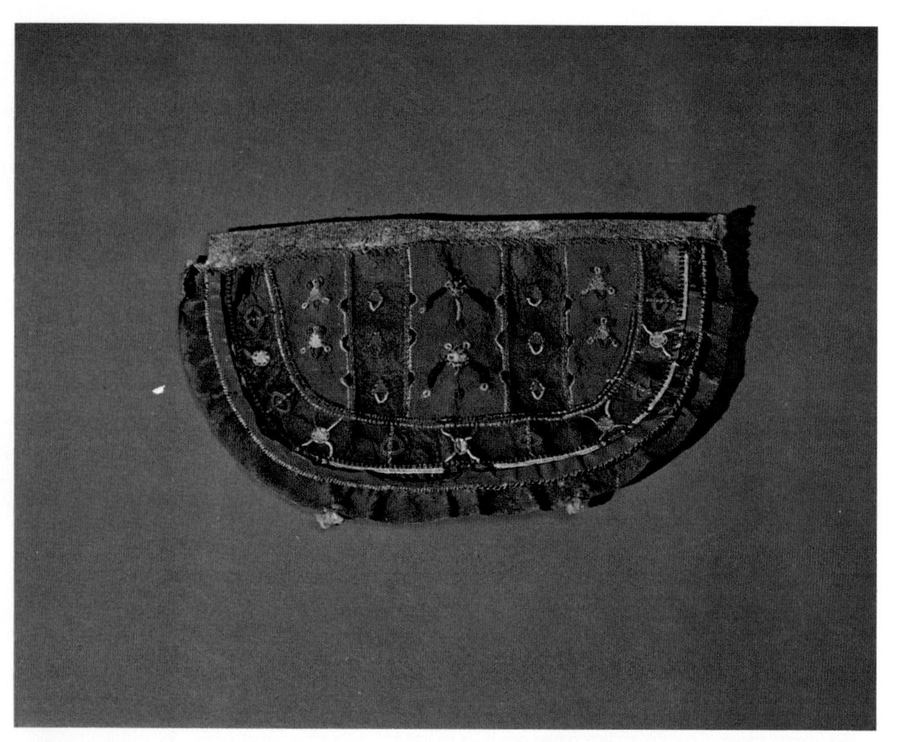

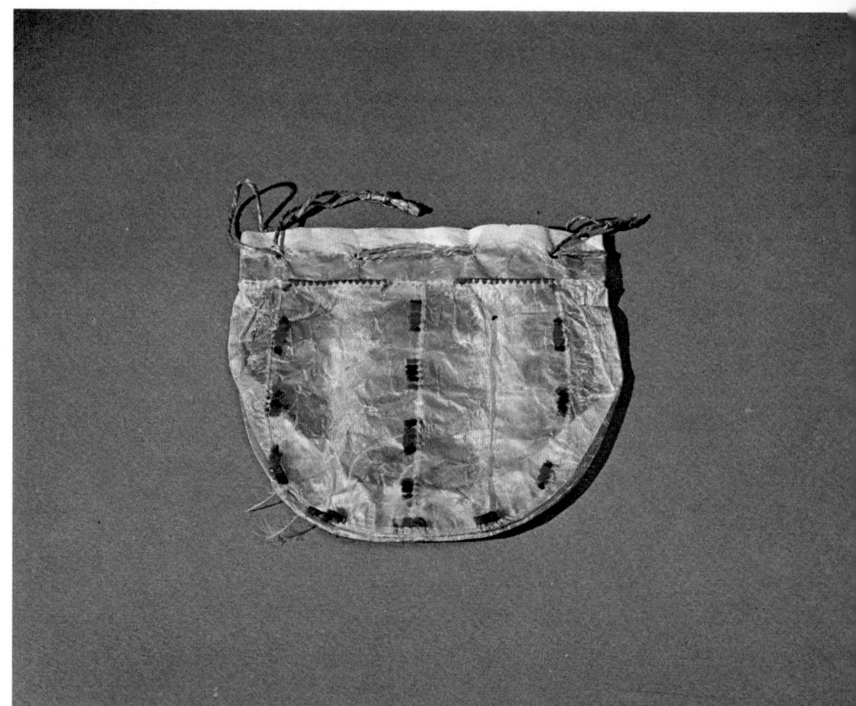

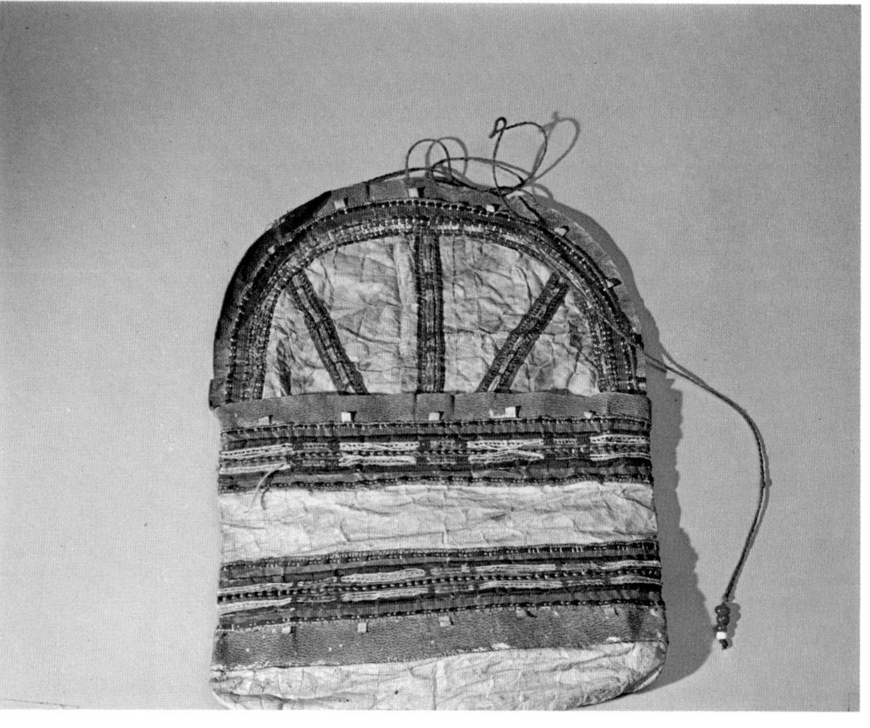

The purpose of this book is to portray the handicrafts of the Eskimo. Not from an archaeological or ethnological standpoint but from the viewpoint of Eskimo artifacts as art. Art in its basic form.

Its purpose is to catalog and identify, in a general way, characteristic objects commonly used by the traditional Eskimo prior to the acquisition of firearms, objects which for the most part are rapidly disappearing through decay or thoughtless handling.

Because the subject matter has a limited range of accessibility, it was thought important to introduce the reader to a visual acquaintance with Eskimo artifacts without requiring extensive research on his part, thereby extending his knowledge generally, and his vocabulary in primitive art especially. To possess an ability to recognize and to identify works of various cultures, is to broaden ones range of human knowledge and perspective.

In general, all artifacts shown date prior to the 20th Century and in a large part, are prehistoric. Designs are basic to man and his environment and are achieved through the use of animal, fish and bird parts — bone, ivory, fur, and skin, others are fabricated from stone, wood, and metal. Artifacts are embellished with engraving, stitchery, and feathers, others are carved or woven with baleen and grasses from the tundra.

The artifacts are photographic illustrations in their actual size giving a true portrayal to the viewer. The artifacts illustrated are for the most part small in scale, light in weight and easily transportable, a feature essential to a nomadic type people often many miles away from their central base in pursuit of game.

In the preparation of this book it was recognized some descriptive material was essential as an explanation of the purpose and use of certain artifacts. However, it was equally recognized that the Eskimo often mended broken objects with parts of others, especially when on an expedition. Often small bone or ivory pieces played dual or multi-use purposes. On occasion, items made for a singular use found their way into costume or personal embellishment, consequently descriptions may be subject to other interpretations, and a broad view must be taken in the interests of absolute accuracy.

Interest in the objects illustrated should lead those specifically inclined to refer to books and documents of a more academic nature, prepared by specializing scholars, for explanations of particular periods, origins, styles and places.

Artifacts such as illustrated here, are becoming difficult to acquire and for the most part are only to be seen by the public in a few scattered museums throughout the world. For this reason it was thought appropriate to publish a book which at bookstores or on the shelves of libraries would be available to all.

This book, then, is to introduce the subject of Eskimo artifacts and their use to people who may not otherwise be afforded an opportunity to see or possess them. Here they have the next best thing, possession by viewing, ownership of the printed page.

The book is divided into two parts:

A. Artifacts associated with the household, fabrication of footwear, clothing and objects of personal use, adornment and recreation.

B. Artifacts associated with survival and the production of shelter, sleds, boats, fishing and hunting gear and various associated implements.

SURVIVAL

Survival is probably the key word to man's existence. To say the word SURVIVAL (to exist) provides a common denominator for all men, is not to exaggerate the fact.

Manners and methods of achieving survival vary with time and place.

To so-called civilized man, the subject, though present, is often lost in daily preoccupation and considered marginally because of built-in protections. But to primitive man survival was a concern always pertinent, close at hand and to be constantly contended with. His, for the most part, was a dangerous life. To him survival was not a frivolous concept, it was basic and limited to the essentials of food, clothing, shelter against the elements and implements for probing the earth, for fishing, hunting, self protection or offensive/defensive action against wild beasts and often other men. To the Eskimo, survival meant all of these things, but under rigidly restricted and dictated conditions. Unlike peoples of more moderate climates — the Eskimo's existence was preluded by the necessity for a continuous confrontation with Nature.

The Eskimo depended upon a cooperative system with his environment, because Nature itself was too antagonistic to overcome. Domination by him could only be an aspiration not an ambition under the conditions imposed.

Practically all of the Eskimo's requirements for food, shelter, clothing and implements depended upon his ability as a fisherman and hunter. His source of supply depended almost entirely on his conquest of other living creatures. Cultivation and tilling the soil was not a part of his life style.

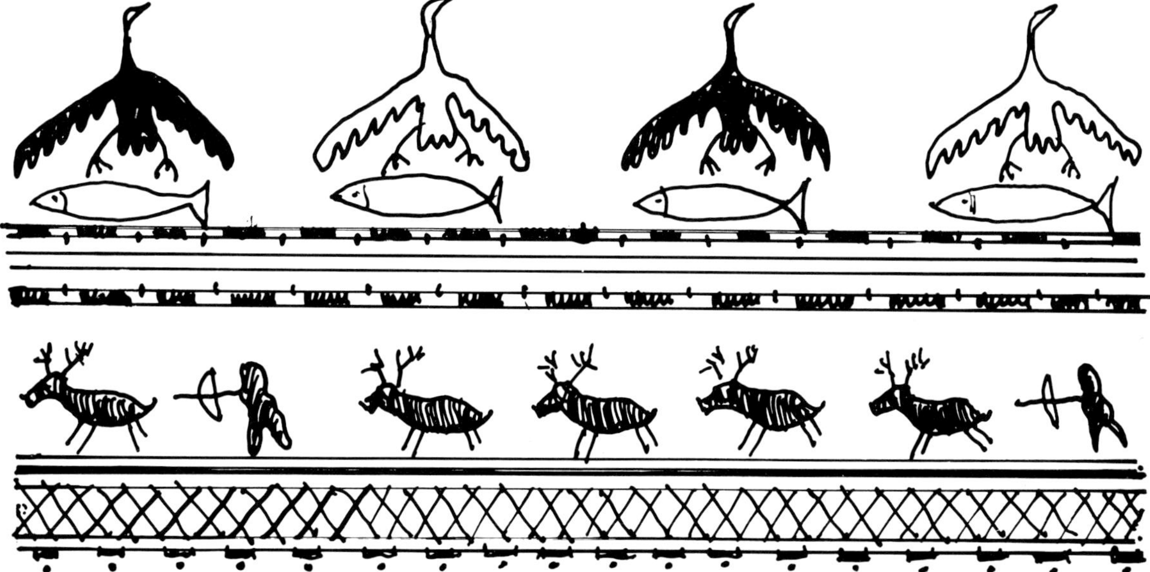

HUNTING AND FISHING

Most mammals excepting inland caribou, were hunted near at hand or in the seas. Fishing was mainly at the mouth of rivers and streams which cross the Arctic and Bering Sea areas.

Winter months presented periods of great difficulty when snaring seals and fishing was necessarily through the thick ice which covered the seas, lagoons and rivers.

The results of hunting and fishing not only provided food in general but also had the residual effect of supplying most of the materials which were so essential to the Eskimos' existence and protection such as skins and hides, ivory, bone, oil and other items from which he made wearing apparel, fabricated tools, shelter, boats, sleds and other implements.

The Eskimo did not wantonly hunt or fish but did so to serve his needs.

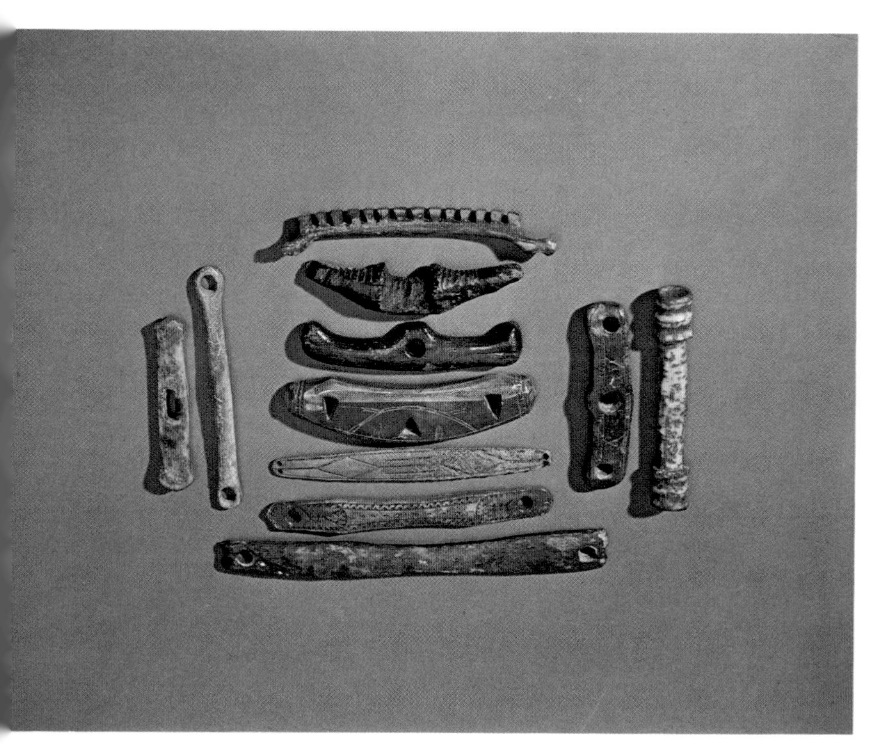

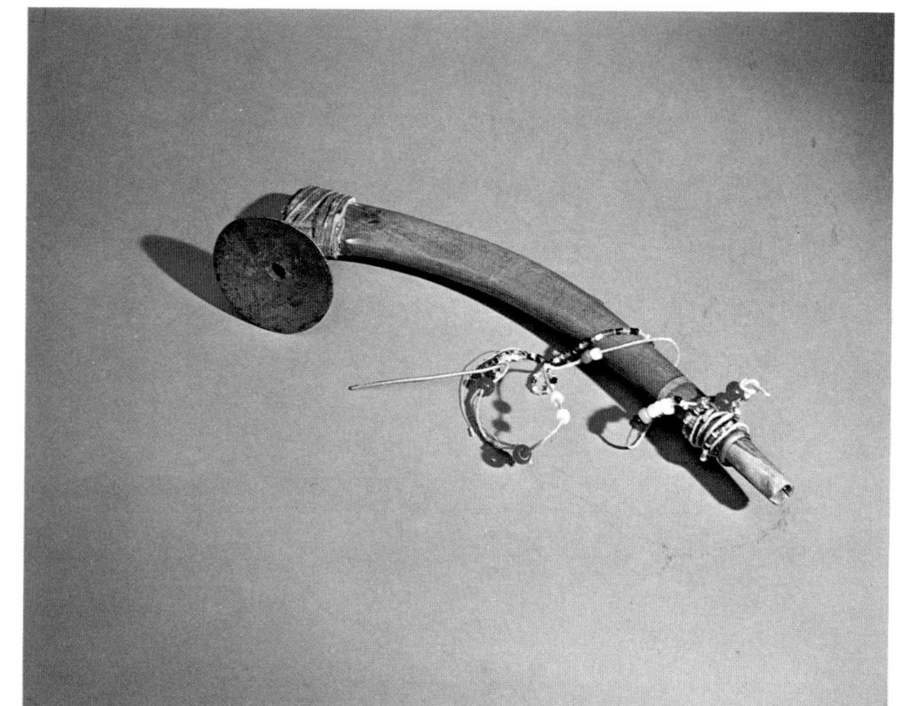

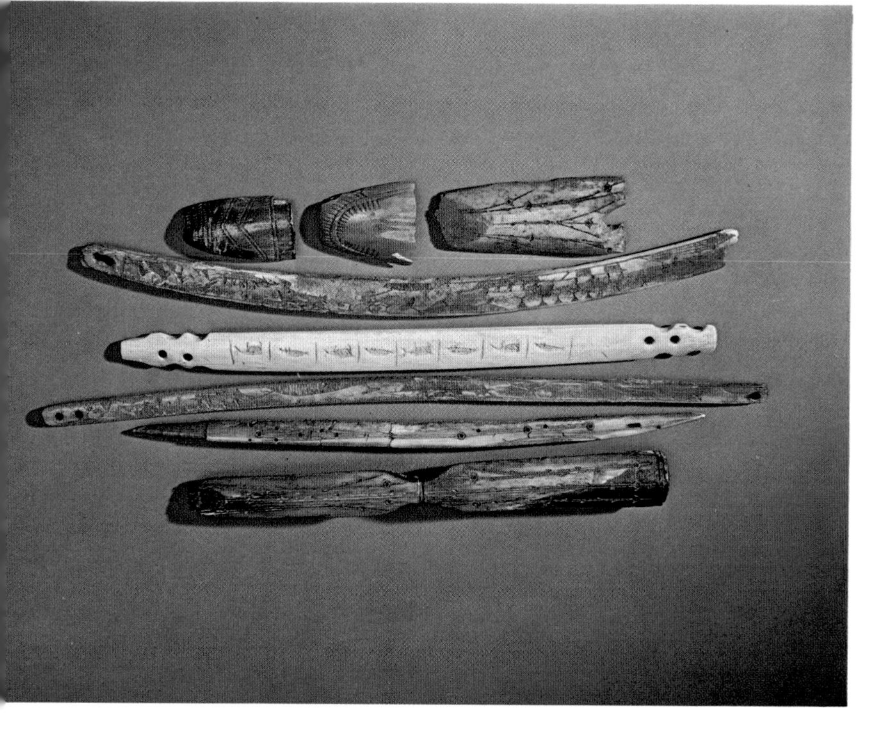

NATURAL RESOURCES

MAMMALS

From large sea mammals such as seals, walrus and whales and land animals such as caribou, muskox, and bear were obtained the Eskimo's greatest riches, hides, skins, ivory, tusks, horns, oils, blubber and other materials. For instance caribou antlers were widely used for tool making, whale bones for shelter framings, baleen for fishing lines and snares.

Smaller animals such as hares, beaver, otter and more diminutive creatures also contributed furs and skins which were often pieced together to make clothing and bags. Tails and bits of fur served as decorative features for parkas, boots and a great variety of items.

FISH

From large fish which inhabit Polar waters, such as salmon, the Eskimos obtained skins for waterproof clothing, boots, bags and wrappings. These skins were meticulously sewn together and often decorated with bits of fur or feathers.

BIRDS

Land and waterfowl in great numbers call the Arctic regions their home. Here they nest and from here they migrate usually via the Isthmus, the natural bird hunting ground of the Eskimo.

Birds contributed their plumage, skins, beaks, talons and bones for decorative features found on Eskimo clothing, boots and bags.

Bird parts play a lesser role in Eskimo implement making, but the bones of some birds, for instance, are hollow and were used for snuff and needle cases.

Mammals, fish and birds were important in varying degrees to the Eskimo but along with them were natural earthen substances which, though accessible only for a short period of the year, were in a sense the finishing constituents of most artifacts.

VEGETATION

From grasses, mosses, roots and lichen, exposed during the summer months, was obtained the raw material for baskets, bags, containers and mats.

Wood such as alder, willow, birch, spruce and pine, while for the most part growing inland, were washed into the sea and in the form of driftwood were retrieved by the Eskimo.

Wood was shaped in the form of boxes, containers, bowls and dishes, shafts for harpoons, spears and arrows, as well as for constructions of shelter, boats, sleds and general implements.

STONE

Hard stone, such as various types of jade, played an important part in the fabrication of cutting edges for tools and other devices.

Softer stone, more adaptable to chiselling, was often converted into basins for lamps, stoves and utensils.

POTTERY

A departure to the Eskimo's adoption of purely natural elements in the making of paraphernalia and devices came in the manufacture of pottery. Containers were molded for household use from combinations of clay, earth, blood and hair. After seasoning these fashioned pieces became stonelike in appearance and hardness.

PAINT

In addition to pottery another significant and creative feature of Eskimo artistry resolved itself around pigment and mineral colorings which were used to embellish helmets, masks, wooden boxes and surfaces of spear shafts and household articles such as dishes and wooden spoons. Colors were generally as follows: White — white clay; Red — bark of alder soaked in urine; Yellow — pigment from ochre/oxide of iron; Black — charcoal mixed with blood; Green — copper oxide. These precious ingredients were sparingly used and were kept in small boxes made especially for this purpose.

HABITATION

In most cases, the Eskimo headquartered in fixed groups numbering from a few to many families in a community. His place of habitation was of no particular aesthetic quality. His principal objective was protection against the weather, particularly shelter against the winter winds and cold.

This he accomplished by seemingly going underground, building structures on which he could pile dirt and sod and which in turn were in season, covered with snow and ice. His house was usually approached by a semi-tunnel trenched in the frozen earth. His accommodations were minimal, a simple room sometimes with utility appendages added to it. The winter house was not generally habitable in warmer months when the ice and ground thawed and flooded its interior.

Often a room of 10 × 14 feet accommodated more than one family.

The construction of a habitation varied with regions. In traditional times, it was comparatively simple, its covering, usually of skins and hides, rigged over a system of staves and poles, sometimes of whale ribs and jaw bones, semi-buried, always rigid enough to carry the winter snow. Later houses meeting the same need specifications were constructed of driftwood or of planks retrieved from wrecked ships. Shapes and the clustering of appendages varied.

But the Eskimo way of life required a nomadic spirit. He was away in pursuit of food a great part of the time, especially when game was migrating. At these times, when traveling, he contrived tent-like structures of poles and skins which were easily erected and disassembled and packed on his sled.

During the winter season when snow covered the ground and particularly in the far Arctic, a snow dwelling (igloo) was built. This was a somewhat temporary shelter and proved most useful for emergency use. Most Eskimos of ancient times erected snow houses on one occasion or another especially while in the open on hunting expeditions.

TRANSPORTATION

Hunting and fishing required mobility. The Eskimo, of necessity, had to be where the game was. The quarry, whether fish, bird or mammal, was mobile and migrated with the seasons; so too the Eskimo trailed in serious search and pursuit.

A means of transportation over the snow-covered land and frozen seas was essential to mobility. The Eskimo's answer came in the form of sleds and boats.

Because these modes of transportation were subject to physical handling, lightness of weight was desirable. This was accomplished by lattice frames and coverings of skins and hides laced and tied with sinew.

For individual use, the Eskimo devised a flat bed sled (unia) which he pulled or pushed across country. At times he utilized the pulling power of dogs. These sleds varied in size and were used to transport bulky objects, often the carcass of animals killed in the hunt.

A second type of sled (kamoti) with side railing, was used for transporting families, household goods, camp equipment and clothing.

Often flat-bed sleds were used to transport the Eskimo's boats across frozen ground or ice to the hunting and fishing sites.

These boats were generally of two types: (1) the umiak, a large open boat, usually measuring about thirty feet long, manned by a number of people and used for traveling and whale and walrus and seal hunts. (2) The kayak, an individually propelled canoe-like craft used for quick transportation from place to place and for fishing and hunting as the occasion warranted.

At times, when at sea, the small hauler sled was hoisted on the kayak in a sort of reciprocal arrangement of land haul, sea haul. Often the Eskimo preferred to carry his kayak overland, grasping the cockpit with one hand and bracing it against his body, bow forward.

Transportation of implements, such as spears and fishing gear, was a complementary process to both sleds and boats.

14

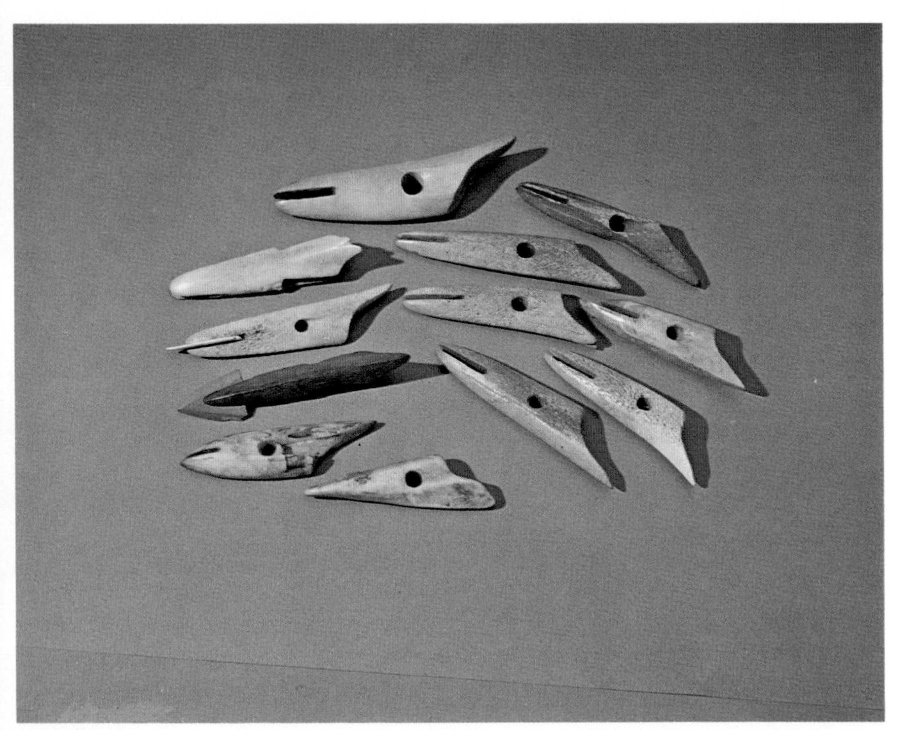

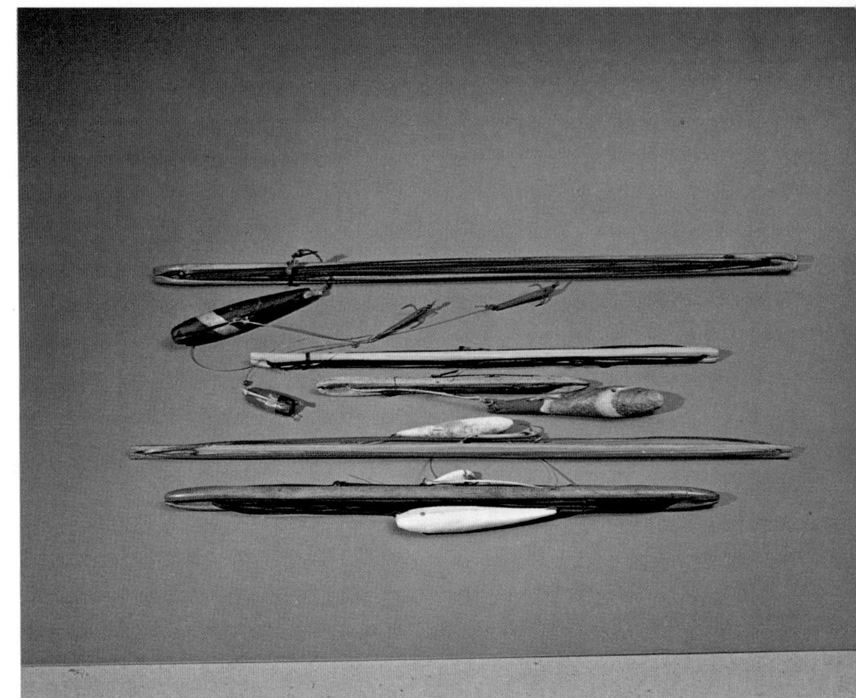

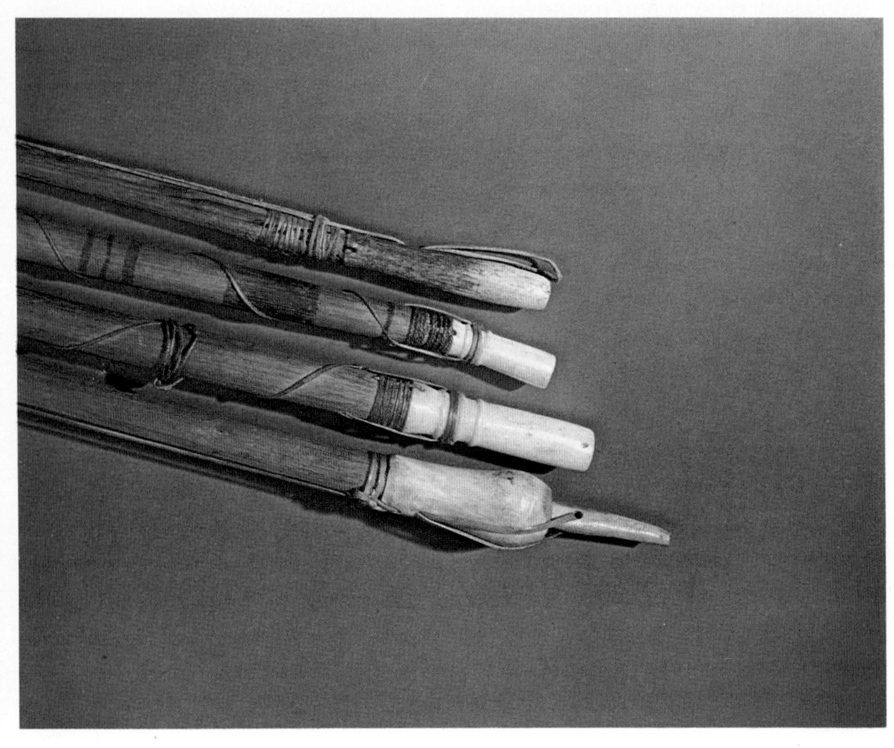

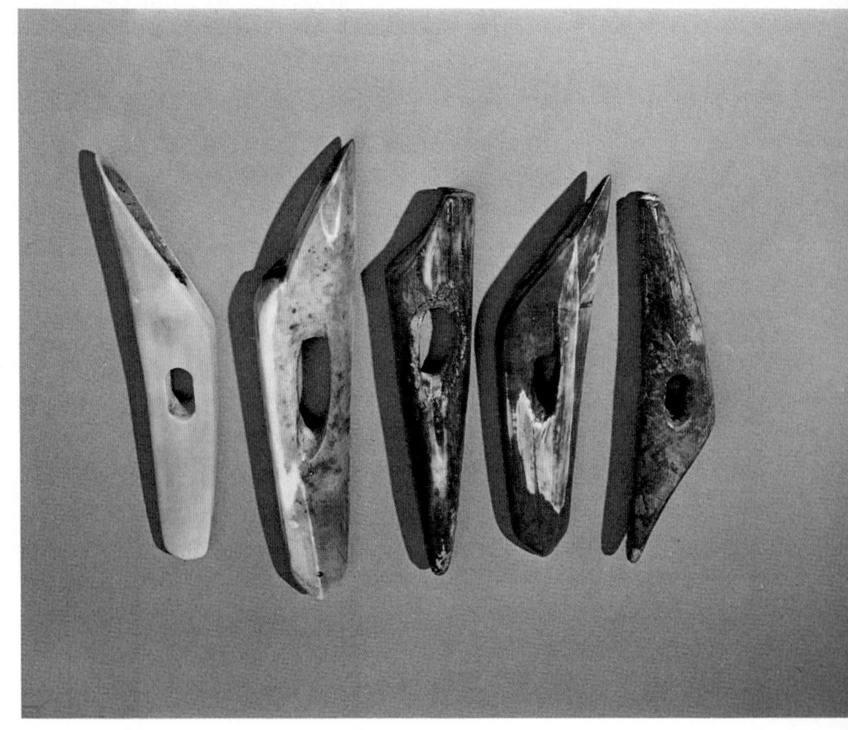

BOOK I

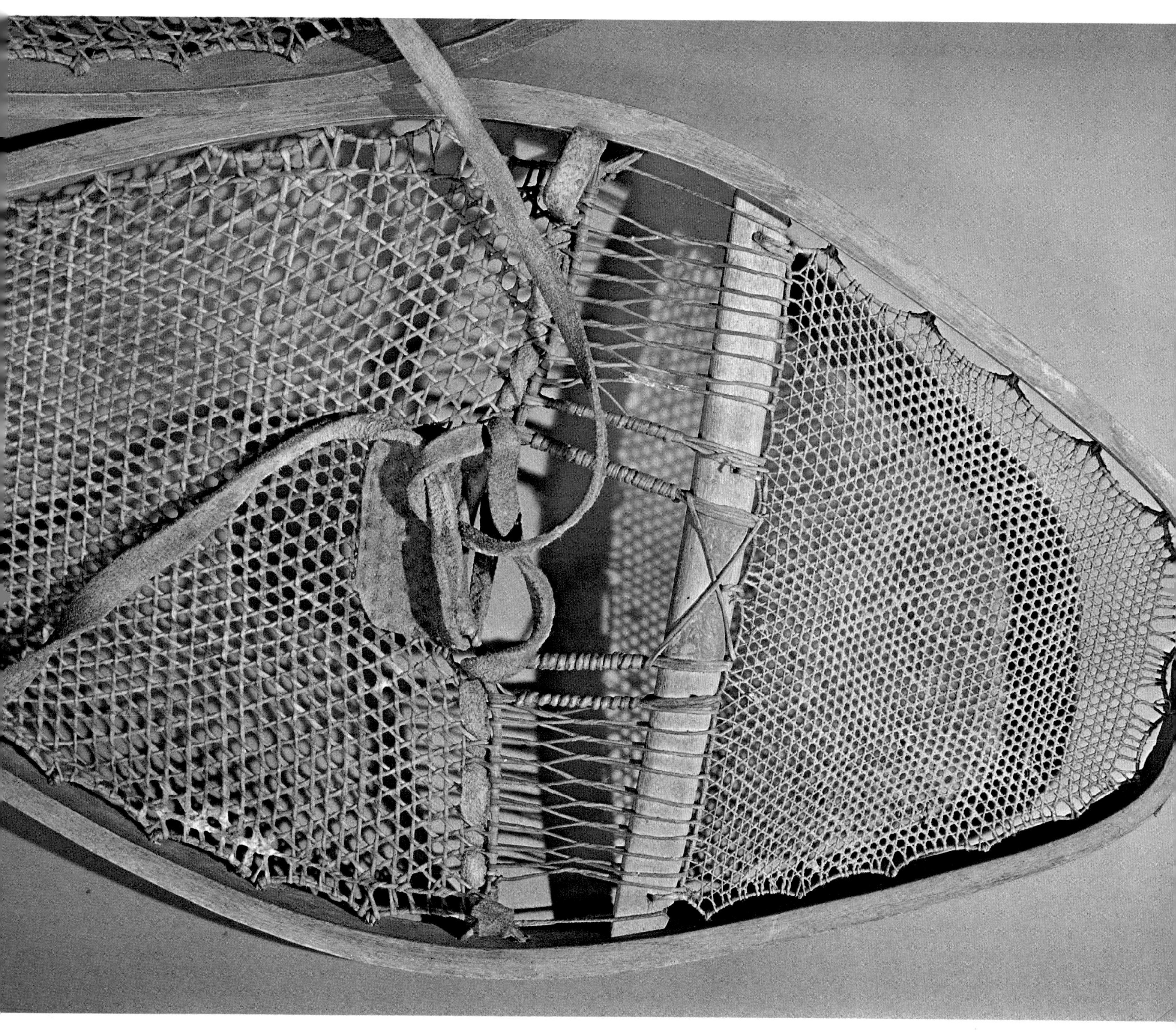

WALRUS TUSKS

The raw material for many implements of Eskimo life. The upper tusk was buried for many years and is known as old ivory because water and minerals leaching through the soil and ice over extended periods of time varied its color from pale yellow to dark brown and black.

BALEEN

Baleen extracted from the mouth of the whale was of great importance to the Eskimo and had many uses such as, lines for fishing and basket making. Baleen is tough, lightweight and flexible. Its fibers run parallel to each other which prevents intertwisting.

Blades or plates of Baleen when boiled for considerable time become soft and can be cut into strips and bent into shapes. Heavier bones from the body of the whale also served many purposes in the construction of shelter or in implement making. Whales in general were a source of oil and food.

ALEUTIAN BASKETS

The one to the left is woven with two colors of grass, a light tan twined around a darker shade of brown. The four part design is applied to the surface with red and dark blue wool. The second basket is fabricated in a triangular hemstitch pattern with the grass separated and caught to the next strand. The applied decoration is red wool.

Actual size of baskets portrayed on opposite page showing details of the weaving.

ALEUTIAN BASKET

A twined open work basket decorated with blue and red yarn.

Actual size of basket portrayed on opposite page.

ALEUTIAN TWINED BASKETS

The first basket is a slightly darker shade of grass than the second basket. The decoration consists of a square pattern using red and black wool.

The finer grass used in the second basket accounts for its smaller weave. The triangular design is black and white wool.

ACTUAL SIZE OF BASKETS PORTRAYED ON OPPOSITE PAGE

AN ALEUTIAN TWINED BASKET

Two shades of blue and three shades of rose thread are applied to the basket in stitches opposite to the twining weave.

AN ATTU BASKET

Extremely fine grass is woven with sometimes as many as forty stitches and thirty nine rows to the inch. The weaving resembles linen more than basketry. Baskets such as this one are decorated with silk or cotton threads applied or woven into the basket.

ATTU BASKETS

The one to the left has a more elaborate design but the right hand basket has a finer weave.

A TWINED ATTU BASKET LID

The lid is woven of fine grass and decorated with thread.

AN ATTU POUCH OF VERY FINE WEAVE

The open twining produces a square type of hemstitching which is another variation of the open work seen in the woven strip opposite.

AN ATTU WOVEN STRIP

The use of this piece is not known. The open twining weave resembles triangular hemstitching and is most effective with the plain twining stitch. The grasses used are several including wild rye and barley.

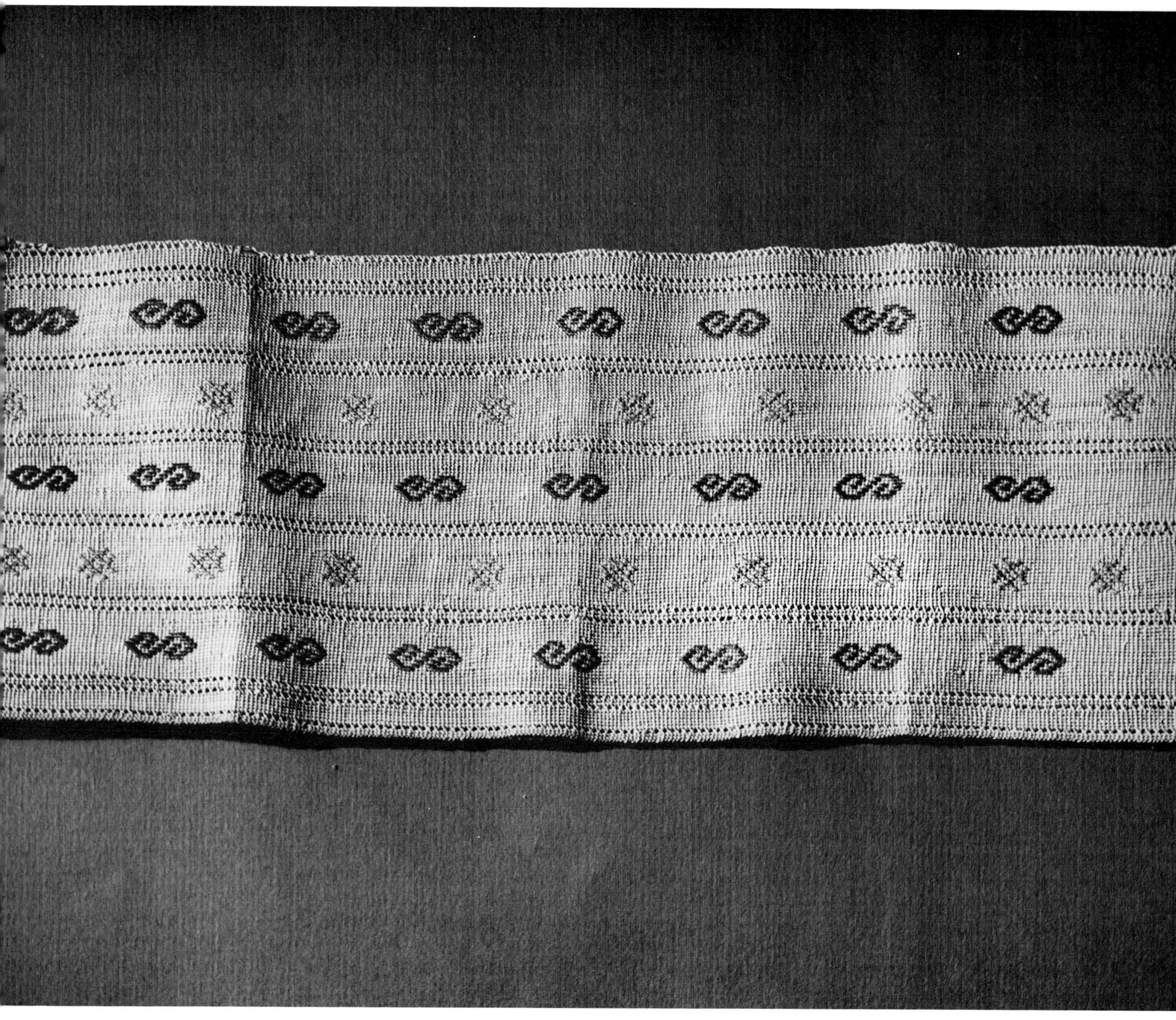

A BALEEN BASKET WITH OPEN TWINING OF WHITE BALEEN

The ivory cover knob depicts a polar bear.

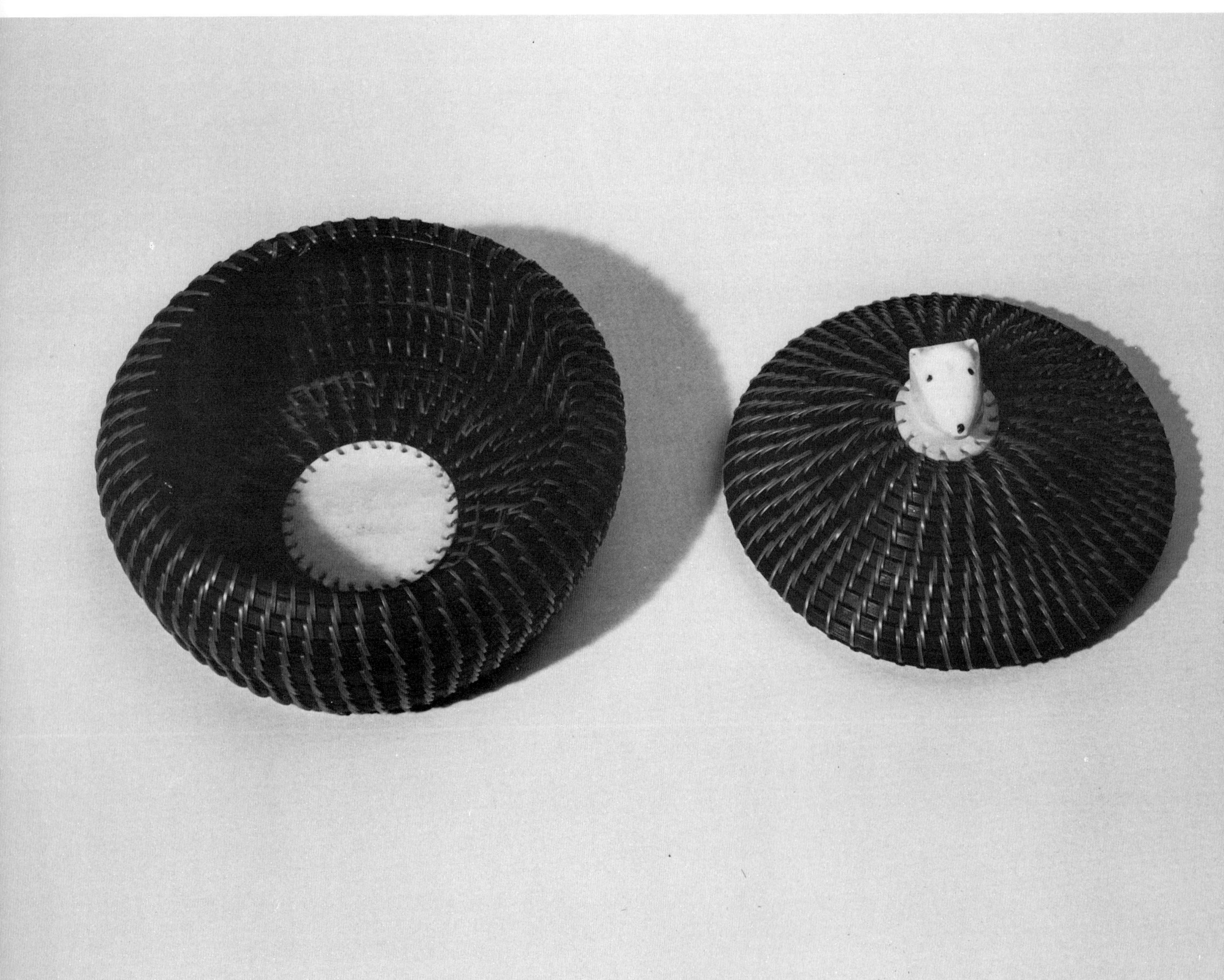

COILED BALEEN BASKET

A fossil ivory knob depicting a seal is woven into the top.

TRINKET BASKET

This basket is fashioned with reindeer and split walrus hide sewn together in strips. The designs are appliqued using dark skin on the lighter background.

The design in the center of the basket shows seals swimming and the tails of whales sounding. A fish trap may be indicated by the undulating line measured off in spaces. The designs on the lid indicate a river with a fish trap.

TRINKET BASKET

Coiled with natural colored and berry stained grass to designate the design. There are fur hairs used in the coils.

ESKIMO COILED BASKETS

The first basket's design is accomplished with colored grass. The second basket's design utilizes strips of seal skin as well as red colored grass which extends around the middle portion. The seal skin decorations are applied not woven into the basket itself.

A COILED ESKIMO BASKET

Decorated with white and black colored twine.

ESKIMO COILED BASKETS

These are made of dried straw like grass and were used for storage of household objects.

COILED GRASS BASKET

There is a decorative line through the center and at the bottom of the basket of darker grass. The knob on the lid is an animal's tooth.

ESKIMO WORK BASKETS

The first has a design sewn into the basket using black cotton twine. The second basket has black cotton thread strands applied around the basket at parallel intervals and seal skin strips threaded through the grass.

Actual size of baskets portrayed on opposite page.

AN ESKIMO COILED GRASS WORK BASKET

This basket is threaded with seal skin strips for decoration. The cover gives a "ginger jar" appearance which appears to be quite oriental.

A FINELY COILED ESKIMO BASKET

Showing the influence of outsiders, namely, the Russians. The decoration is sewn on the basket not woven into it. A close look at the tree bough at the center left will recall the delineation of trees on ivory carvings. The scallop top rim of the basket shows an expertise acquired in basket making.

A WOMAN'S WORK BAG

Use of two colors of skin and decorated seams done with stitching. The embroidery colors are from berry and other dyes. It is interesting to note the very narrow strips of skin appliqued in color varients on the top flap, and the white cord left unstitched on the pocket, and how their use accomplishes a most sophisticated design.

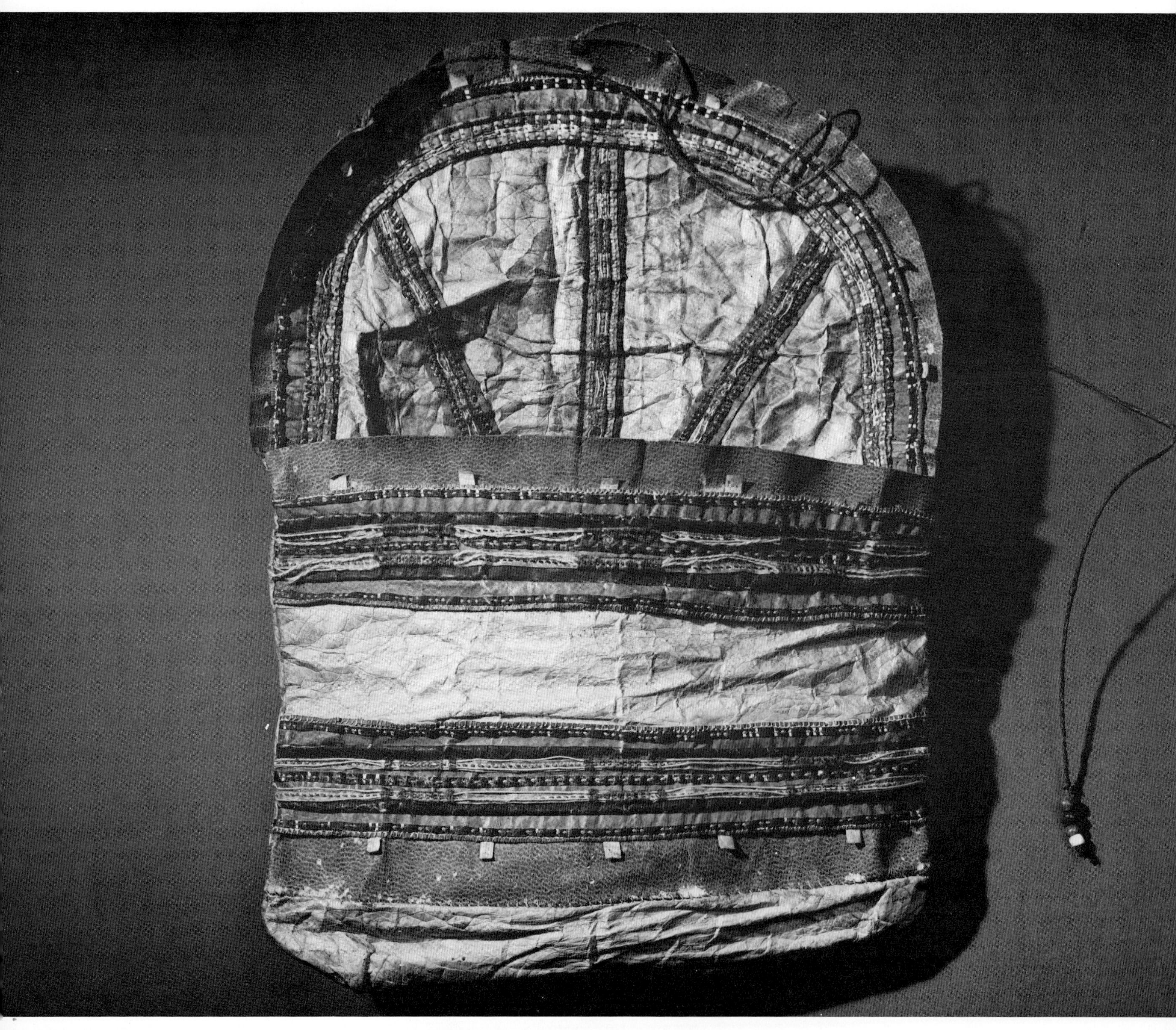

A FRAGMENT OF DECORATED SKIN

Portion of a woman's case or bag in which sewing tools were kept. It is decorated with red, blue, and white bits of skin appliqued and stitched. The designs are in a type of button hole stitch worked in circles and oval shapes. This kind of bag varied in length and contained one or more pockets. When not in use, the bags were rolled up and secured with an attached tie, and fastened with a cross piece thrust through the tie.

A BAG

Made of transparent seal intestine sewn with very fine sinew and decorated with bits of fur and feathers.

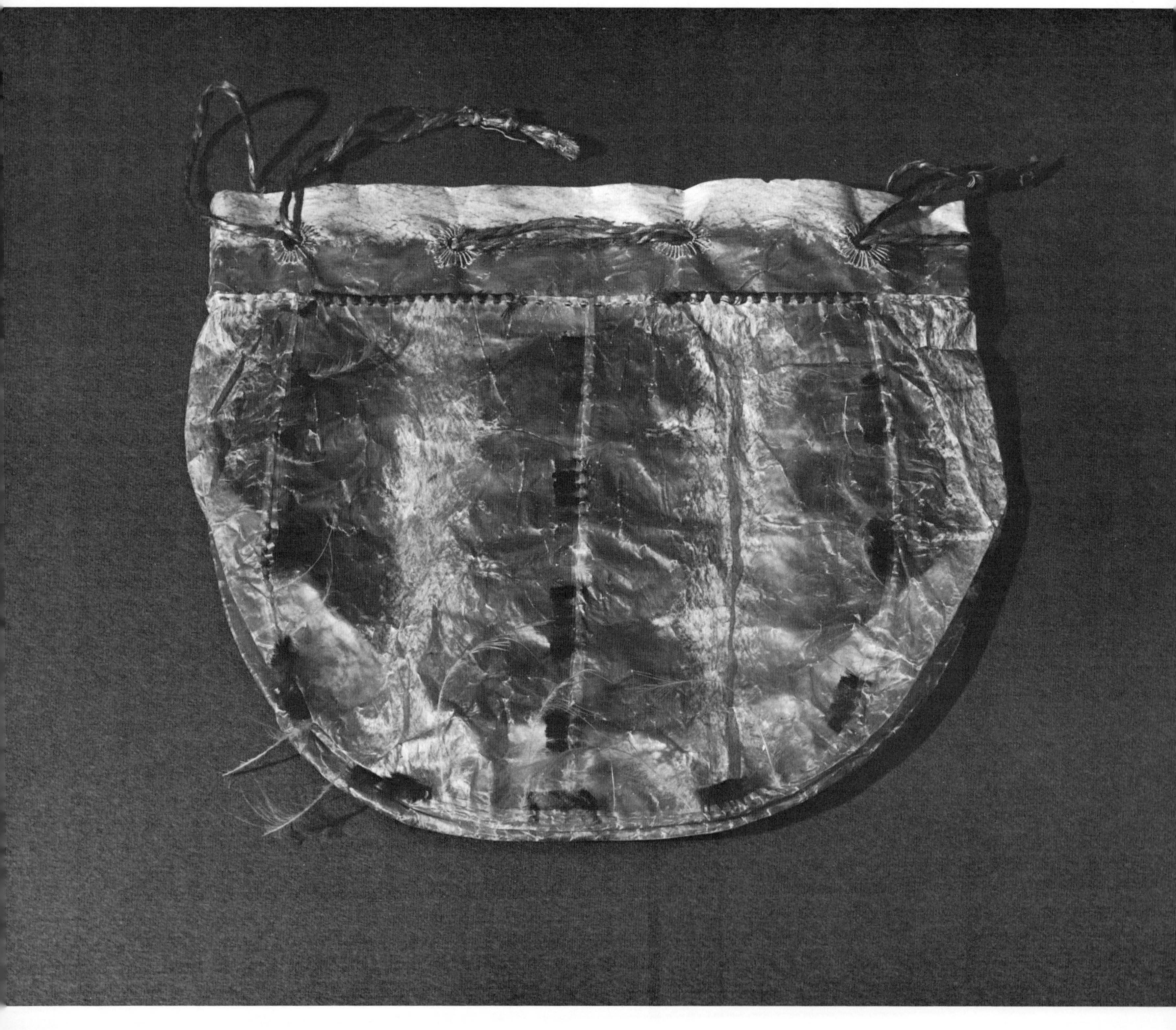

SMALL BAGS OF PIECED TOGETHER HIDE

1. Seal skin and white deer skin are stitched together in a design using fine dyed sinew. The top most piece of this bag is intestine doubled for a draw string channel.
2. This bag made of dark seal skin and deer hide has oval cuts of hide sewn together with sinew in a chain stitch.

A BAG

Made of tanned seal skin and bleached deer hide sewn with black dyed sinew. The circles are appliqued using the same black sinew.

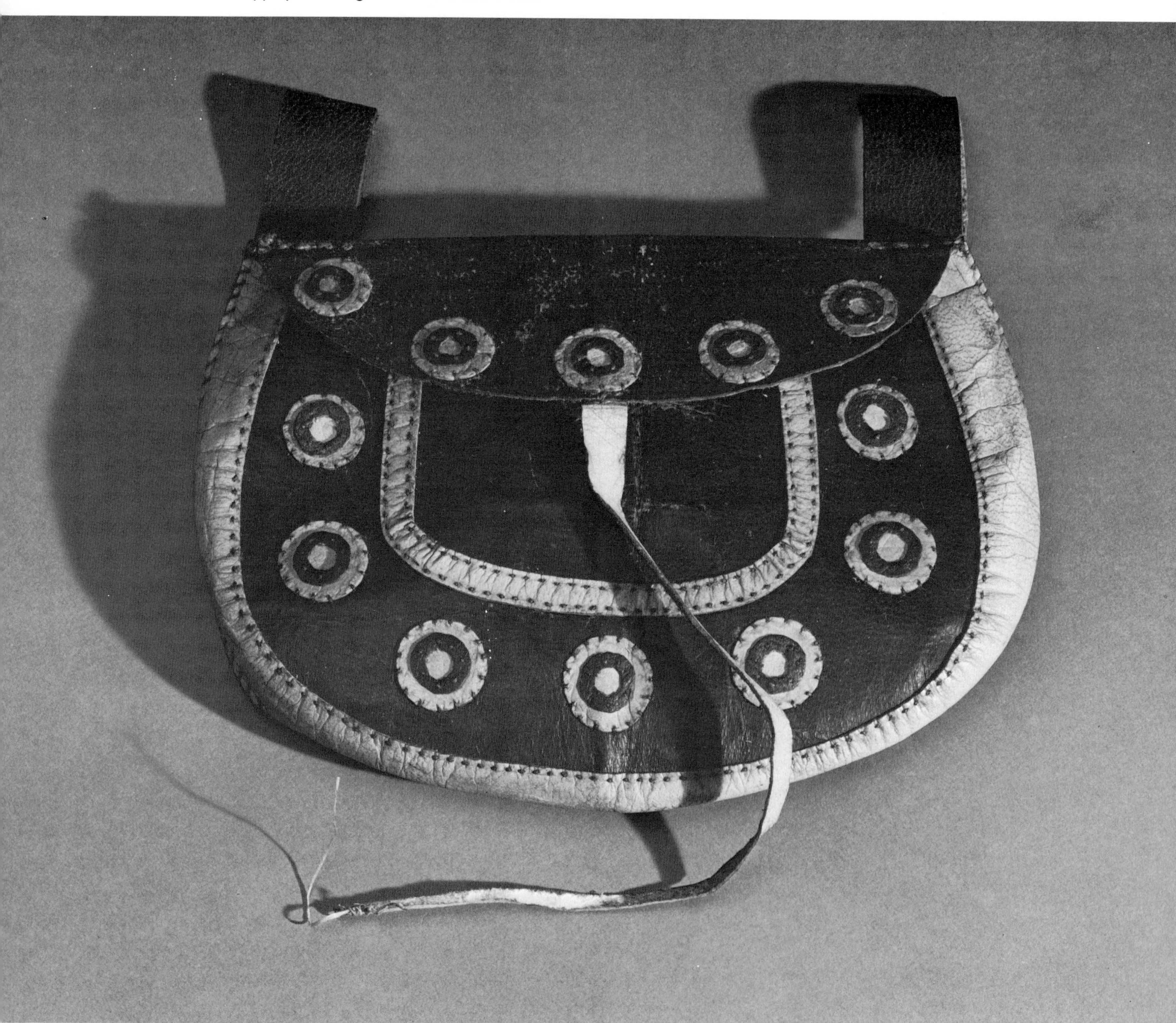

A BAG

Made of bleached and regular deer hide sewn with sinew. The two seal skin flaps are to enable one to wear it on a belt.

A BAG

Of white deer skin and seal skin. This may have been intended for some kind of storage since it is lined with seal intestine making it waterproof. The stitching is done with sinew.

A BAG

Of deer hide and seal skin sewn on a welting of deer hide which emerges at the top as a handle. The welting reinforces the bottom of the bag keeping the contents from breaking through the joined skin.

A BAG

Repaired with canvas probably sometime after 1900. There was nothing left apparently but the cover decorated with sea bird feet and seal skin applique.

A SEAL SKIN BAG

Appliqued with white skin for decoration. The stitching and embroidery is done with fine sinew gathering small bunches of fur over and over to create the design.

A BAG

Made from two feet of water fowl. It is stitched with fine sinew and the top edged in bleached hide with an edging of cloth.

A BAG

Made of sinew netting probably reindeer leg tendon, which is fastened to two strips of seal skin worked to a velvet like finish and sewn together with fine sinew cord. The cotton thread embellishment is a later addition meant to "beautify" the bag. Small strips of marmot fur were attached for decoration.

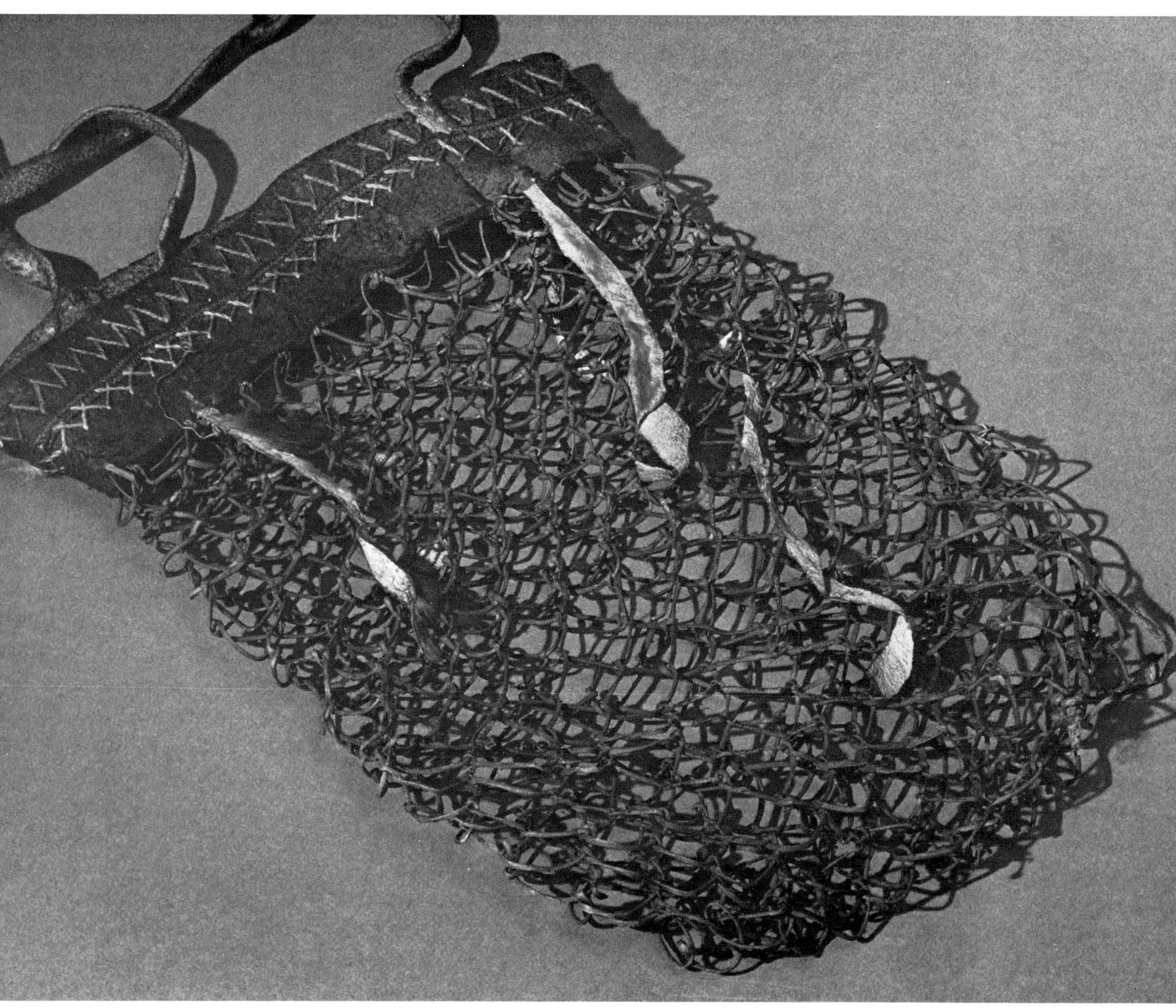

AN OUTER GARMENT

A model of a waterproof garment made from seal intestine. The edges of the sleeves are faced with seal skin providing reinforcement for a drawstring which enables the garment to be tightly drawn around the wrists. The hood of the garment is also drawn about the head in the same fashion. The frocks are worn over other clothing during wet weather, at sea as well as on land.

AN OUTER GARMENT

A model of a waterproof garment of seal intestine sewn in horizontal strips. This little frock is decorated with yellow "bird toes" sewn by twos at intervals along the seams.

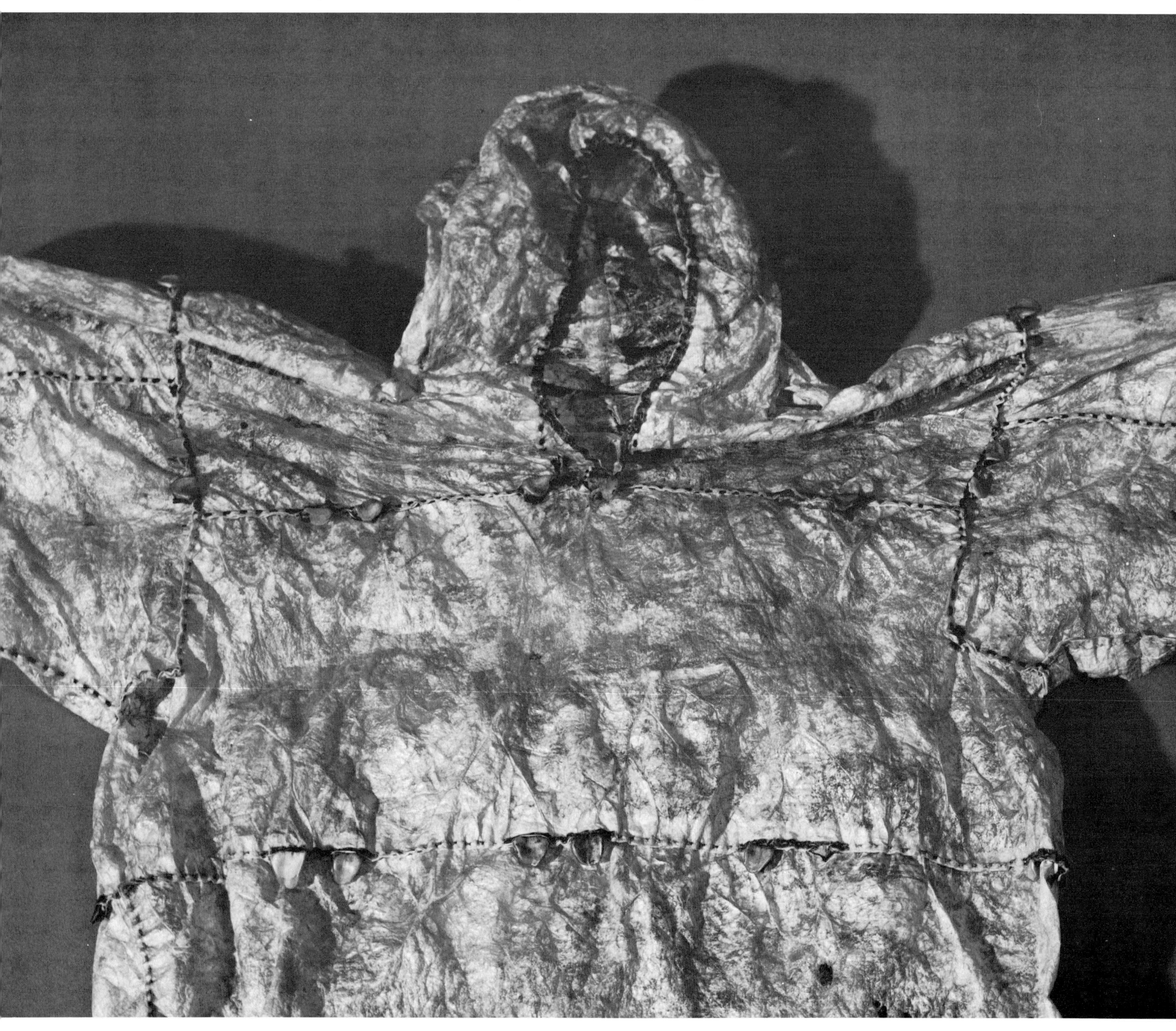

A BELT

Made of seal skin which has deer teeth sewn on in a pattern. The fastening is a large ivory button. The two rings of beads at the extreme left are purely decorative.

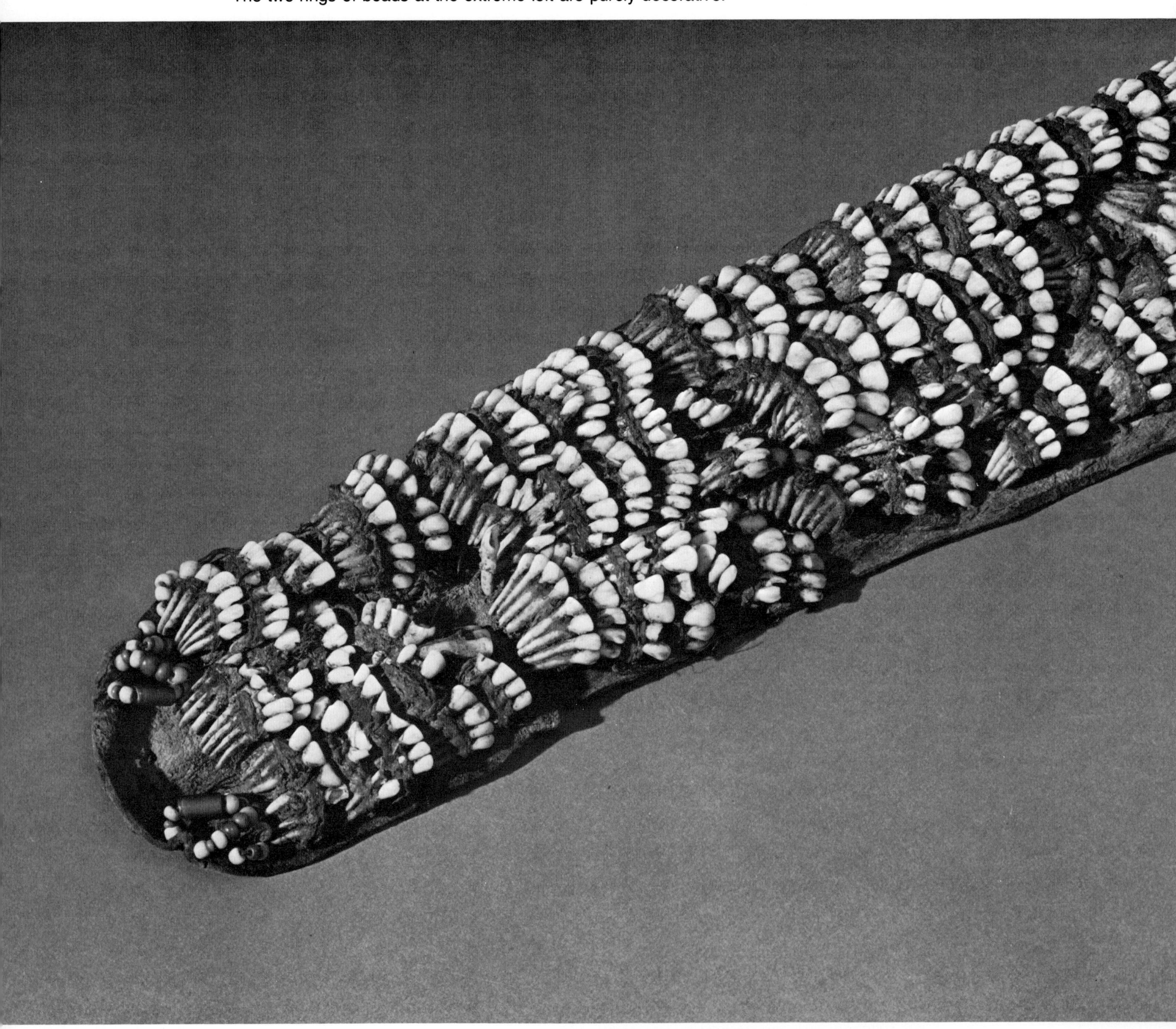

A BELT

Made of seal skin appliqued with darker skin and embroidered with bits of reindeer fur caught with fine sinew. The belt fastener is an ivory double seal head.

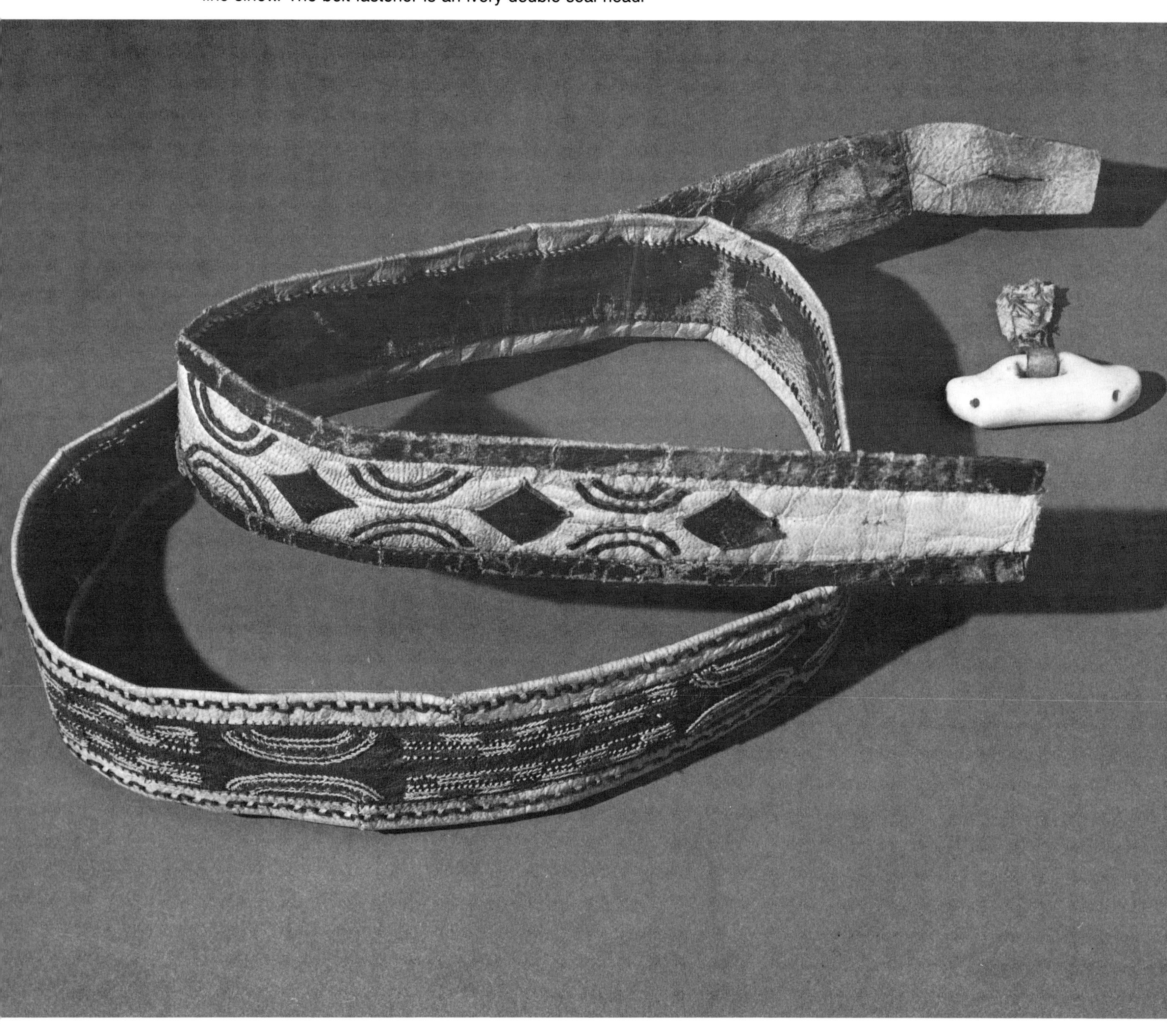

BOOTS

Made from tanned fish skin have a heavy fish skin sole attached to the leg section. The stitching is done with small twisted sinew. The top of the boot has a doubled fold of wool cloth. The tips of the strings are decorated with dark and white seal skin fashioned to resemble tassels. The boots were oiled. Less privileged Eskimos generally used fish skins for garments and other wearing apparel although women's sewing bags, clothes bags, and such paraphernalia were often made from the same type skin.

ACTUAL SIZE OF BOOTS PORTRAYED ON OPPOSITE PAGE

A detail showing the gathering and fitting of the fish skin sole to the boot top and the stitching used to join the skins. The stitching is done with twisted sinew.

BOOTS

Made of tanned seal skin with hard tanned seal skin soles. These are summer boots. The hair is removed from the skin which is oil tanned for waterproofing. The skin is dyed a reddish brown with tree bark. The soles are crimped and are almost black. The top band of light seal skin has a channel for a drawstring and is decorated with applique of skin strips and red skin dots. The boot ties are seal skin strips.

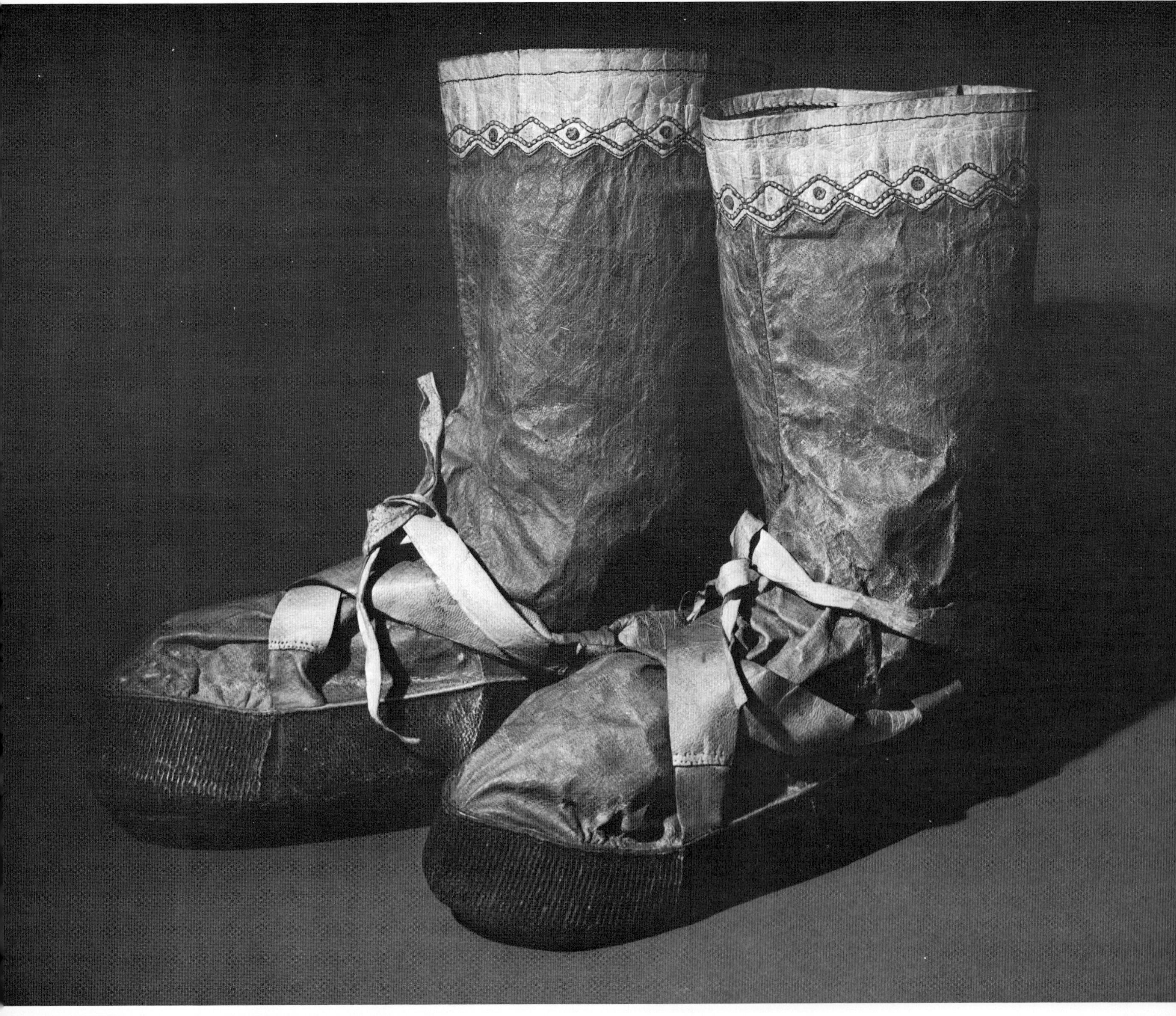

ACTUAL SIZE OF BOOTS PORTRAYED ON OPPOSITE PAGE

Detail showing the decoration. Note the neat mend in the right boot.

BOOTS

A pair of child's boots. The hair has been left on the seal skin. One can see the small pieces of skin which are probably left overs sewn together to make these small boots. The toes are not creased. An attempt was made to decorate the boots by using contrasting colors of skin.

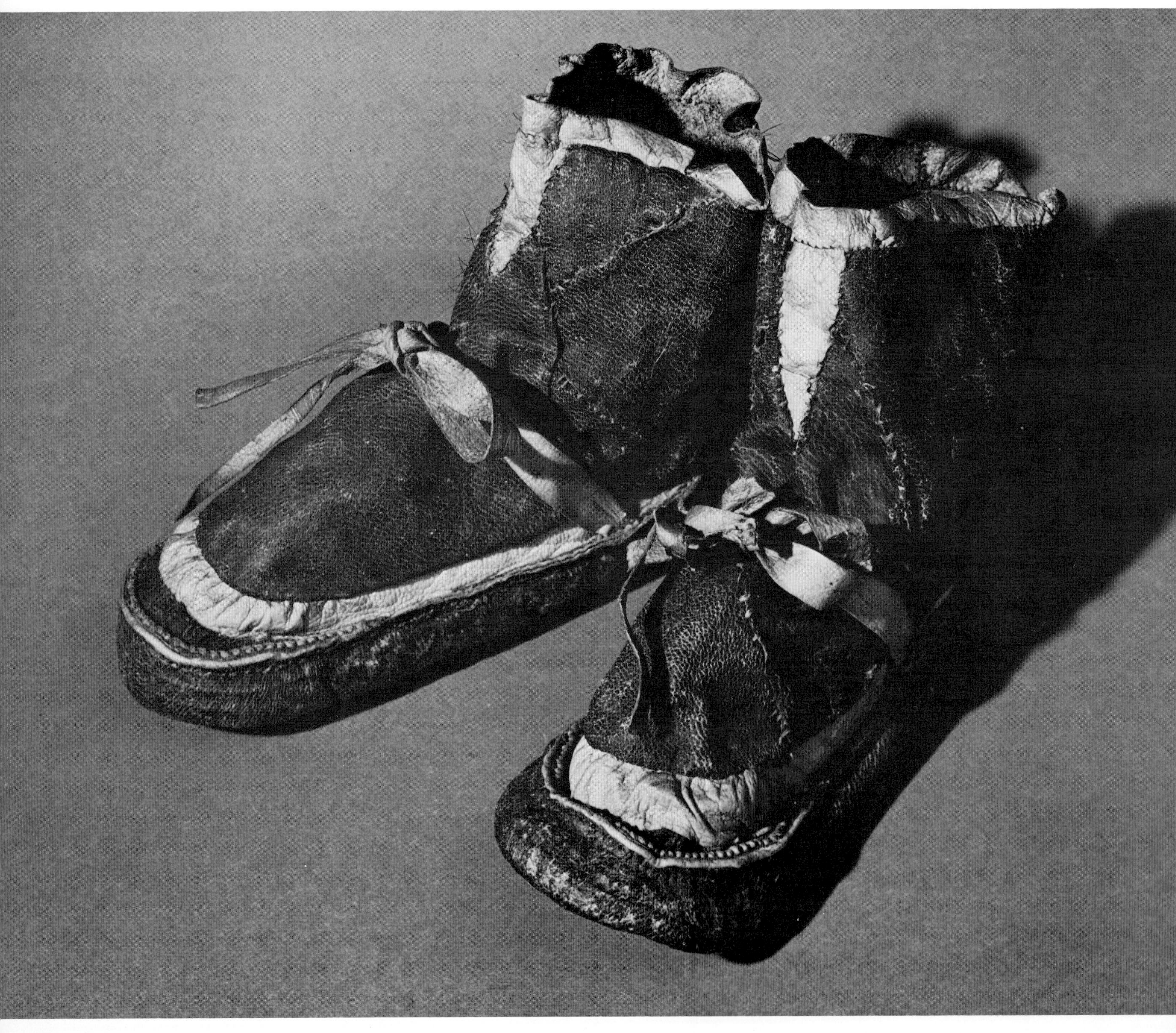

A PAIR OF GRASS SOX

Used in all seasons with boots. These were to keep the feet comfortable and dry.

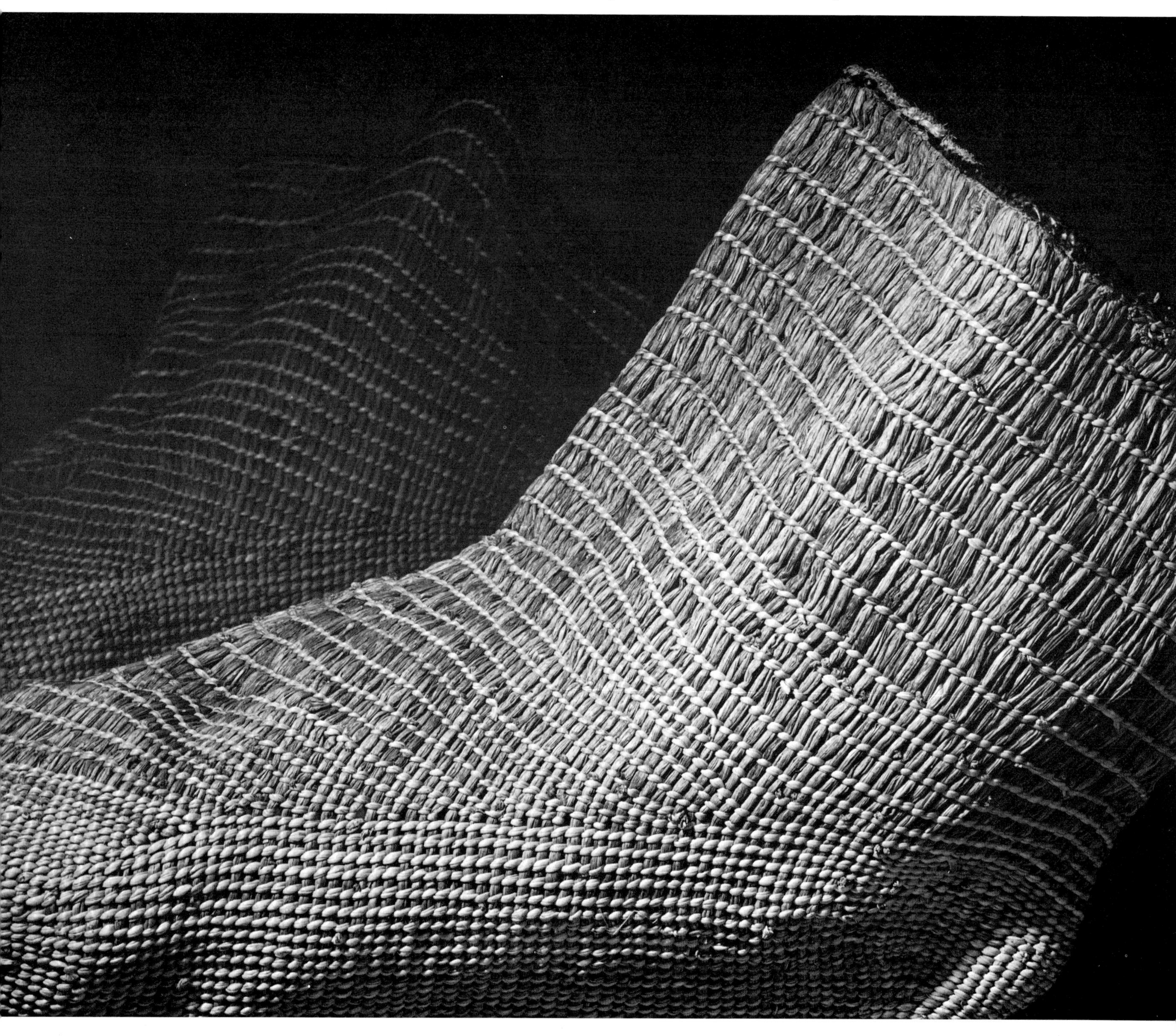

A FRAGMENT FROM A BOOT TOP

Showing the decoration done in fur ingenuously divided and stitched down after having been laid on in small bits ranging in colors of black, white, and brown. The wide center strip is seal skin and the strips above and below are parchment color and brown deer hide.

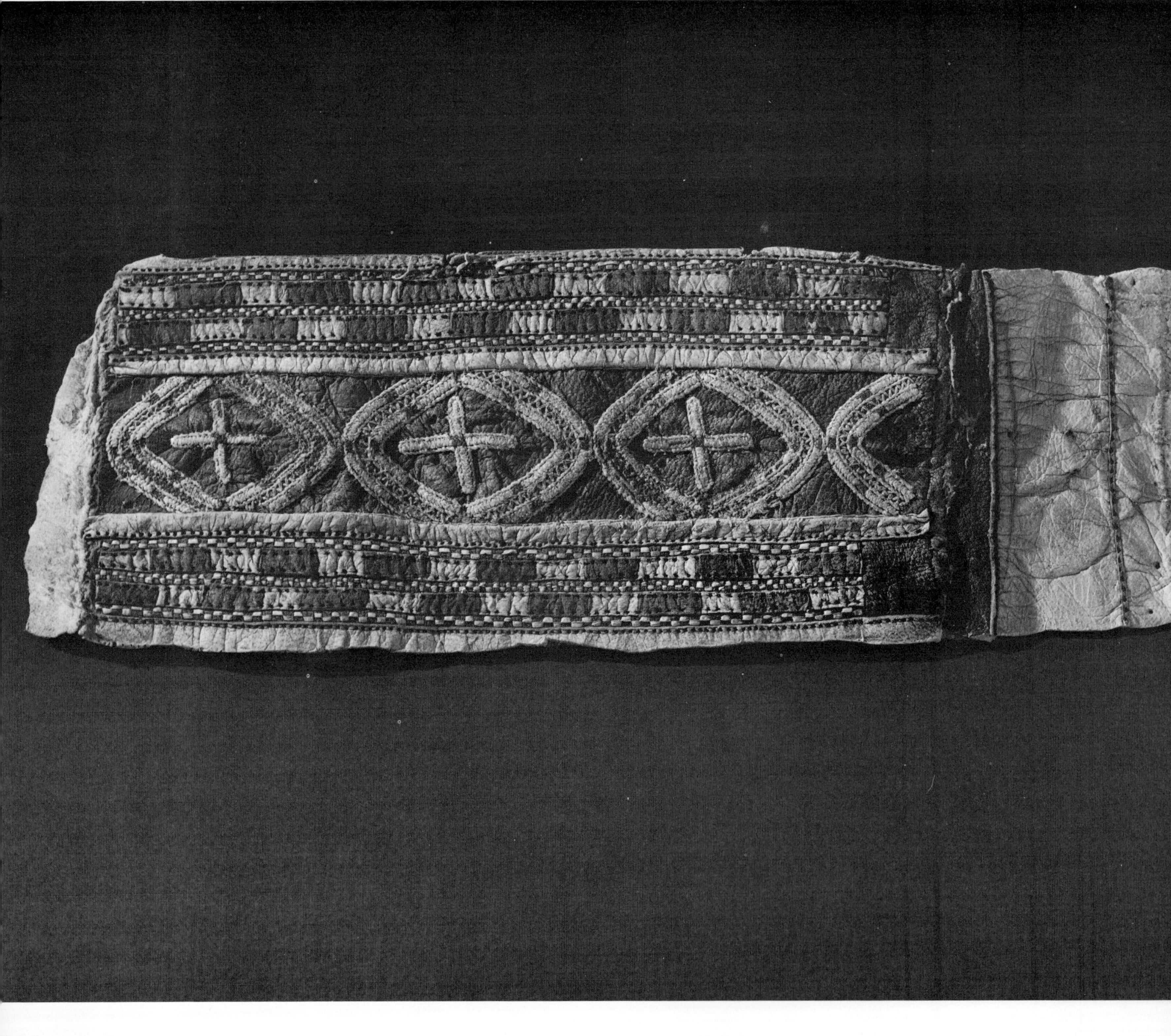

A FRAGMENT FROM A CHILD'S BOOT TOP

This is fashioned in fur hairs and thread on the upper part, and thread alone through the dark seal skin lower section. The colors are dark brown, light brown, and parchment.

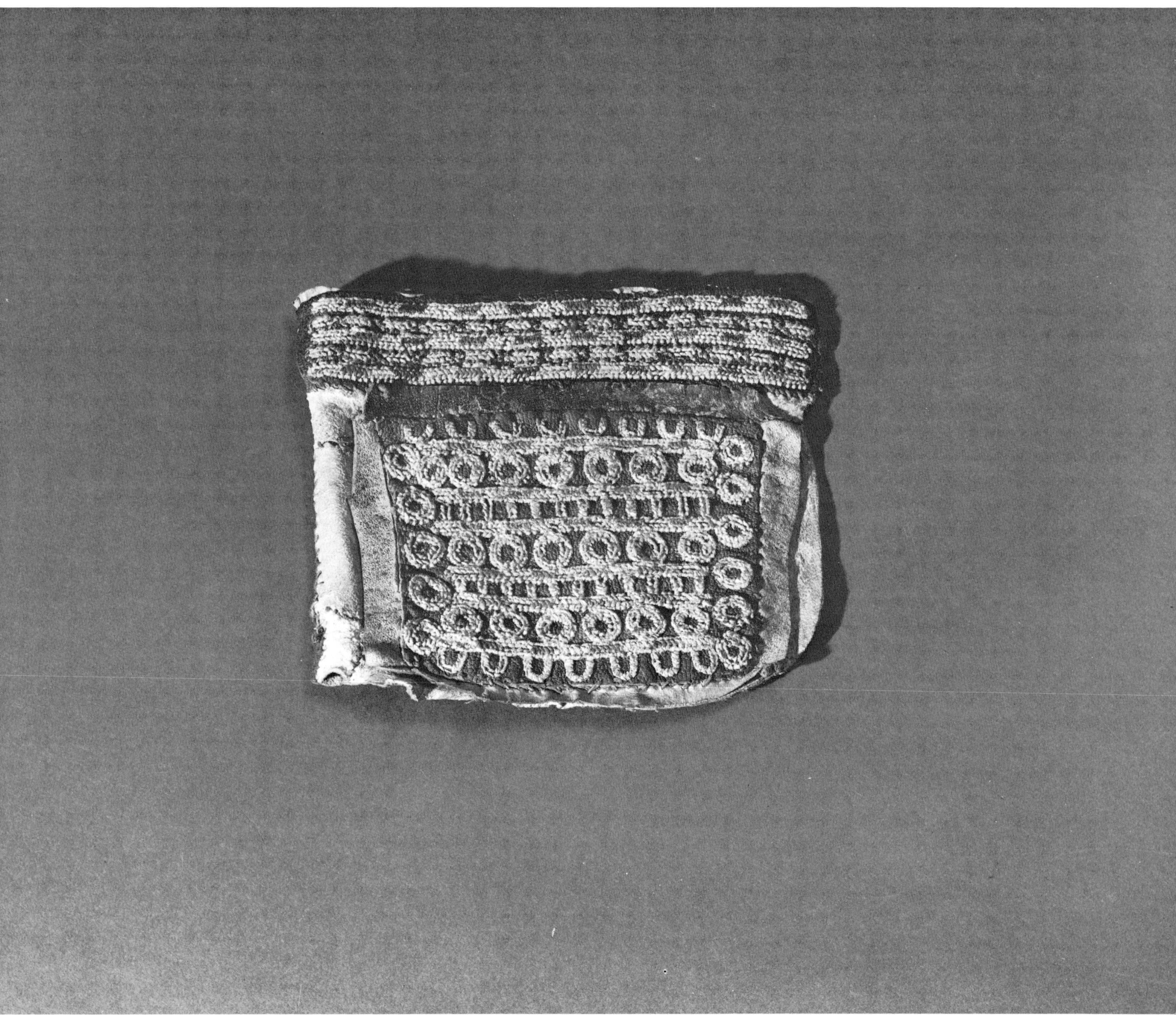

EARRINGS OR HAIR DECORATIONS

Constructed of beads strung through ivory spacers. These spacers are drilled through both sides of a flat ivory piece, enabling the wearer to thread beads in a parallel design, to hang on the hair or attached to a loop or earring to be suspended from the ear.

Animal skin spacers are also used the same way, pierced at short intervals so the thread passes through separating the beads. The rods holding the bead threads are only to keep them together.

EARRINGS

With ivory fastening hooks for inserting into holes in the ear lobes. The beads are light blue Peking glass trade beads with cobalt blue beads nearest the hooks. This type of earring was worn with the beads extending from ear to ear under the chin.

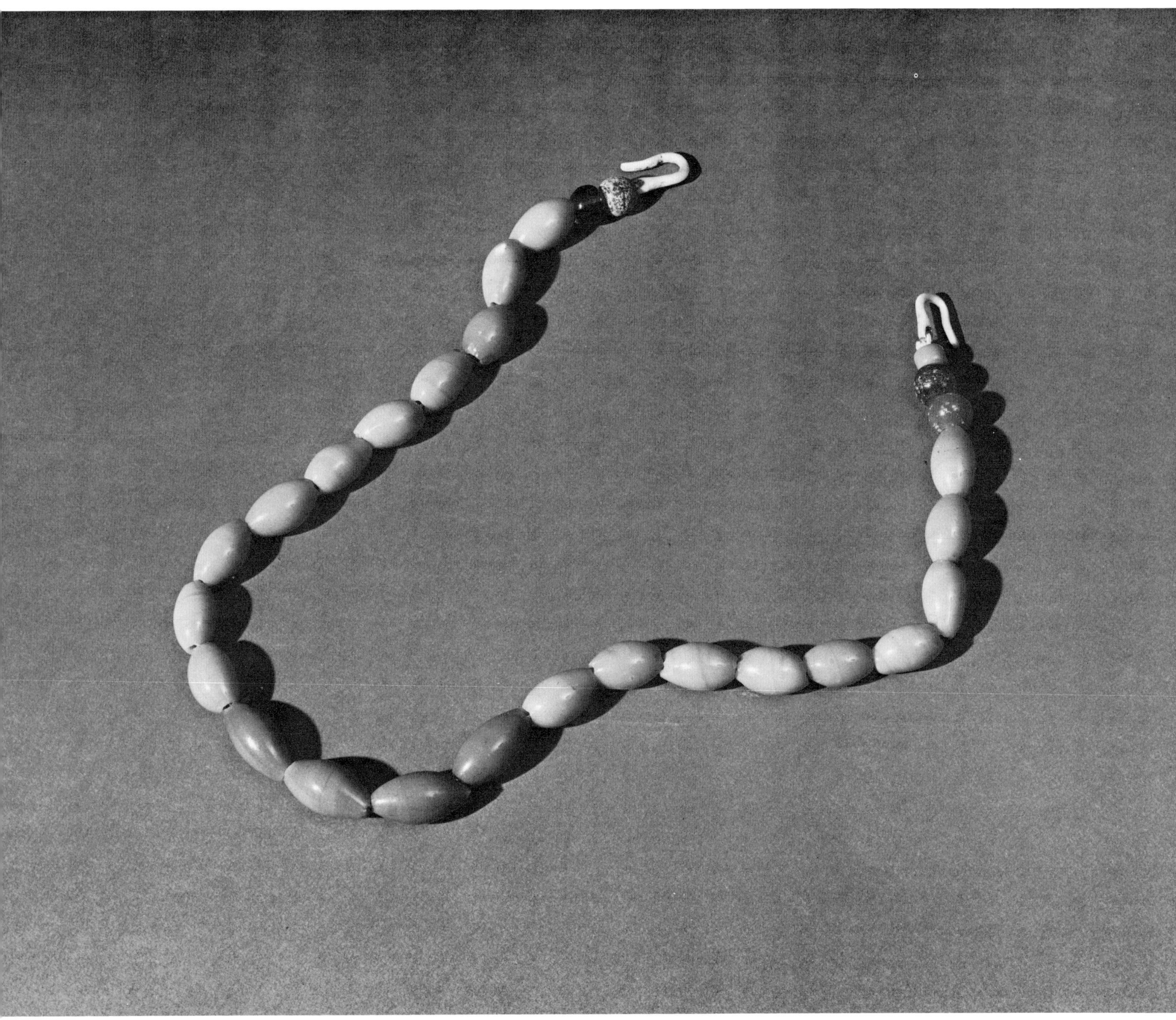

LABRETS

Very old labrets of ivory and stone, 1-5 are ivory, and #3 once had an inset. #6 is a beautifully made stone labret.
7 & 8. Ivory
9. Bone

PERSONAL DECORATIONS

1. A sickle shaped labret worn by women. These labrets are often decorated with beads which hang below the chin. 2. An ivory fish pendant from an earring. 3. & 4. Two ivory earrings consisting of a hook to wear through a pierced ear and the pendant on which was hung beads or other decorations. One hook is lost. 5. The ear might be pierced in several places not only through the center of the lobe but around the outer edge of the ear above the lobe. This earring was worn threaded through two or more of these holes. 6. & 7. Pendants made from animal teeth etched at the upper end of first and the lower part of the second. 8. An ivory walrus earring pendant. 9. An animal tooth pendant etched with dots and totem marks. 10. A seal shape pendant decorated with small holes which have been filled with a black substance similar to graphite. 11. An animal tooth with etched lines. 12. Two ivory seal earrings. 13. A pendant of fossil ivory. 14.-18. Hair fasteners or pins.

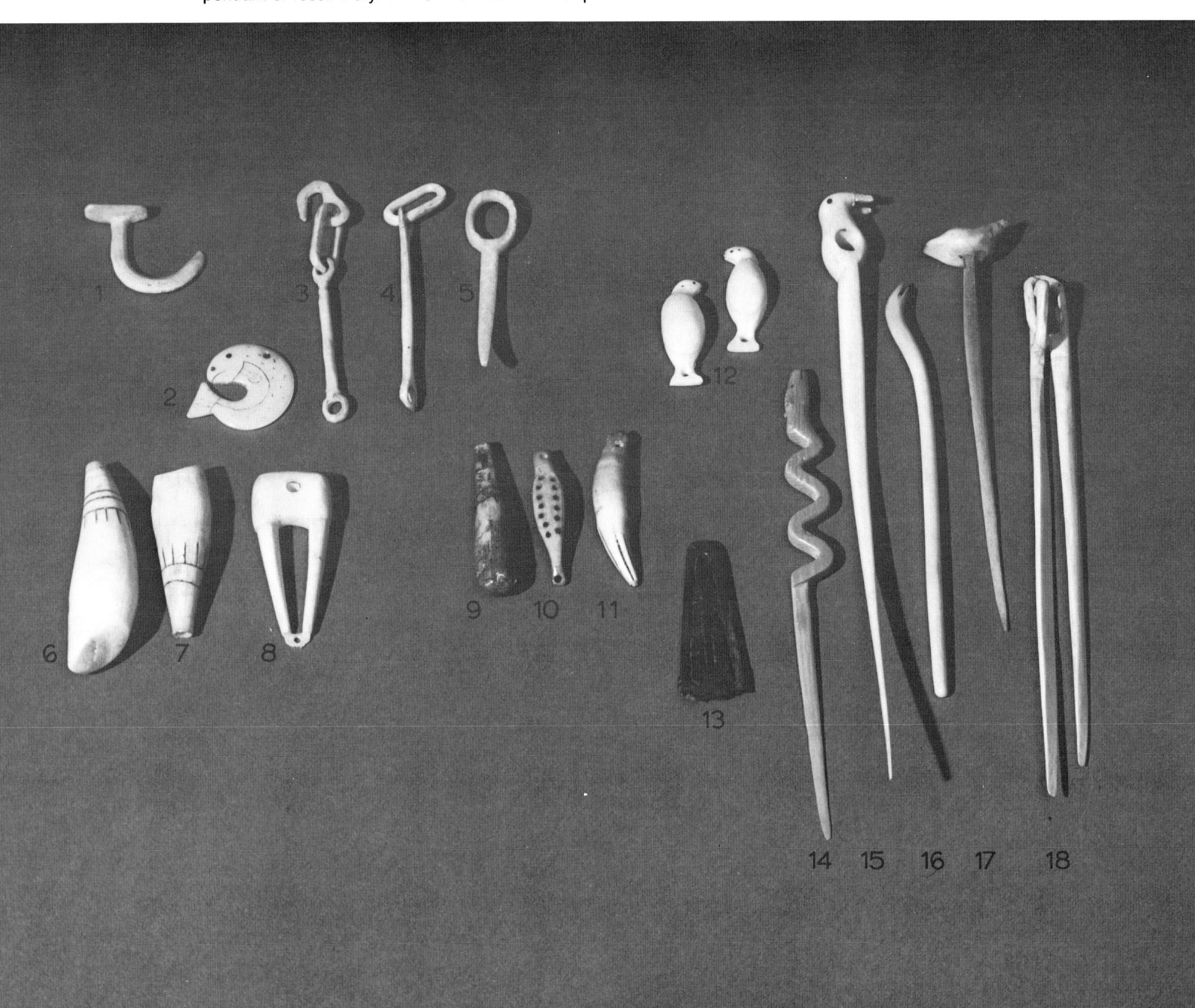

LABRETS

Worn by the men they were somewhat smaller than those worn by women. These labrets are black stone, a mottled lignite, and white stone. The hole in the labret, lower line, is for the placing of a bead.

LABRETS

Various designs several with holes for beads. These are all ivory with the exception of the large white labret with the bead hollow which is bone.

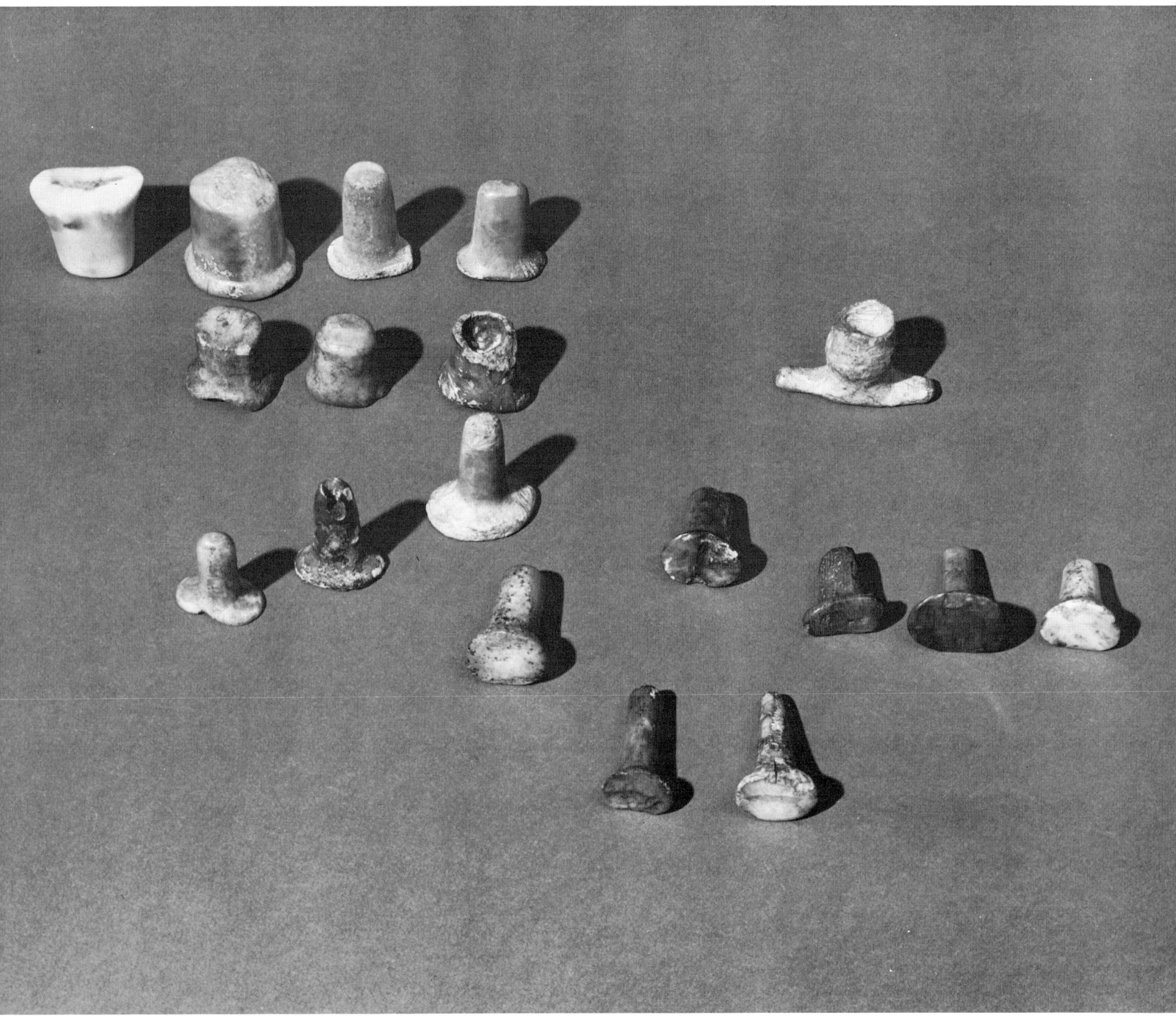

A NECK ORNAMENT

The holes in the bottom are for attaching decorations or charms.

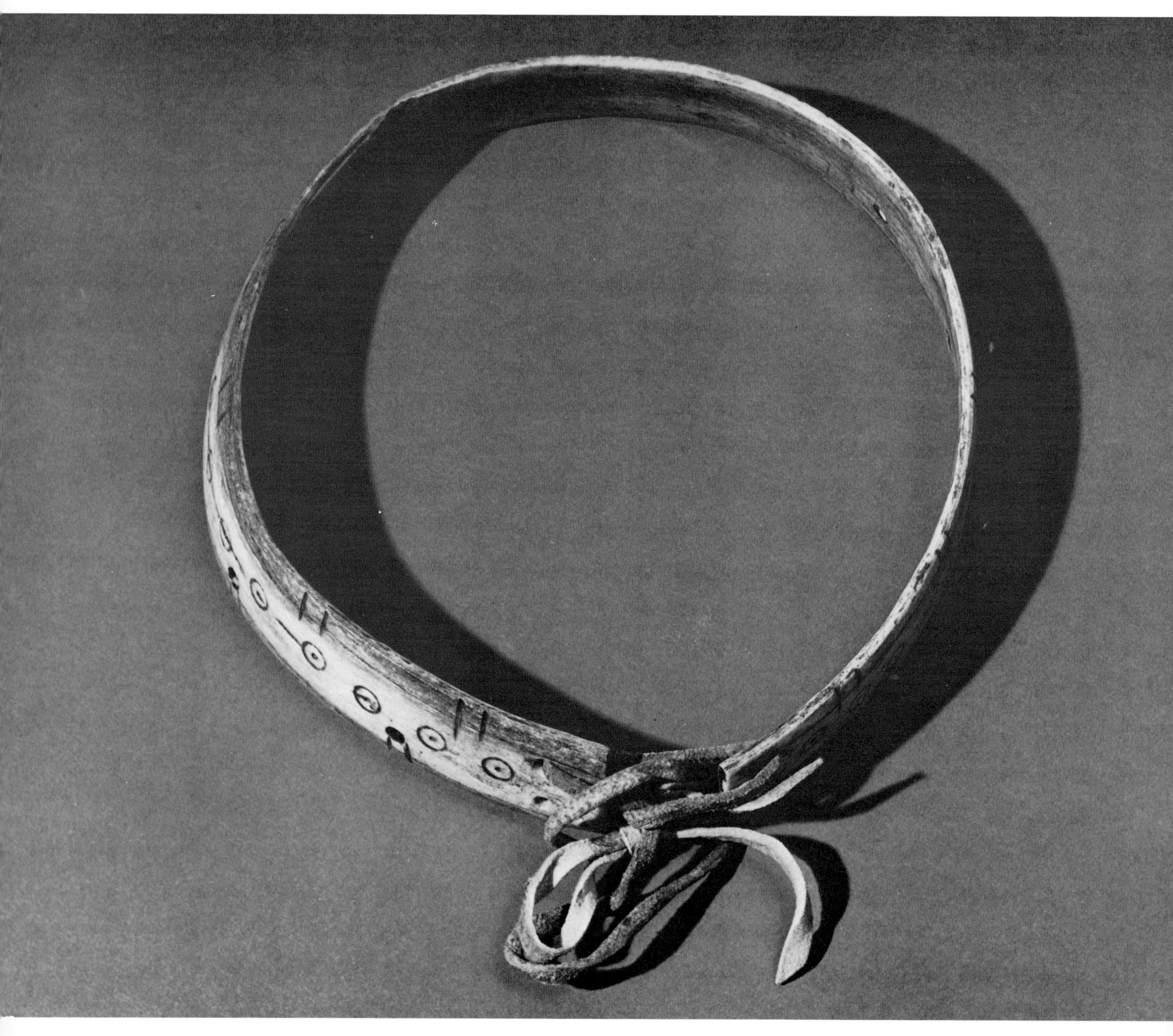

MISCELLANEOUS IVORY ITEMS

1. An ivory object of uncertain use. The raised flaw in the ivory was etched around the outside with a line and ray like cuts. There were two small heads at the top connected by a line similar to the decoration around the flaw.
2. & 3. These wrist guards are from an excavation. They are very thin and their design is more ornamental than later examples.
4. A fragment of ivory similar to the wrist guards decorated with circles.
5. Two ivory pendants or earring parts.
6. An ivory fastener.

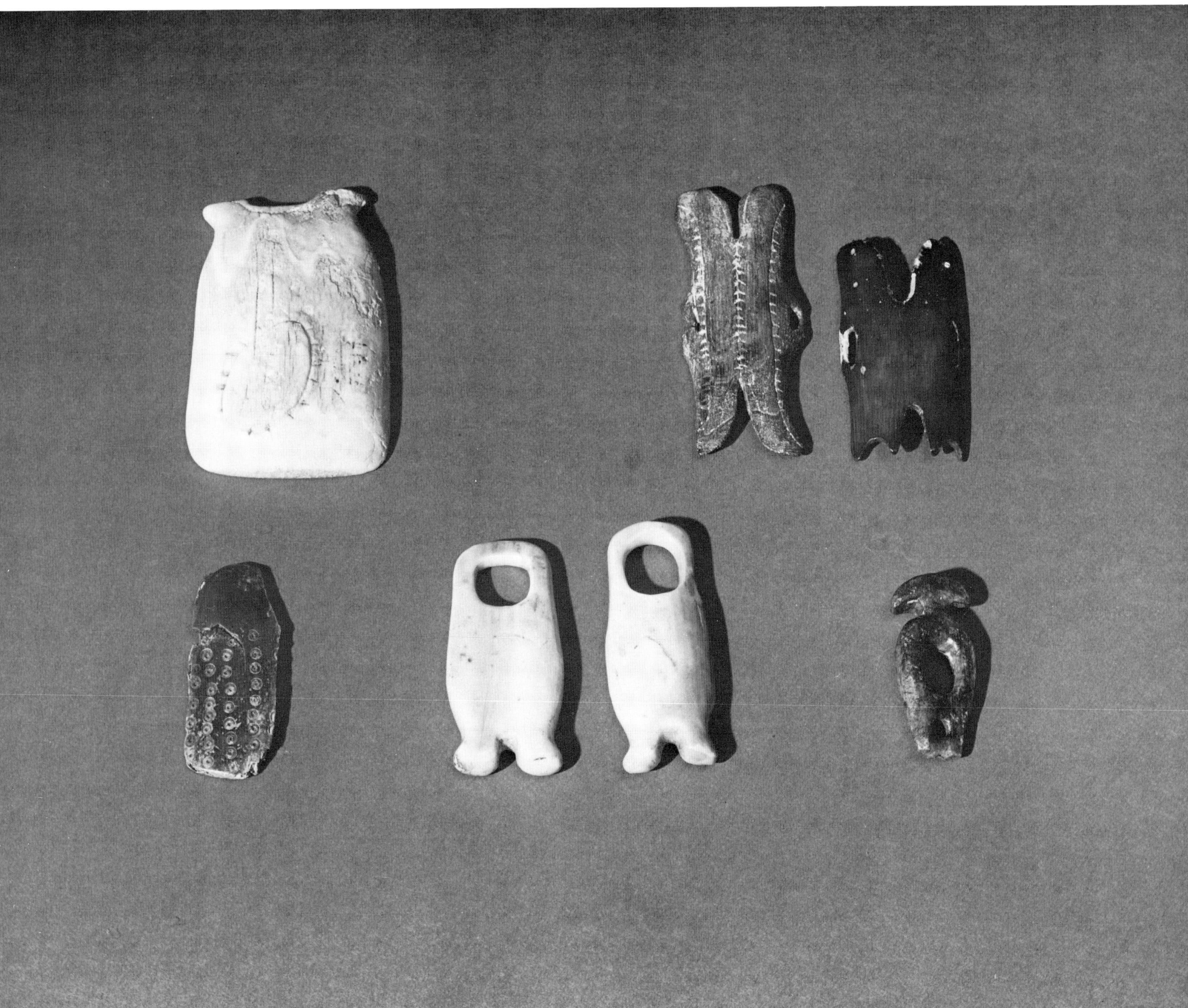

MISCELLANEOUS IVORY FASTENERS AND BUTTONS

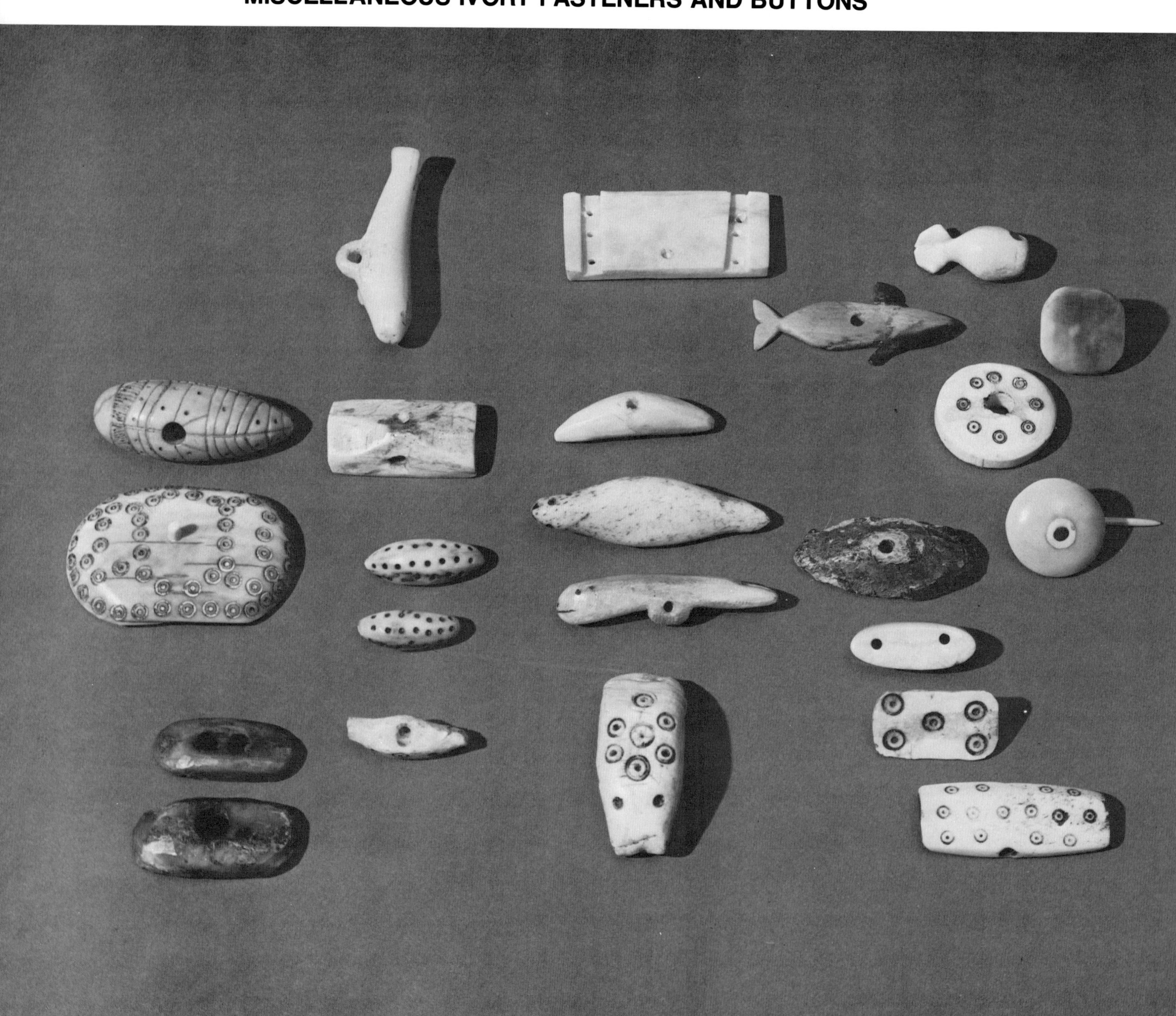

MISCELLANEOUS IVORY ITEMS

1. An ivory belt fastener decorated with incised lines.
2. Probably a trinket box top. There is a lip on the underside which fitted an opening. On the left side is a hinge type arrangement in which a peg is still embedded. A green pebble is set into the ivory and lines are incised around the circle.
3. A crudely shaped and decorated ivory stopper top. There is a groove around the bottom to receive a cord.

MISCELLANEOUS ITEMS

1. A mouth piece for a float. 2., 3. & 4. Spear rests for a kayak. 5. A water or oil bag plug. 6. A spear guard in the form of a whale's tail. 7., 8. & 9. Cord joiners. 10. Spear guard. 11. Bag plug. 12. & 13. Spear guards. 14. A seal carved cord joiner with a pebble caught in one hole. 15. The broken half of a pivot rod for a swivel. 16. Probably a belt fastener. The larger hole at the bottom has been broken. 17.-20. Finger rests. 21. Belt fastener. 22. A cord joiner. 23. An ivory sinker which was once a carved seal. 24. A bird shaped finger rest.

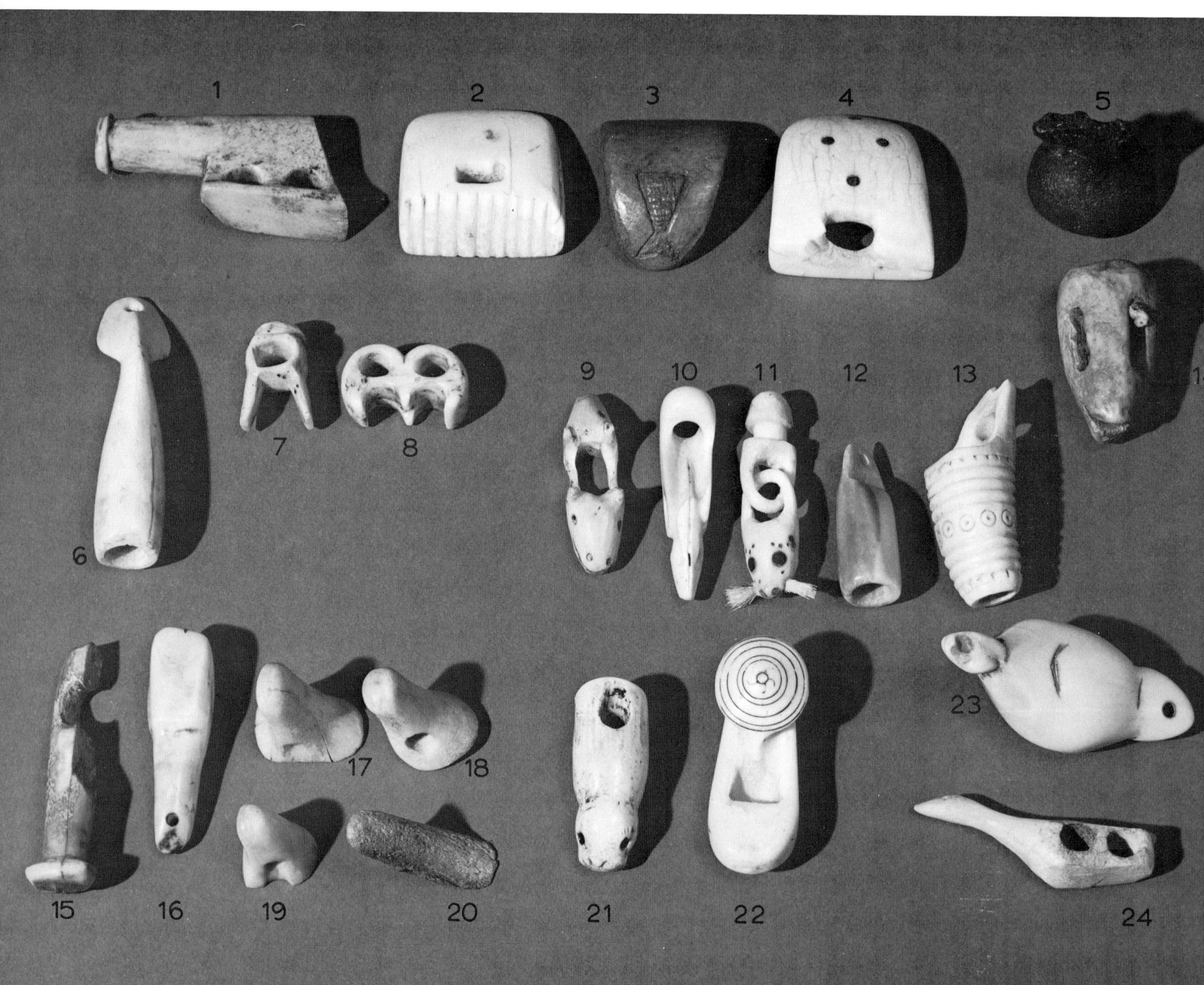

MISCELLANEOUS ITEMS

1. A block to hold a swivel bolt. The ivory has been grooved around the edge.
2. Decorated ivory buttons with carved shanks.
3. A small ivory button with two recessed holes in the underside.
4. A fastener with a catch to engage a loop.
5. Two ivory pieces probably parts of earrings.
6. A block for a swivel bolt. Numbers one and six are for a similar purpose. A round length of horn or wood with a large head was inserted through the middle hole and was allowed to rotate. The bottom of the bolt or pin had a hole to secure the cords. Swivel blocks were used for staking out dogs or wherever cords had to be kept untangled.
7. An ivory button with a carved shank.
8. An ivory button with sunken holes.
9. A larger ivory button with two holes drilled through.

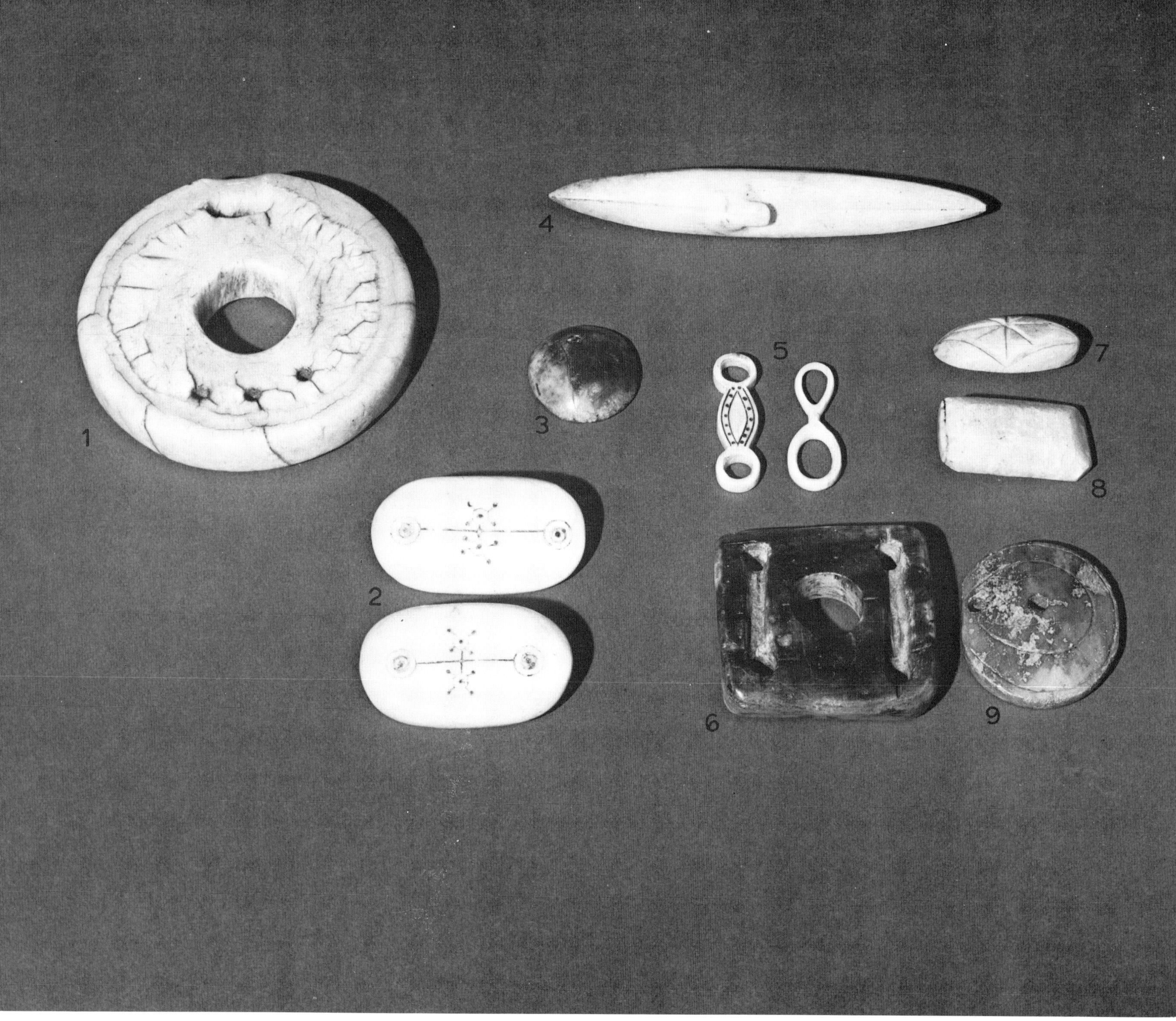

IVORY HAIR COMBS

Carved with bear heads on the tops. The comb on the right has a bird like figure scratched on its surface.

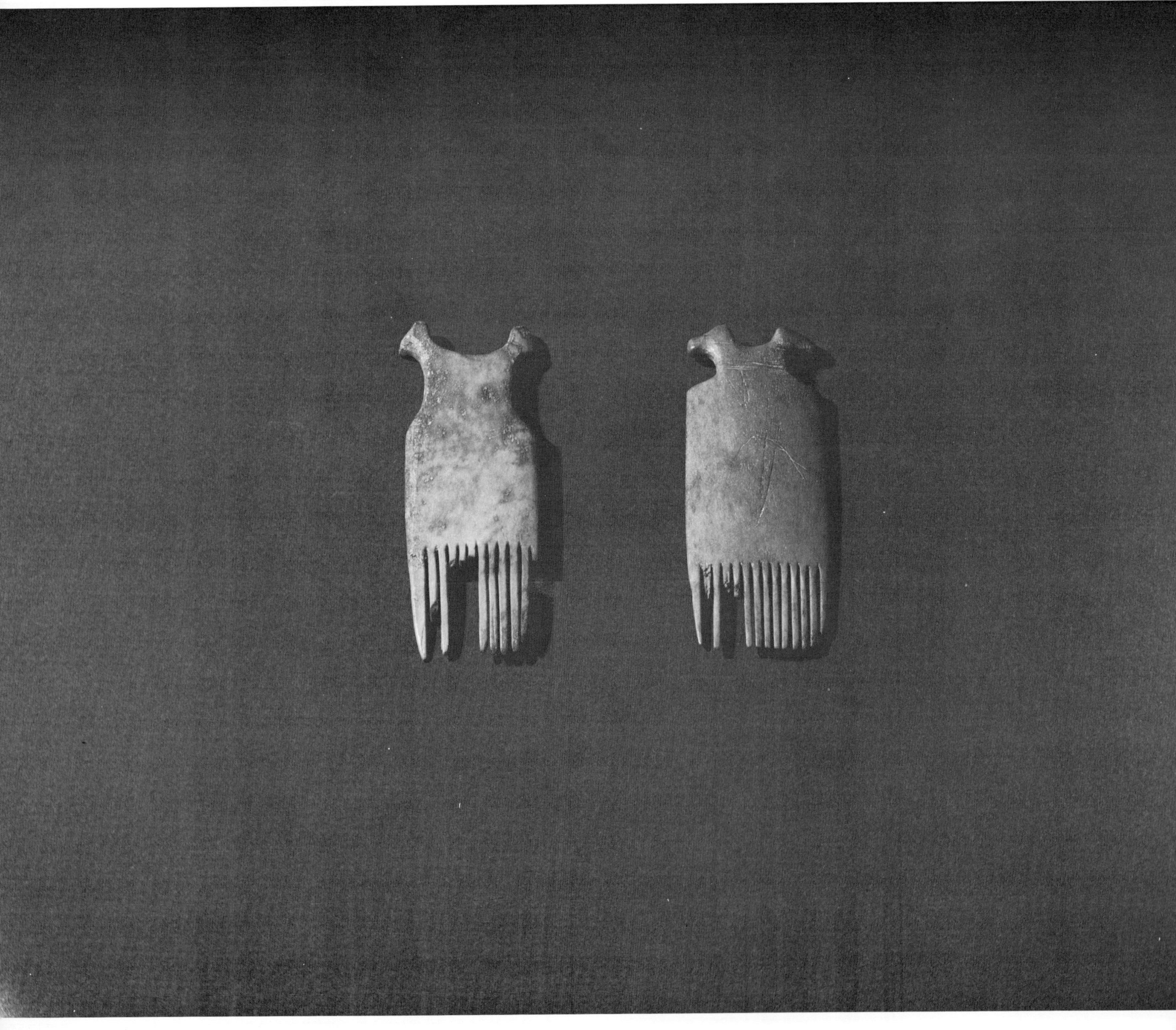

IVORY COMBS

Borders with etched designs.

IVORY AND BONE HAIR COMBS

Somewhat elaborately designed, the materials are shaped and formed to suit the artist. The animals on the handles are seals and bears.

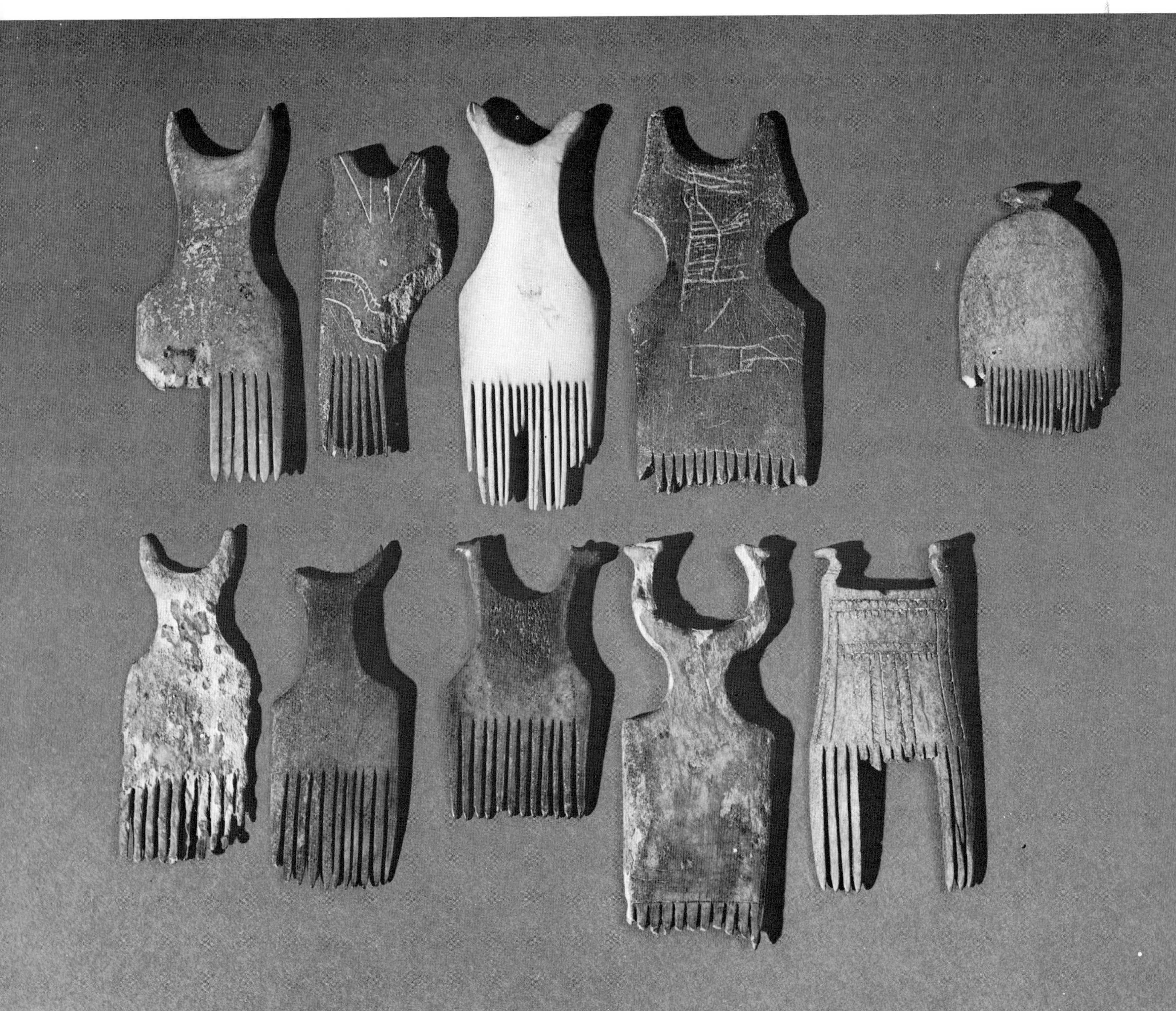

IVORY COMBS

Designed and decorated by their makers. The second and third combs on the top row have insets of light green stones resembling raw jade.

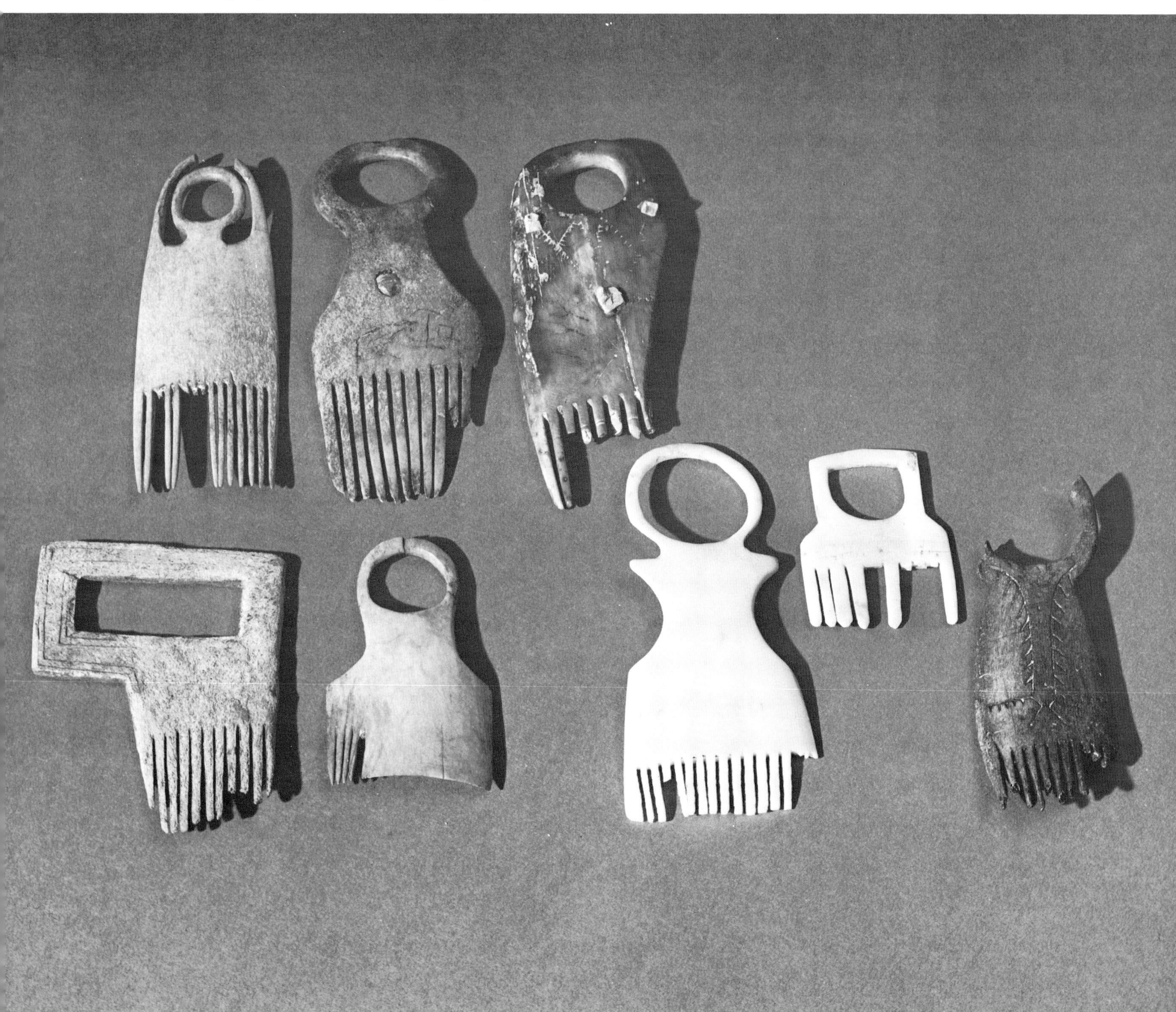

IVORY COMBS

Of varying shapes showing designs and variety in outline enhancing their appearance. The last comb in the first line is the scapula bone of some small animal.

IVORY AND BONE HAIR COMBS

Etched with border designs. The reindeer etched on the second comb from the bottom left is framed with a simple line and a "ground" line which gives perspective to the scene.

BONE HAIR COMBS

These show the variety in their design. Etching and decorations on several of these are almost completely worn off.

IVORY AND BONE DEER SKIN COMBS

1. A bone hide comb used to clean skins of hair and vermin. This comb is hollowed out antler.
2. & 3. Two long handled combs made from rib bones.
4. A piece of mammoth ivory roughly cut into a comb.
5. A flat ivory skin comb with a substantial handle.
6. A bone skin comb with course teeth on one end and finer teeth on the other.

IVORY COMBS USED FOR GRASS PREPARATION

The two combs drilled with holes could have been attached to work bags. The comb on the left portrays a male figure, the face shows tatoo marks and the ears are pierced through.

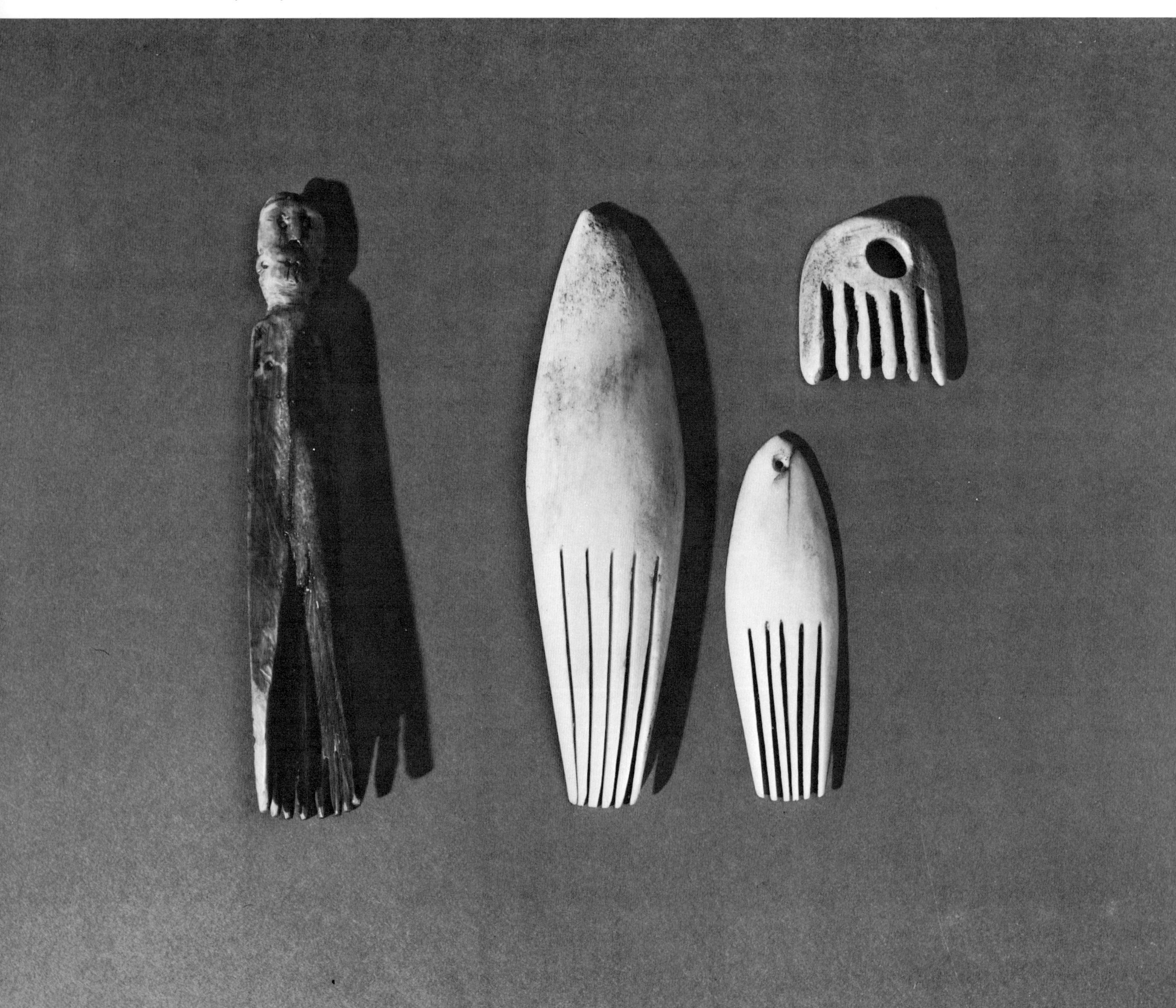

These are the same combs as on the opposite page showing on the left the "female" side of the comb, there are tatoo marks around the lower lip, two labret holes, and the ears are pierced. The material from which this comb is made is mammoth ivory.

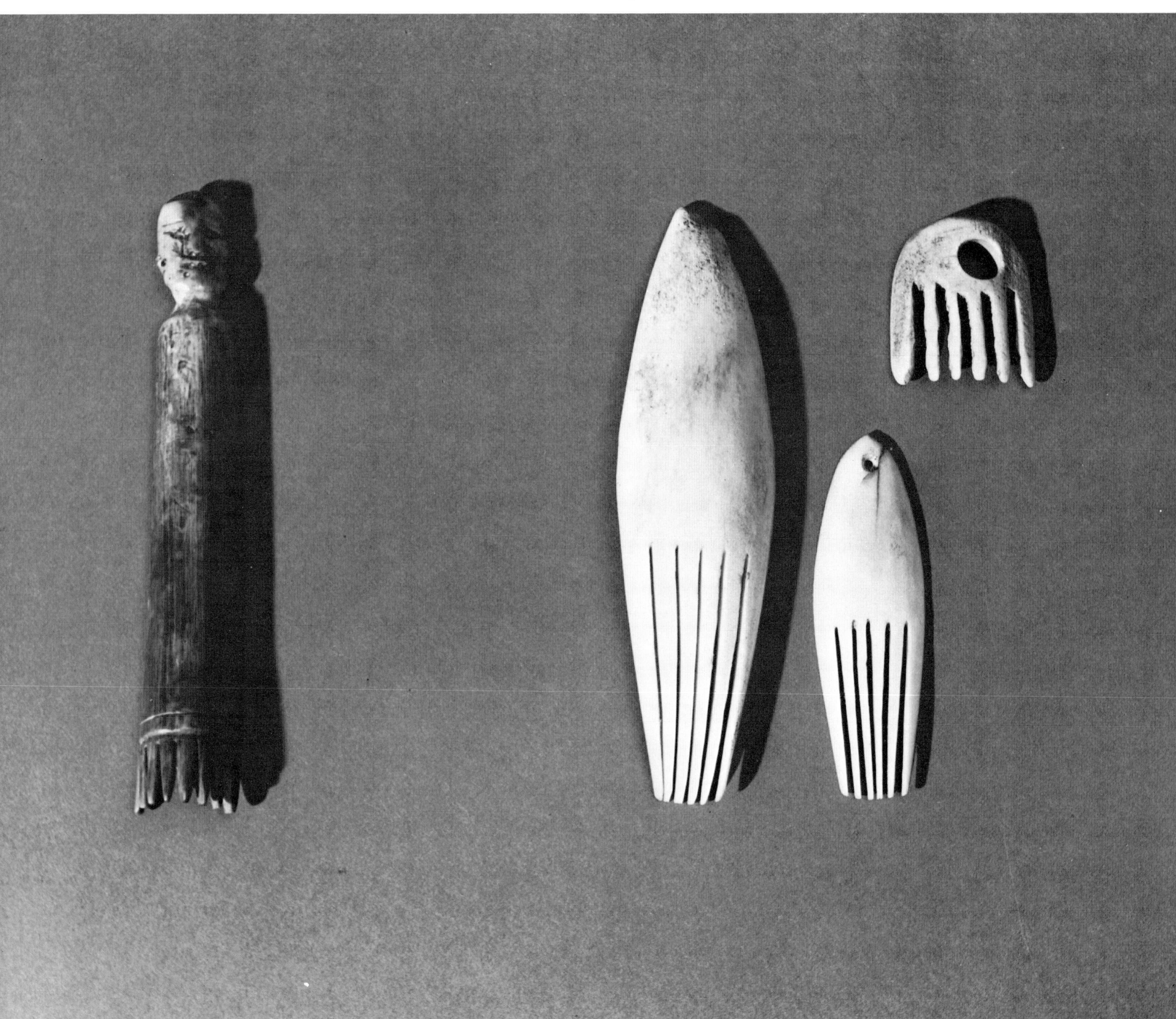

MISCELLANEOUS FASTENERS USED ON WOMEN'S BAGS

1. An etched ivory fastener used on a woman's sewing bag to secure it after being rolled closed and tied with a cord.
2. An ivory fastener to be used with a cord.
3. An ivory handle with whale tails some worn smooth. The green insets are stone.
4. An etched ivory fastener.
5. An etched ivory fastener with a copper eyelet instead of a pierced hole.
6. A small etched ivory fastener.

7. & 8. Etched ivory fasteners.

9. An ivory handle with whale tails and an umiak with its crew. Another umiak was broken off.

10.-11. Small ivory handles.

12.-13. Ivory fasteners for securing rolled sewing bags.

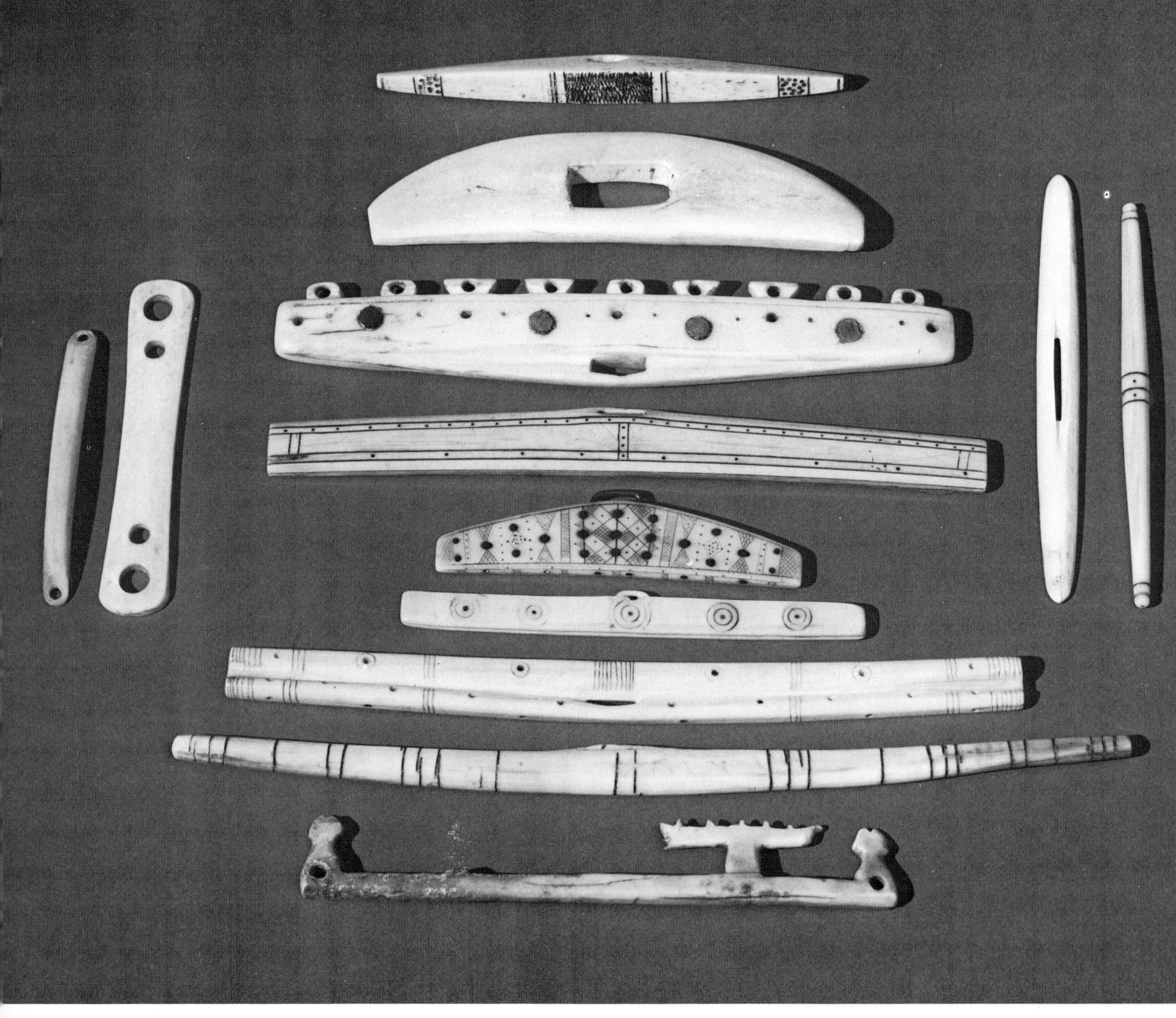

BAG HANDLES OF VARIOUS DESIGNS

1. A deer horn handle with bear's heads carved at either end.
2. An ivory handle with etched whale tails and a line around the edge.
3. An ivory handle with carved whale tails still to be seen on the right side.
4. A bird's head with the eye accented with etched lines appears on the right. The continued handle forms the bird's body. The handle is bone.
5. An etched ivory handle which once had figures or whale's tails on the left side.
6. An ivory handle with one remaining whale tail. This handle had eyelets and rings for attaching, the whole ensemble being carved from a single piece of ivory.
7. A small etched bone handle.
8. An etched piece of ivory probably a hunting tally which was used for a handle. There are sunken holes on the under side for attaching but they were placed there when the ivory was appropriated for this use. This is an example of using one artifact to make another.

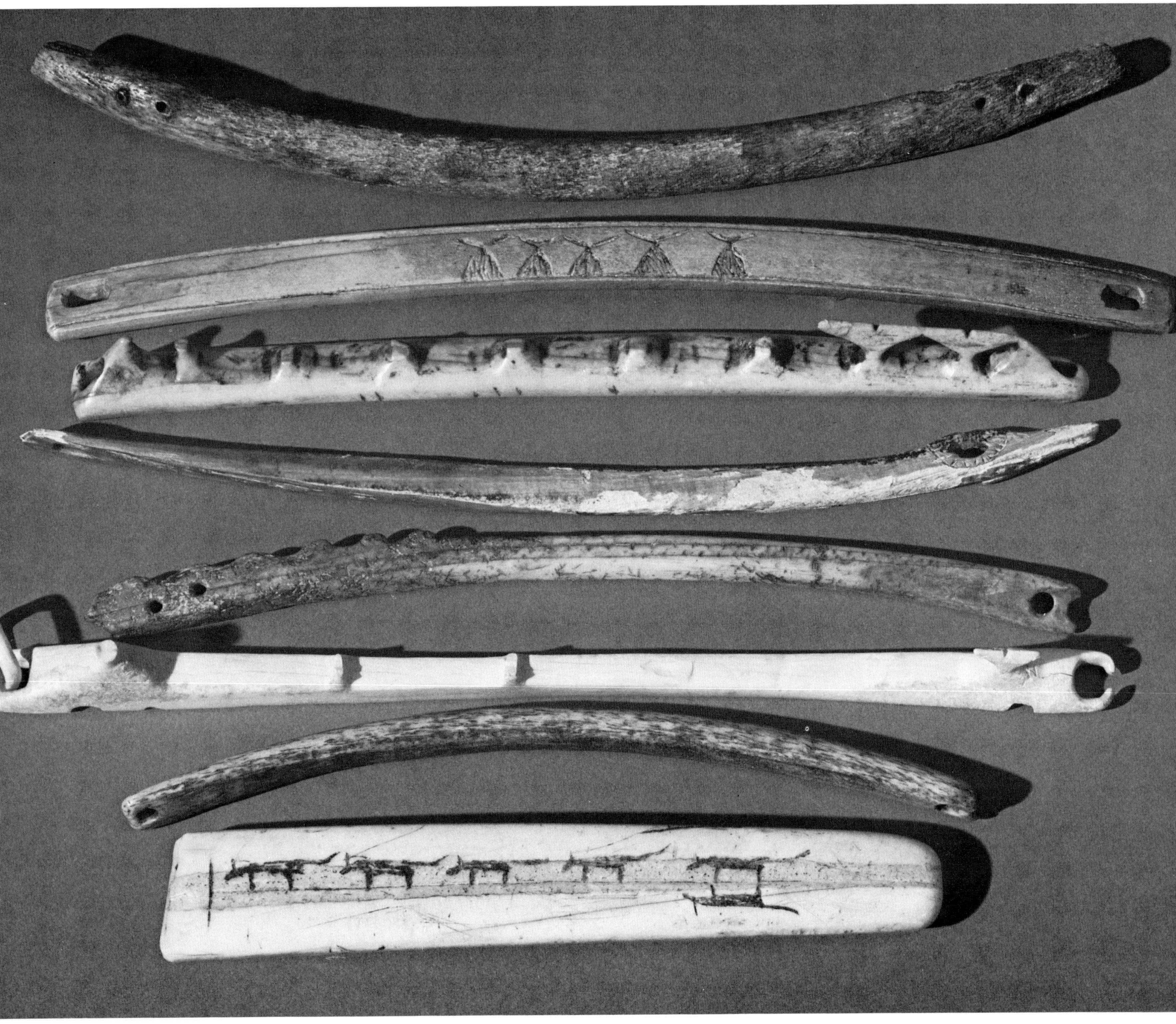

MISCELLANEOUS ETCHED ARTICLES

1. An ancient artifact, its use is not known.
2. An ancient decorated spear point.
3. A bag handle with the story of a whale hunt.
4. A bag handle with seals and reindeer.
5. A drill bow decorated with the story of a hunting expedition. The reverse side shows a hunter falling out of an umiak and being rescued by a man leaning overboard extending his hand. This side shows reindeer, walrus, whales and two umiaks and their occupants. The other parts of the bow are similarly etched.

6, 7 & 8. are parts of artifacts. The fragments are very old and decorated in an early style.

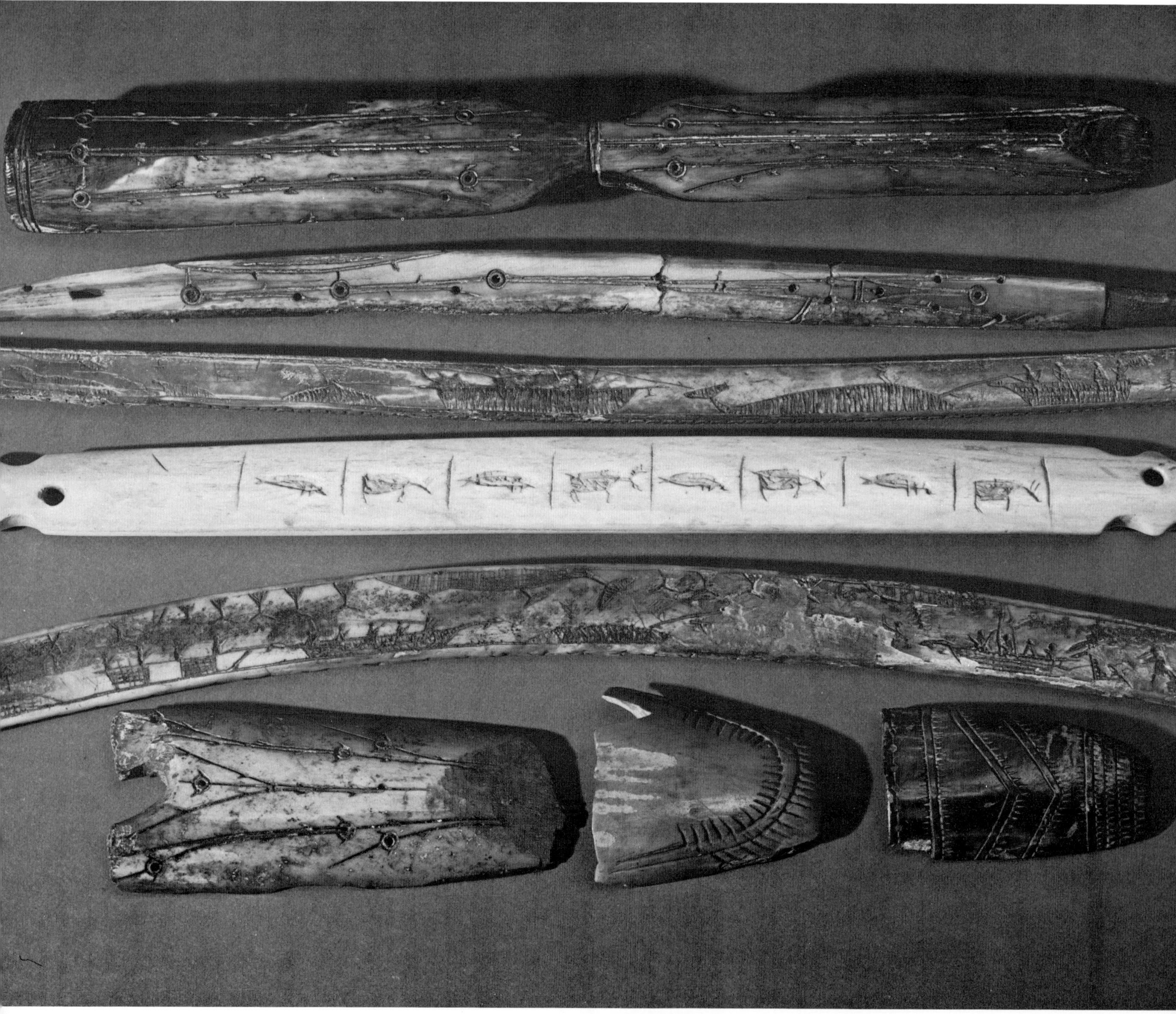

MISCELLANEOUS HANDLES

Several handles are carved on the ends with animal heads, others are etched, the incised lines depicting scenes or designs. The placement of the holes indicate the many ways there were to fasten handles to articles.

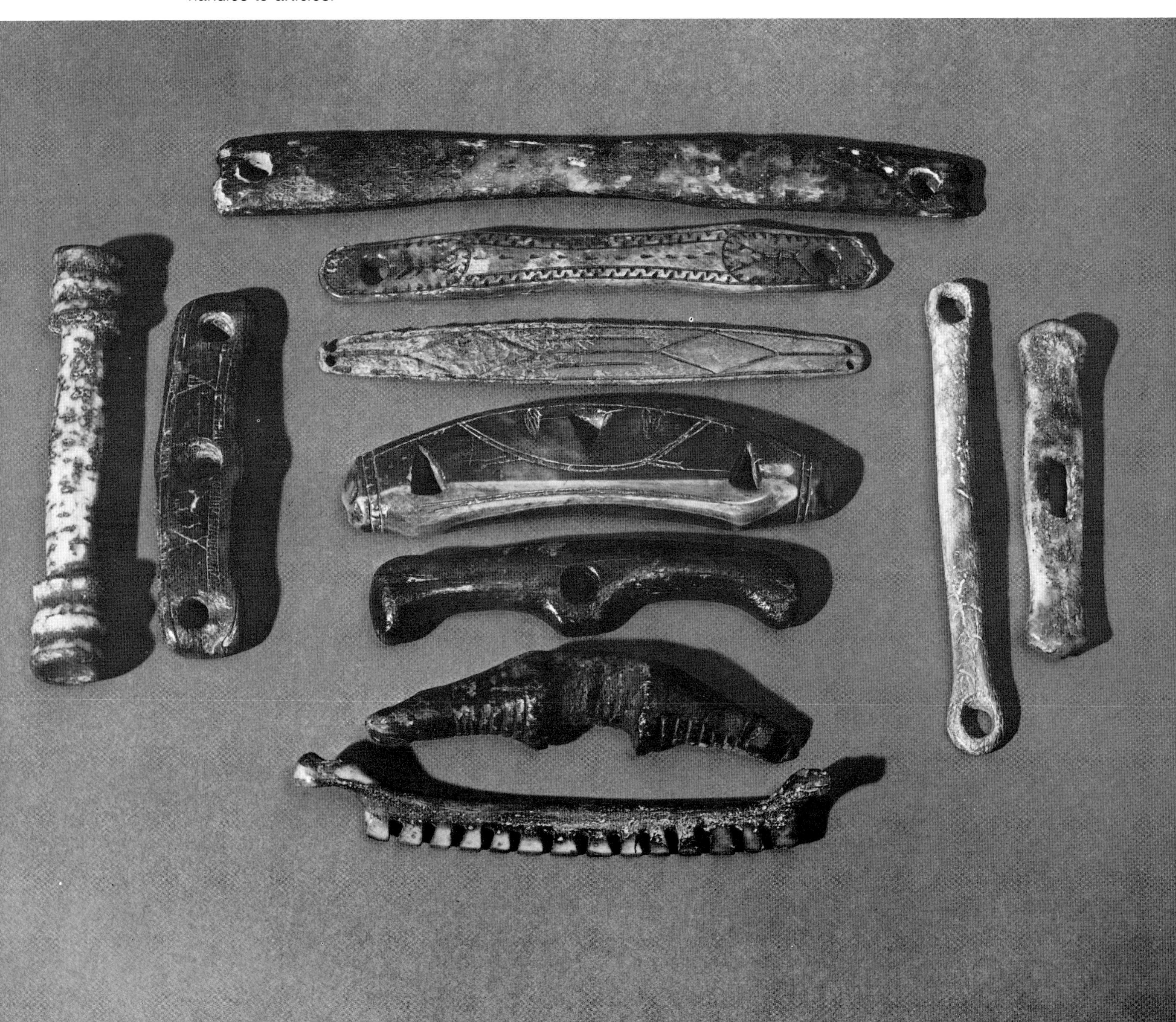

MISCELLANEOUS SMALL BOXES

1. A tobacco box of bark over hide secured by stitching through an ivory joiner which covers the bark where the pieces come together. Stitching is baleen. A piece of seal skin attaches the wood top to the box. 2. A box made of bark notched and interlocked. The bottom is wood secured with baleen pegs. The wood top has a seal skin loop handle. 3. A bark box with a second piece of bark wrapped around the shell. The outer shell reinforces the box since there is no stitching. The bark has been indented for decoration. A well fitted bottom is secured by wood pegs. 4. Hide formed into a box and covered with bark overlapping to create not only a pleasing decoration but a secure fastening for the ends. The top and bottom are wood. 5. An oval box made of birch bark over bent wood. The bark is cut to interlace securing the ends of the bark and forming a decoration. Brown horizontal lines are applied to the box at random. The wood bottom is attached with rawhide ties. The top has a rawhide cord which not only serves as a handle but secures a snuff tube made of a hollow wing bone.

FUNGUS ASH BOXES

1. Bone with ivory pegs and an ivory lid. The loop handle is walrus hide. The bottom is wood.
2. Baleen closed with baleen stitching. The bottom is a fitted wood piece and the lid, wood with a baleen loop.
3. A box made of bone with a wood lid and fitted bottom held by wood pegs. Fungus was burned and the ash mixed with tobacco. This combination was formed into pellets or quids.

SMALL TRINKET BOXES

1. A trinket box of walrus ivory. The decorations etched into the ivory depict summer habitations. A modified seal tooth design circles the box. The top and bottom are wood. The handle is a narrow strip of rawhide. 2. An ivory box etched with reindeer and a simple form of the raven totem. The circle and dot is a common decoration on ivory carvings along with single lines. The top and bottom are wood. A carrying cord is inserted through a hole in the side of the box secured by a knot. 3. An ivory snuff box. There is a tree represented also a whale lightly scratched on the side. A figure variously described as a seal's spirit or that of a walrus appears on the other side of the box. The top is secured by a strip of seal skin threaded through two holes which makes for a secure closure when the cord is pulled tightly. The top is attached through a hole in the side of the box. The bottom is wood. 4. An ivory box the bottom of which is part of the core of the walrus tusk from which it is carved. The etching is in simple lines used on very early artifacts. 5. An old ivory box with a fitted wood bottom and a wood top which has a rawhide pull.

SMALL TRINKET BOXES

1. An old trinket box of whale bone with a seals head on the bottom probably to serve as a wrap around catch for cord attached to a top. There are two simple lines grooved around the top.
2. An ivory box with two walrus. The box appears to be a very old one and shows it was etched at one time.
3. An old ivory box with two seals. This box has had etched decorations which are now almost obliterated.
4. One side of an old ivory box with a seal's head on either side.
5. An ivory box made in the shape of a whale's body with an etched design.
6. A typical fitted wood top with a sinew pull.

SMOKING PIPE

This pipe's stem is hollowed out wood in one piece carved and tapered at the mouth end. The brass bowl has a long neck and is flared considerably. A small hole has been cut to receive the bowl which is tightly held by shoulders secured with rawhide. There is an opening on the bottom for nicotine, also one on the center front which is closed with a spent brass cartridge shell. The mouthpiece probably was furnished with a metal end at one time. Brass rings are set into the stem and a nicotine picker is tied to the pipe with a gut line strung with beads.

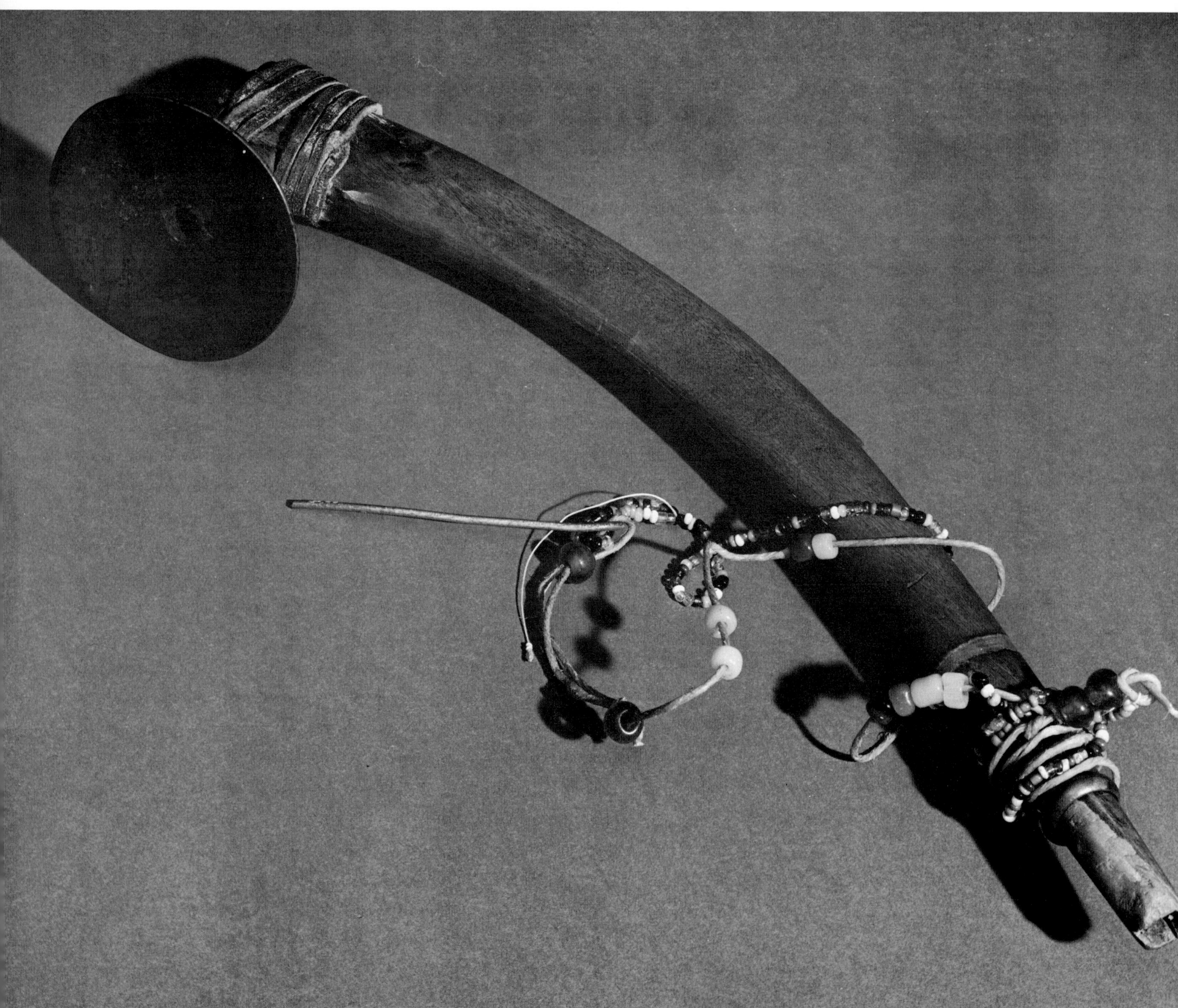

SMOKING PIPES

1. This pipe's bowl is lead made with shoulders for attaching to the stem which is split lengthwise, hollowed, and held together with a continuous piece of seal cord. A nicotine opening is in the front of the pipe.
2. This primitive pipe has a bowl of bone tapered to two shoulders by which it is secured to the wood stem.

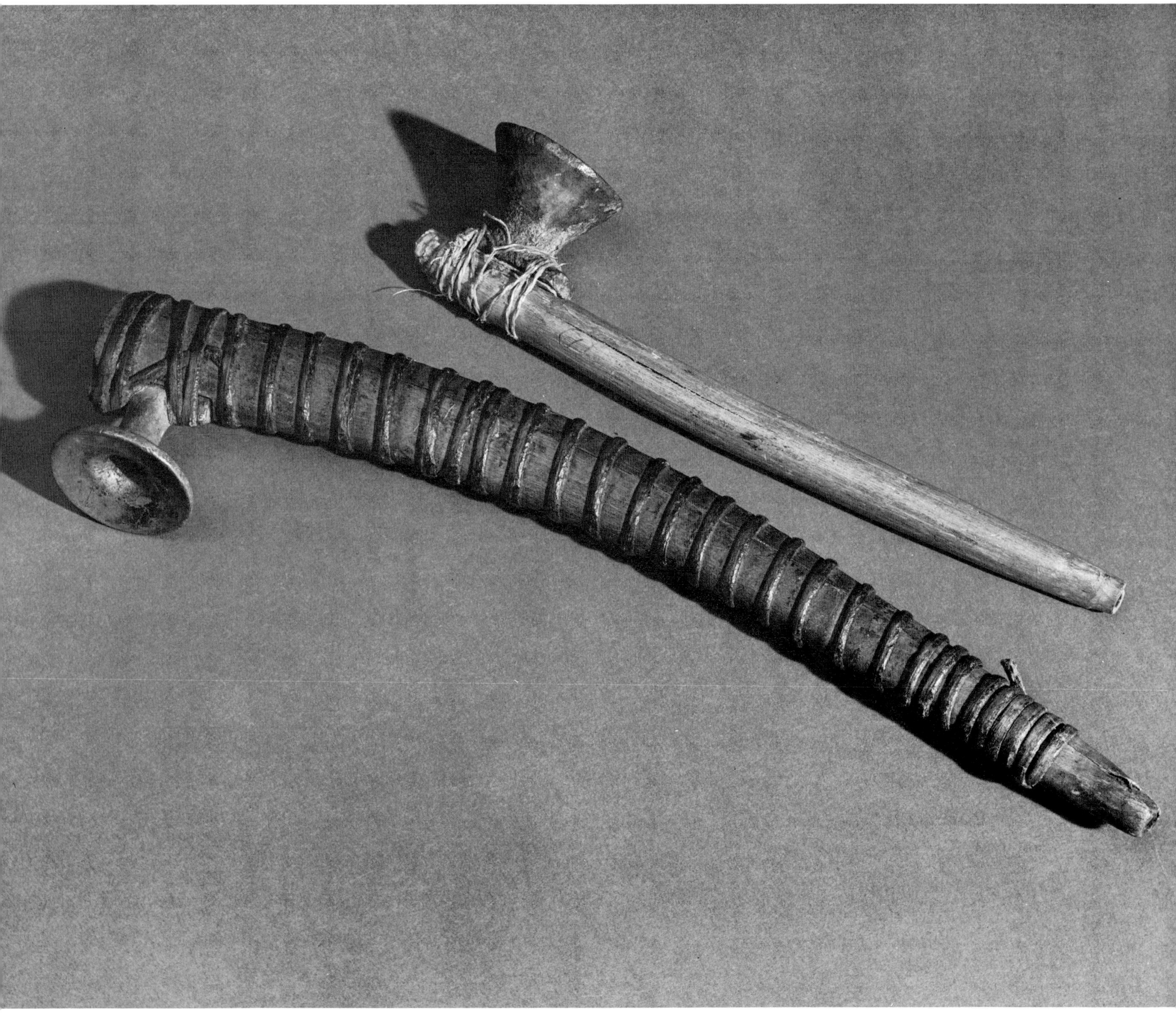

SMOKING PIPES

Two eskimo pipes of wood and lead. Both pipes have a lead stem fitted into a wood body.

1. This pipe may be of Siberian Eskimo manufacture. The lead is fitted into the wood so neatly it is hard to find where it is joined. There is a nicotine opening in the underside of the pipe. The lead pounded into the wood for the design is very neatly done and although it seems to be only a pattern may mean to show summer dwellings or a summer encampment. The flared bowl is Asiatic in design.
2. This pipe from St. Lawrence Island has a lead mouth piece flared at the end and the bowl somewhat raised has a flat top. There is a nicotine opening at the front of the pipe. If one looks carefully the thunderbirds can be seen which form the design.

THREE IVORY PIPES WITH IVORY BOWLS

1 & 3. The stems are etched with hunting scenes and follow the natural line of the tusks. The first pipe exhibits in its etching an interesting story including a man's encounter with a bear.

2. This pipe is considerably influenced by outsiders. The bowl is separate. The original mouth-piece was replaced by this later one.

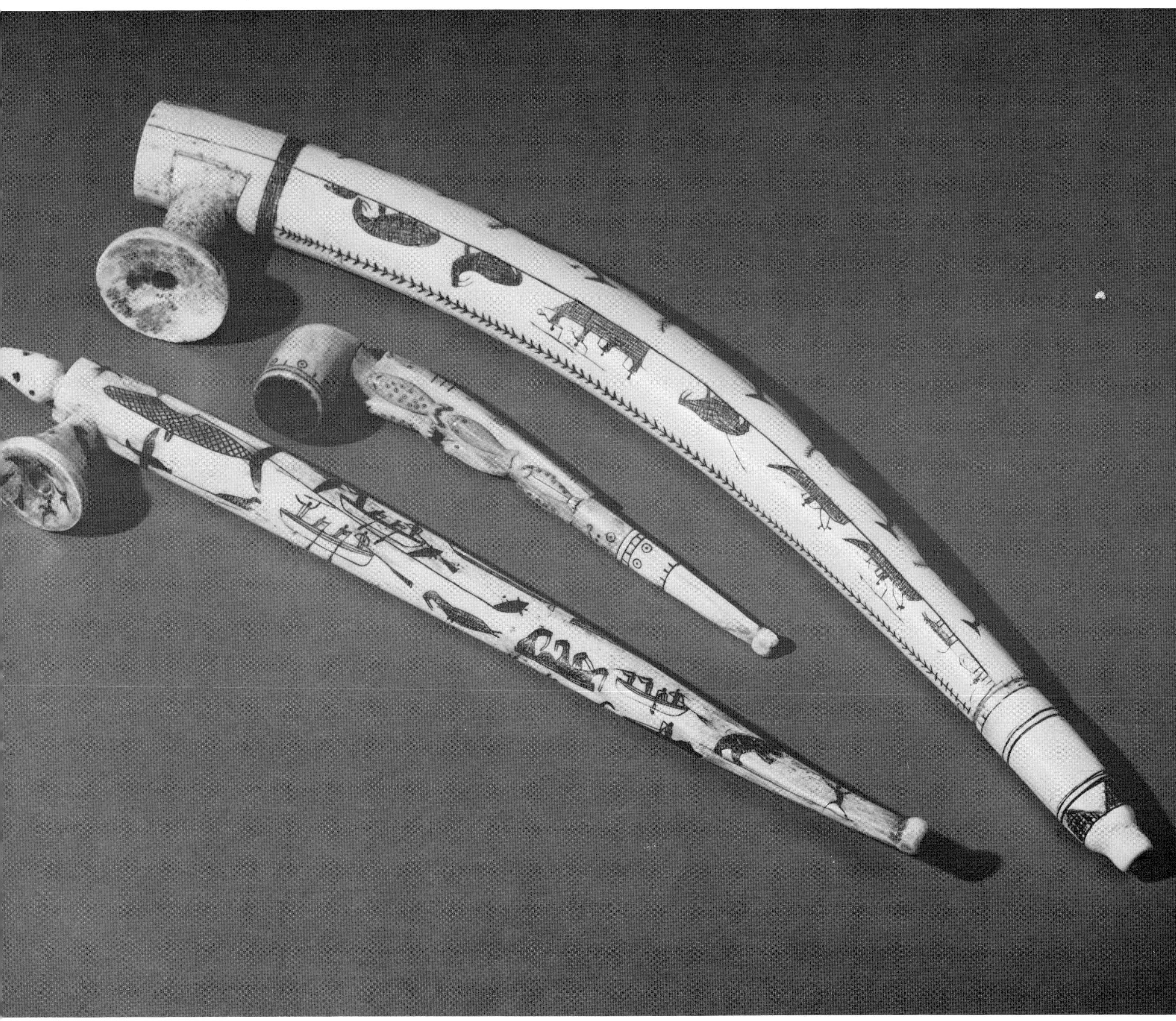

BACK SCRATCHERS

Ivory discs having sharp beveled edges fixed to wood handles through a hole in the center of the disc.

WOOD HANDLES

These were probably parts of dippers or ladles and are carved to represent left to right, a seal and two bears.

The center figure has a resemblance to the bear mask on page (163) in its general expression.

FIRE MAKING IMPLEMENTS

Like most primitive people, Eskimos made their fire by friction using materials one against the other to cause a spark which was caught by a piece of tinder or dust. These are fire making implements. The bow, the drill cap, and a fire stick. This stick was used later as a drill, the metal point inserted into the very hard wood. While a slab of soft wood was generally used as a fire maker, this ivory piece sparked very well, the dust still igniting with little effort.

The drill cap socket is metal evidently replacing the original one and patched into the wood. Note the neat plug at the left side of the socket. The drill cord handle is ivory.

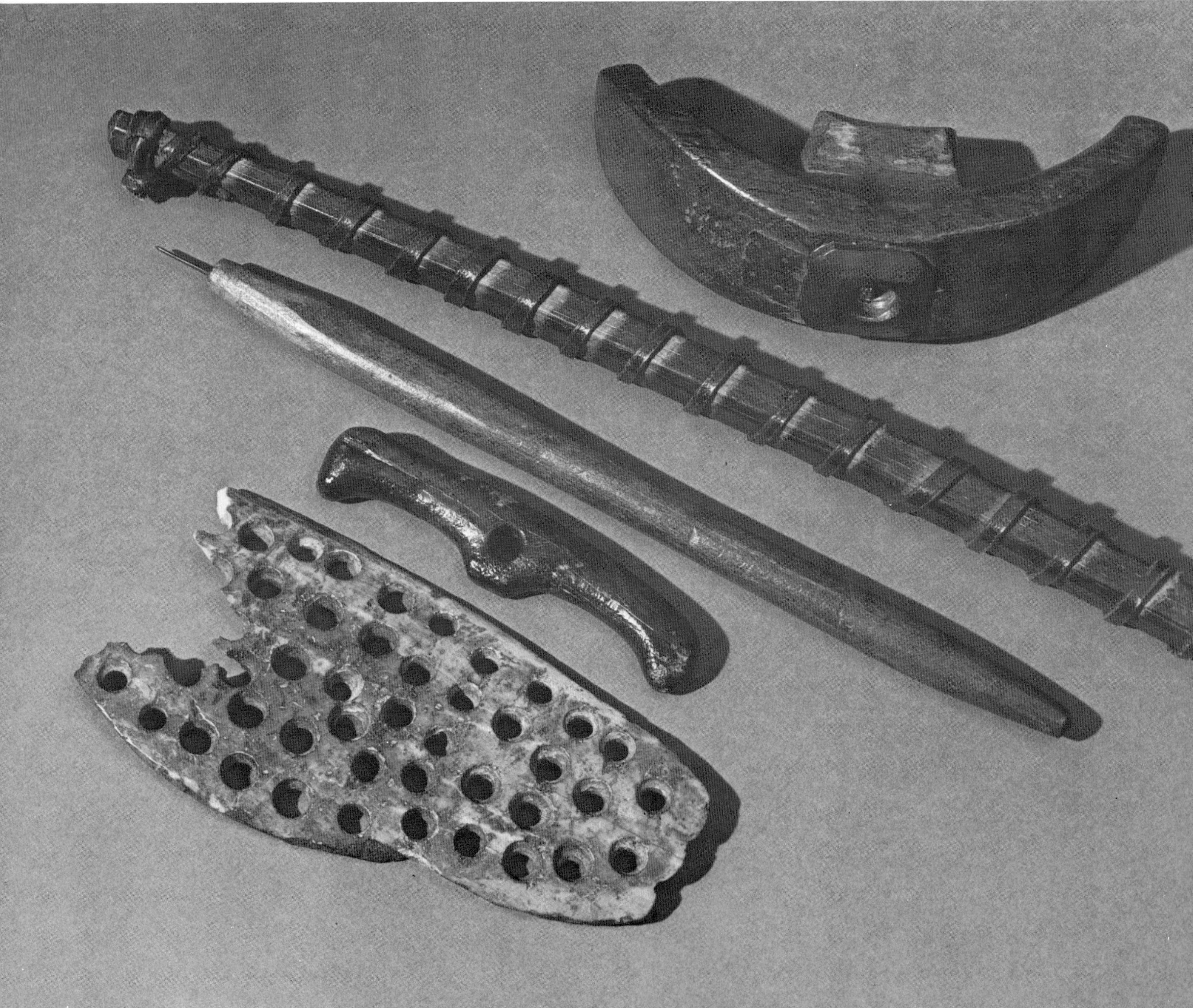

OIL LAMP

A small oil lamp probably used when traveling. The form is similar to the typical large houselamp used by the Eskimo which serves for lighting and warming his place of habitation. The material is gray stone which has darkened with oil and soot.

OIL LAMP

A lamp of hard gray stone which has a double ridge accommodating two wicks.

OIL LAMP

This stone lamp similar to ones found on the eastern Siberian coast is sub-oval in outline, deeper in the back, and slopes upward to a wide ledge in front. A stone ridge cut through the center crosses the ledge for holding a wick.

OIL LAMPS

To the left is a fragment of a lamp to which a seal skin cradle was applied. This pottery lamp made of earth, fur and blood among other things, may have been a child's toy or a hanging lamp. To the right is a saucer like lamp of stone with a gradual deepening of the bowl.

A WOOD FOOD BOWL

Grooved around the outside and mended in two places with baleen.

A WOODEN FOOD DISH

A well made wooden food dish, decorated inside with grooves, a single wide one around the top and three around the bottom. There is an indication of once having had red color on the outside of the dish.

A DISH OR DIPPER MADE FROM MAMMOTH IVORY

Only one handle remains of the four originally cut into the ivory. A split down the middle was mended.

A WOODEN FOOD DISH

A well made food dish cut from a single piece of wood shaped with a rim flattened around the top. There are indications this dish was colored red on the outer surface at one time.

A WOODEN FOOD DISH

Made from a plank, the wood is shaped and hollowed out. A thicker wood strip secured around the upper edge, is chamfered to fit neatly together, and is secured with bone or wood pegs. The dish was colored red at one time and grooved around the top strip for decoration. The creator of this dish did a superb job of joining the one piece lower section to the top edge. One can barely see where they join.

A WOODEN BUCKET

Made from a thin strip of spruce closed at the overlapping end by sewing with rawhide. The bottom is fitted into a slight channel and secured when the sides are drawn tight. These buckets were used for water and other liquids as well as blubber and meat. This example is a smaller version. The sizes range from very large tubs to cup size. They are often equipped with a skin carrying handle. Buckets may be colored and grooved for decoration.

A DIPPER

Made from steam bent wood having the ends sewn together with rawhide and fitted with a closed bottom. The handle is cut to resemble an animal. The top has incised lines around it, the base a groove. The dipper is painted red on the outside.

WOOD SPOONS

Lower example is a long handled wood spoon, the bowl of which is painted with red ochre. The red also occurs in the middle of the handle and at the end. The mythical animal in the bowl, a seal's spirit, is black as are the lines of the spoon.

Above is a wooden spoon undecorated except for a groove, the full length in the center of the handle.

WOOD LADLES

The ladle on the right continues to ooze oil. It is mended at the lower left corner with baleen. The ladle on the left has a more elaborately shaped handle.

MISCELLANEOUS SPOONS

Ivory spoons of various shapes with holes for ties. These were worn on the person while traveling about.

MISCELLANEOUS SPOONS

Left: An ivory spoon bowl and a bone skimmer.
Right: A ladle made of bone.

A SEAL SKIN WORK BAG

With a set of skin working tools. (Some woman's personal collection.) The small handles to the right are for women's bags which roll closed for storage of their sewing implements. The handles may have other uses such as sharpening needles #9, creasing skin #8, or making holes #7.

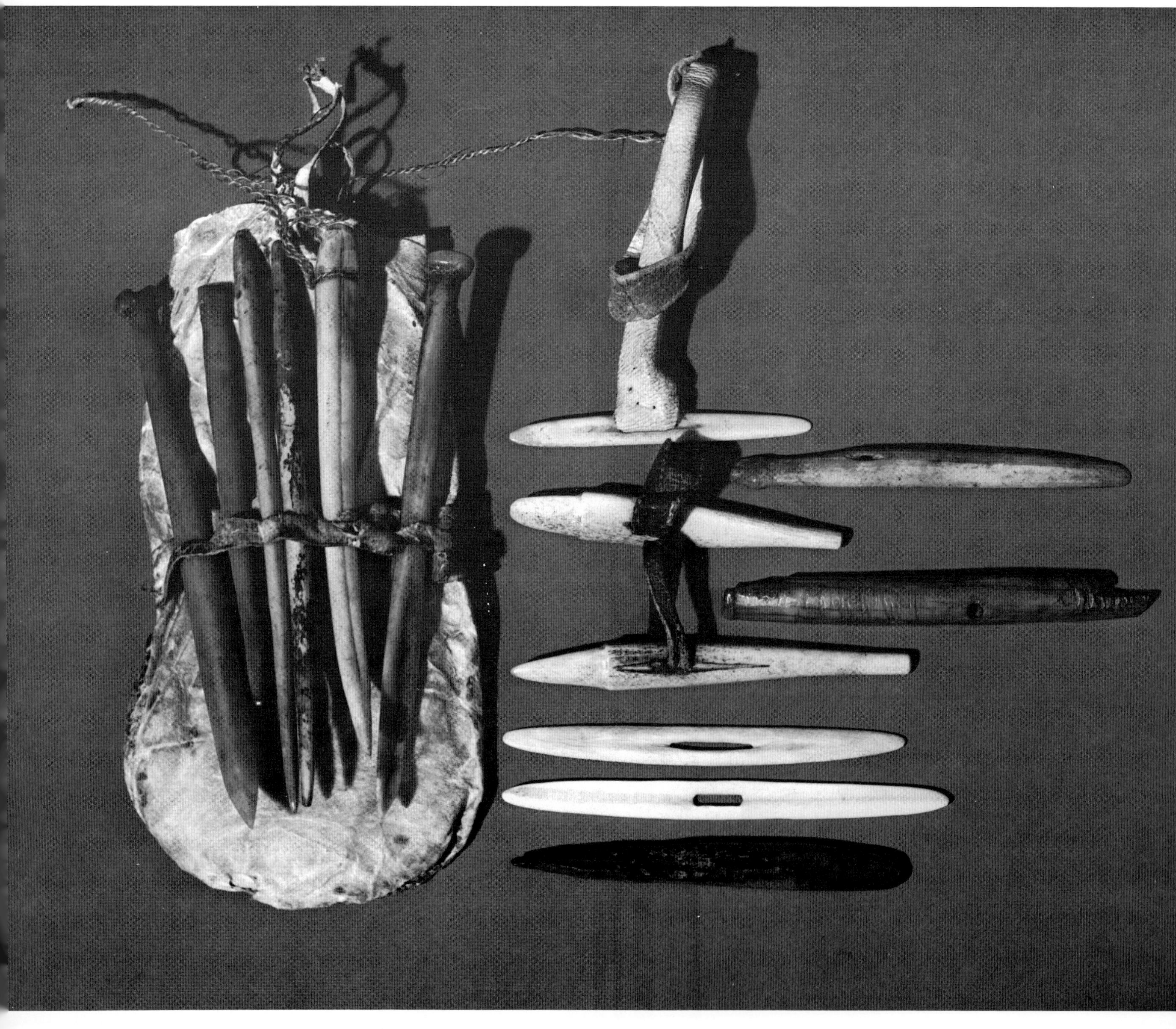

BODKINS, SCRAPERS, CREASERS

Bodkins are sharp ivory instruments used to make holes in skins so that they can be sewn with ivory needles. The sharp pointed examples are bodkins. The flat articles are skin scrapers or creasers.

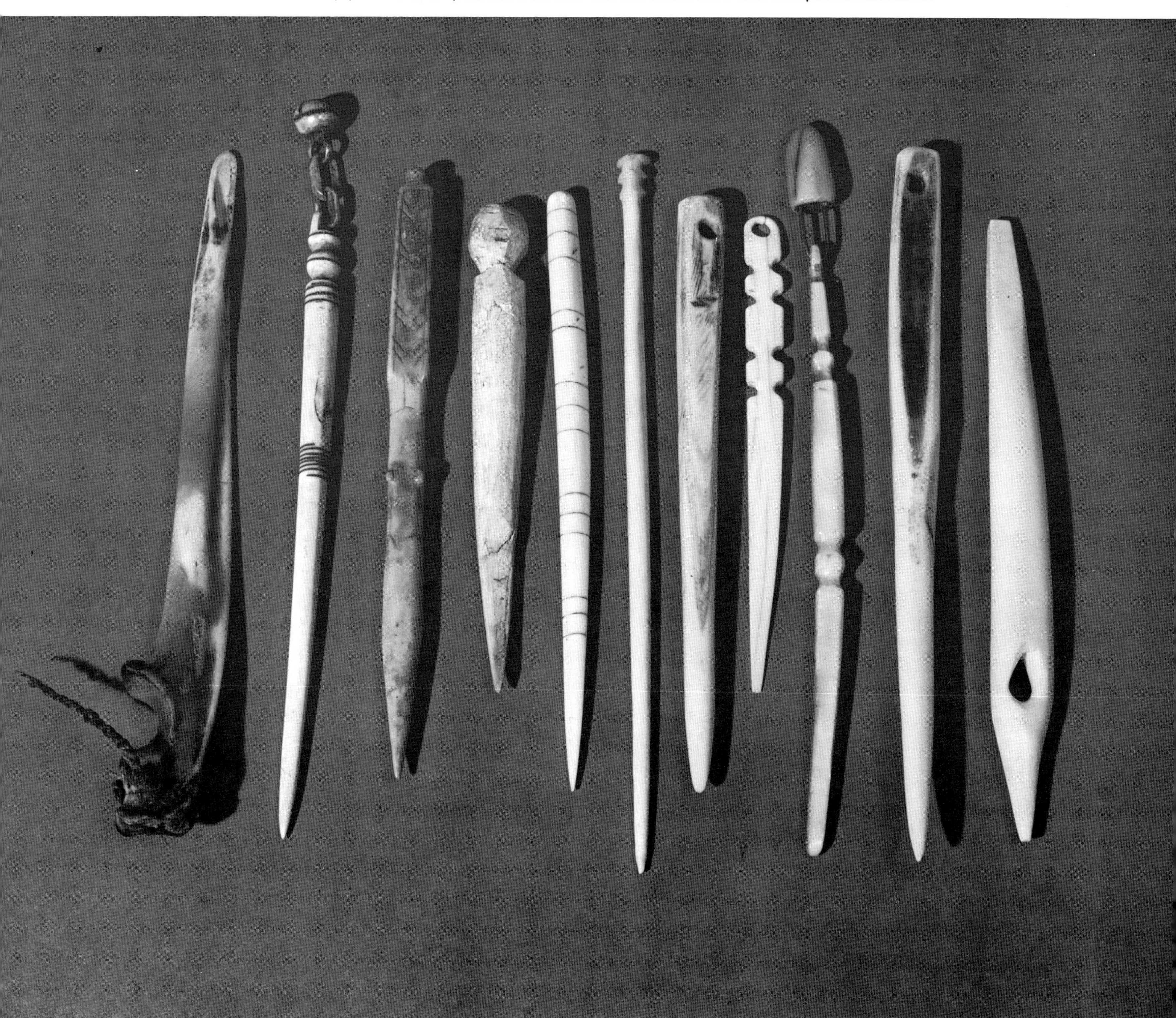

NETTING NEEDLE AND DIVIDERS

The ivory seal is a netting needle with a broken point. The compass shaped articles were probably used to measure material and stitch lengths.

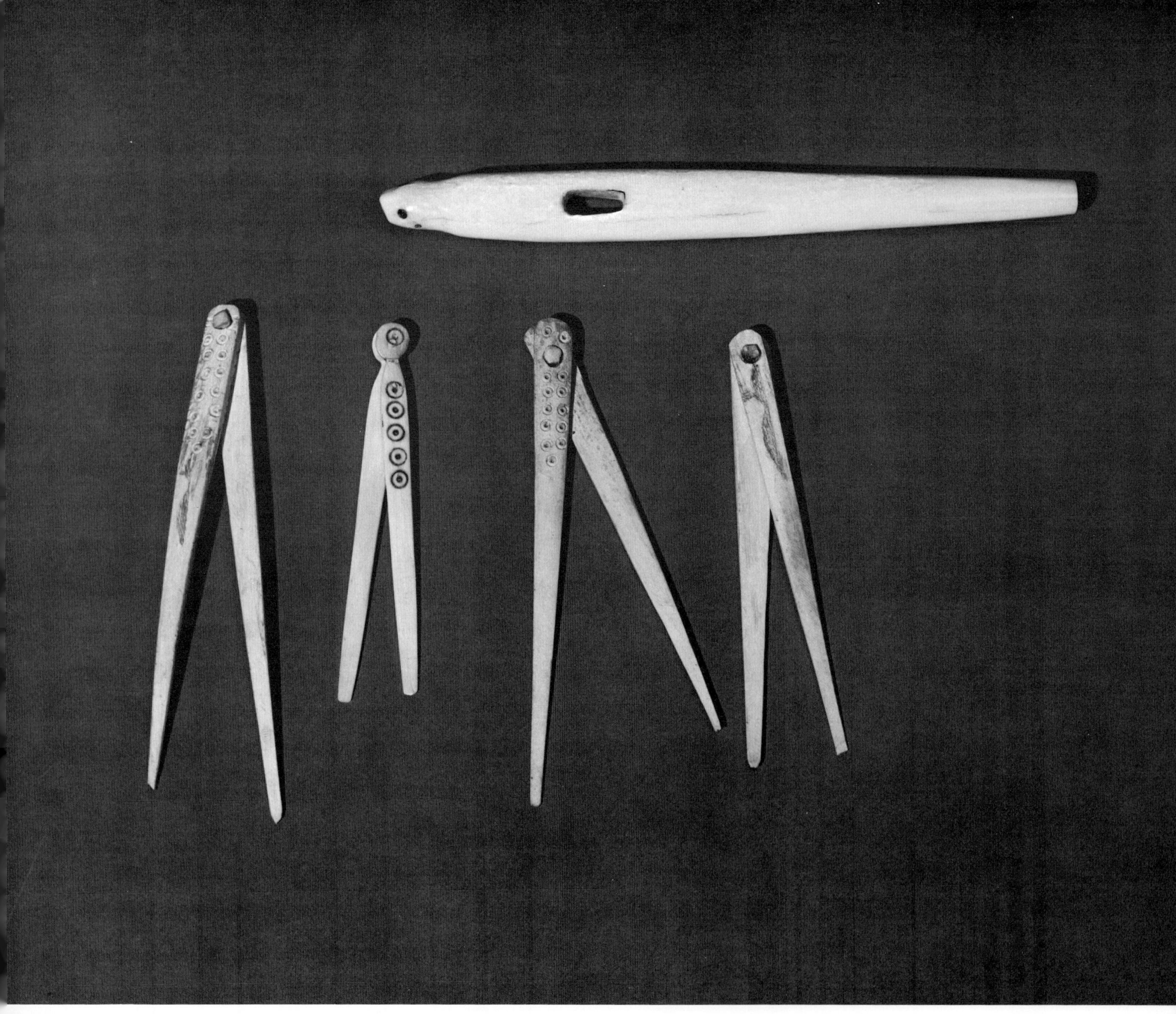

MISCELLANEOUS SKIN WORKING IMPLEMENTS

Bodkins and two single parts for spacers 4-5.

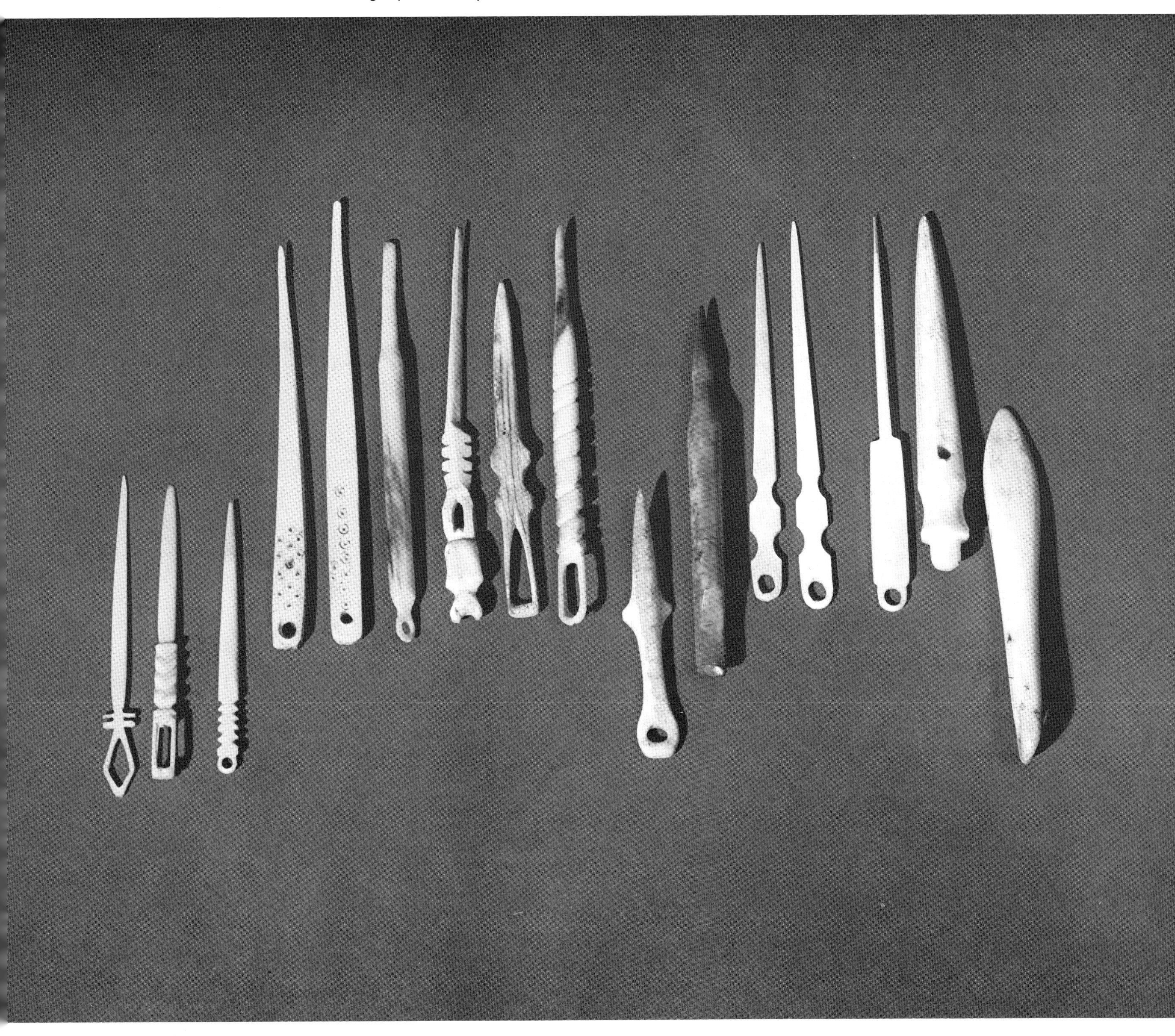

MISCELLANEOUS NEEDLE CASES

The case to the left has a sharpener attached made of hard black stone, and a thimble guard as part of the case.

Thimbles were made of tough seal skin and were generally oval in shape. They were secured by pulling one end of the skin, which was tapered, through a slot in the center of the thimble skin, thereby making a rough circle which was easily hung from a hook shaped holder, such as the sharp spur on the above.

Needles were ivory and were stuck into a hide strip which was pulled through the case protecting them from being broken or lost. Many cases had stoppers while others depended upon several strips of hide to stopper the container. In such an instance there might be several implements attached to a single case such as a creaser, a bodkin, and a sharpener.

The fish at the far right has a very sharp tail which was probably used as a bodkin. The mouth is stoppered with a piece of wood. Needles were contained inside the fish which was tied to a work bag, through the two sets of holes shown on its back.

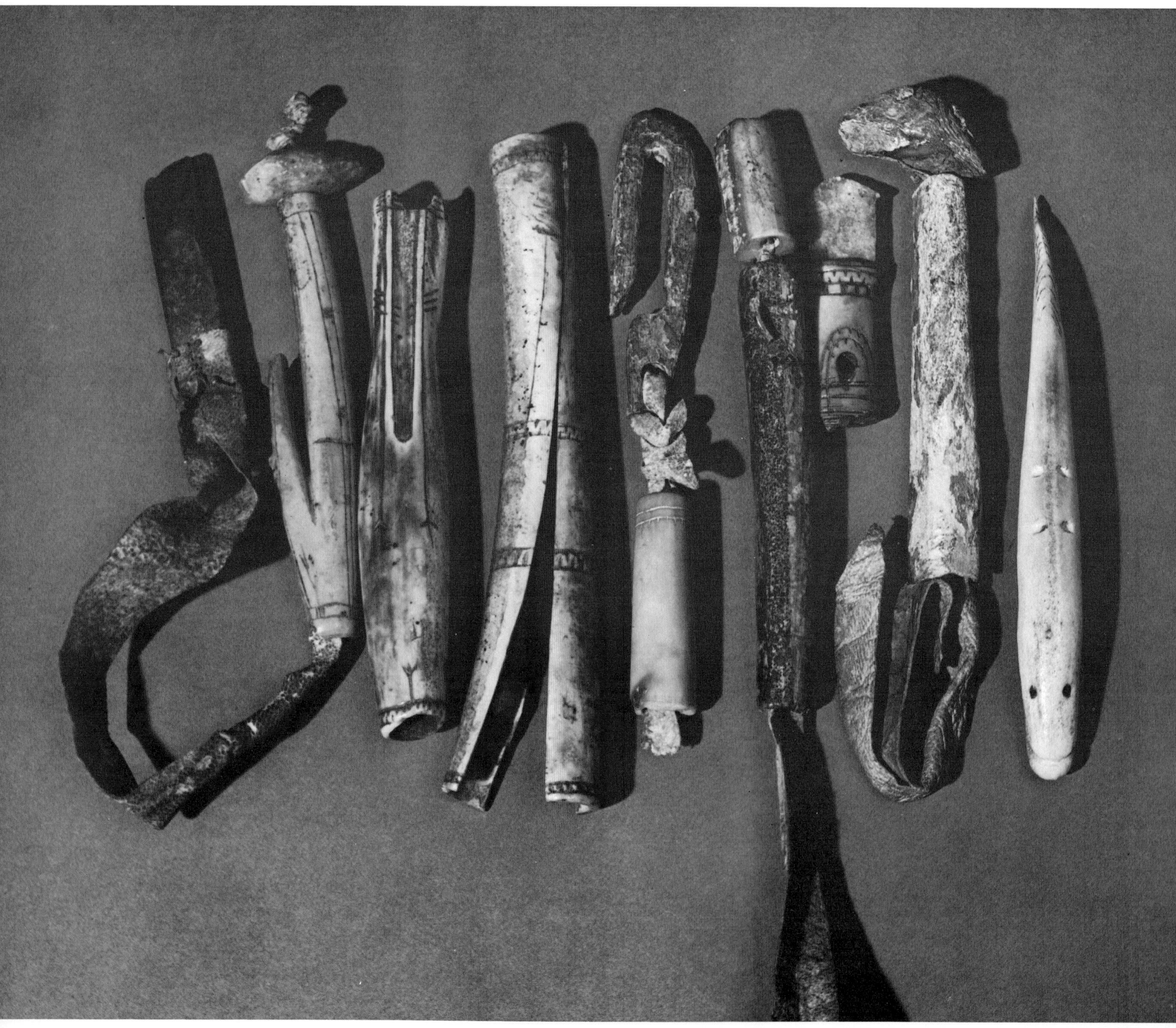

MISCELLANEOUS THIMBLE GUARDS

An arrangement made expressly for keeping seal skin thimbles. The skin circles were pulled down over the complete guard or caught on the hook, through the joining hole in one end of the thimble skin.

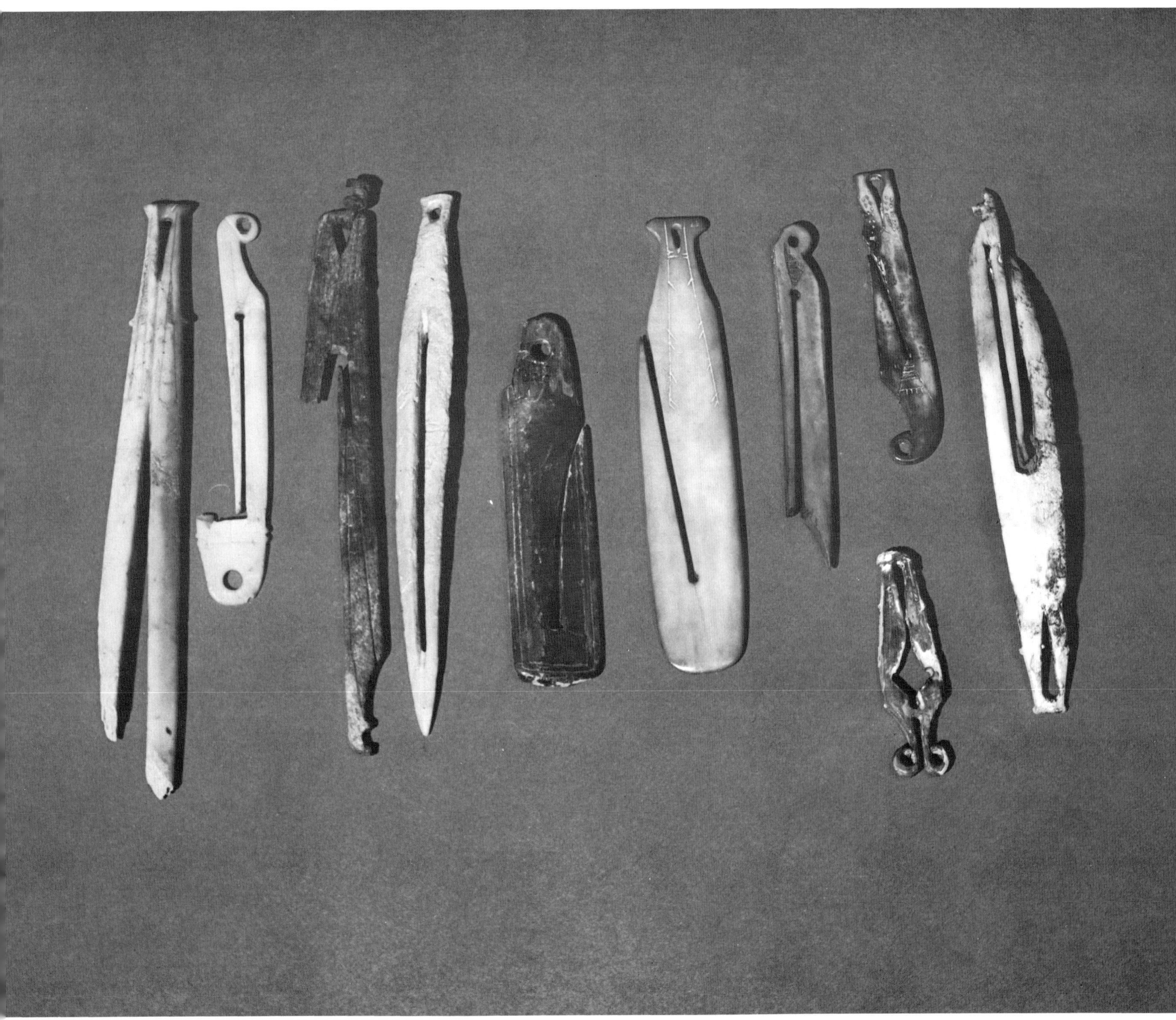

MISCELLANEOUS HOUSEHOLD ITEMS

1, 2, 3 & 7. Tom cod rod line guides.
4. & 8. Skin softeners.
5. A netting needle.
6. A sinew twister.
9. An etched skin softener.

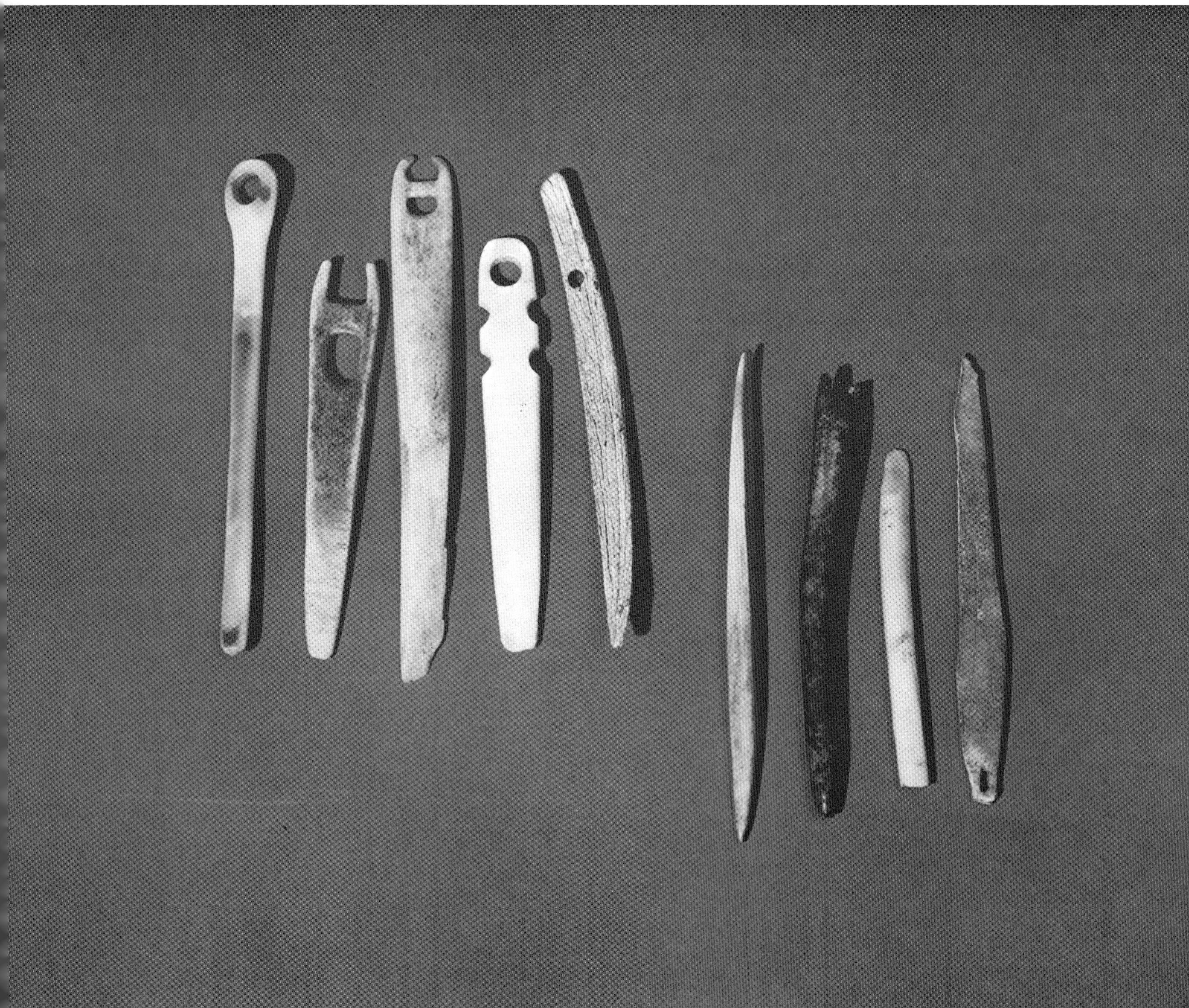

SINEW TWISTERS AND SMALL COMBS FOR MAKING SEWING CORD.

Sinew from reindeer legs, because of its length and strength, was used for making "sewing thread". It was dried and pounded then separated into shreds with combs similar to those below (left). It was later twisted using sinew twisters (right) and finally, wound until used.

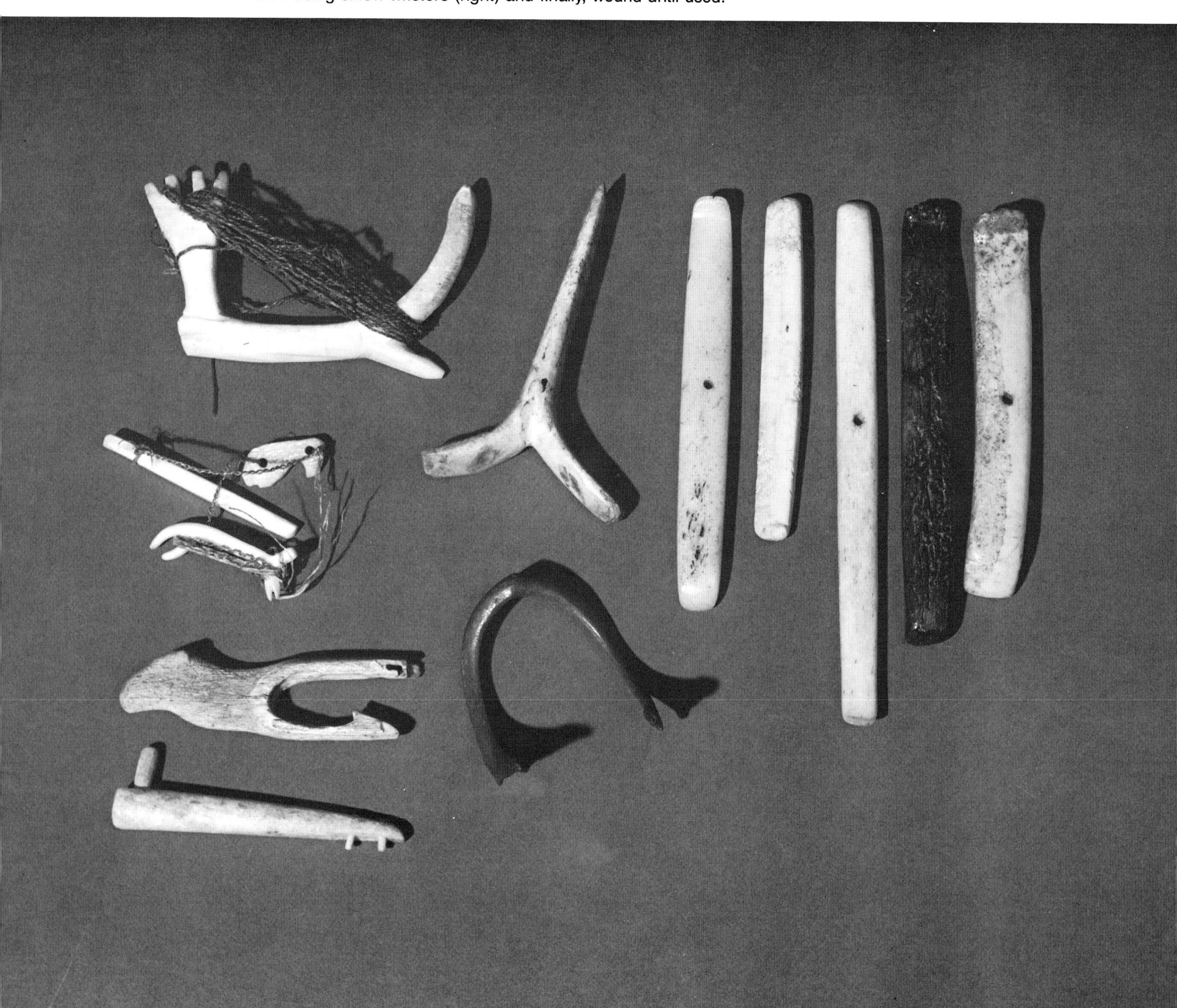

MISCELLANEOUS BOOT SOLE CREASERS

Generally larger then those kept in a woman's work bag. They are etched and shaped making for great variety and design.

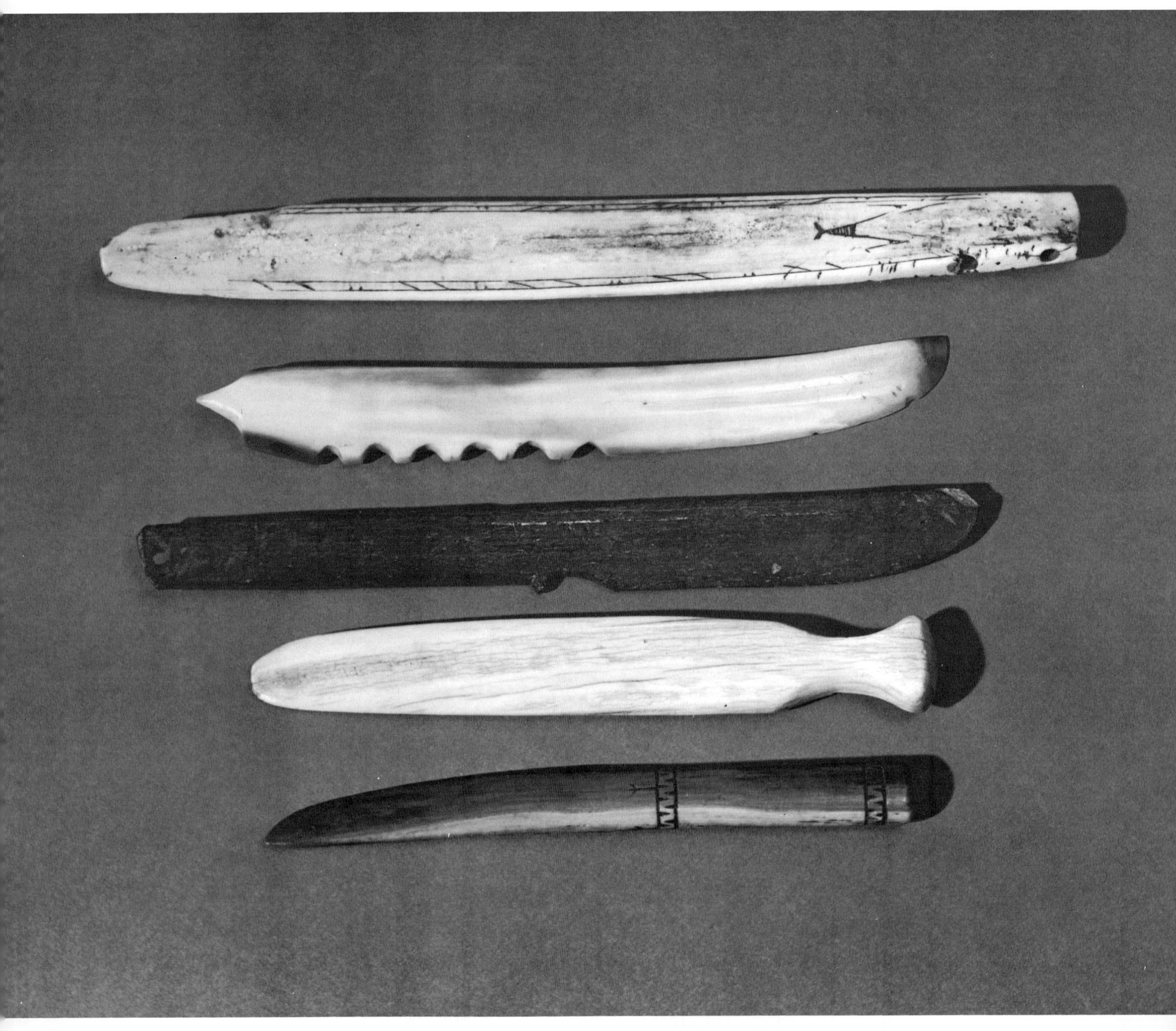

SNUFF TUBES

The upper box was at one time a woman's needle case but was appropriated for a snuff container judging from the dark residue on the inside. In the center of the box there is a tally of some kind with a circle around a central dot.

The lower two are snuff tubes which were used to take snuff from boxes. Tubes were made from hollow bird bones and were often decorated. They were frequently attached to a snuff box by a cord. One end of the tube was placed in the snuff and the user inhaled the material through the other end into the nostrils. Women were the principal users of snuff which may account for the needle case being used as a snuff box.

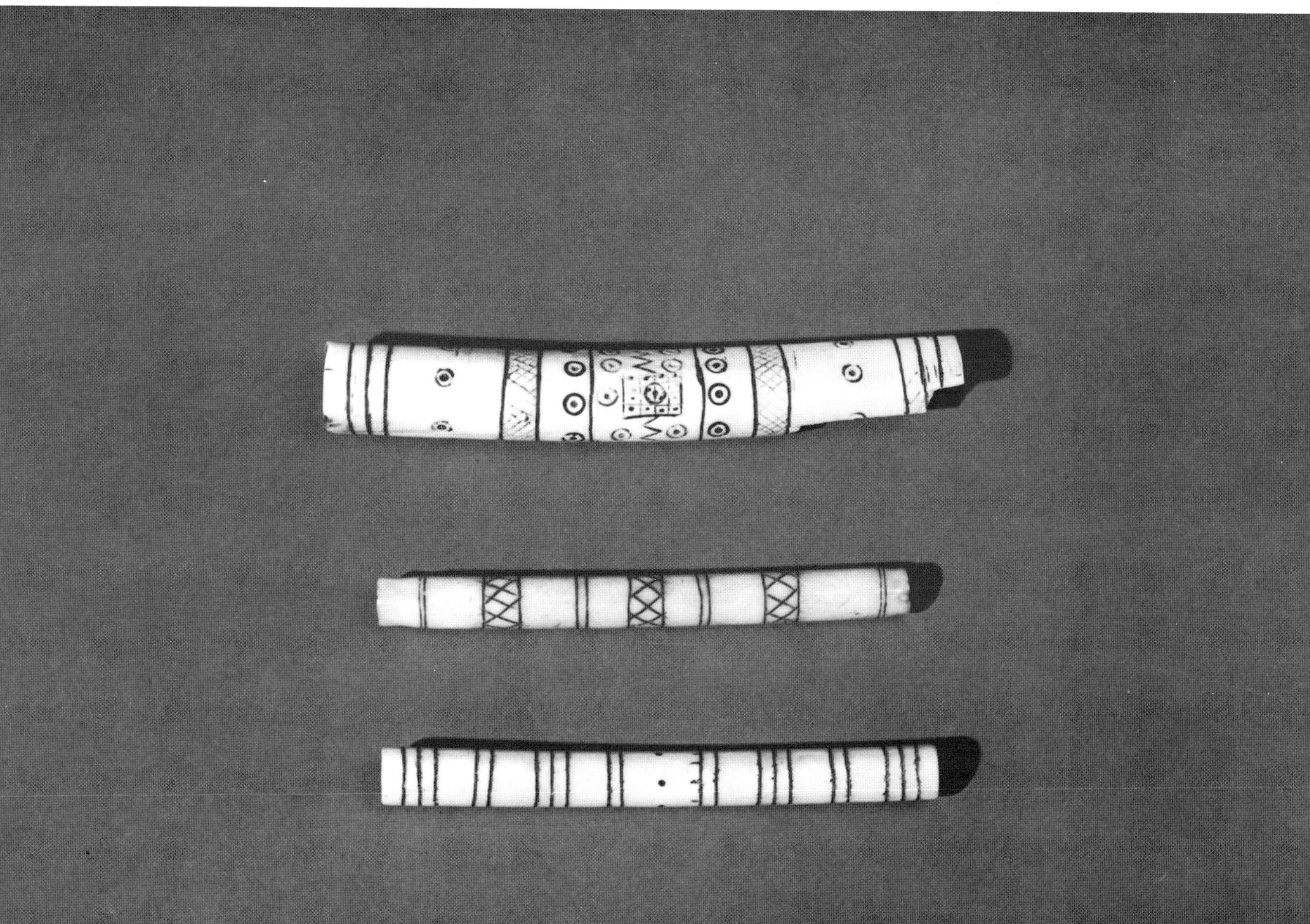

WOMEN'S SKINNING KNIVES

The two upper examples have bone handles, the first has a stone blade, the second a slate blade. The bottom handle (left) is ivory and the blade metal. The fourth handle (right) is a wood bird with a slate blade.

MISCELLANEOUS IVORY HANDLES FOR WOMEN'S SKIN AND FISH KNIVES

A blade was inserted in the slot and secured with pegs. The handle at the right top, has two seals heads on its left side. The second handle on the lower left side has comb type teeth to soften hard spots in skins.

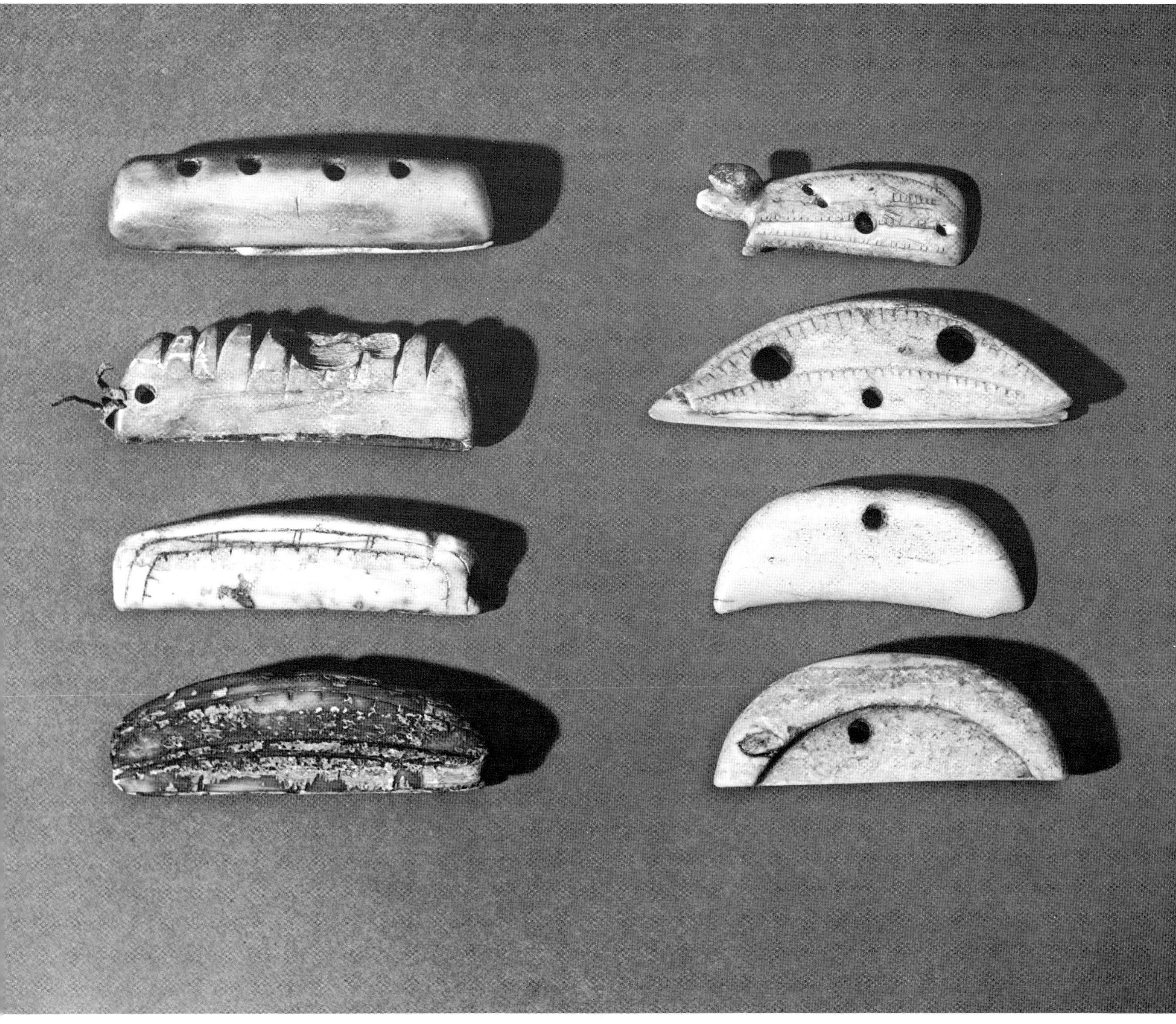

WOMEN'S KNIVES

Used for cutting up fish and game. The first has an old bone handle and slate blade, the upper right handle is also bone. The two lower handles are ivory and of the same general design but of different size.

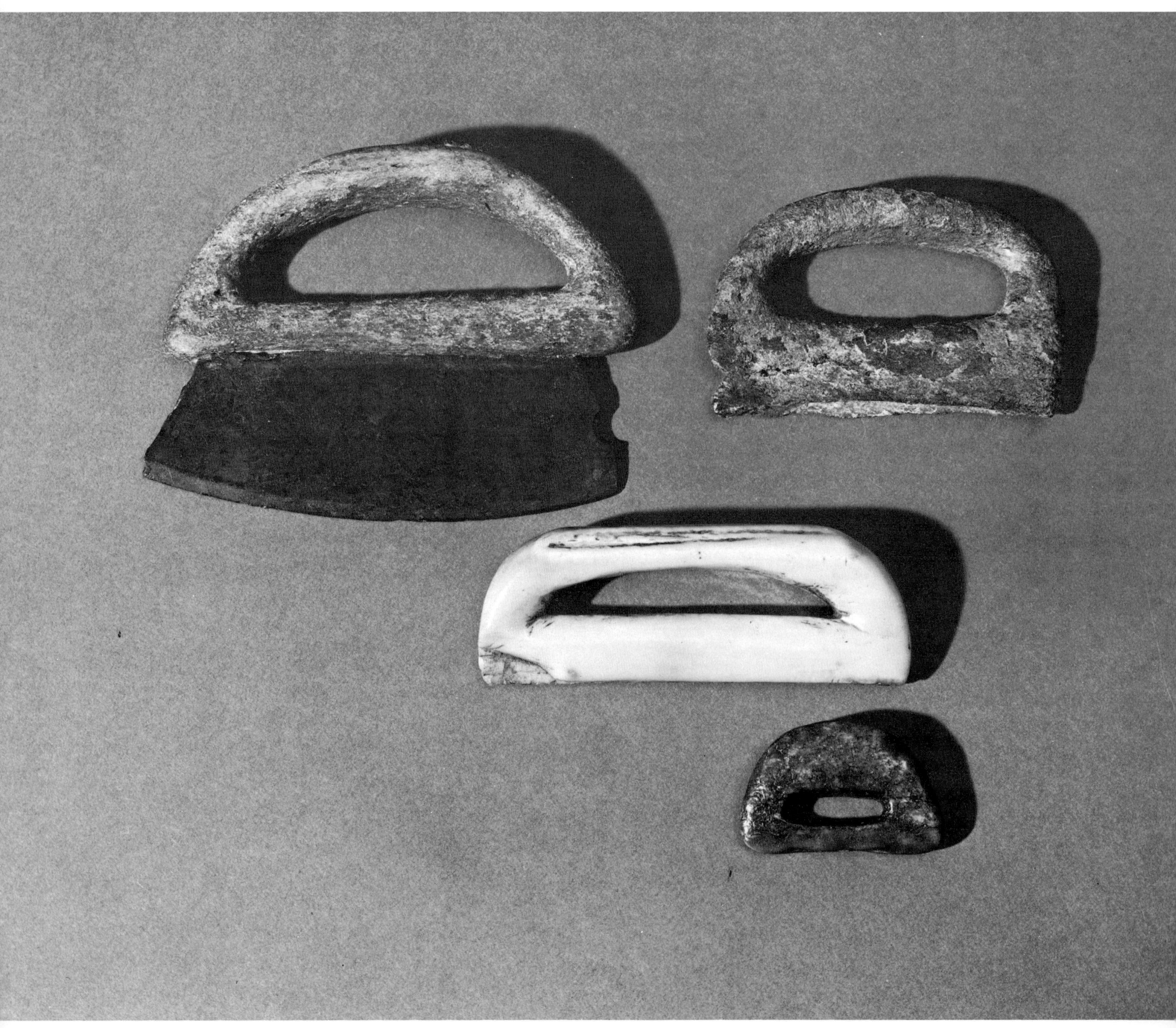

HANDLES FOR WOMEN'S KNIVES

The upper left handle is bone the others are ivory. The blades were fitted into the openings on the bottom of the handles.

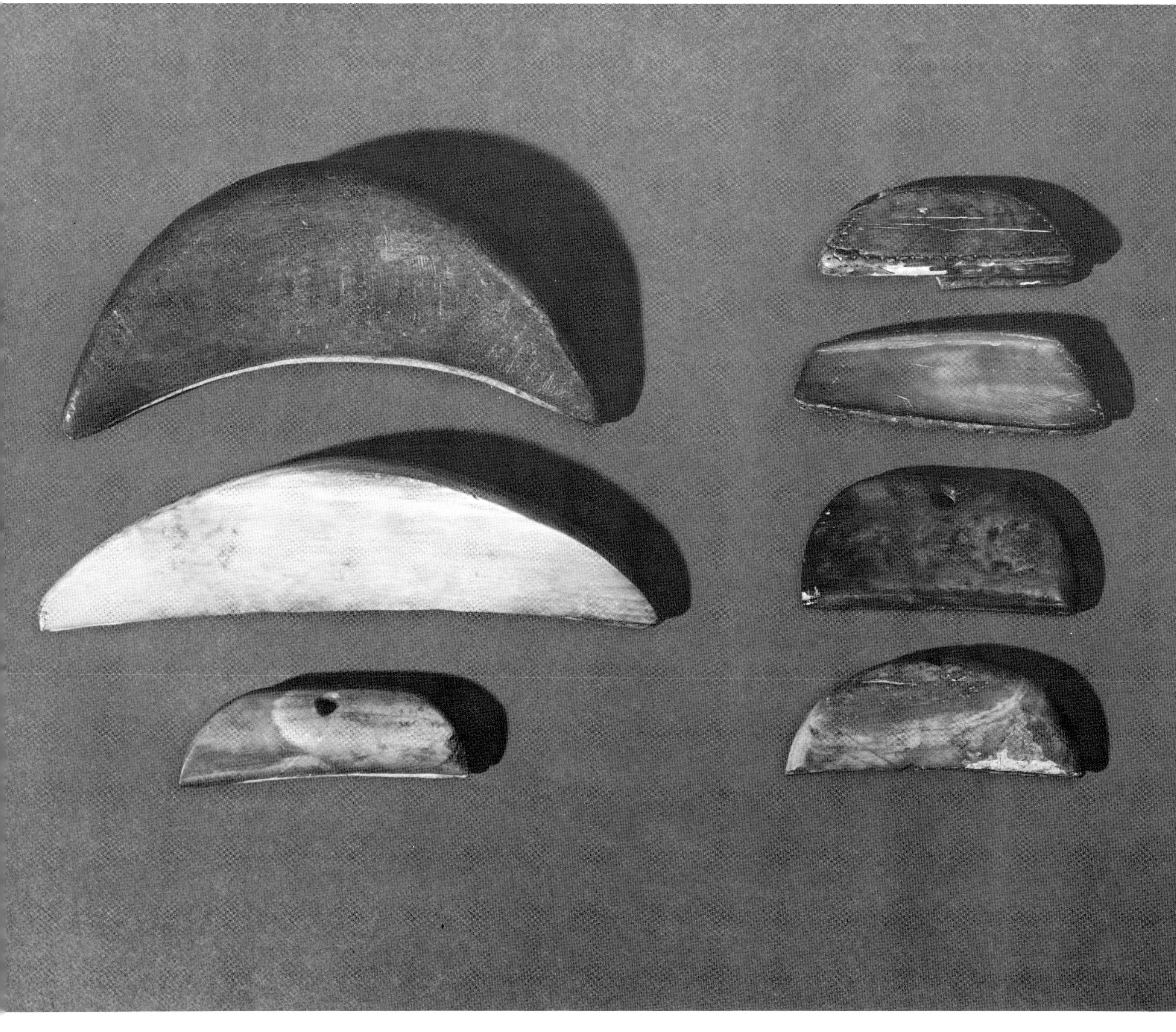

AN OLD IVORY SHAPED AND DECORATED IMPLEMENT

The use of this artifact is uncertain, it may have been a skin softener.

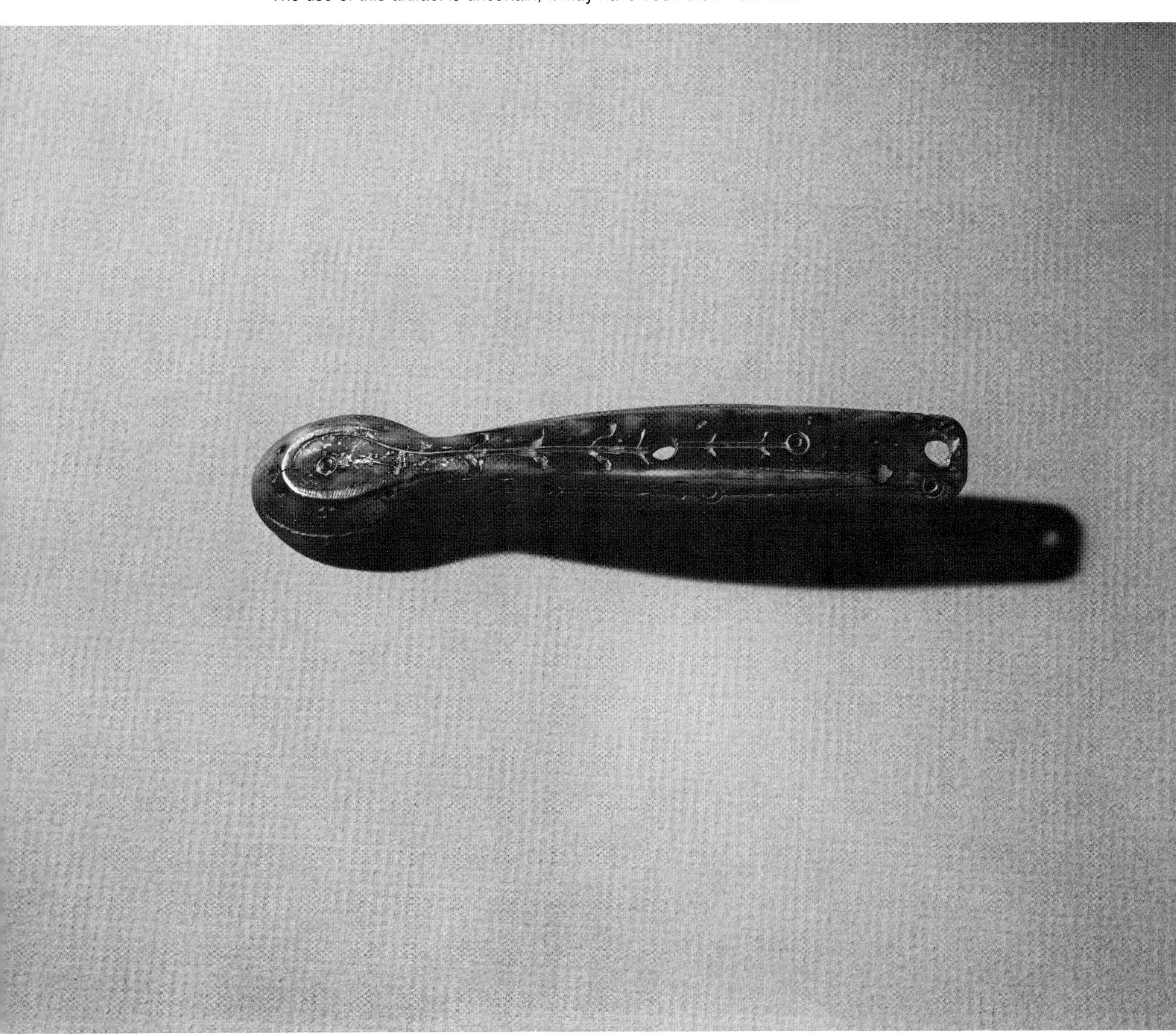

A REINDEER HORN ROOT PICK

Used by women to dig out edible grass roots. This is a superior tool showing great care in its manufacture.

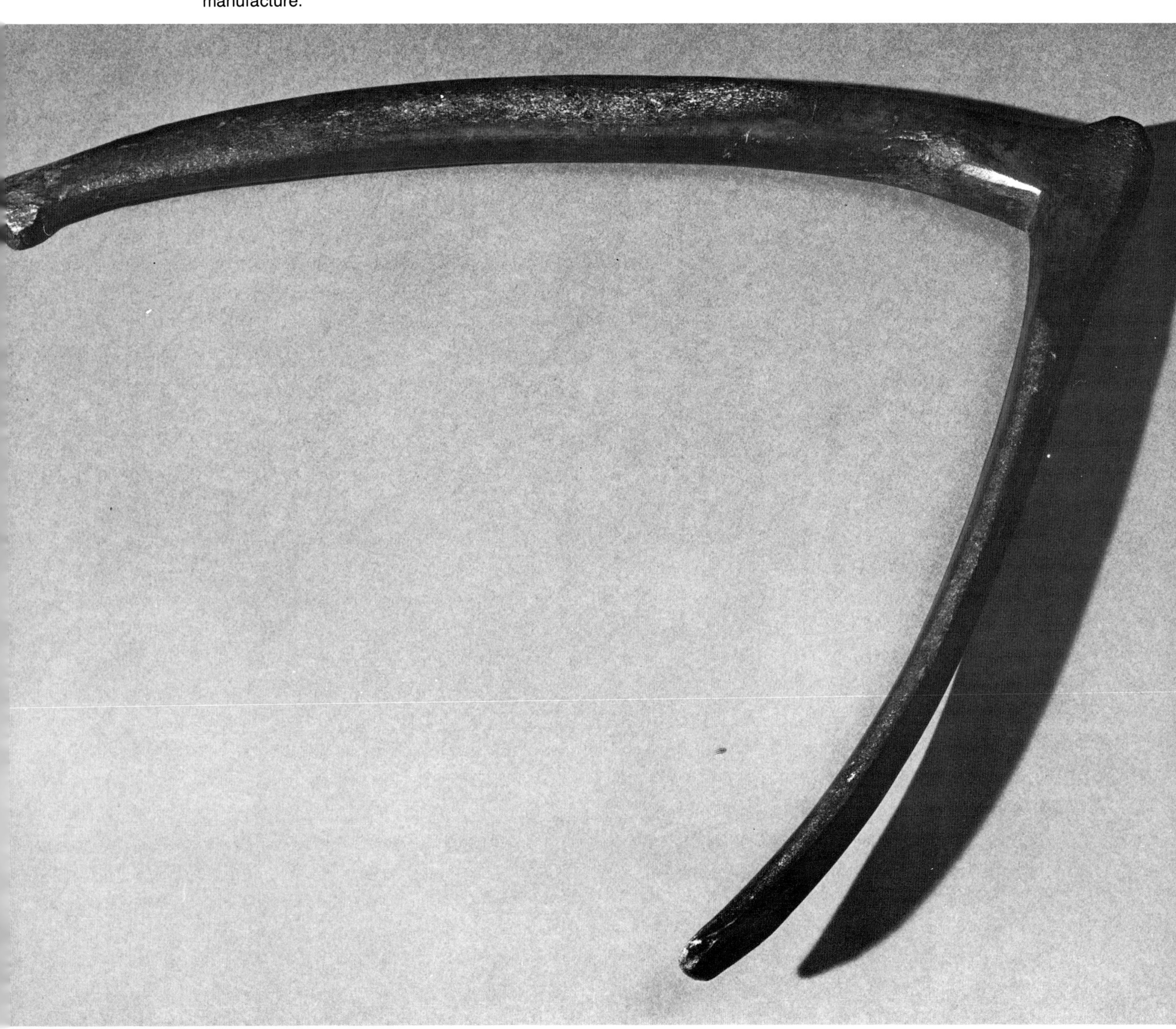

BONE SHOVEL EDGES

Wooden shovels were generally used to clear away snow and dig through drifts. The bottom of the shovel was often fitted with an edge of bone or ivory grooved to receive the wood and extending beyond it to form a sharp edge. These extensions were fastened to the wood with pegs.

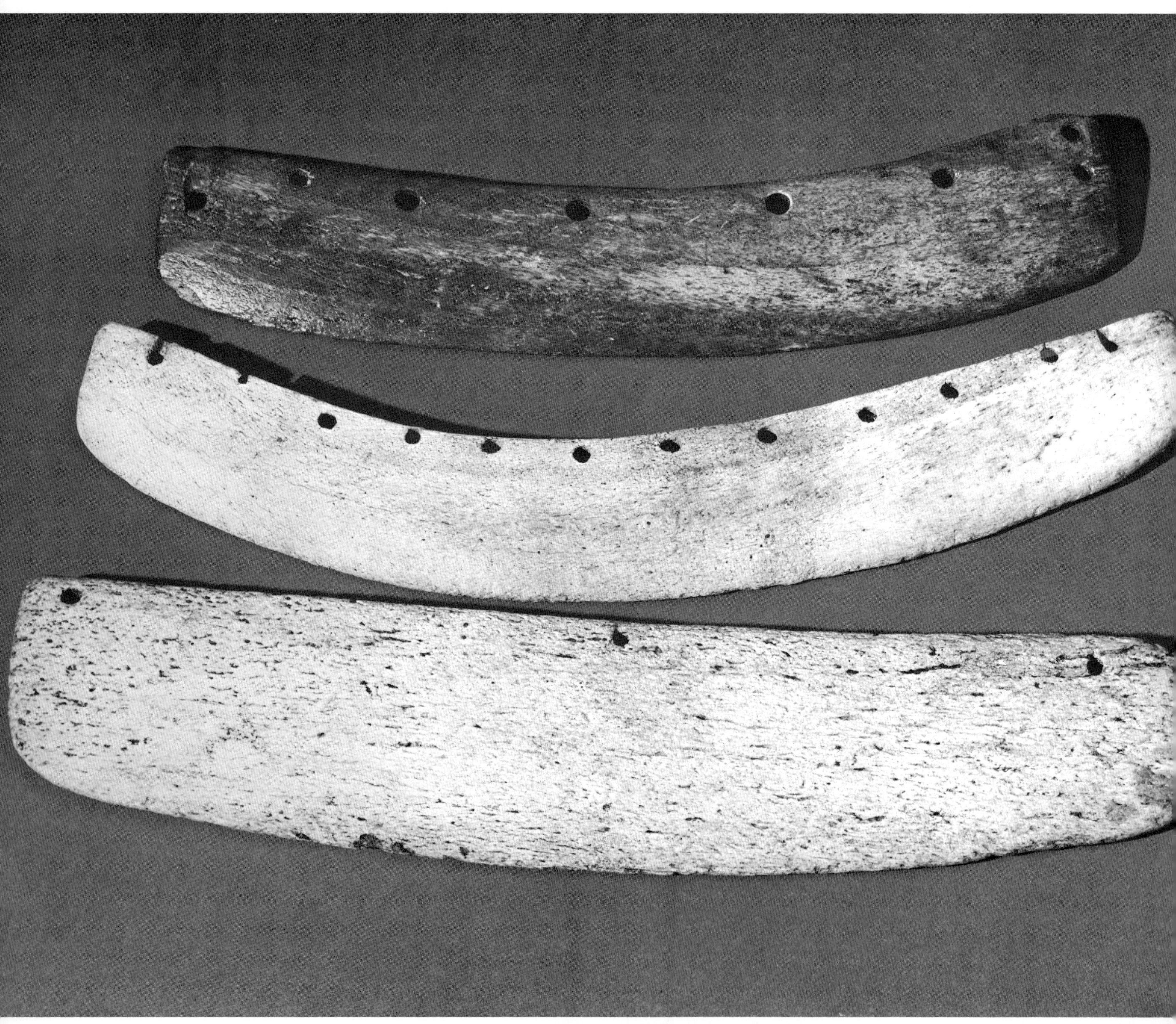

SNOW KNIVES

The upper two artifacts are antler snow knives with bear heads. These were used to beat snow off clothes and boots. The white bear was cut off from something, perhaps a similar knife.

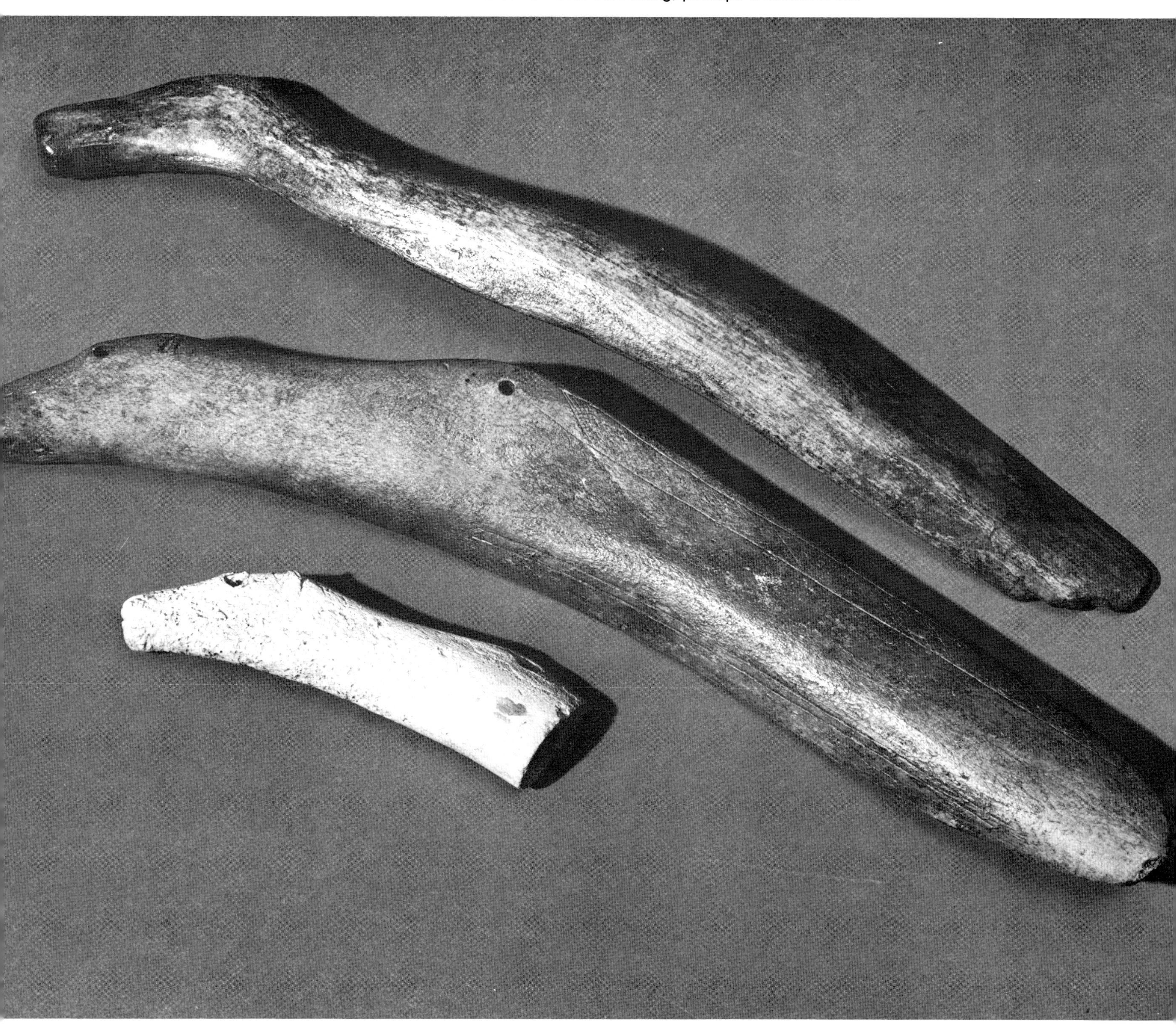

FETISH FIGURES

The figure on the right holds a shamen's property between its feet.

FETISH FIGURE

A spear point with a carving of a human face on the end. This likeness was obviously not carved for decoration but was probably a fetish. It is not noticable except while examining the point carefully. It was probably a superstitious hunter making his presence known to the animal hit by his weapon.

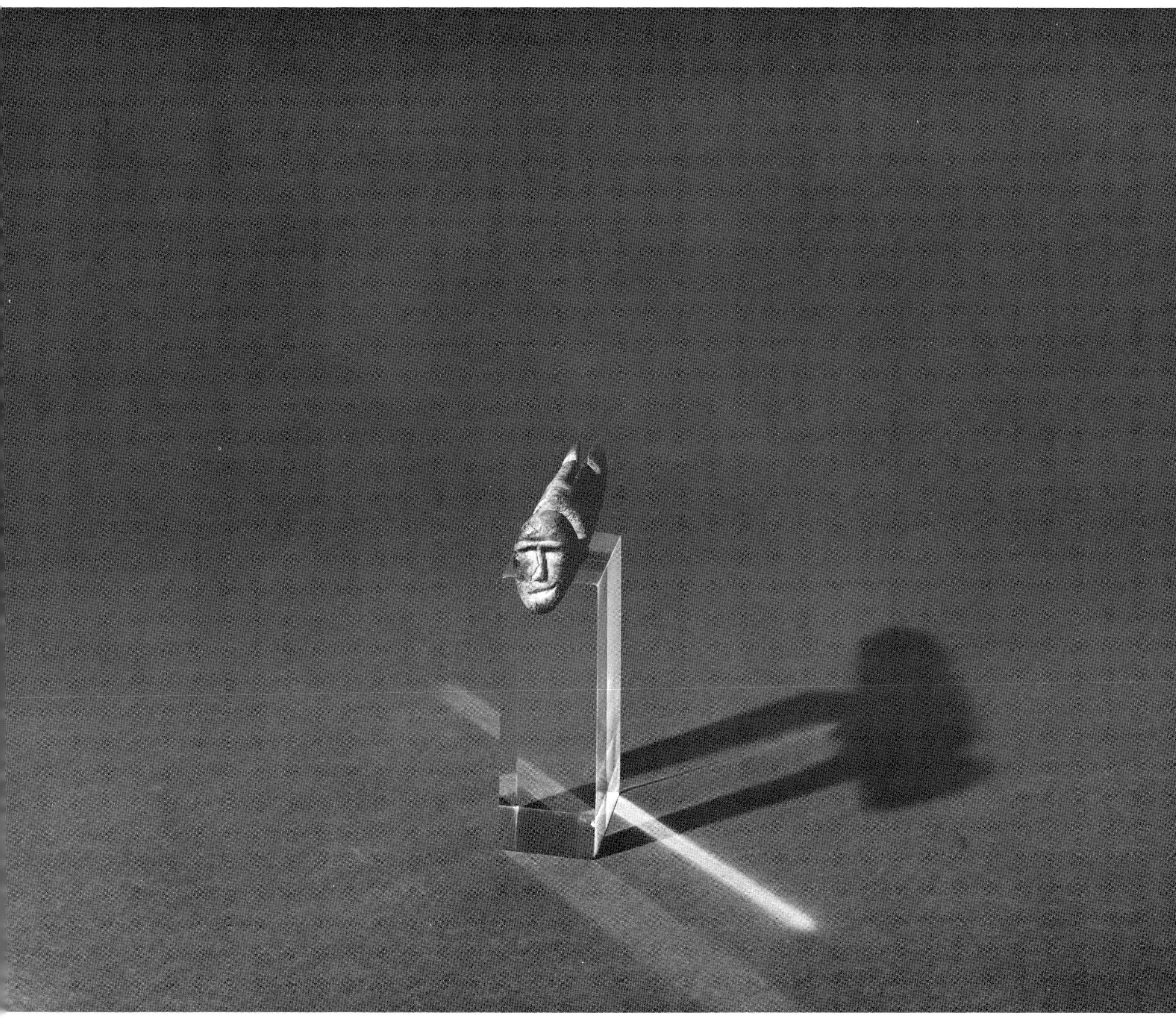

MISCELLANEOUS IVORY FIGURES

Ivory animals from an excavation were probably toys. The seal figure at the left has a hole at the tail indicating it could also have been a sinker.

MISCELLANEOUS IVORY FIGURES

1. This may be a figure which broke while being carved or did not please its carver. It was not finished but was discarded which was the custom.
2. This figure's head is shaped, the nose clearly carved and the mouth provided with teeth. The body is realistic even though only black dots mark the breast and navel. There are tatoo marks around the mouth.
3. A fetish figure of a seal. There is a minimum amount of carving which suggests the ivory itself inspired the creation. The large eyes only slightly indented are filled with graphite.
4. A small ivory mask. Some small articles similar to this were carved for toys. This does not seem to be for that purpose.
5. An ivory effigy representing a fetus which was carved for a fertility fetish.

CHARMS FOR HATS AND OTHER ARTICLES

Bear heads similar to those in the lower part of the picture are fastened on a float rack. Walrus heads are often seen on hunting visors. The pin like seal is an earring.

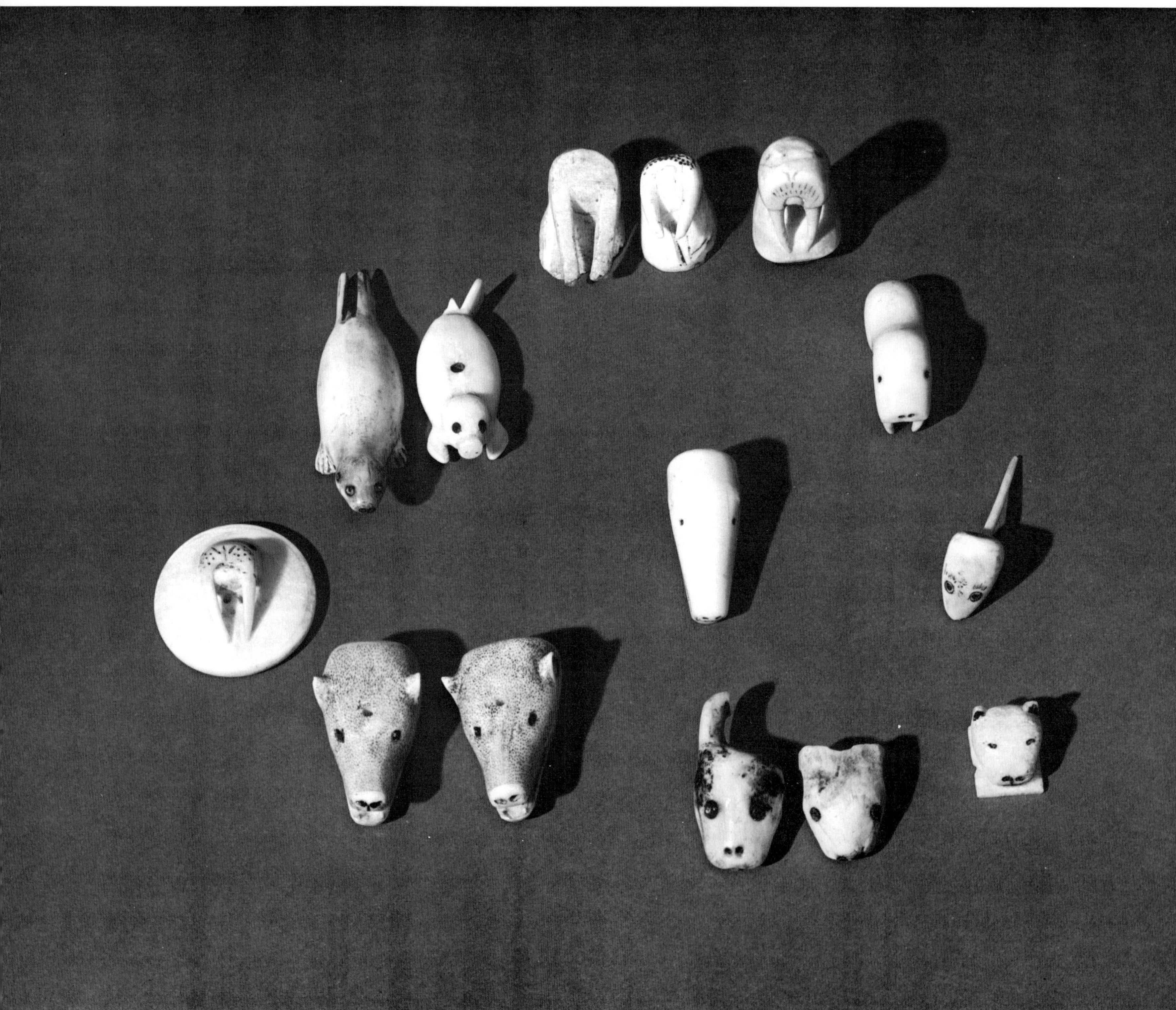

BONE TOY FIGURES

Ivory was used for toy carvings generally in the coastal regions where it was plentiful. Bone seems to have been used where there was little ivory and wood used where it was available.

1. The animal with a figure on each side, over its back, represents a story in folklore. The animal in the story is a bear. These figures being bone may have been carved by Tundra people who knew the story but not necessarily the contours of a bear.
2. A bone reindeer or caribou figure which has lost some of its antlers. There are two small eyelets carved along the side indicating a rein or other trappings were used with this animal.
3. An arctic rabbit, carved from the same type of bone as the other two figures, shows considerable life when seen standing on its legs. The primitive carver captured the spirit of the animal with a minimum of material.

MISCELLANEOUS FIGURES

Animals and birds were carved by fathers for their children. The materials were ivory, wood or bone. Many show great skill and perception. These figures are ivory and the first three, upper left, are especially interesting since they were made to sit. The forelegs are usual but the back legs are only indicated. The first of the sitting animals has inset legs the other animals are carved from one piece. The animal at the lower right of the picture, probably a bear, is also meant to lie down but these legs are indicated by pegs placed flush to the body.

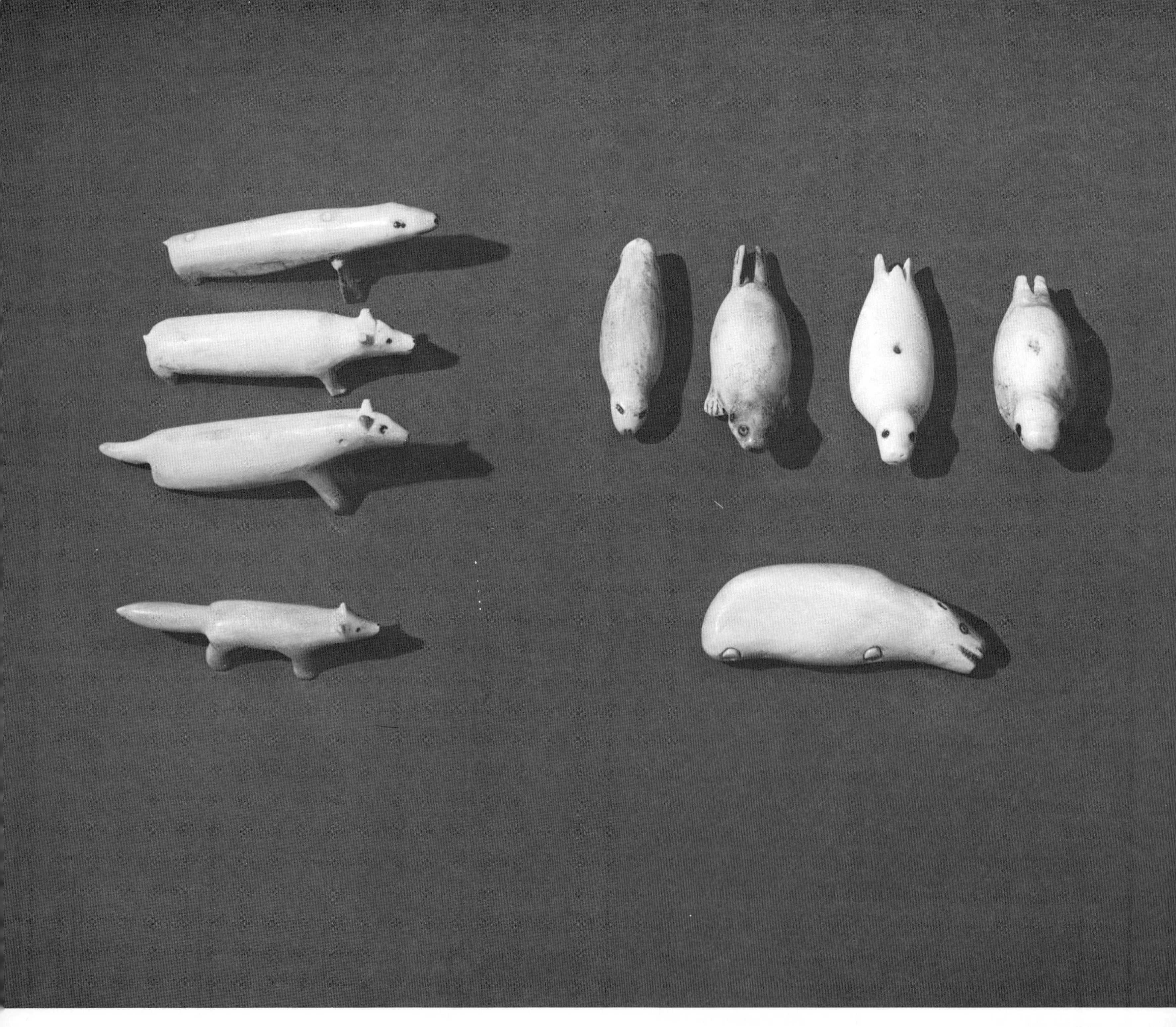

IVORY WALRUS FIGURES

The upper one carved from one piece of ivory, the lower one having separate tusks.

These two carvings show the problem carvers have with walrus ivory to be able to manipulate the material so that the core does not detract from the finished article.

OLD IVORY FIGURES

Three excavated artifacts from St. Lawrence Island. A bird, a bear, and a seal.

OLD IVORY FIGURES

Three carvings from St. Lawrence Island.

Upper: A polar bear carved in the old style. This carving was "brought up to date" by blackening the mouth and eyes with what appears to be mud mixed with soot applied to the original lines in the ivory.

Middle: The remains of an ivory polar bear. This example, like the one above it does not have individually carved legs but a block cut all in one shaped to resemble legs when viewed especially from the side.

Lower: An ivory drum handle which was made for a small frame. The whale's tail serves as a hand grasp.

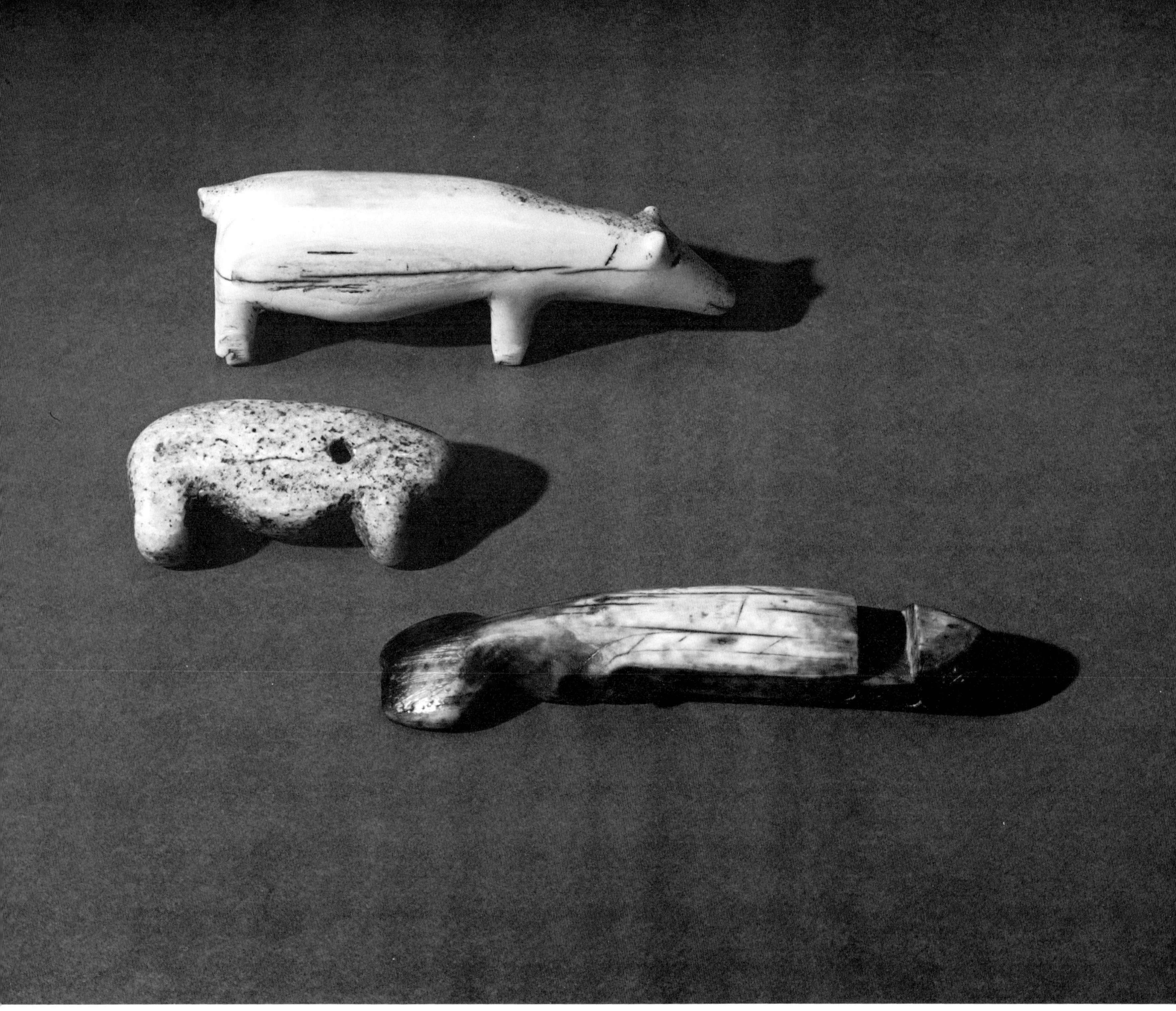

IVORY FIGURES

These whales appear to have no use other than as fetishes which were important to hunters.

IVORY FIGURES

Three polar bears carved before 1900, show not only skill in their execution, but also knowledge of the anatomy of the animal. Old ivory, brown and black colored from being in the ground, serves to highlight the muscular development of the brown bears. The white ivory bear has the long lean look of the polar bear which being a swimmer has in reality, a different body than that of Kodiak or other land bears.

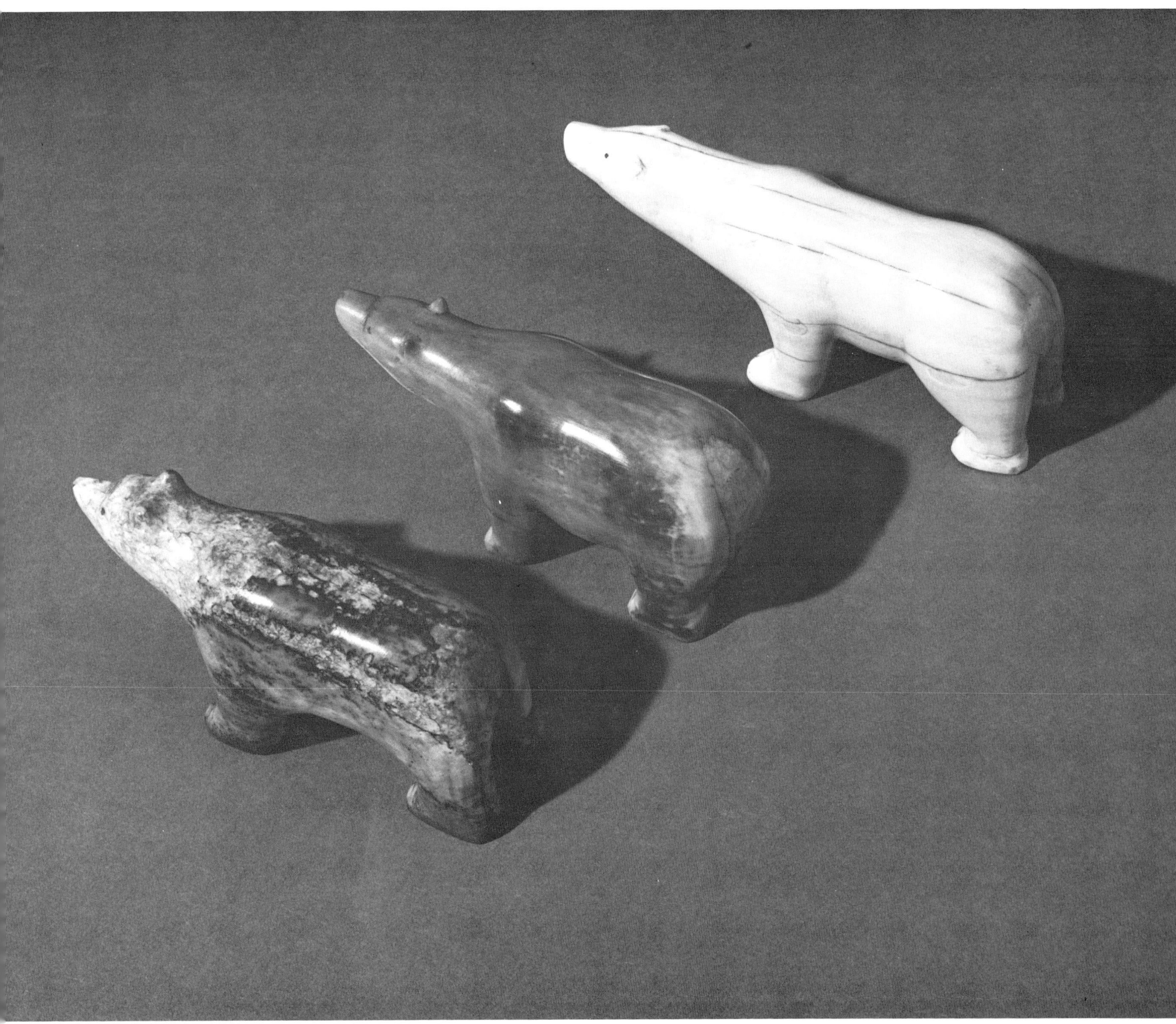

DRUM FRAMES

Wood frames for drums which look alike but are quite different in their construction.

The smaller hoop is bent wood which is fastened together, not overlapping end to end by sinew. An ivory band fits over the juncture on the inside and is drilled to receive pegs which fasten into the hoop, holding the ends together securely. The larger hoop also of bent wood comes together but has been shaped at the juncture, on both sides, to receive a single carved piece of ivory long on the inside, tapered to the ends, pierced and pegged to the wood with ivory dowels. This piece is shorter on the outside and made to fit in an x shape, securing the wood through its tapered ends to the ivory with dowels. The wood does not meet because of the ivory joiner.

A thin parchment like cover made from seal or walrus bladders was stretched over the frames and tied securely by sinew, round and round in the groove on the outside of the hoop. The drum handles have been made to fit each frame by cutting a square notch the width of the wood and ivory reinforcement. They are fastened to the frame with ivory pegs. The smaller drum has an ivory handle while the larger drum has a bone handle.

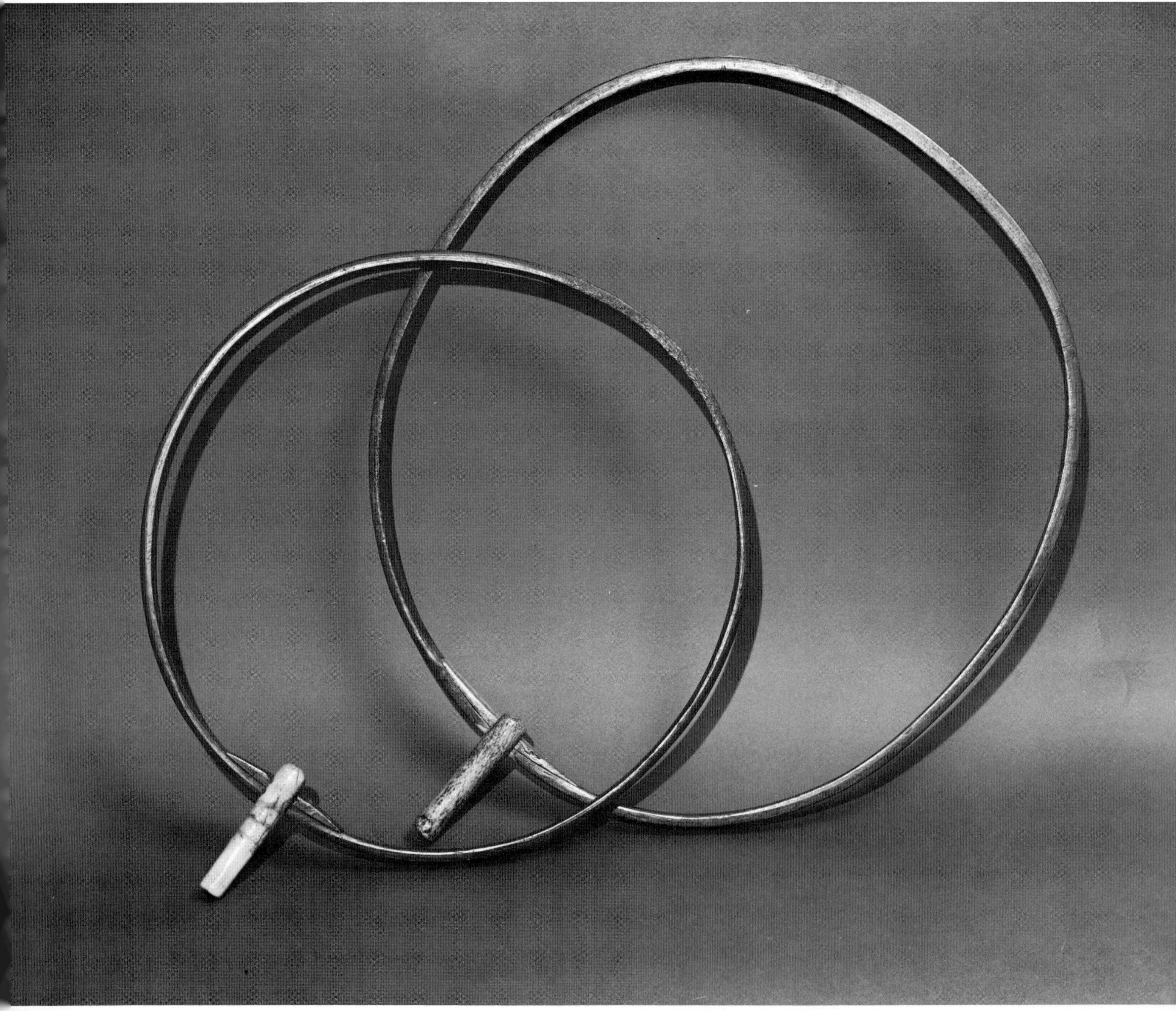

Actual size of drum fastenings and handles shown on opposite page.

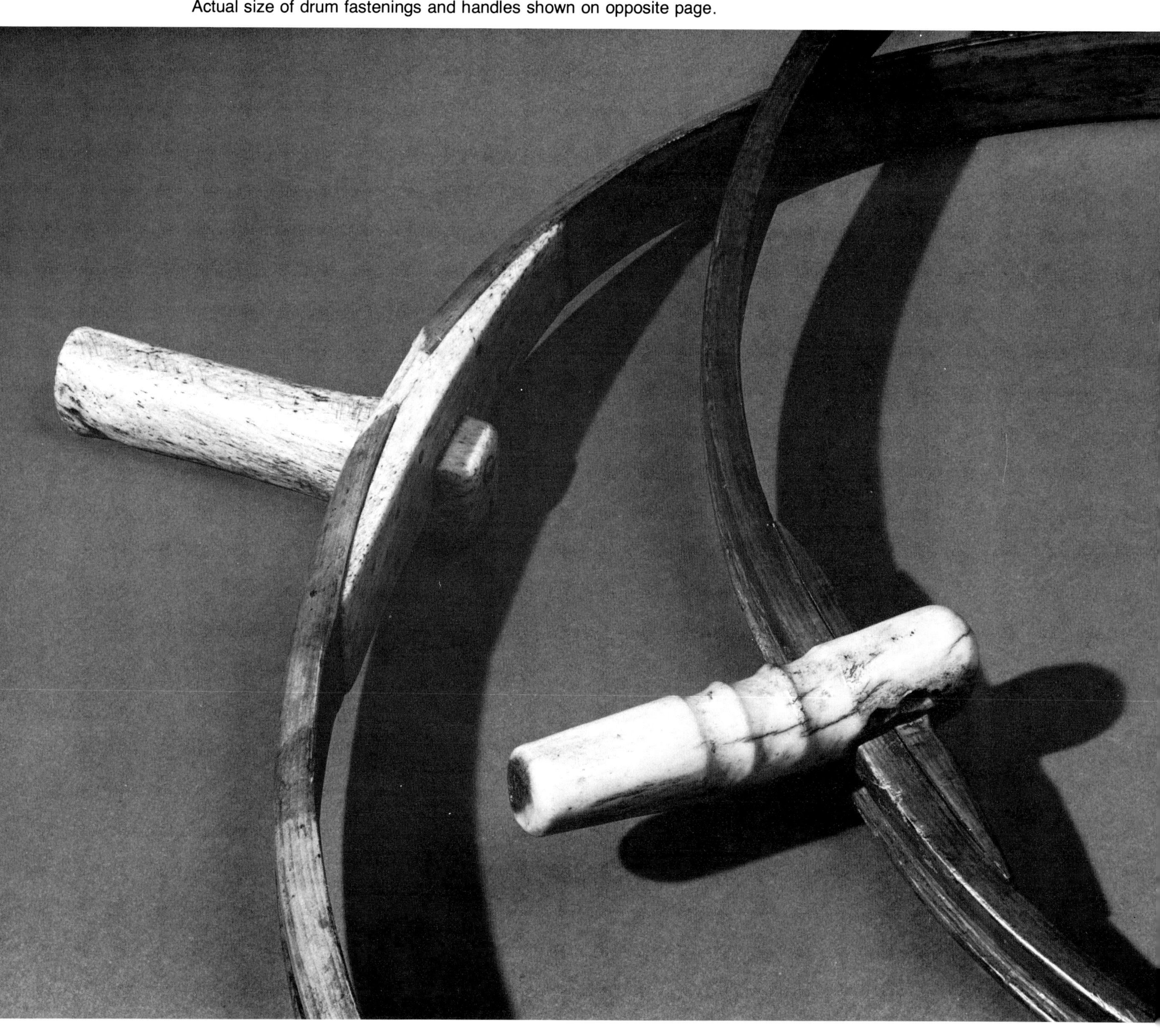

DRUM PARTS

1. An ivory baton for beating time on a stick for songs and dances.
2. & 3. Ivory reinforcements for joining drum ends together.
4. & 5. Ivory handles showing the notches for fitting drum frames and the holes to receive sinew for tying the handles to a frame for more strength.
6. A similar handle without tying holes but a peg hole in the small lip.
7. A reinforcer piece inserted into a drum handle to show its relative position. This ivory handle has the head of a bear with his paws covering his face.
8. An ivory reinforcing piece showing the great variety of securing holes. No two drums were exactly the same although the designs were similar.

SPINNING TOP (TEETOTUM)

Tops were used by children on the mainland and through the islands. The design idea was generally the same, but the shapes differed in that some were thin edged, some were spun with a stick and cord, while others followed the ingenuity of the maker and his own idea of a top. This ivory top and stick is spun by working the spindle upright between the two palms. This top spins a surprisingly long time.

A PAIR OF BALLS USED IN A GAME

They are seal skin with the fur left on. Red dyed skin is appliqued in designs on the tops and bottoms.

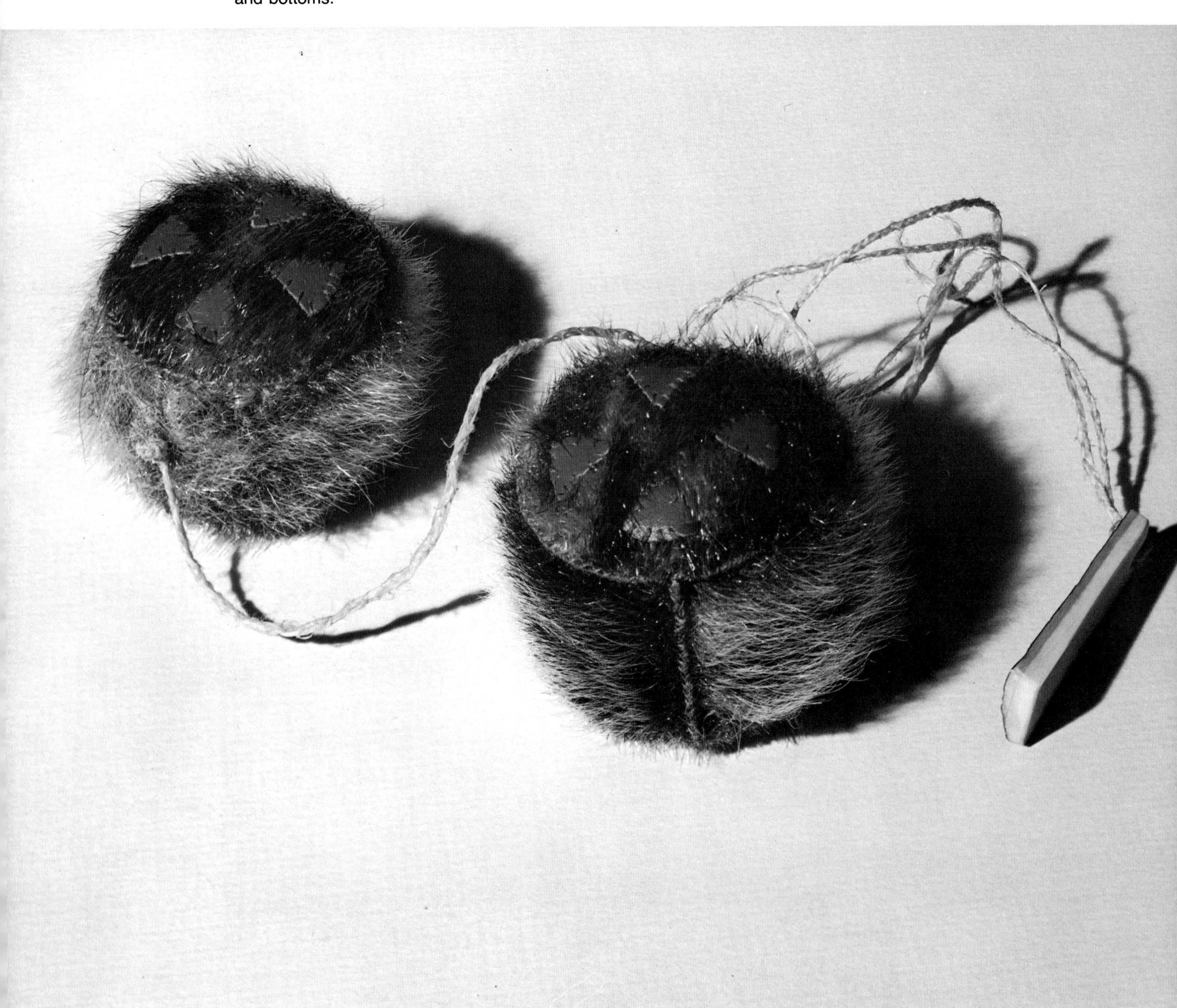

FOOTBALLS MADE OF SEAL SKIN STUFFED WITH DEER HAIR

The small decorations are colored patches of hide.

MISCELLANEOUS IVORY FIGURES

Ducks, geese, and murres carved for toys. An auk is first in the center rear group. Several of these little carvings are decorated with small dots. The dark ivory group were excavated on St. Lawrence Island.

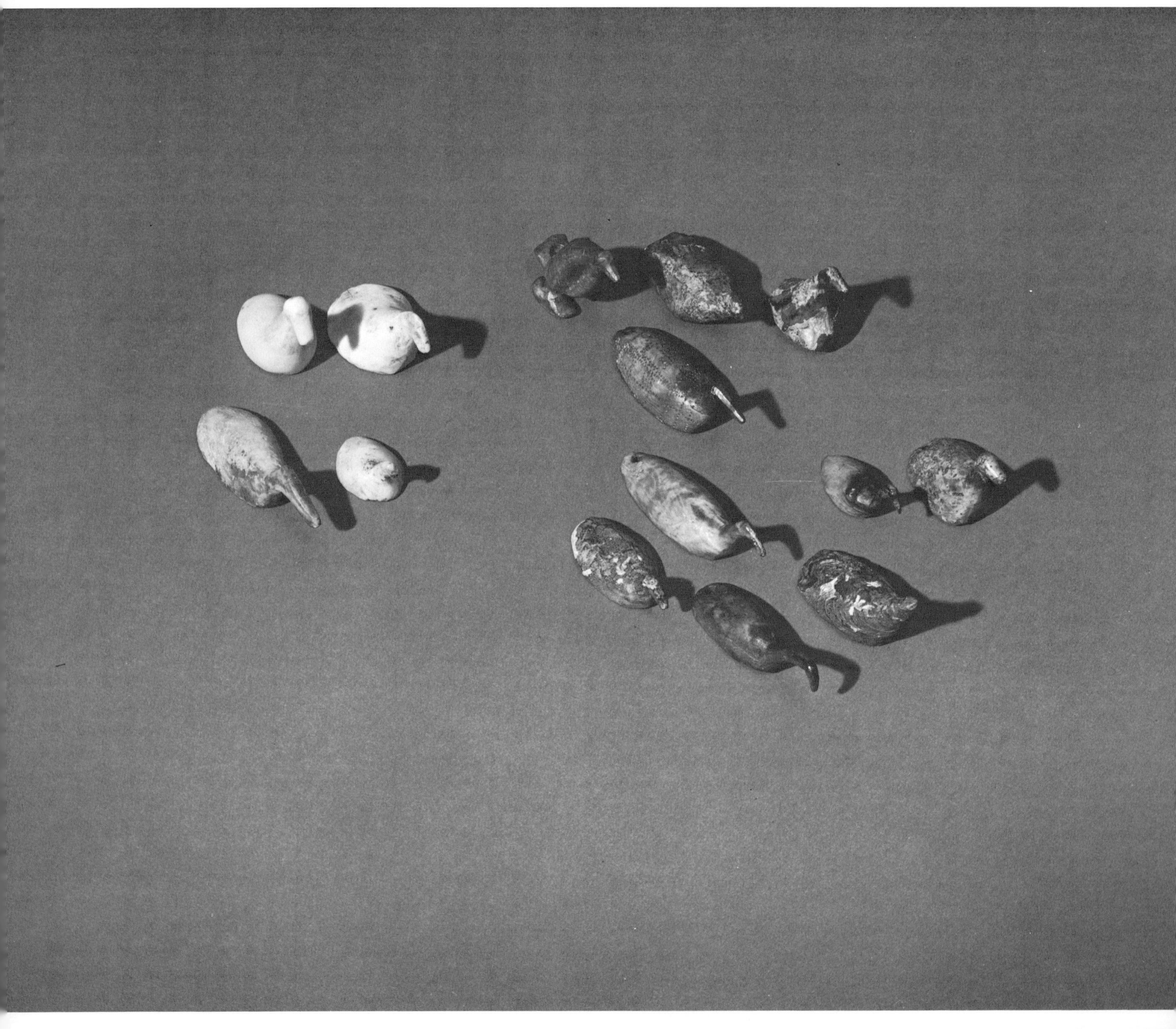

GAMING FIGURES

Decorated bone and ivory pieces used in a gambling game.

A SPIRIT MASK

Masks such as this one represented the spirit world. The inspiration for their design came through a vision, a dream, or a personal experience. Songs or stories were a property of these masks, they may have had dances associated with them. This expressive example was made by gouging out the wood rather than carving the features. The back was washed with a fragile white chalky substance but was otherwise left untouched. The extensions were rubbed with black and the small wood dangles attached with sinew.

ACTUAL SIZE VIEW OF THE MASK PORTRAYED ON THE OPPOSITE PAGE

Showing the carving technique and the use of the wood grain to achieve the design.

A WOODEN MASK

This is a smooth well carved mask representing a human face. The teeth are bits of wood set into place. The black lines are a whaler's mark. Traces of a labret outline are on either side of the mouth.

The border of the mask has holes for wood pegs which held deer skin or other fur to represent a winter hood. This mask depicts a human face without distortion which is somewhat unusual. The back of the mask has been carved out.

A WOODEN MASK

This mask carved and modeled to represent a human face has the mottled wood of a buried piece which it was. The raised ridge above the eyes denote the brows and the other features, mouth, nose, and eyes are quite natural. A wood plug was inserted on the left side of the mouth but rather than a labret, seems to be a patch repair. There are holes around the mask for affixing fur. The back is carved out.

A WOODEN MASK

A mask realistic in design, and carved with concern for natural appearance. The raised carving shows the eybrows and the well formed nose and eyes.

The mouth of this mask was not provided with teeth and only a single hole was drilled on either side for tying. There are dots on the lower chin indicating a tatoo. Traces of red ochre remain on the mask. The back is carved out according to the facial details. The wood is very thin.

A WOODEN MASK FRAGMENT

The remains of a realistic mask which apparently once had a full set of ivory teeth of which three remain. There are also labret holes on either side of the mouth. The carved teeth are interesting since they resemble the cutting on natural teeth one sees in ancient Mexican skulls. The two holes at eye level were for attaching cords.

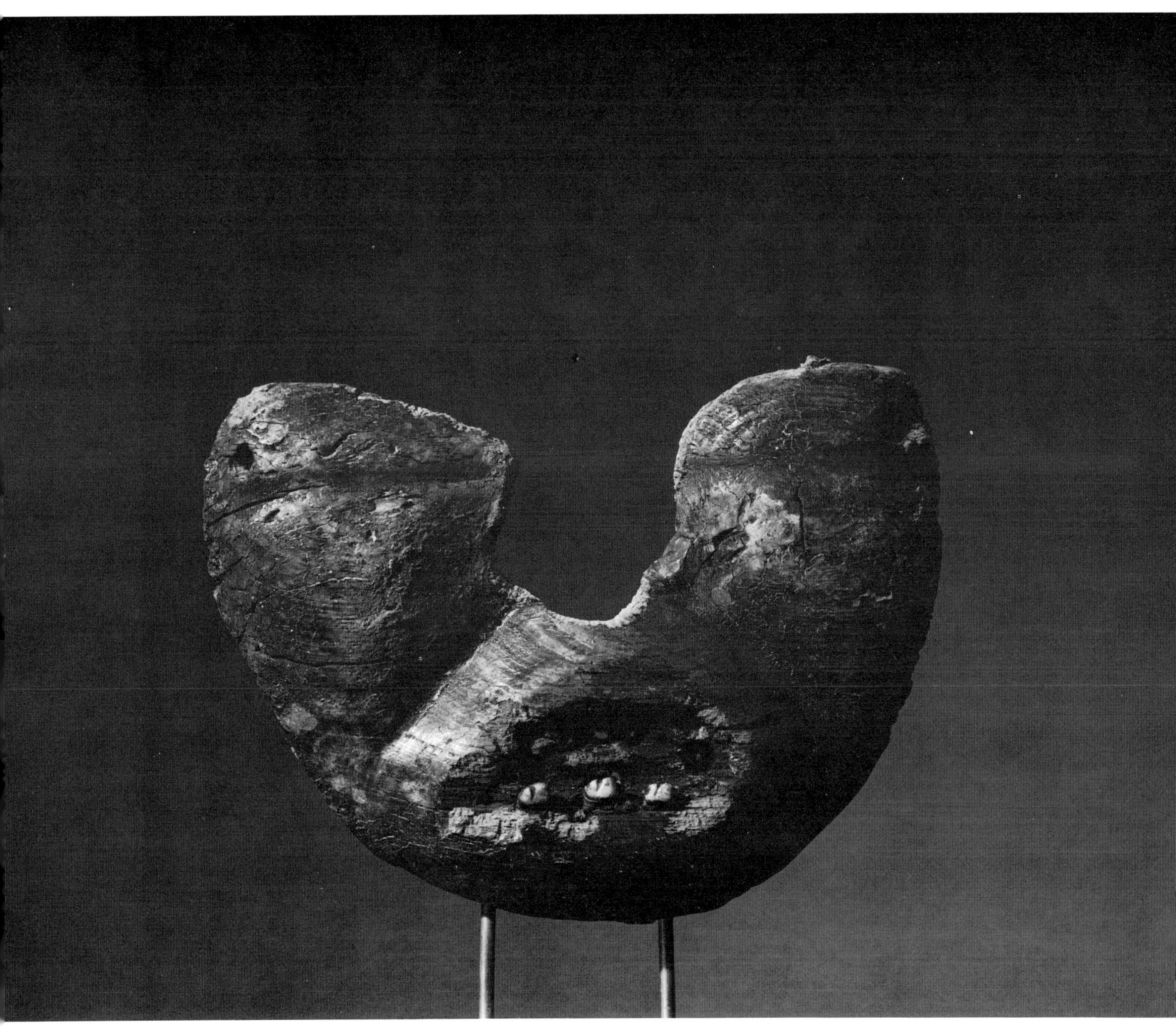

THE REMNANTS OF AN EXCAVATED MASK

This mask is interesting for the tatoo marks seen clearly below the lower lip.

A SPIRIT MASK

Portrayed in the form of a bear's head, was buried but fortunately enough remains to see it was well conceived and expertly carved. The tongue, eyes and general contour leave no doubt as to what the maker had in mind.

SNOW KNIVES

These snow knives were used by children of both sexes to play at cutting and shaping snow. Knives were made of ivory, bone, or wood and often showed great skill and design quality.

1. A well made knife which still shows etched designs on the hand hold.
2. An ivory knife decorated with lines and circles. The lines generally are simple forms of the raven totem.
3. An ivory knife with a bird's head and knots representing swimming seals.
4. An ivory knife with a bear's head.
5. An ivory knife with seven small circular knobs on the hand piece. The blade is etched with the raven totem and circles.

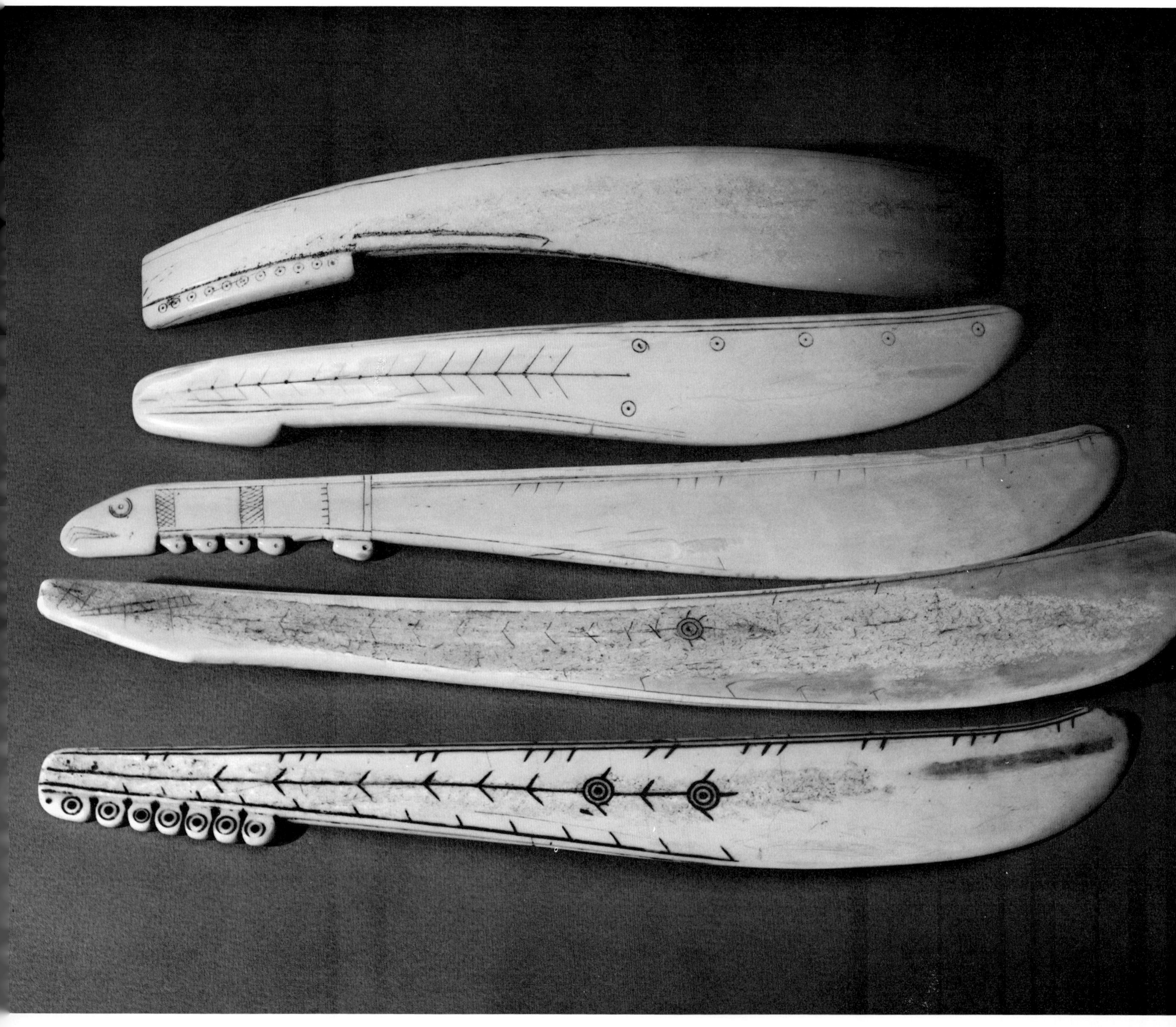

SNOW KNIVES

1. An ivory snow knife with a murre head and totem designs.
2. A snow knife of bone with a driver and his reindeer sled. This design was inspired by an outsider, a Laplander. Laplanders came to Alaska at one time at the invitation of people who hoped to make an industry out of reindeer management.
3. A small ivory knife carved and etched with totem marks.
4. A whale bone knife very nicely shaped but undecorated.

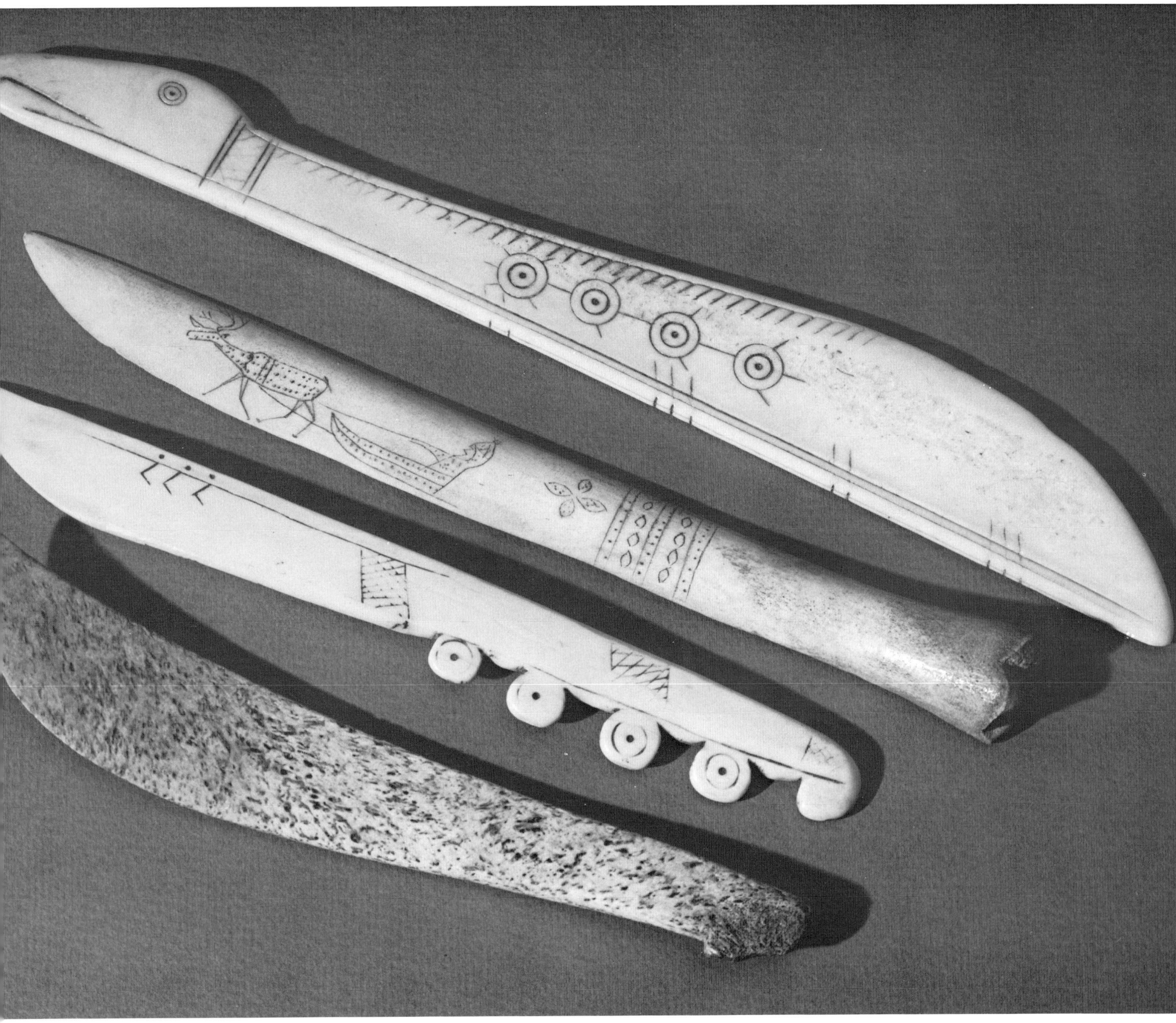

A WOOD HUNTING HELMET

This conical shaped wood hunting helmet is joined in the back and secured with a strip of wood which is sewn into the hat with sinew to keep the wood together. It is painted white with a red stripe and a red border. The white paint is not regular lead paint but is more of a wash, the red color contains the same ingredients as the white wash, is true red but not brilliant. The colors are subtle and appear to be quite durable. The decorations are ivory carvings thought to be fetishes tied through the hat with thongs. The feathers are held in place by a grass ring into which they are secured.

ACTUAL SIZE OF HUNTING HELMET SHOWN ON OPPOSITE PAGE

Showing attached wing like decorations, designed with engraved circles and seabird's head.

WOODEN HELMET SHOWN ON PAGE (166) REAR VIEW

The back of the hunting helmet showing the wood reinforcing strip which holds the hat together. The strip is sewn through the hat with rawhide. These strips were also made of bone or ivory. The grass feather holder is held with a strip of skin and twine used to mend the ring at a later date. The feathers were knotted at the top to give a decorated look to an otherwise ordinary feather. The white chalky wash used for paint by the Eskimos can be clearly seen in this picture.

ACTUAL SIZE OF REAR OF HELMET SHOWN ON OPPOSITE PAGE

A SUN VISOR

A visor made of a piece of wood fitting around the head with the front extending out to form a shade. This example is cut from a thin piece of wood bent, steamed and fastened to fit the wearer. A groove extends around the center of the visor and the edge has a slight groove.

A SUN VISOR

A wood hunting visor which has a rawhide cord to attach it to the head. The upper part of the visor is carved in such a way as to permit it to fit closely to the forehead. The edges of the visor are grooved. There are signs of red color.

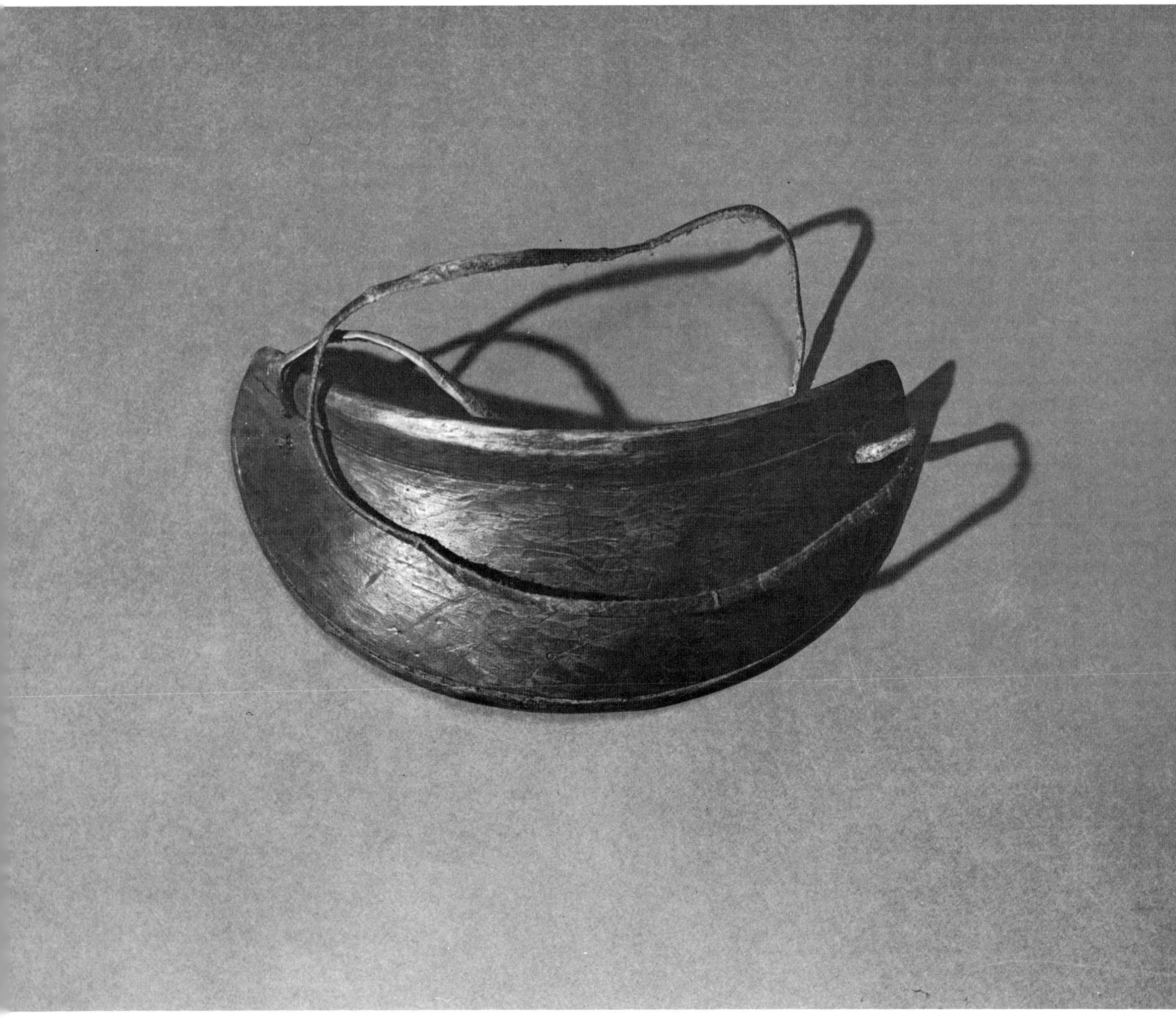

SNOW GOGGLE

Used to save the eyes from sun and snow glare. These are snow goggles of wood in a spectacle shape. There are narrow slits for vision and a visor serving as a shade over the eye slits. The nose piece is formed to provide a close fit to the face.

SNOW GOGGLES

Upper: Snow goggles providing a continuous eye slit filled in at the center and capped by a visor. The nose piece has been shaped. Notches at the top of the goggles and at the bottom facilitate air circulation around the eyes. These are especially well made and have been mended with a thin strand of gut. The wood is very thin.

Middle: Wood goggles with a visor. The eye channel was not cut continuously making the eye slits separate. Lamp black was rubbed on the inside to further guard against the glare. The nose space is cut out.

Lower: Visored goggles having separate eye slits and a shaped nose piece. The visor has been notched in the center forming a kind of eyebrow effect.

Goggles were fastened by tying a cord around the head, the cord being secured through holes in the sides of the goggles. This example still has twisted cord on one side and a piece of sinew on the other.

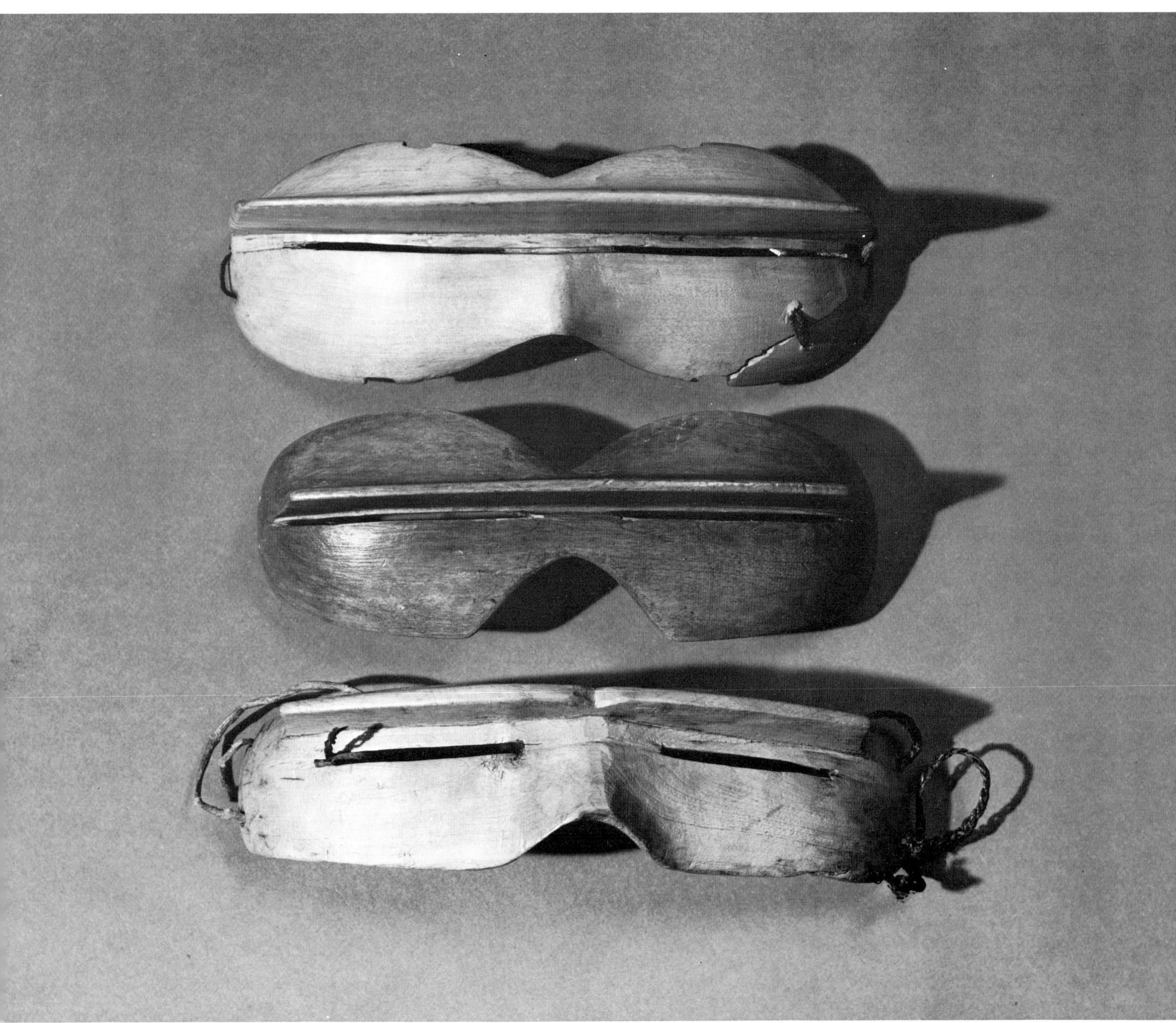

SNOW GOGGLES

Top: Wood goggles extending out from the face and closed squarely at each end. These are not as closely shaped to the face as other types. The forehead projects slightly to form a visor like edge.

Middle: Back view of wooden goggles hollowed out for the eyes and nose. The sides are square and are probably to be covered by a hood.

Lower: An unfitted goggle which rests on the hood better than on the wearer's face.

SNOW GOGGLES

Top: These goggles are cut to fit the face closely. A trough shape piece of wood concave inside and convex on the outer side has a section cut out for the nose. The eye slit is continuous. There is no visor.

Middle: Bone goggles probably a deer antler with a cut much like a pair of eye glasses. The slits are wider and the goggles extend out farther from the face.

Lower: A narrow spectacle goggle of wood. The slits are separate and the nose space is cut out. The top is cut in an undulating line very narrow at the nose bridge.

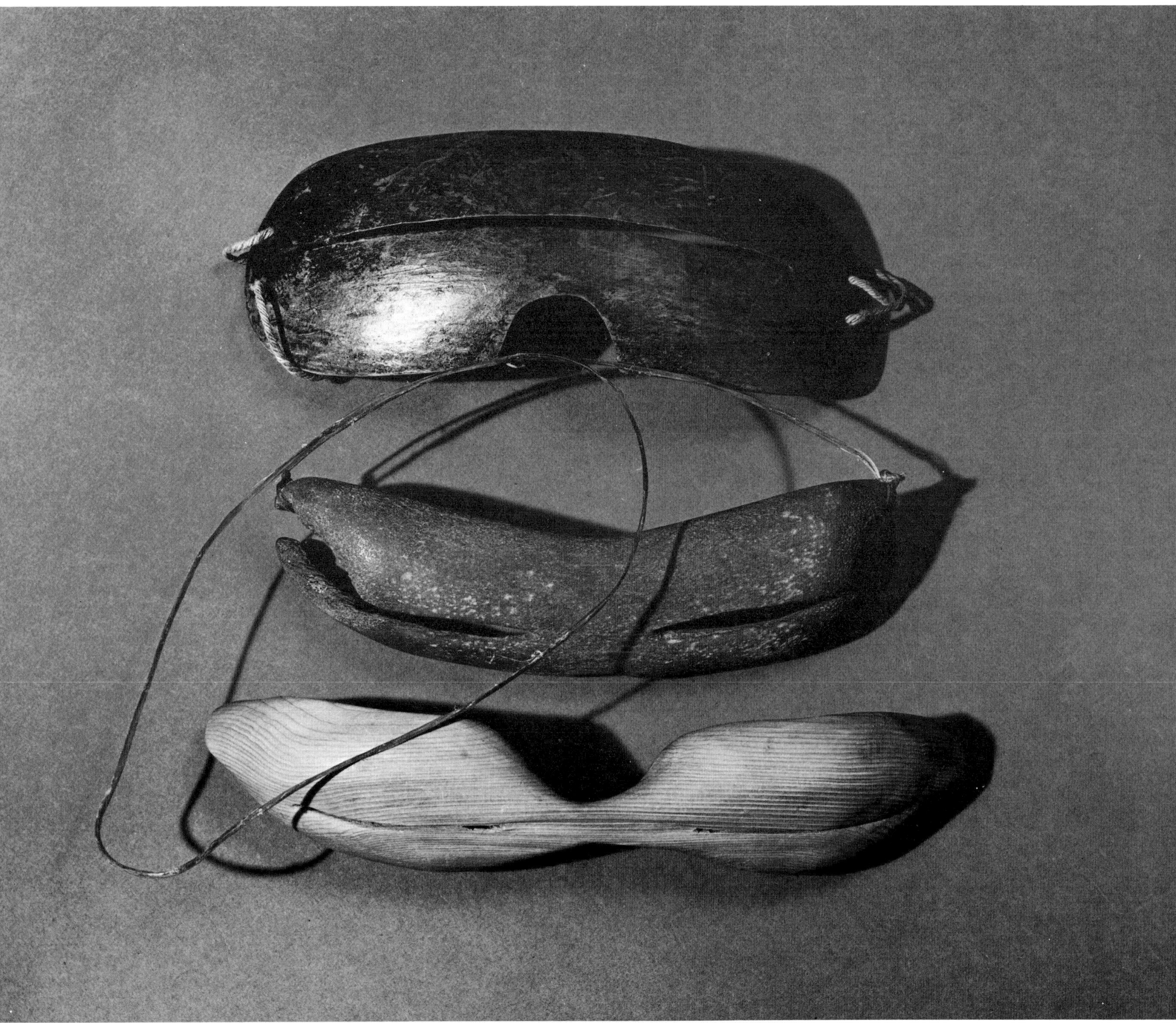

SNOW GOGGLES

Flat wood funnel shaped goggles, the slit is wide having the upper front border projecting beyond the lower. A notch is rounded out for the nose and the inside darkened with lamp black.

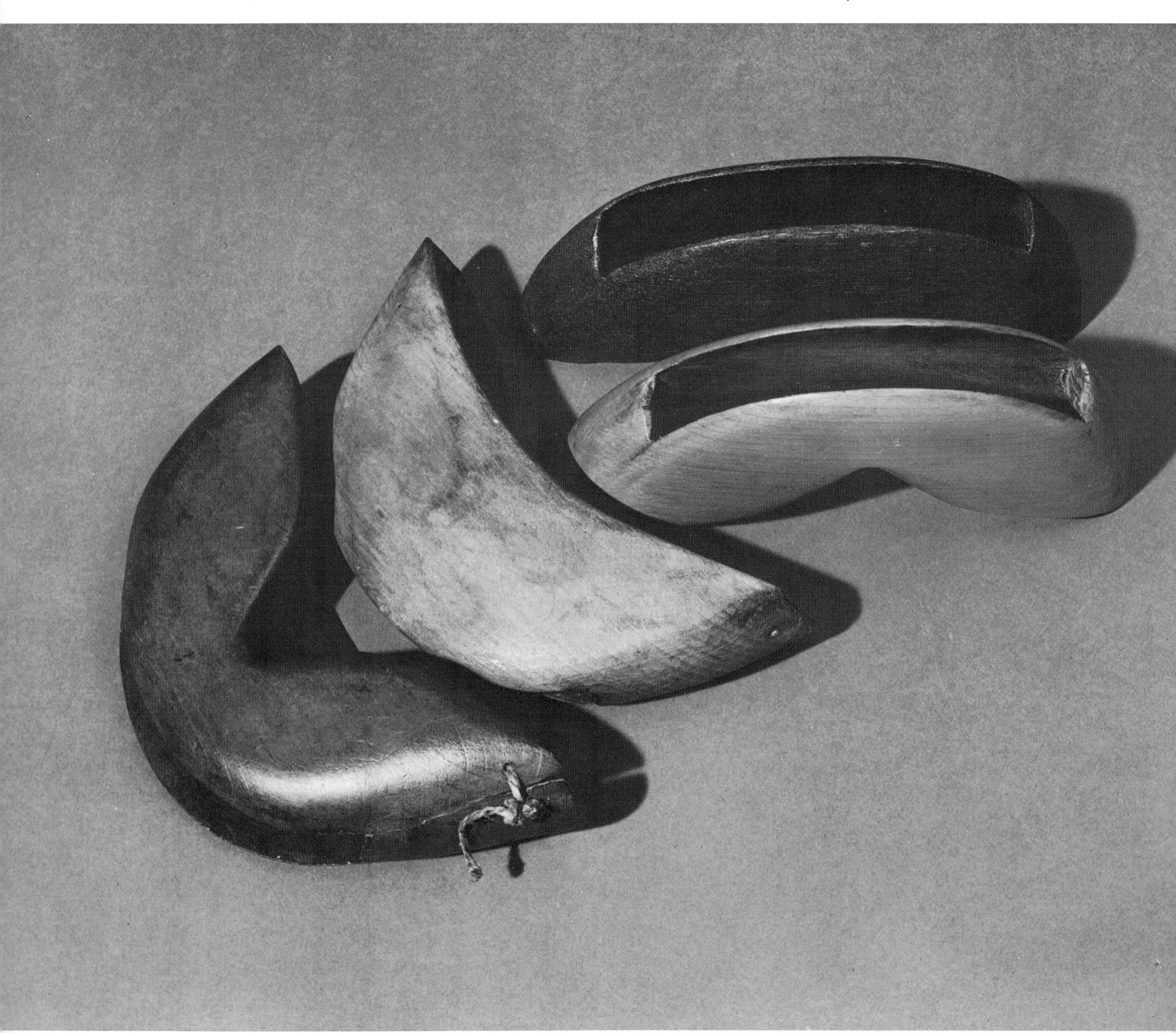

SNOW GOGGLES

Top: Contemporary goggles made of bone. The shape is similar to older wood goggles but the material makes them much heavier.
Middle: Bone goggles made to resemble an older style.
Lower: Ivory goggles with wider eye spaces and a carved nose notch. The sides are shaped down from the eye space to bring the goggles closer to the temples and cheek bones.

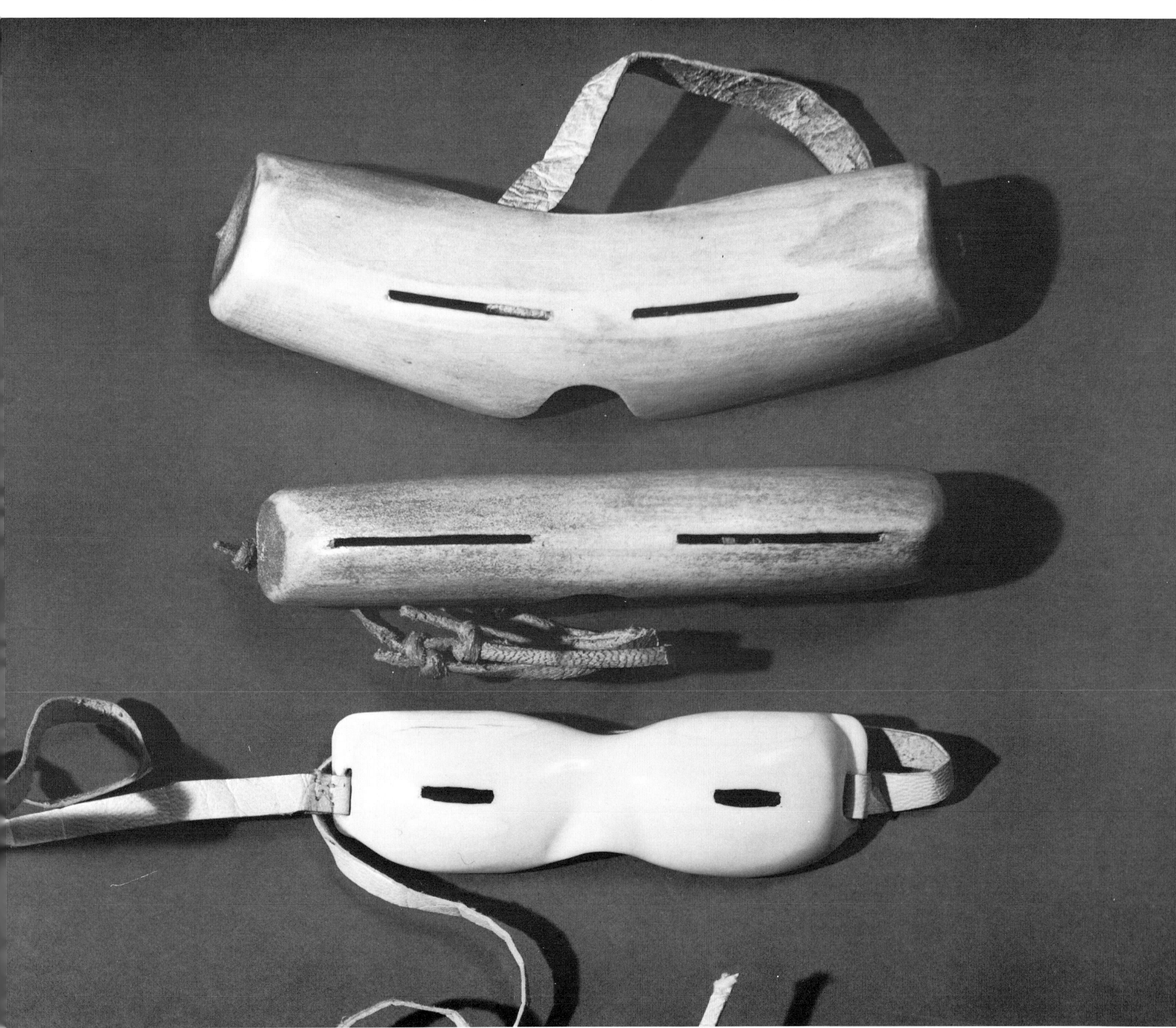

A LARGE DOLL

The wood face is painted a dark red and the eyes and mouth of ivory are etched to simulate pupils and lips. The doll is dressed in seal, reindeer, and marmot fur in the fashion of regular clothing. The skin body is stuffed with fur hair.

WOOD AND IVORY DOLLS

Dolls of ivory and wood. The third figure from the left is a doll from St. Lawrence Island of ivory long buried. The larger doll of wood has a groove around the face which at sometime held a hood in place. This doll was also excavated on St. Lawrence Island.

MISCELLANEOUS TOYS

Dolls were used by children both on the mainland and on the near islands. Many had proper anatomical parts.

1. A wooden doll carved with separate arms. 2. An undelineated wood figure from St. Lawrence Island. It is thought, the remoteness of this settlement from others was the reason for the plain design of their dolls. 3. A stuffed cloth body enclosed in a seal skin baby carrier. Fringe extending from small sleeves, must have been meant to represent the hands and fingers seen on either side of the head. 4. Fur frock decorated with white skin, left open at the bottom and a round hole in the hood front. A stick is put through the frock and shows through the hood for the face. Only the apparel is any trouble to construct, the doll is replaced by inserting another stick. 5. A rudely carved ivory doll with very small dots in a triangular pattern through the center. 6. Although small masks were often carved as toys, they were also used as fetishes. 7. A rudely shaped wooden doll. Although the body is a block of wood the facial features are expressive giving the doll considerable character. Figures such as this one were often the upper part of a stuffed body. Garments in the prevailing styles were made for the dolls. 8. A doll having no outstanding features except well defined arms and recognizable hands, one in front and one in back. 9. A wood dog carved with a bushy tail. The legs are separate and placed in holes in the body. 10. A wooden whale with flippers set into slots on the body sides.

BOOK II

IVORY CARVING

This carving is from the lower Yukon. The ivory walrus tusk is carved to represent a two man kayak with a bear's head on the prow. This piece was probably made for sale but the figures have the form and design of old figurines and the decorations both on the craft and bodies give the idea of the custom of embellishing persons and property. Boats were often decorated with mythical animals to ward off evil.

A MODEL OF AN UMIAK

Showing the frame usually of driftwood cut and lashed together with rawhide cord strung through holes in the parts to be joined. The frame of the Umiak varied in length and was covered with heavy walrus or seal skin with the hair removed. The skin was shaped to the frame and lashed to the rails on the inside. After drying, the skin and lacings became taut. Seal oil was applied to the cover time after time and allowed to dry until the boat became watertight. In the interest of safety water proofing was a continuing process and necessary after several expeditions.

ACTUAL SIZE OF MODEL SHOWN ON OPPOSITE PAGE

A detail showing the interior construction of the Umiak and the method of fastening down the sheathing of walrus skins.

MODELS OF KAYAKS

Small boats used along the American coast and close in islands were known as kayaks. They differed somewhat in design from place to place but were generally similar in construction. The frame was made of small wood strips running lengthwise joined at the bow and stern. Curved ribs ran horizontally between the long strips and were fastened to them with cord. A rail of strong wood fitted into the rib tops. The frame was covered over with tanned seal skin except for the manhole which was left in the top. The coverings were oiled and the seams calked with tallow. Single passenger kayaks were used until later times when two and three passenger craft were introduced by Russian traders, who used them to travel around manned by the Eskimos. The natives themselves, did not use these larger versions preferring the single kayak in their own pursuits.

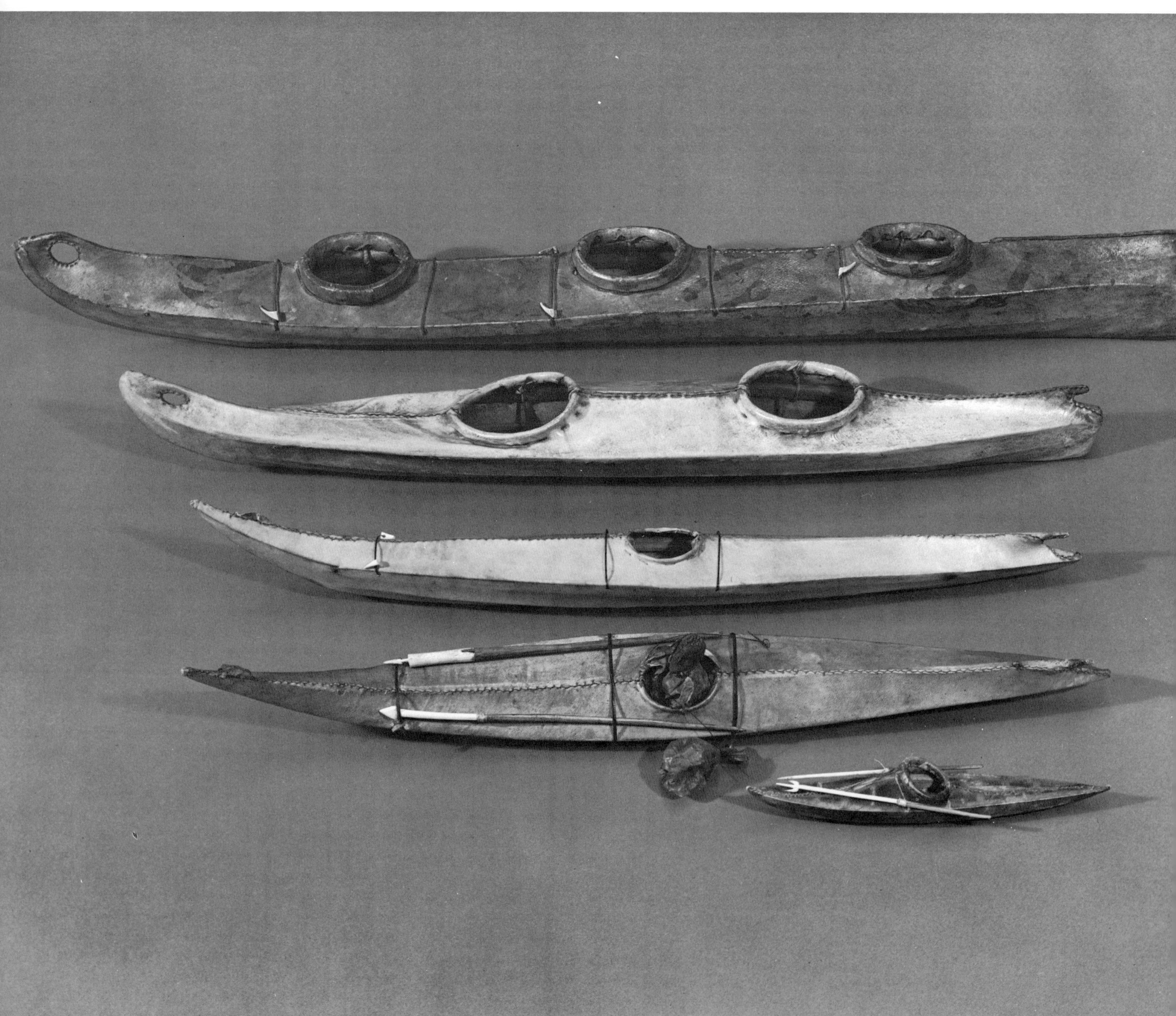

A BONE GUARD

In the form of a polar bear. It is secured to the frame of an umiak or kayak through the holes near its feet.

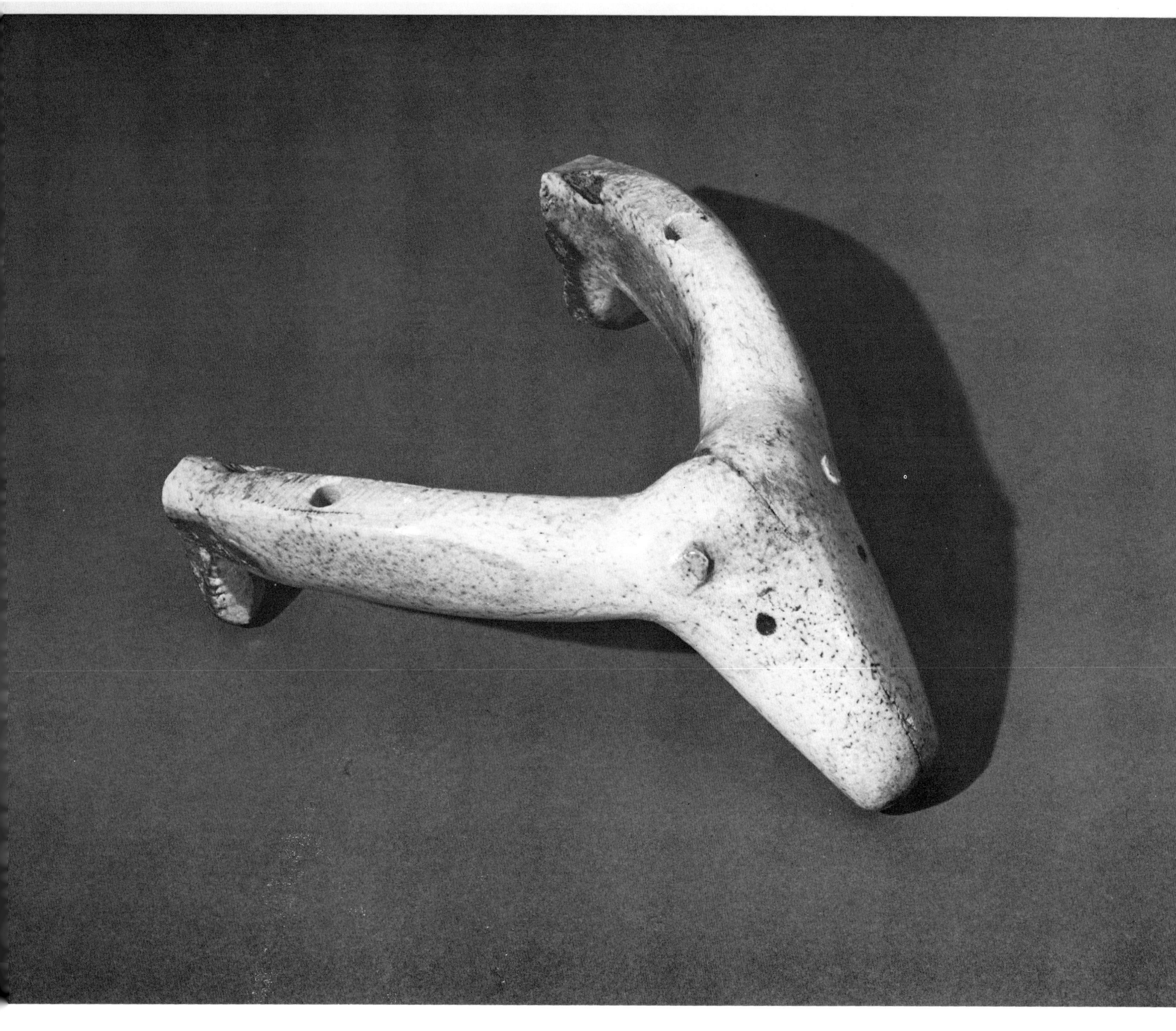

A BONE GUARD

Made from an animal jawbone. The holes for decoration and for keeping the bone from splitting are filled with baleen inserts. The eyes are carved ivory button-like pegs.

A BONE GUARD

A polar bear made of a single animal bone. The bear's eyes are ivory pegs set into a piece of baleen.

A SPEAR BOARD

With a float line in position on the board. The line is made of walrus hide and has an ivory cord attacher showing on the left and a cord handle in the shape of a seal, on the right. The spear board was used on a kayak.

ACTUAL SIZE OF SPEAR BOARD SHOWN ON OPPOSITE PAGE

Ivory bear charms are fitted and tied to the edge of the spear board.

PRONGED HOOKS

Each carved from one large piece of bone. These had the same general use as the single tined hooks shown on opposite page

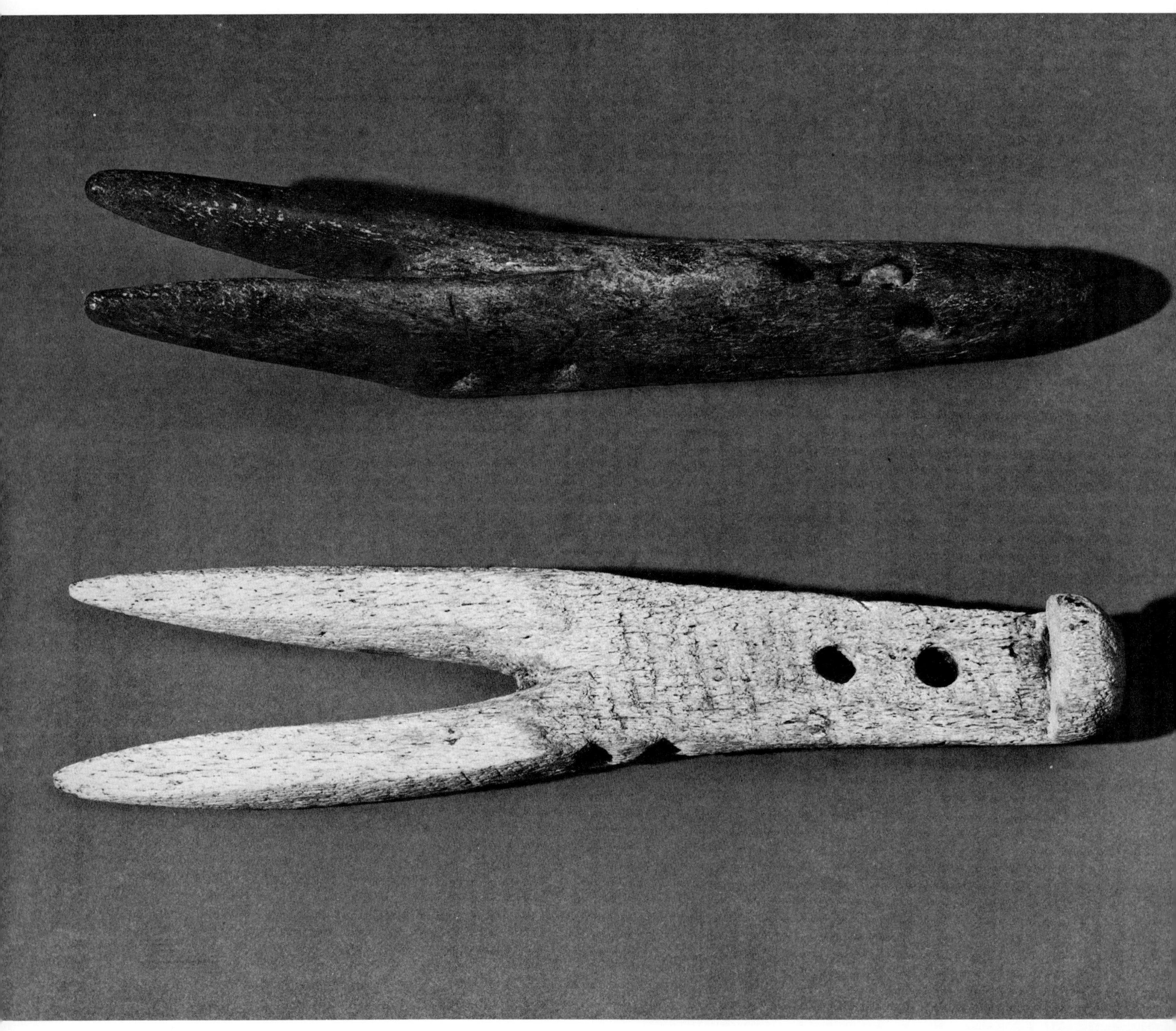

BOAT HOOKS

These were made in a number of ways and differed according to the locality. They were designed to fit securely to the end of a pole for the heavy work of clearing ice. These hooks are bone and by their holes and shape show how the lashing kept them secure to the pole. Similar hooks were used to haul animals and to hold them while being flensed. When used as blubber hooks, the handles were shorter, about two or three feet. These three hooks resemble blubber hooks used with a short handle.

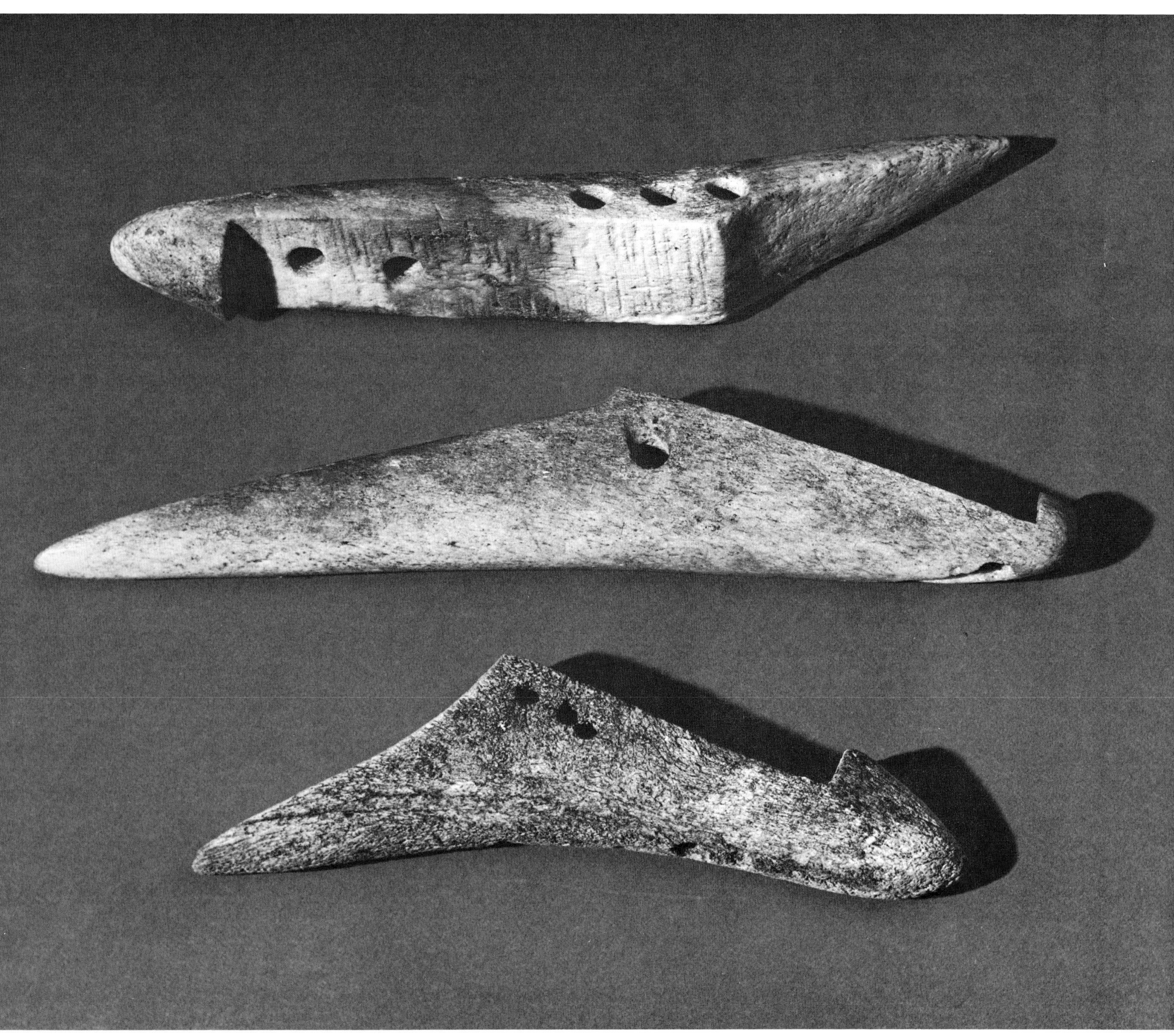

BOAT HOOKS FOR UMIAKS

Were generally larger than those used with kayaks. These three bone hooks lashed to long poles were used to push away ice and when landing among rocks. The poles were generally six to eight feet long.

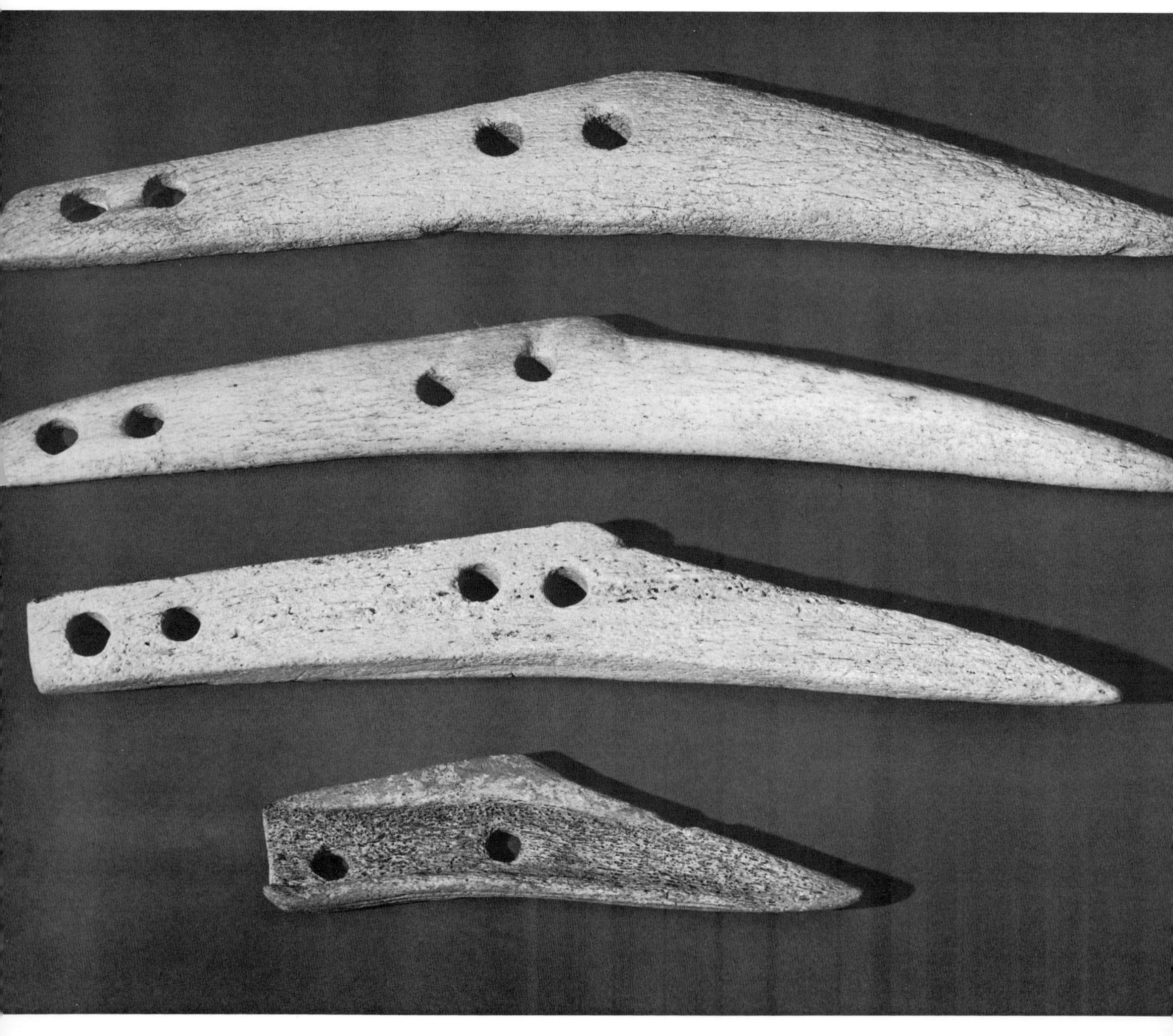

IVORY AND BONE BLOCKS

Used in rigging Umiaks. The lines etched into the first two blocks not only make an attractive design but are practical as well, keeping the cord from slipping.

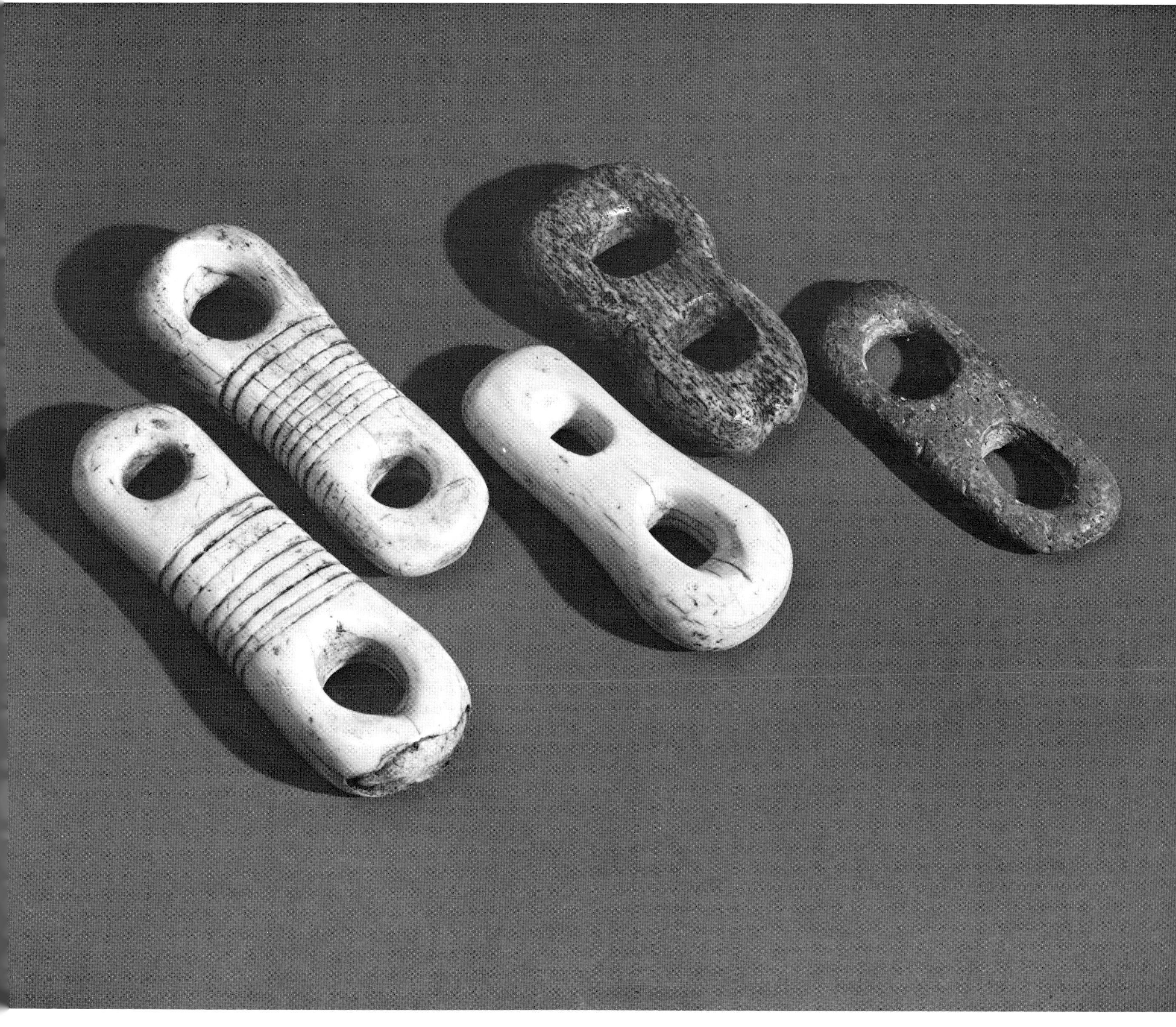

A MODEL OF A HAND SLED

These sleds were light weight and were used for short hunting trips being hauled by the hunter. When the ice broke up, they were used to transport kayaks back and forth from the land to hunting and fishing sites.

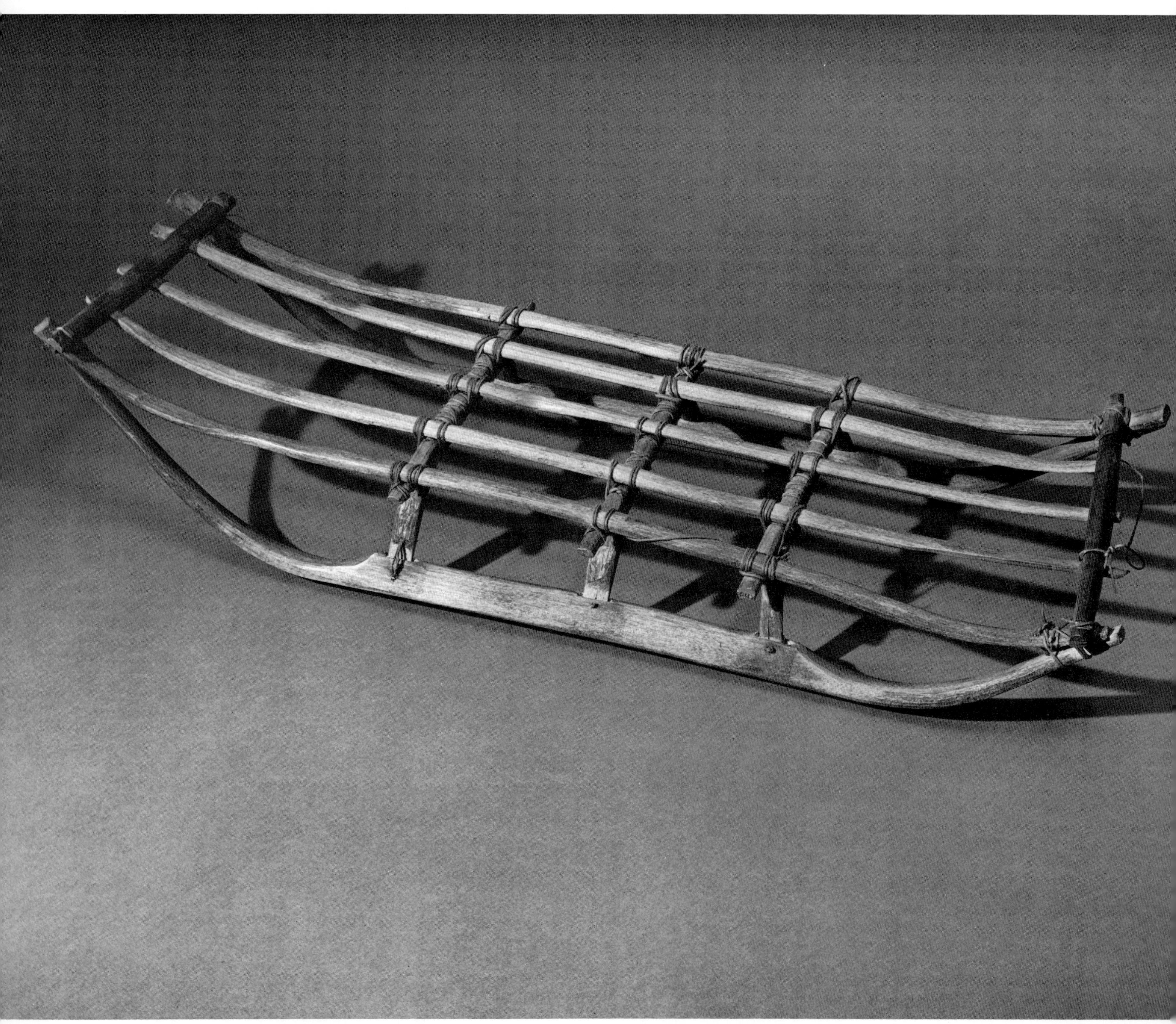

ACTUAL SIZE OF MODEL SHOWN ON OPPOSITE PAGE

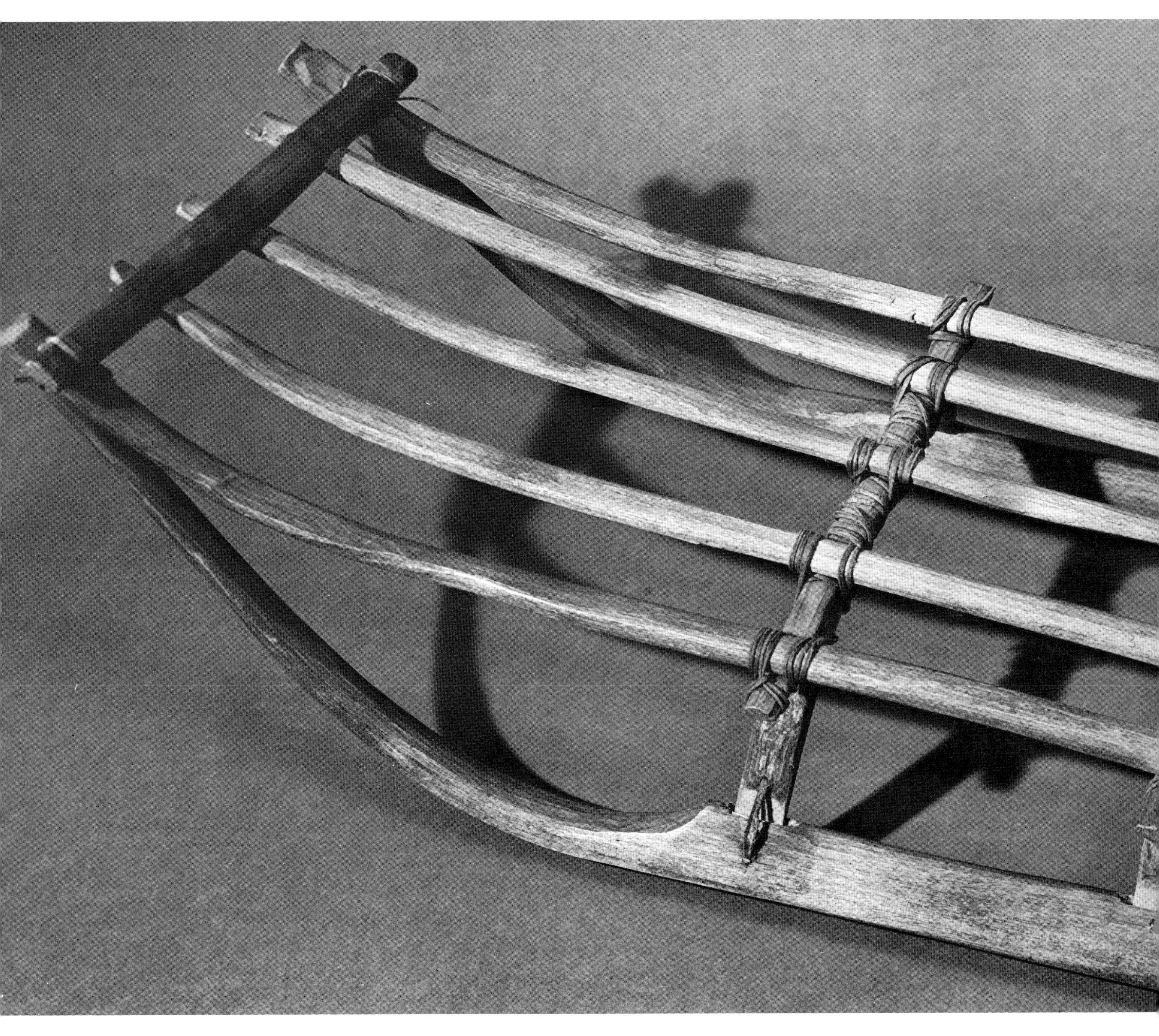

SLED RUNNERS

Wooden runners of larger sleds were often equipped with bone or ivory strips to enable them to travel better. These are three ivory sled runners showing the holes for attaching to the frame.

Upper: This runner was secured with thong threaded through the holes at the tip and along the top. The sled shoe seems to have fitted over the top of the runner judging from the wear marks, which would indicate the runner and sled were made together according to a plan.

Middle: This runner was notched to fit a shoe and was secured to the sled with lashing through the large hole.

Lower: This runner is not notched but the hole is similar to the middle example where it was lashed to the sled.

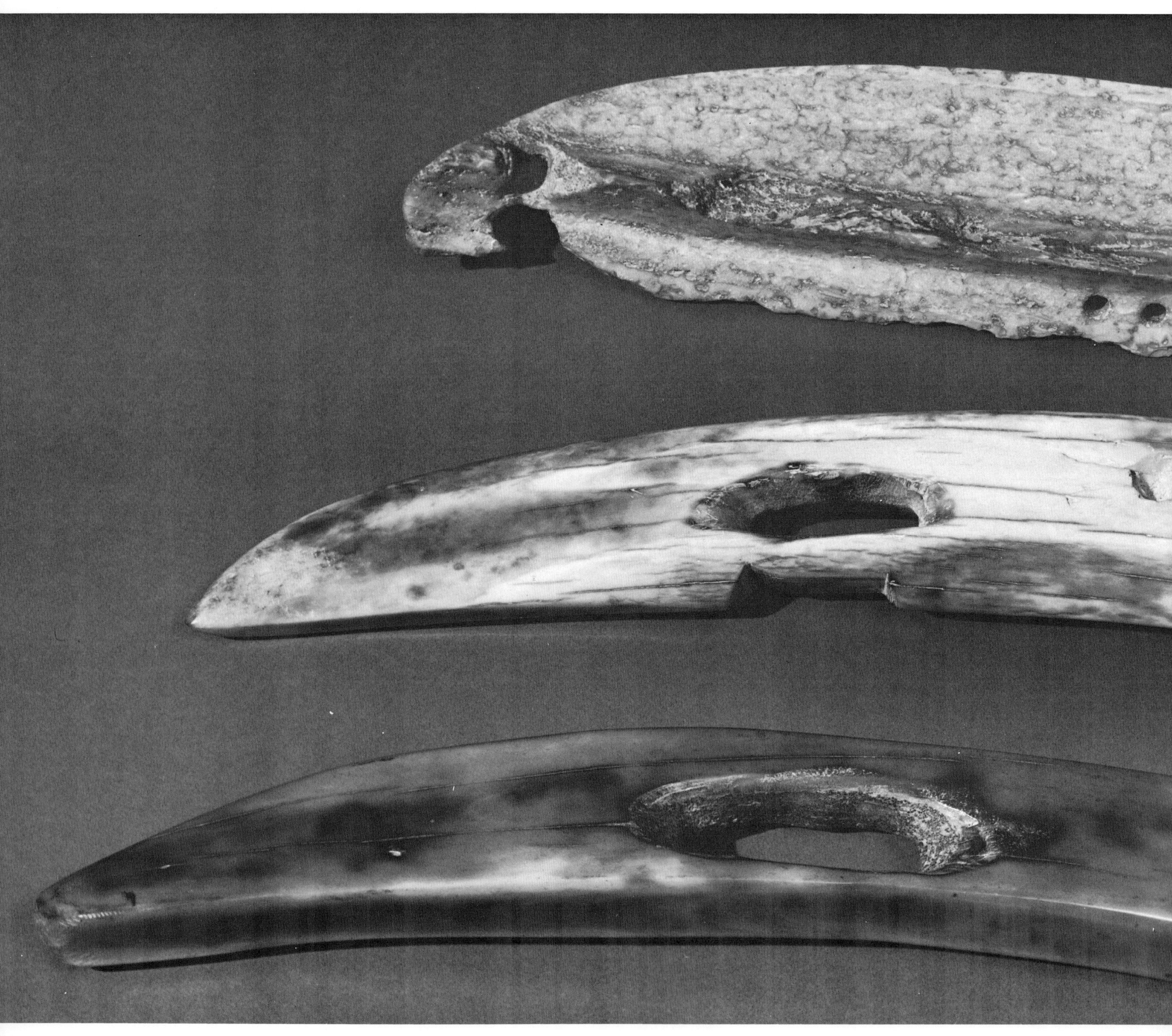

ICE CREEPERS

Were attached to the sole of the boot to prevent slipping while traveling over ice. Some creepers were channeled others were turned up at the ends to fit more closely to the boot. Creepers were tied to the boots with cords part of one showing in the spiked specimen.

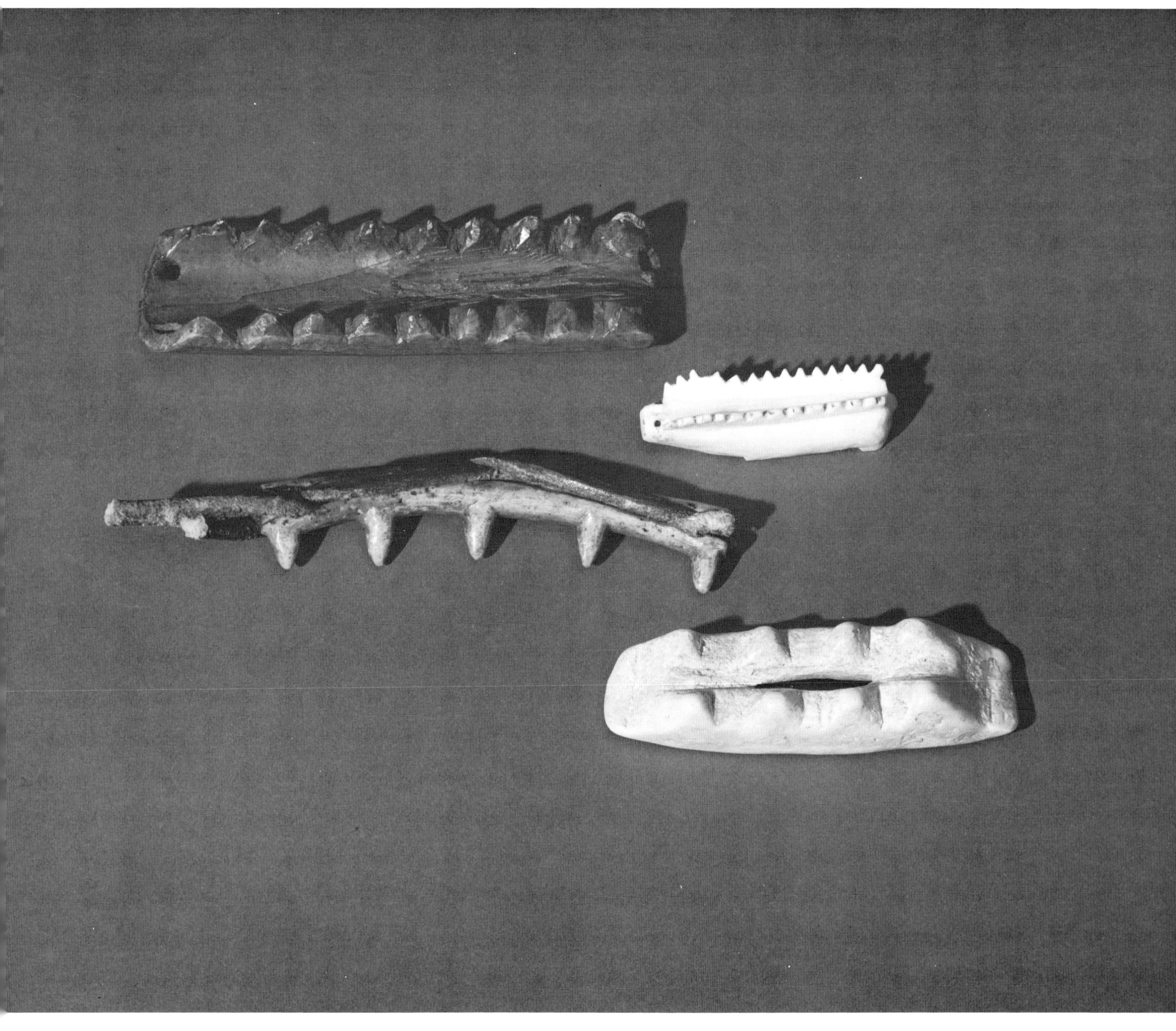

SNOW SHOES

A pair of snow shoes made of bent wood the ends fastened together with two cross bars in the center, one in front of and the other behind the foot rest. The webbing is twisted sinew in a small weave and in a larger weave to facilitate walking over soft snow. There are other designs made expressly for sea ice and rougher snow the difference is principally in the length and width of the shoes and the density of the webbing.

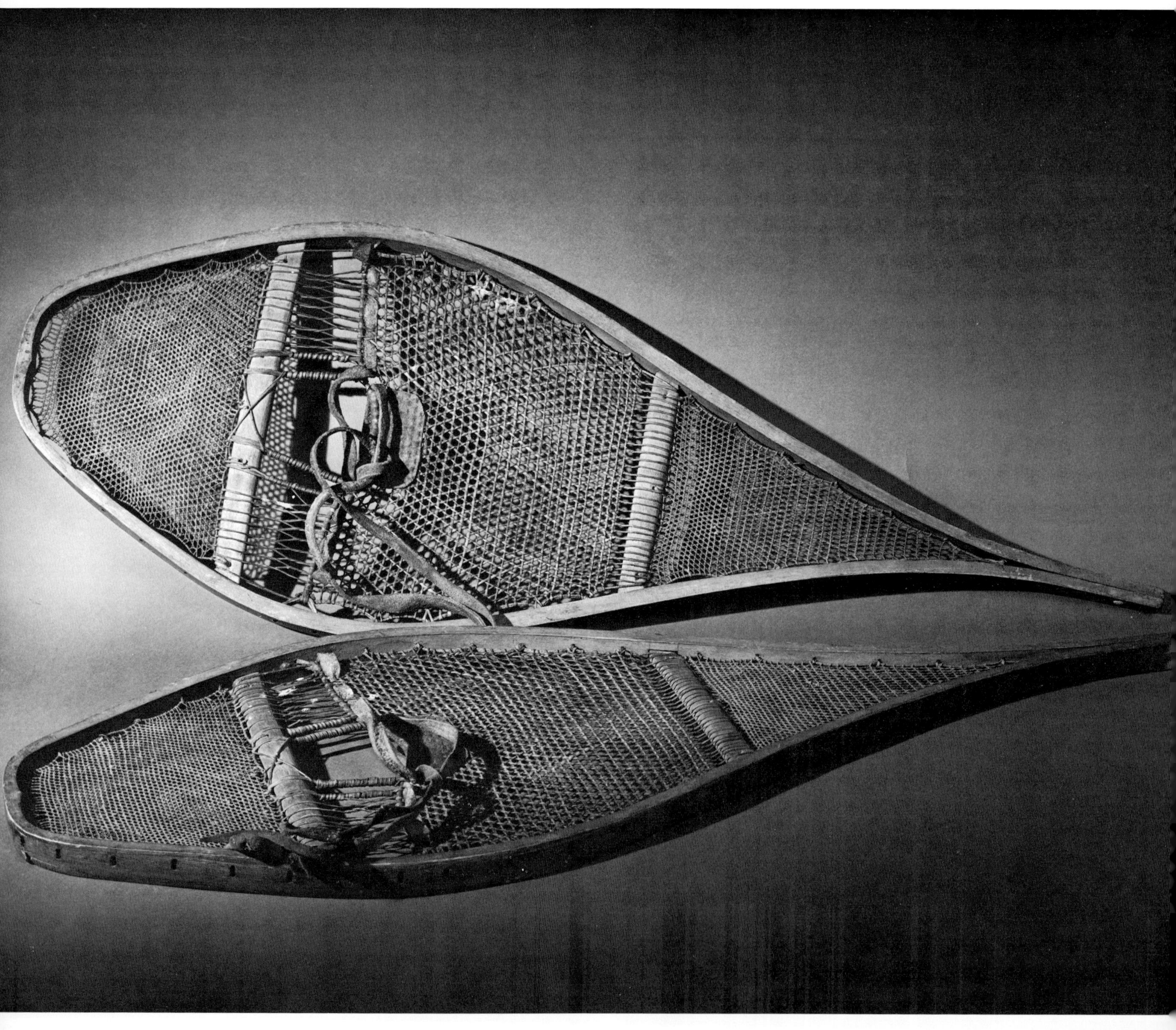

ACTUAL SIZE OF SNOW SHOES SHOWN ON OPPOSITE PAGE

Detail of a snow shoe which was used mainly for soft snow since it is more densely woven with larger and finer net and secured to the foot with strong rawhide.

ICE SCOOP

The upper side showing the position it would be in when used on a handle fastened to the bone at the top of the picture. The rim is deer horn which was bent and secured with rawhide. Webbing was fastened into the holes on the bottom and woven usually in a hexagonal pattern to form a net. The handle was generally thirty to thirty six inches long. These scoops were used to skim off ice fragments which formed constantly over the fishing hole in freezing weather.

The eliptical shape of the scoop, with the point in the front, made it a very efficient tool.

REVERSE SIDE OF SCOOP SHOWN ON OPPOSITE PAGE

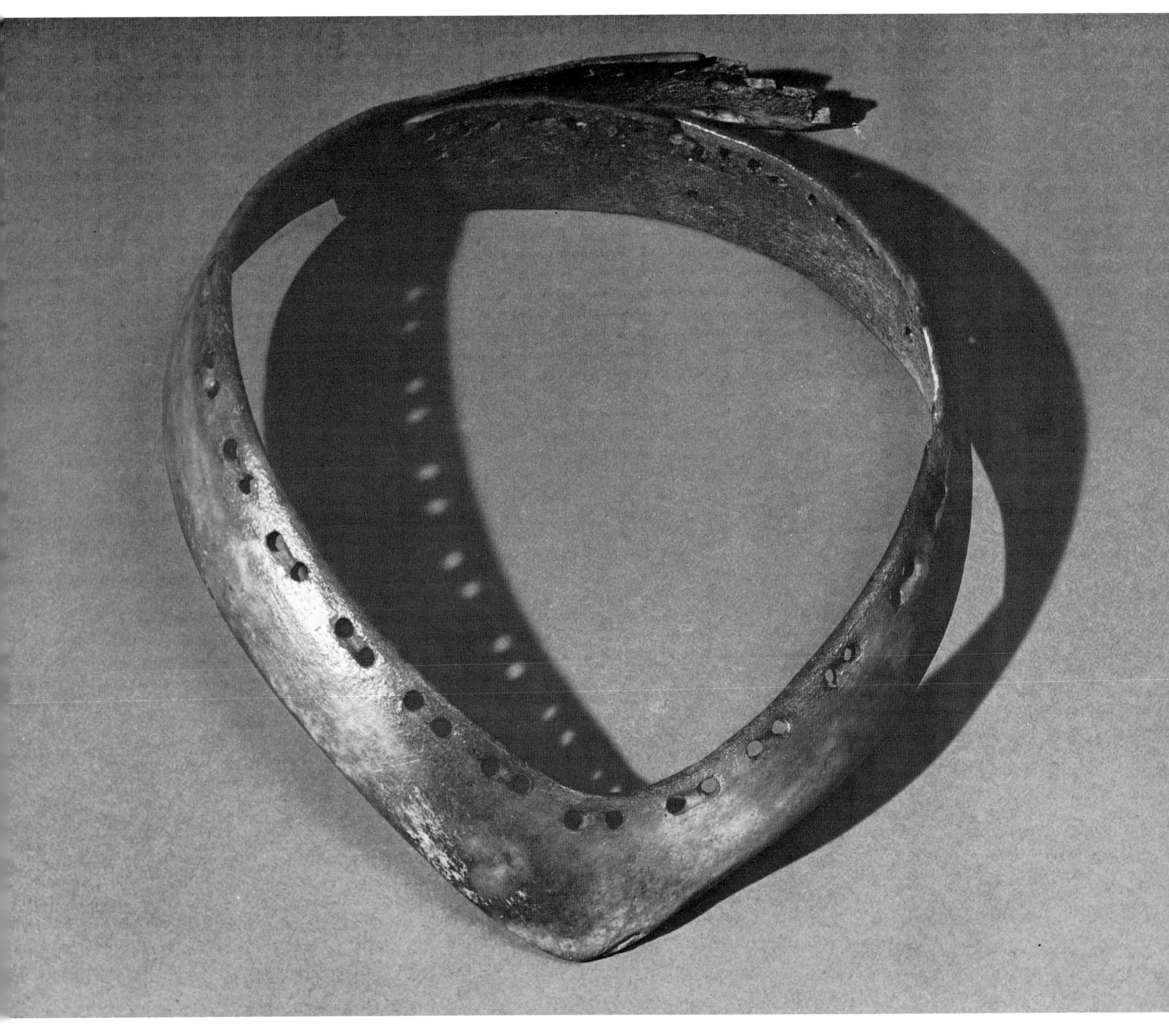

IMPLEMENTS FOR TOM COD AND SCULPIN FISHING

Numbered top to bottom:
1. A stick for winding the whale bone fishing line. The sinker is of black and white carved stone with a hole at either end to attach to the line and to the leader and lures. These two lures are red dyed ivory with four unbarbed metal hooks fitted through the larger end. Two blue glass beads and a duck toe terminate the line. 2. This lure is red dyed ivory with a lead center band. The carving resembles a large insect having white eyes and two forelegs decorated with blue beads and duck toe tips of bright yellow. Hooks of this type were mainly used when fishing for sculpin. 3. A shorter shuttle of bone having a baleen line and a two piece sinker of black and white stone fitted to a black stone end piece. These two parts are precisely cut and held together with white whale bone ties. Holes in the head allowed a piece of sinew to thread through holding a hook at each end. 4. A wood fishing stick with white whale bone line. The sinker is ivory and a hook of ivory with metal points is attached to the sinker at the line end. There is no hole at the head of the sinker. 5. A wood fishing stick with a black whale bone line. The ivory sinker has black stone eyes in the head making it a realistic white fish. The hook is an ivory piece carved to resemble a small fish with a hook protruding from the body.

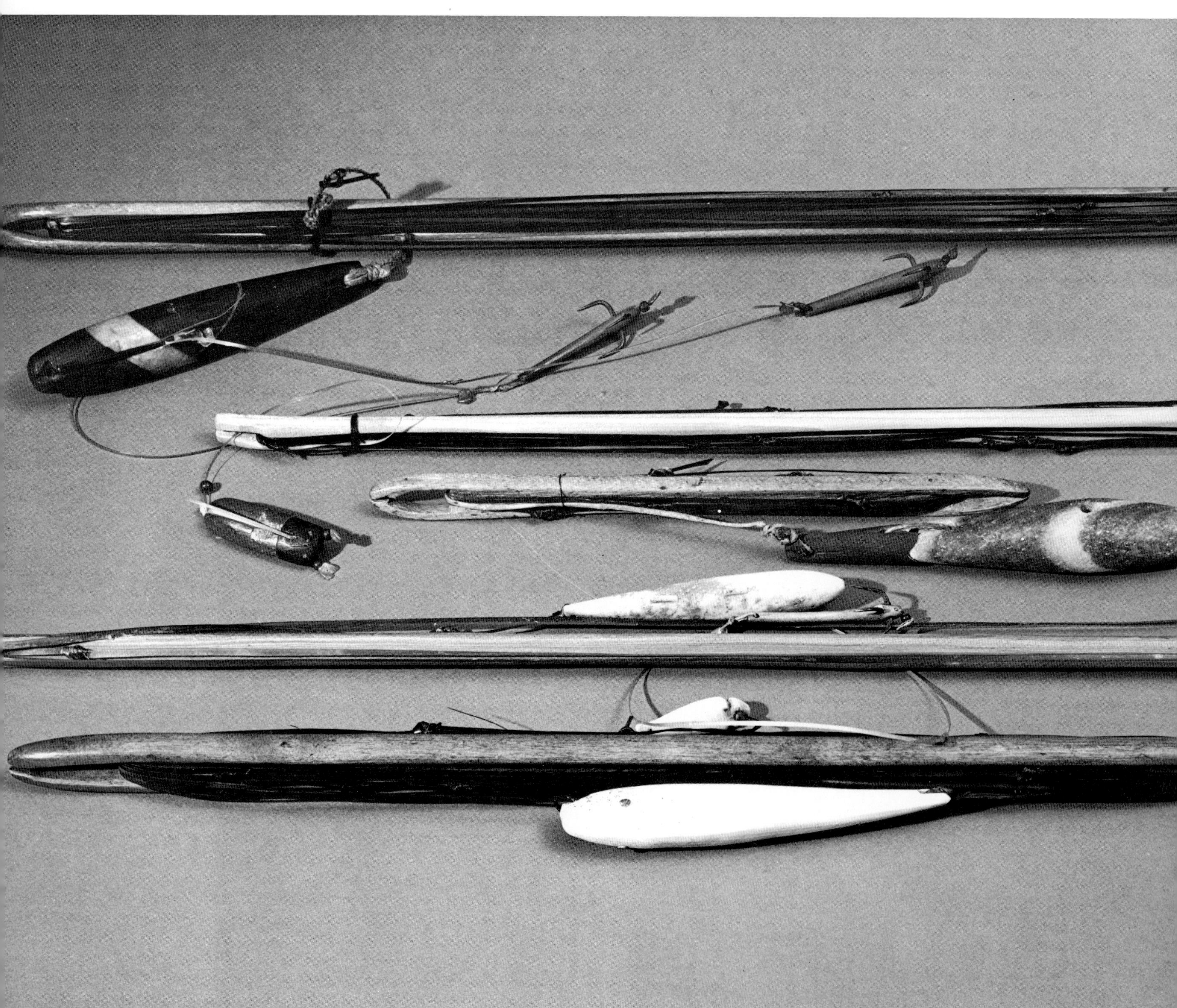

TOM COD FISHING STICKS

Numbered top to bottom:

1. A wood stick with a baleen fishing line. The knotting of the baleen shows the usual way it was joined.
2. A bone fishing stick showing the slotting through the center which helped to keep the line from being bulky.
3. A well finished wood stick with a fine baleen line.
4. A stick with a wide center and long end points rather than the rounded type. This stick is exceptionally well finished and shaped with a guide line inserted against the slightly raised sides where the baleen fitted into the stick.
5. A crudely made stick which may have been a shuttle for the storage of finished line.

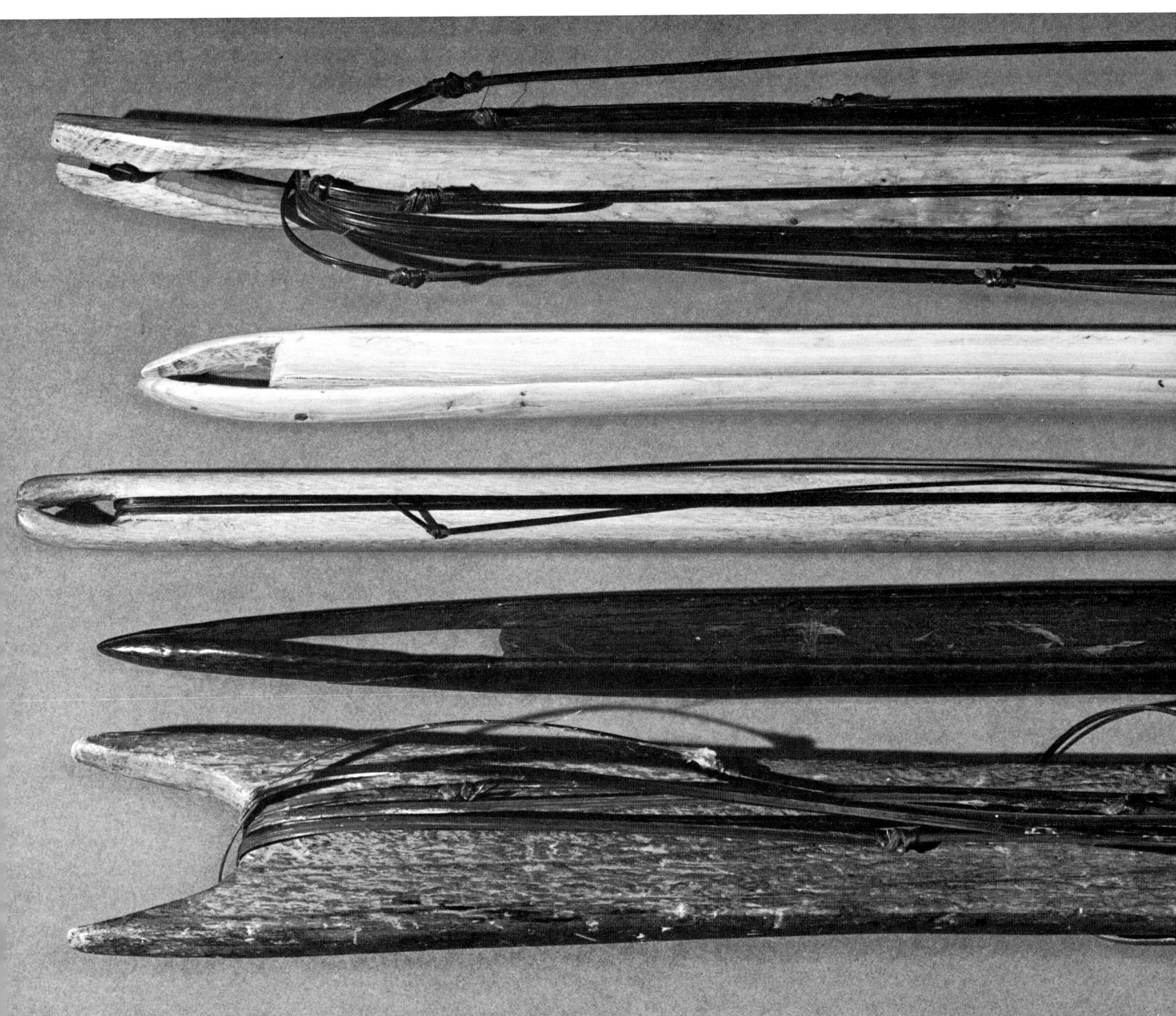

MISCELLANEOUS FISHING ITEMS

1, 2, & 3. Seal skin pouches for keeping small fish hooks and lines.
4 & 5. Are fish spear heads with lines and sheaths.
6. A hook used to catch wolf fish. It has an ivory shank and a metal hook.
7 & 8. Are ivory models of floats used on retrieving lines here used as sinkers.

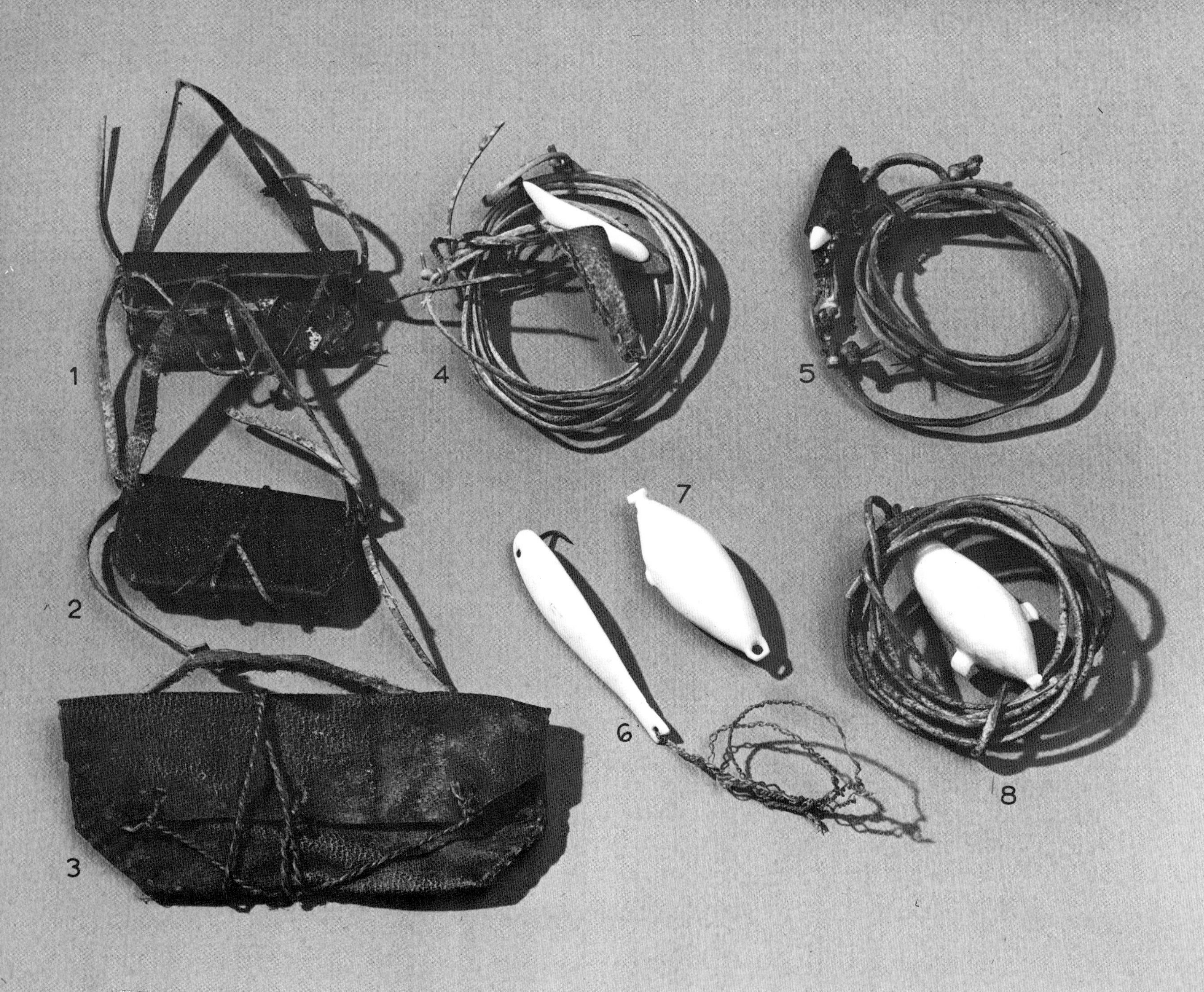

HOOKS SHOWING A DIVERSITY OF DESIGN

1-2. Two dark ivory shanks with metal hooks set into the ivory.
3. A float model used as a sinker.
4-5. White ivory shanks with metal barbs.
6. A decorated shank with metal hooks. This hook resembles a seal collector although it seems to be too small. The seal etching shows one being dragged and this may be its purpose.
7. A fish spear head and sheath on a line.
8. A double pointed ivory hook carved in one piece.
9. A decorated ivory shank with an ivory barb.
10-11. Two small ivory shanks with metal barbs.
12. A sinker and fish spear head in its sheath on a line.

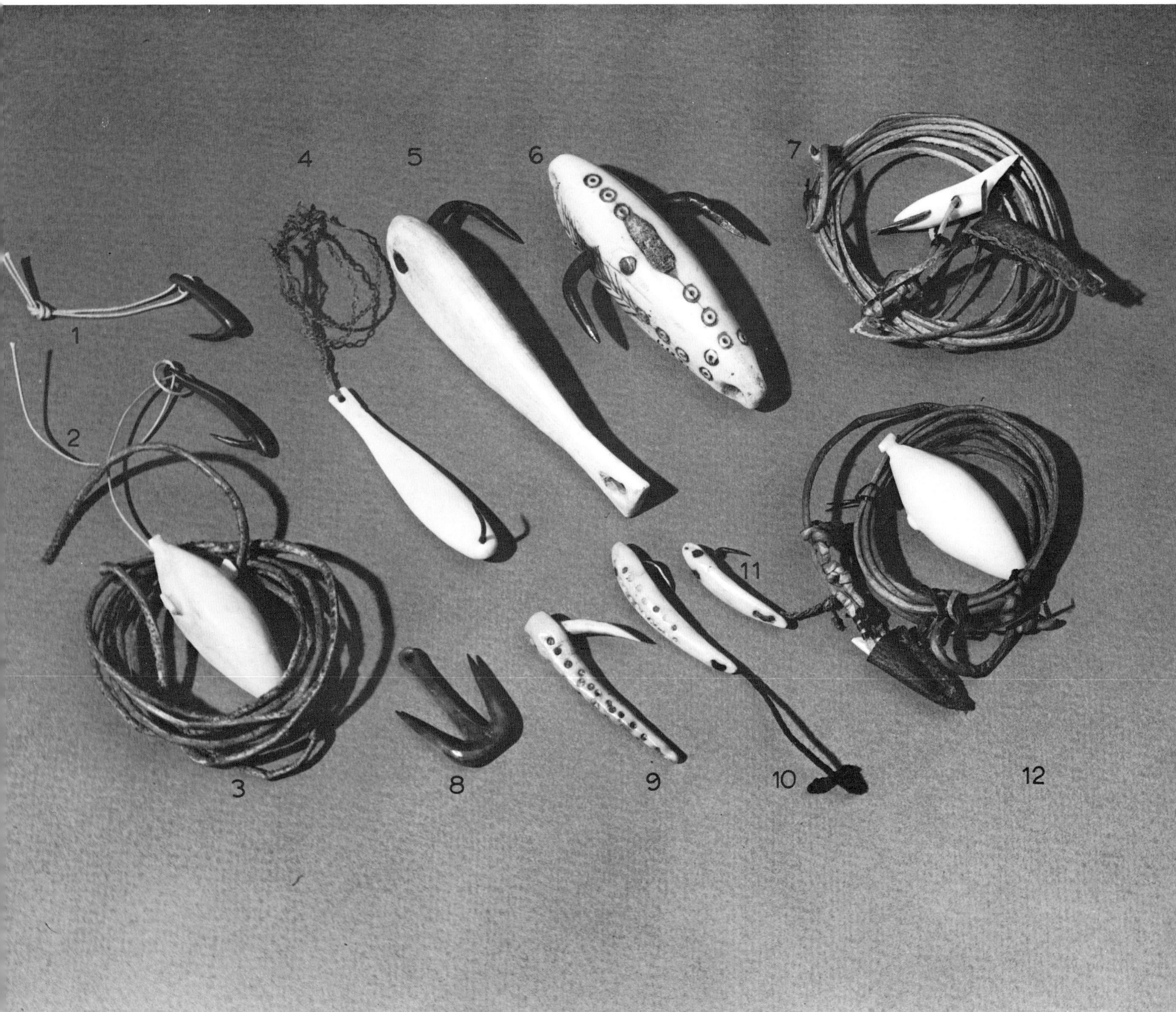

FISHING HOOKS AND SINKERS

Were unique in their design often resembling small fish or other creatures.

1. A hook is on the underside of this two color ivory lure. Pieces of red thread are tied to the lure.
2. A similar lure has dark ivory fastened to a white ivory piece with small copper pegs. This lure has white ivory inlaid for eyes. The hook protrudes from the underside. Two eyelet holes one on either side allow for threads.

3.-6. Ivory sinkers resembling small fish.

FISHING LINE SINKERS

Sinkers shaped like fish in ivory and bone showing various types of holes used to attach lines.

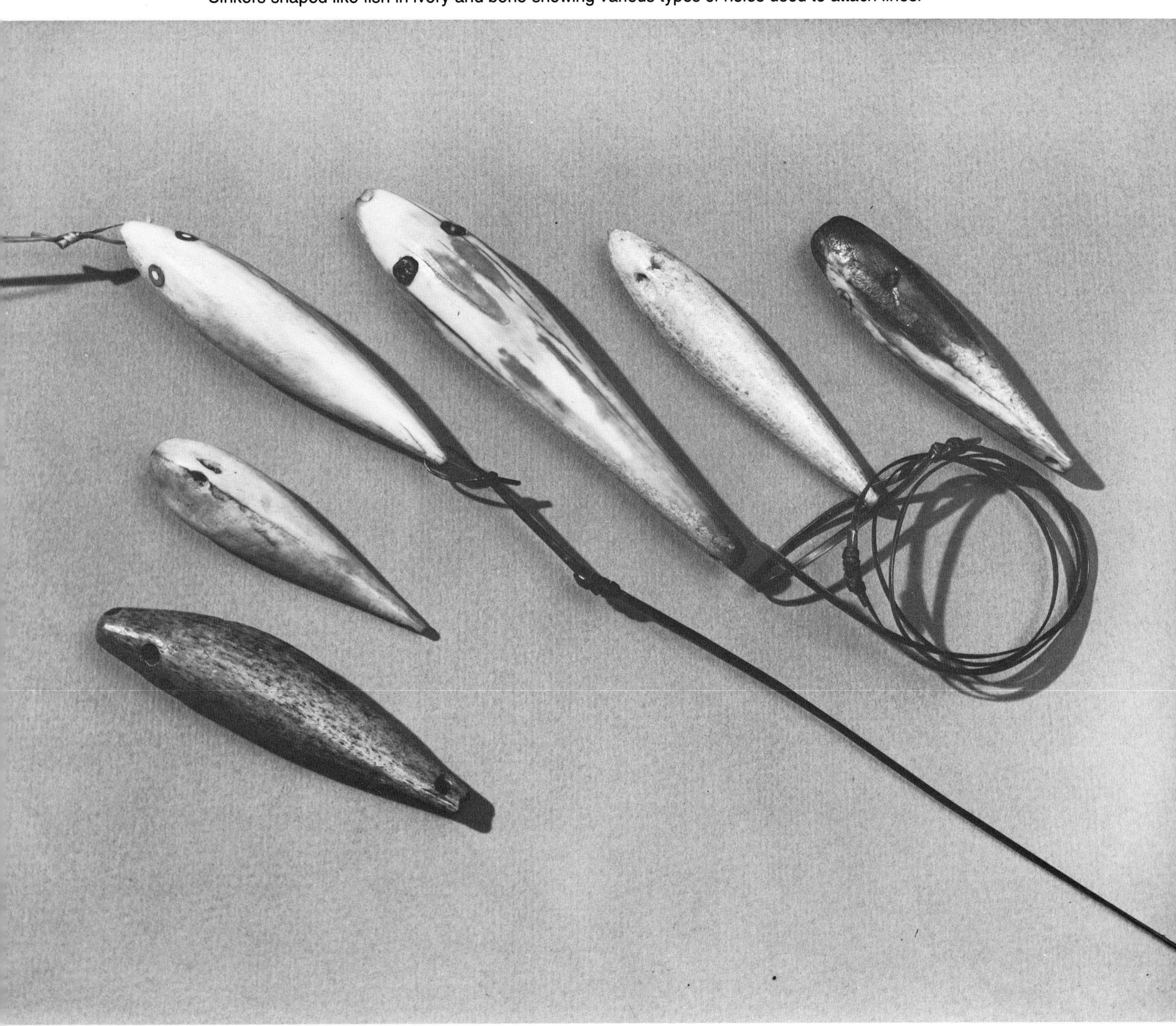

MISCELLANEOUS ITEMS

1. A seal retriever used to fasten seals for hauling when collected after a hunt.
2-3. Ivory shanks with metal fish hooks attached through the ivory.
4. An ivory shank with hooks notched into the ivory.
5. An animal retriever with metal hooks forked at the ends. The line has a round ivory cord handle showing the method of tying.
6. An ivory fish hook with the metal set through the ivory.

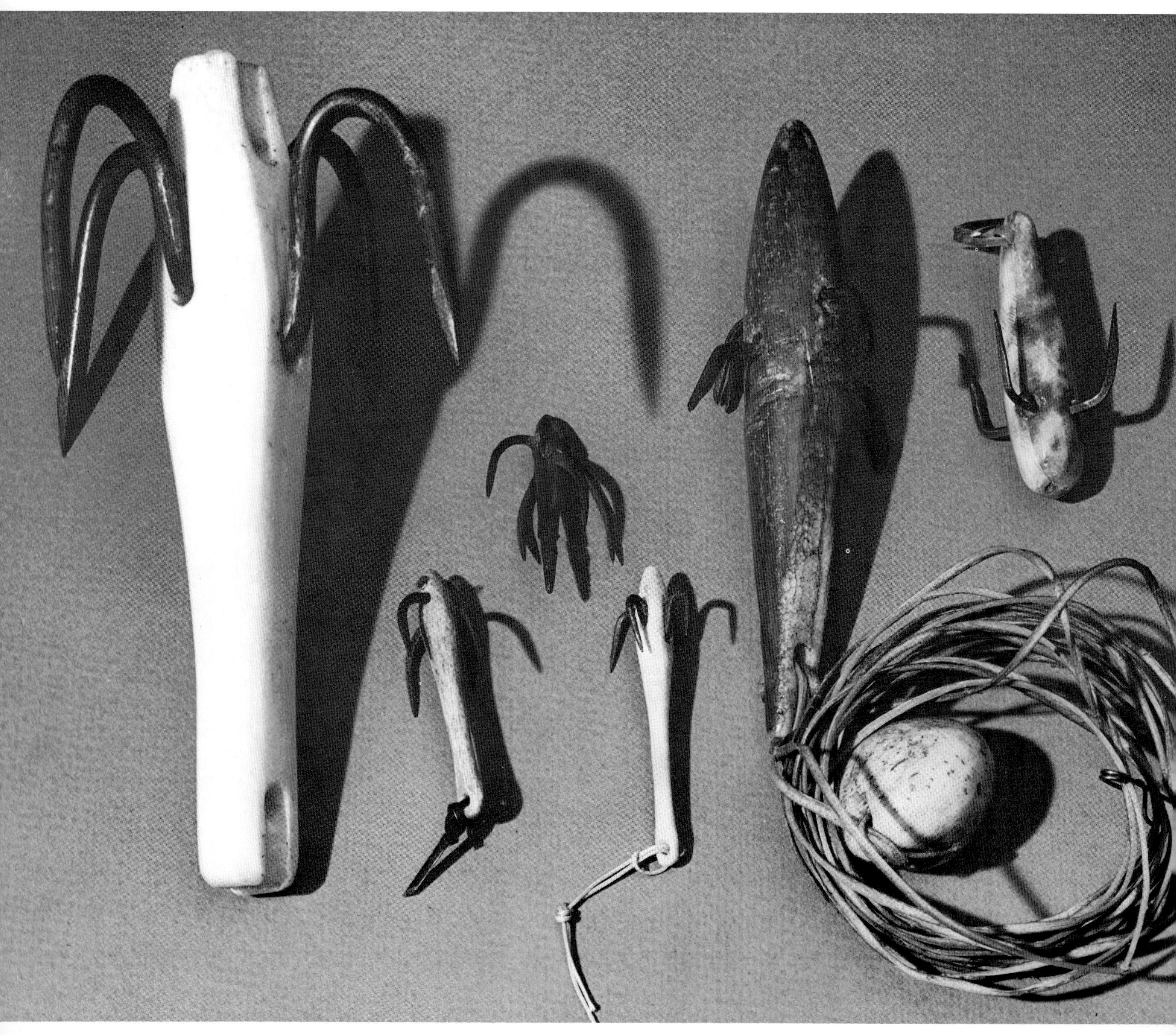

A RETRIEVING HOOK

Used to fasten dead animals, such as seals, together so they could be transported after a hunt. The body of the collector is wood with metal barbs fastened securely. The wood caps protect the points when not in use and were secured to the collector with rawhide ties part of one showing at the left.

MISCELLANEOUS ITEMS

1. A fish arrow shaft and socket for a detachable point.
2. A shaft with a small socket for a detachable point. When the fish is struck the point separates, the shaft becomes a drag impeding the fish's escape.
3. A bird spear with an ivory single barbed point.
4. A bird spear with a single point barbed on one side. Three barbs on the shaft arranged in this fashion were usual on this type of spear.

5 & 6. Two small spears with seal spear points.

7. A barbed spear point.

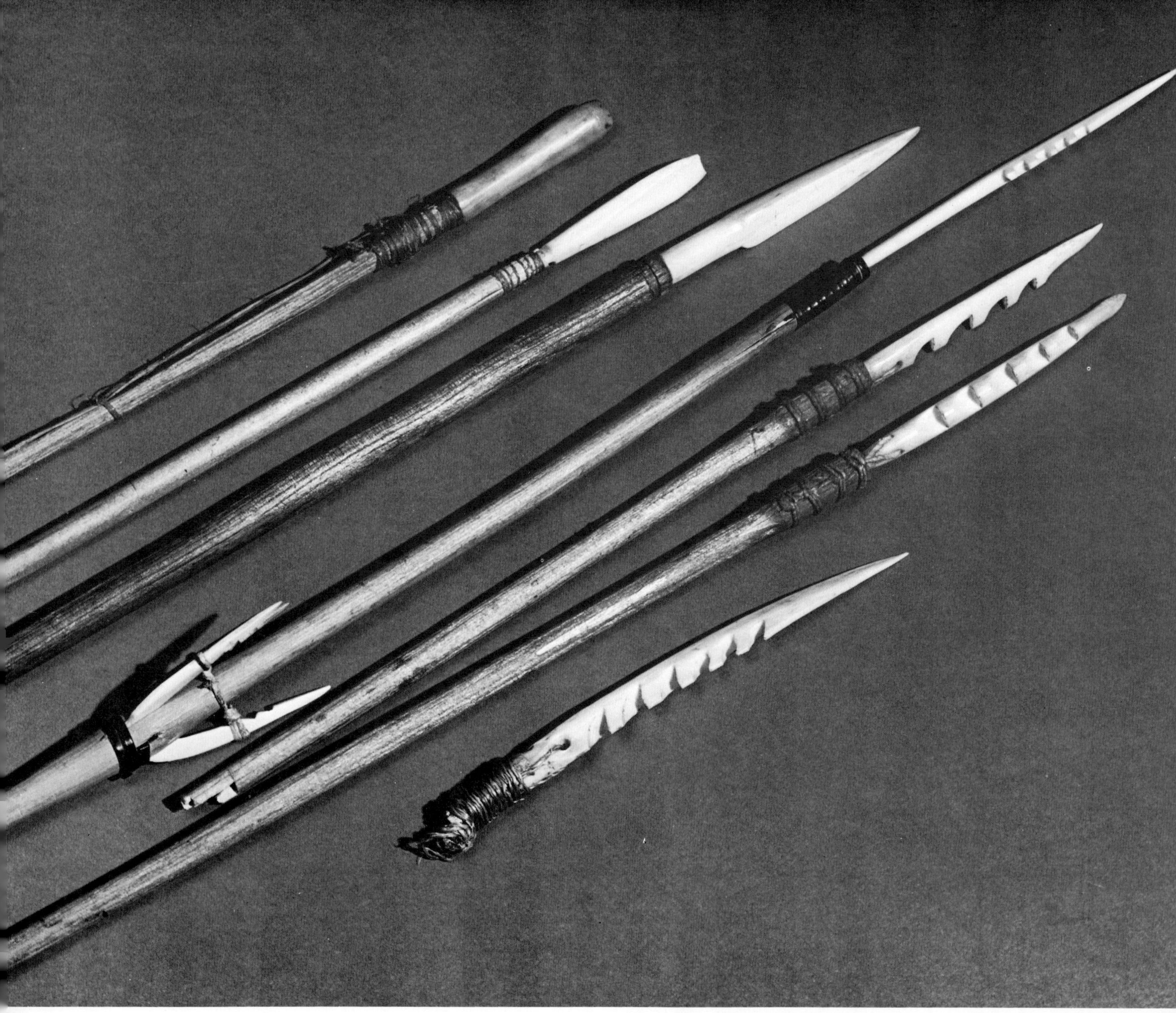

MISCELLANEOUS ITEMS

1. A bird spear with only two points. Note the small barbs on the ivory shaft, left corner.
2. A bird spear showing the serrated barbs on the points. One point is broken.
3. A fish spear with three points.
4. A fish spear with a center point and shaft weight.

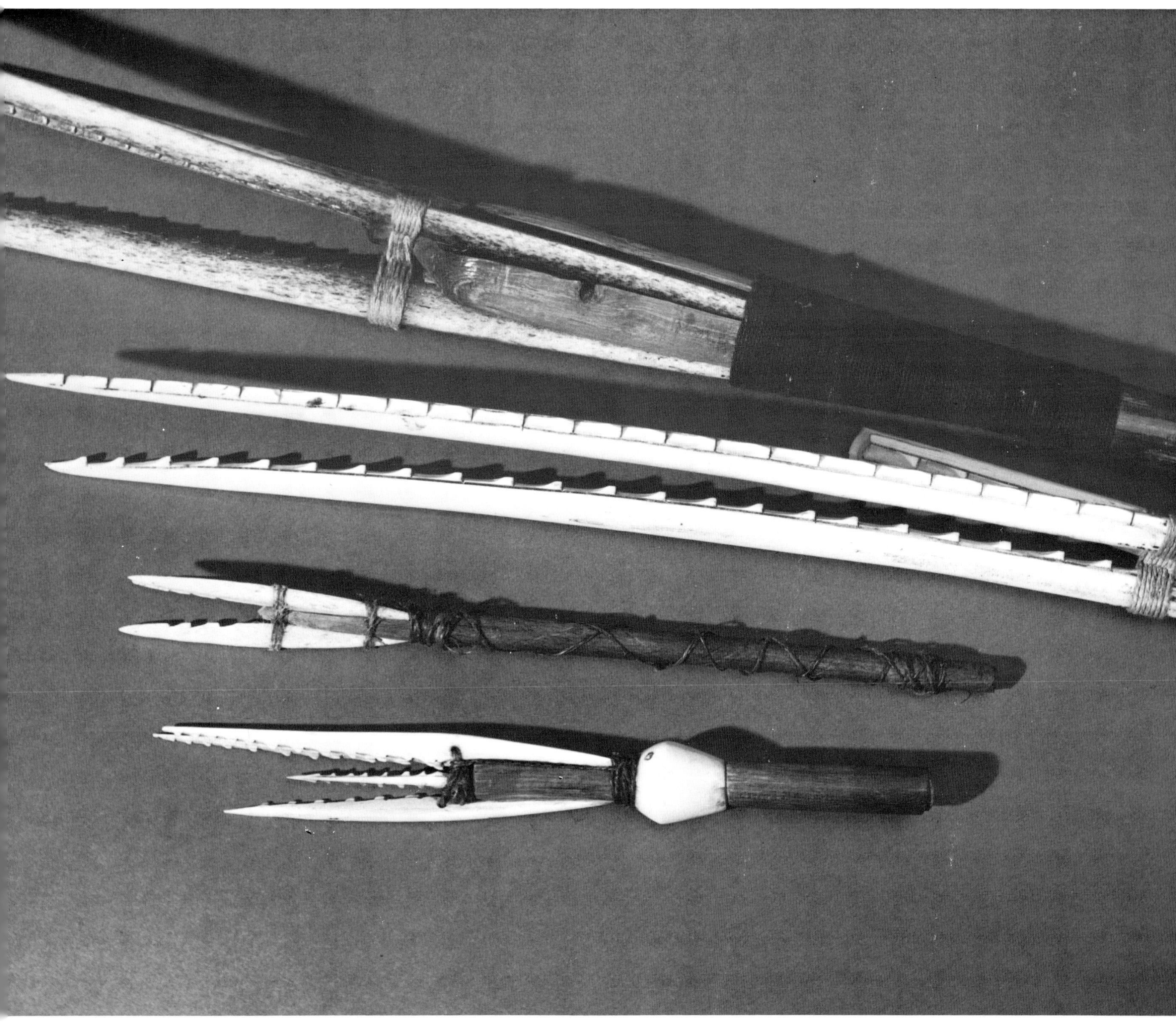

MISCELLANEOUS BONE AND IVORY BARBED POINTS

Examples of ivory points barbed in various ways to suit the hunter. One is aware of the skill of the maker especially when his crude tools are considered and the beautiful results are seen. These points assume the character of works of art.

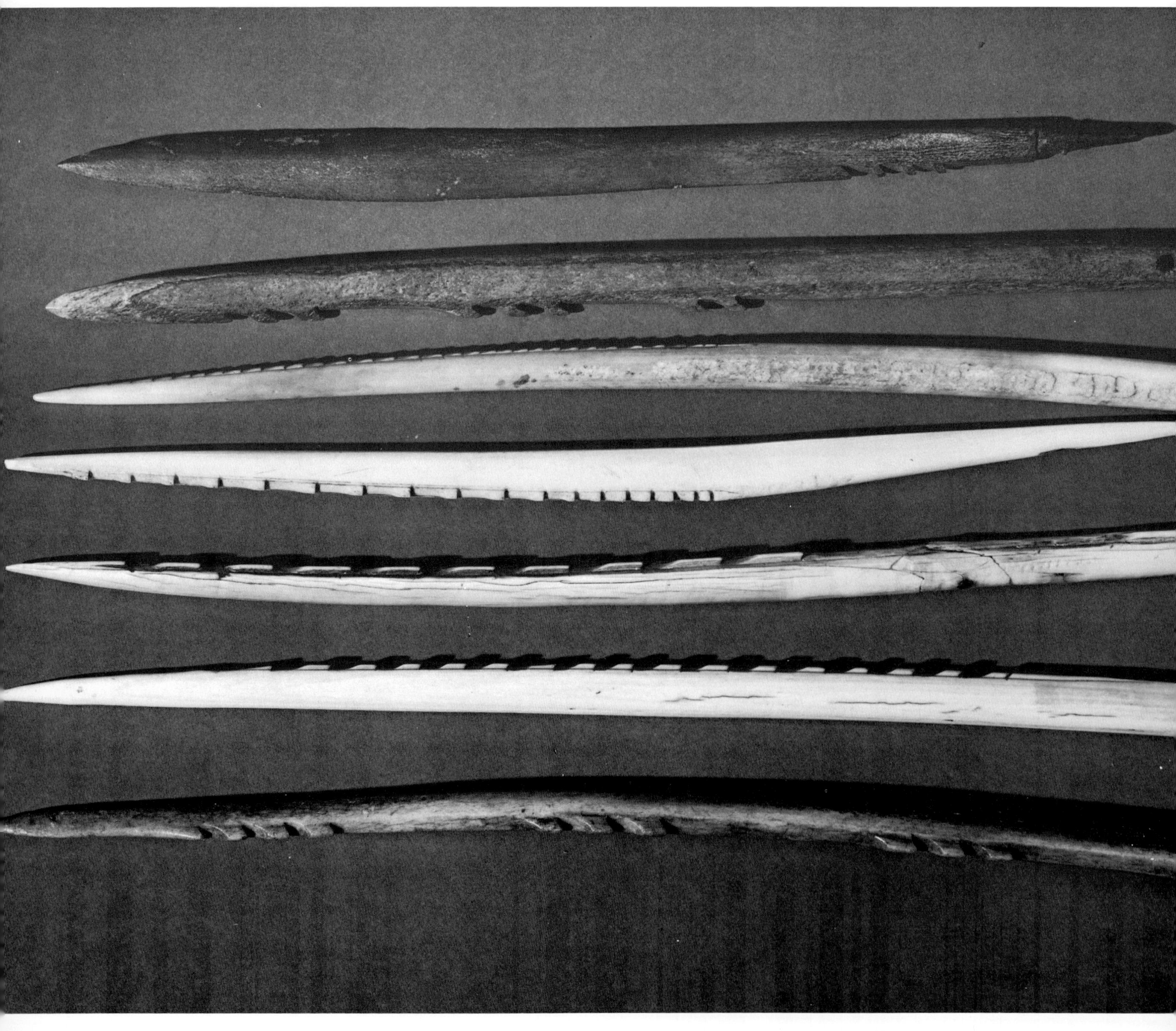

MISCELLANEOUS BONE AND IVORY BARBED POINTS

The Eskimos took great pains with their hunting tools. Here are spear points showing a variety in the barbs cut into them. The third example from the top is a bird's tongue which is naturally barbed, it was shaped, as shown on the right end, to fit into a projectile.

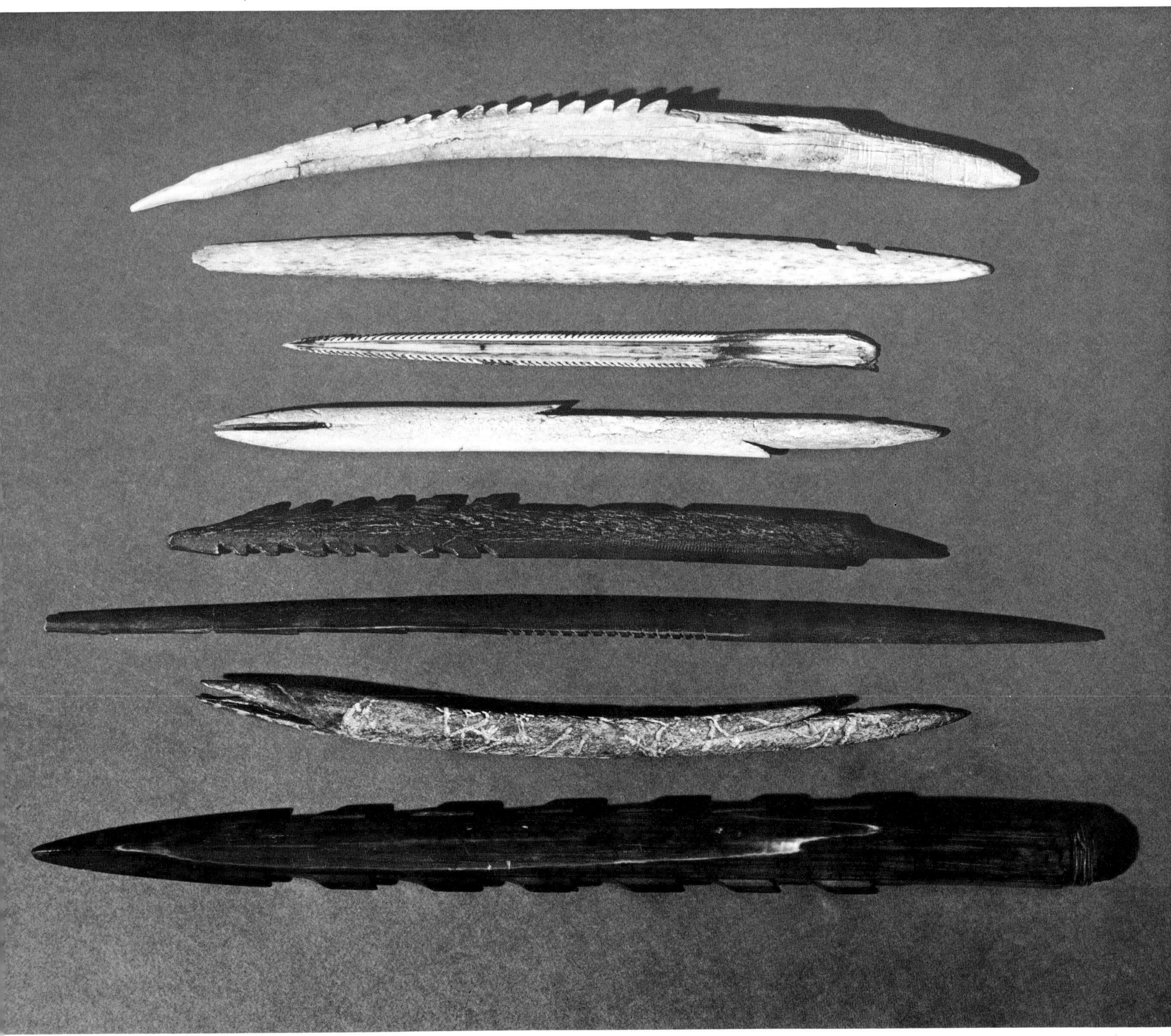

LARGE GAME SPEARS, GROUP 1:

1. A spear for large game having a heavy shaft, a spear head at the right and a socket at the left for a harpoon head. The seal in the center of the shaft is a cord joiner.
2. A spear for large game with a heavy shaft reinforced at the right end with an ivory piece. There are two finger rests at the center of the shaft. The foreshaft is lashed onto the shaft with rawhide.
3. A spear for walrus or large seals with a separating point inserted into the socket at the left and a thrusting spear on the right end.
4. A shaft with a spear on the right end, a finger rest on the shaft, and a long socket on the left which has a separating point on a foreshaft.

BIRD SPEARS, GROUP 2: These spears are fitted with long tapered points barbed on one side. The first spear had three points (one is broken) the second spear has four. The shafts are not feathered and were usually from three and three quarters feet to four and a quarter feet long.

SHORTER SPEARS FOR SEAL HUNTING, GROUP 3: These four shafts have thrusting points on the right ends. The heads of the first two spears have sockets which are bulb shaped; the other two are more slender. The second spear design is similar to a walrus spear.

SPEAR SHAFTS WITH FEATHER INSERTS, GROUP 4: The head on the first spear has no point but is rather a stunner type. The second spear has a socket and separate point. Feathers were inserted onto shafts for flight direction or to turn the shaft in flight.

GROUP 5: Shafts with small spear ends and sockets for points.

SPEAR SHAFTS

The first two shafts show the arrangement of feathers and their cuts. The three lower examples show the fastening of spears to the shafts. The one spear has been scored on both sides.

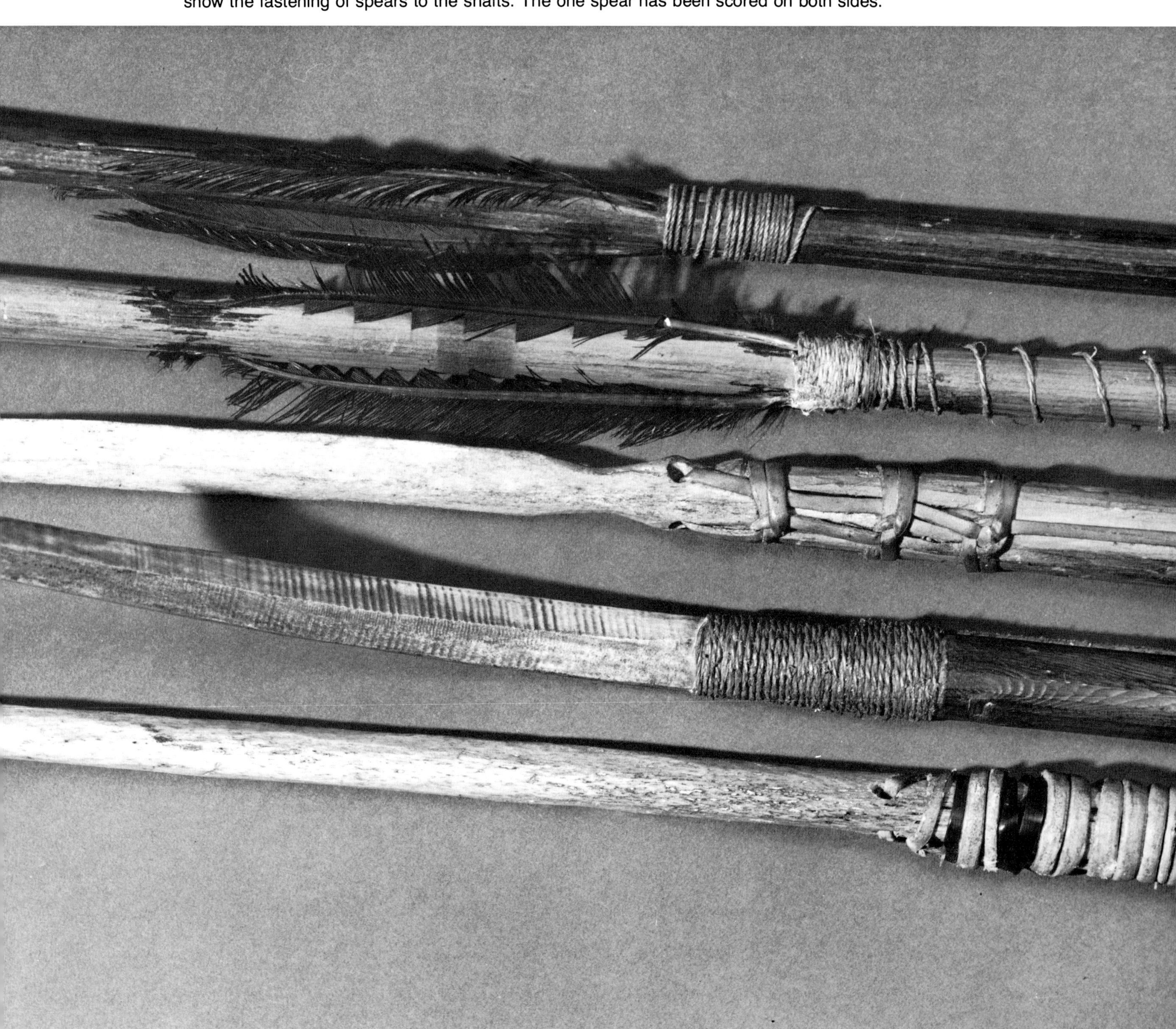

DETAILS OF WALRUS AND WHALE SPEARS

Numbered top to bottom:

1. The thrusting spear on a shaft
2. A socket and point.
3. A socket on a walrus spear.
4. A whale harpoon head detail. The socket is short and thick. The foreshaft is tied securely into the shaft with rawhide.

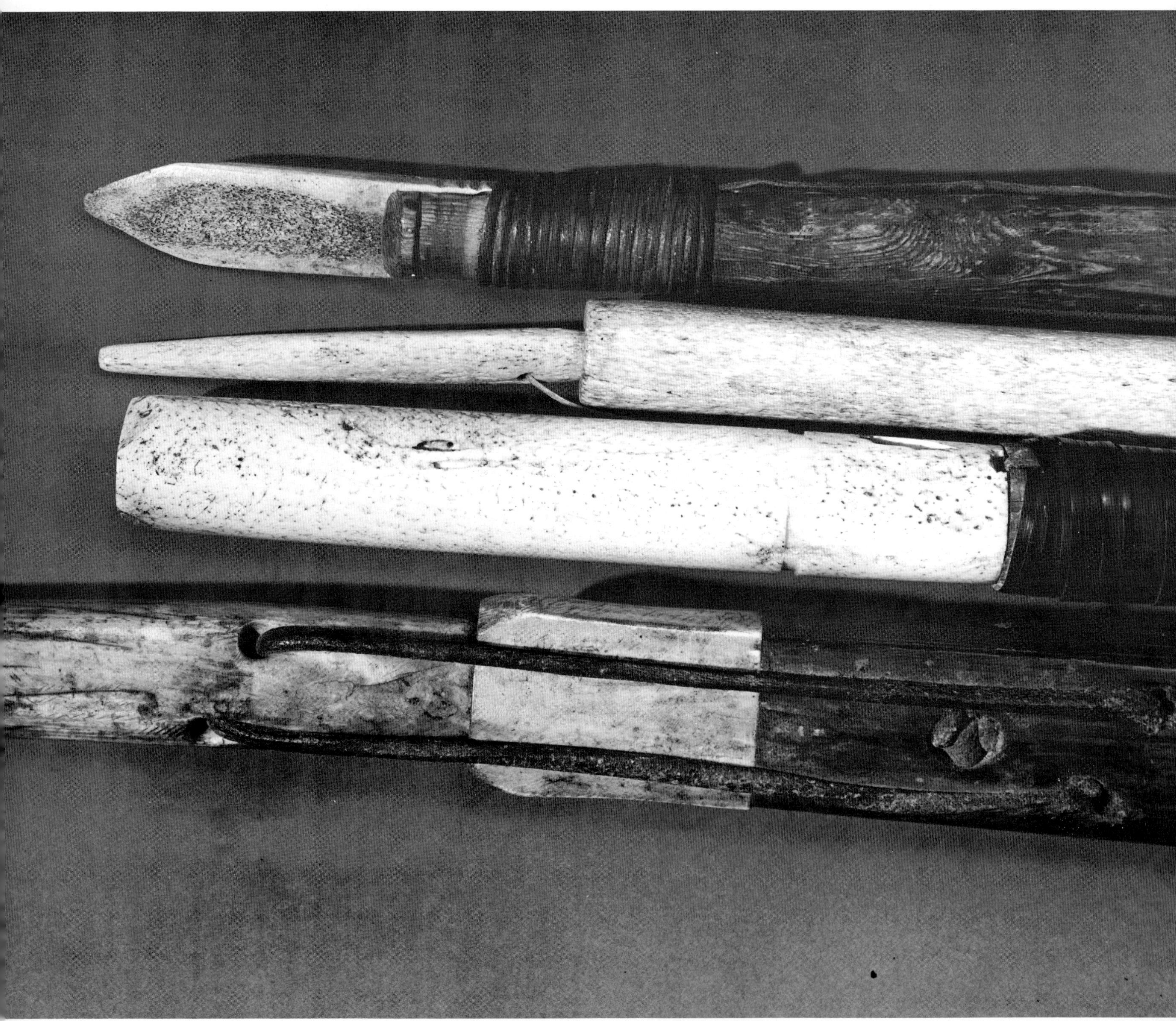

SPEARS FOR WHALES AND LARGE WALRUS

Were larger and heavier than ordinary spears.
Numbered top to bottom:

1. A socket and point for a walrus harpoon.
2. The spear end of a retrieving harpoon.
3. The broken thrusting spear end of a harpoon.
4. An ivory terminal on a harpoon shaft.

SPEARS USED IN HUNTING SEALS AND WALRUS

Numbered top to bottom:

1. An ivory foreshaft for a seal spear.
2. A foreshaft and barbed separating point.
3. A walrus harpoon head.
4. A shaft with short socket.
5. A shaft showing the rawhide, line, socket and spear head attached to the line.

FOUR SPEAR SHAFT SOCKETS

Showing the care in their manufacture and variety in their design.

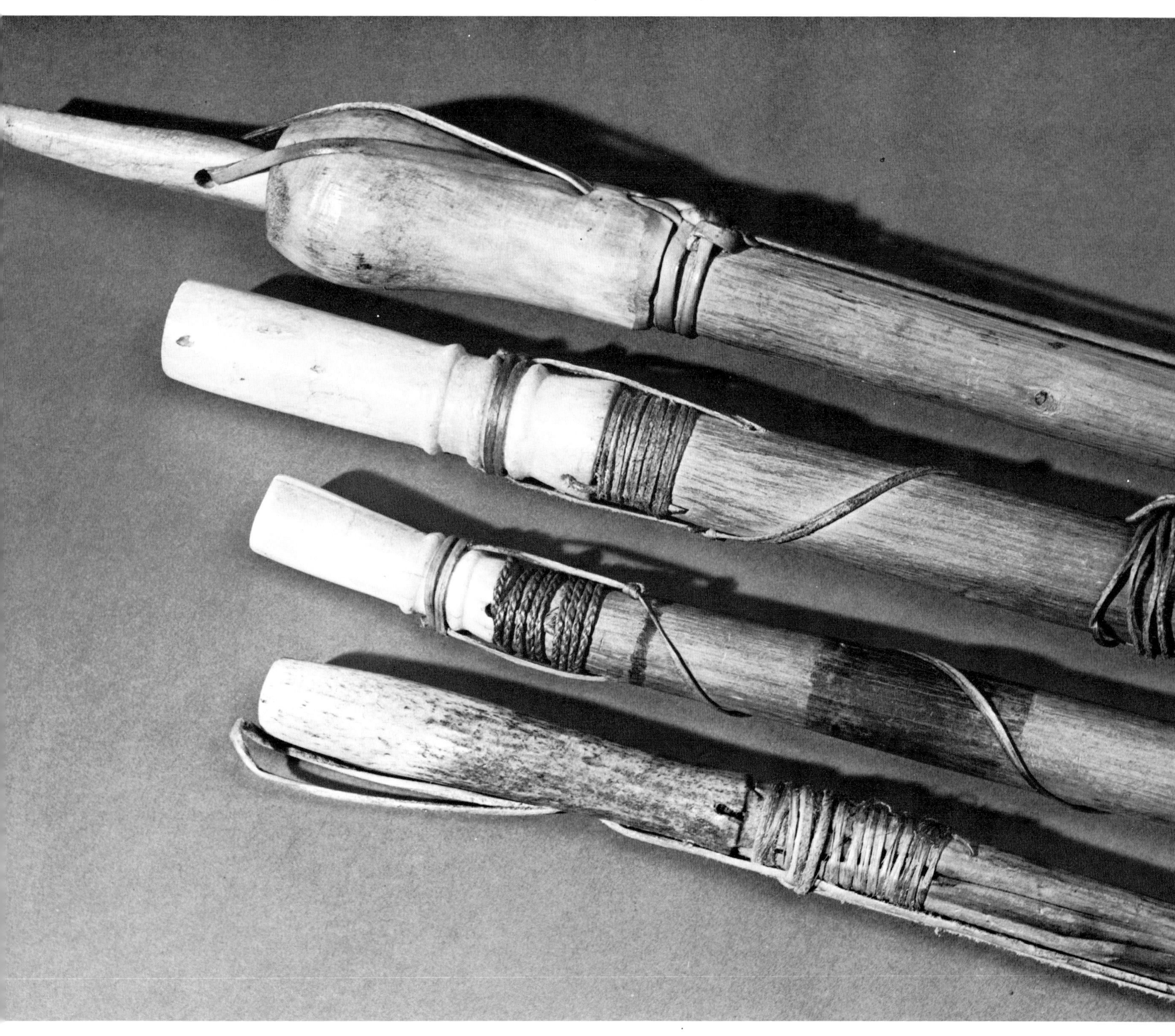

SHAFTS OF LARGE SPEARS

Showing the placement of several types of finger rests. Some rests are fastened to the shaft with pegs; others are tied.

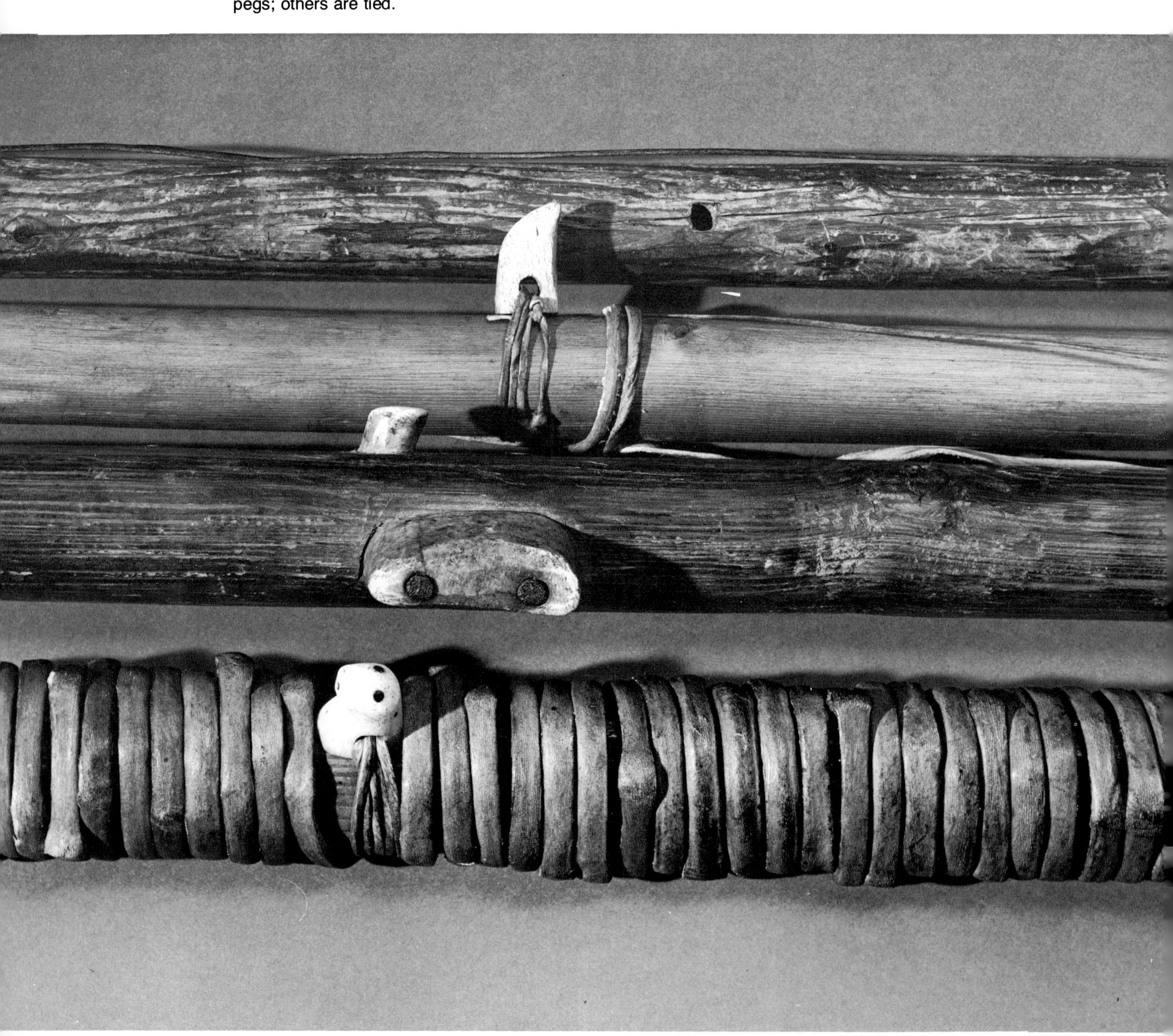

ARROW HEADS FOR KILLING BIRDS

Bird points were blunt headed but often had notches cut into the head especially if they were square. These are round heads.

The center white ivory point is unusually well made.

The point, top row right, still has a piece of the shaft, also the point on the right lower line.

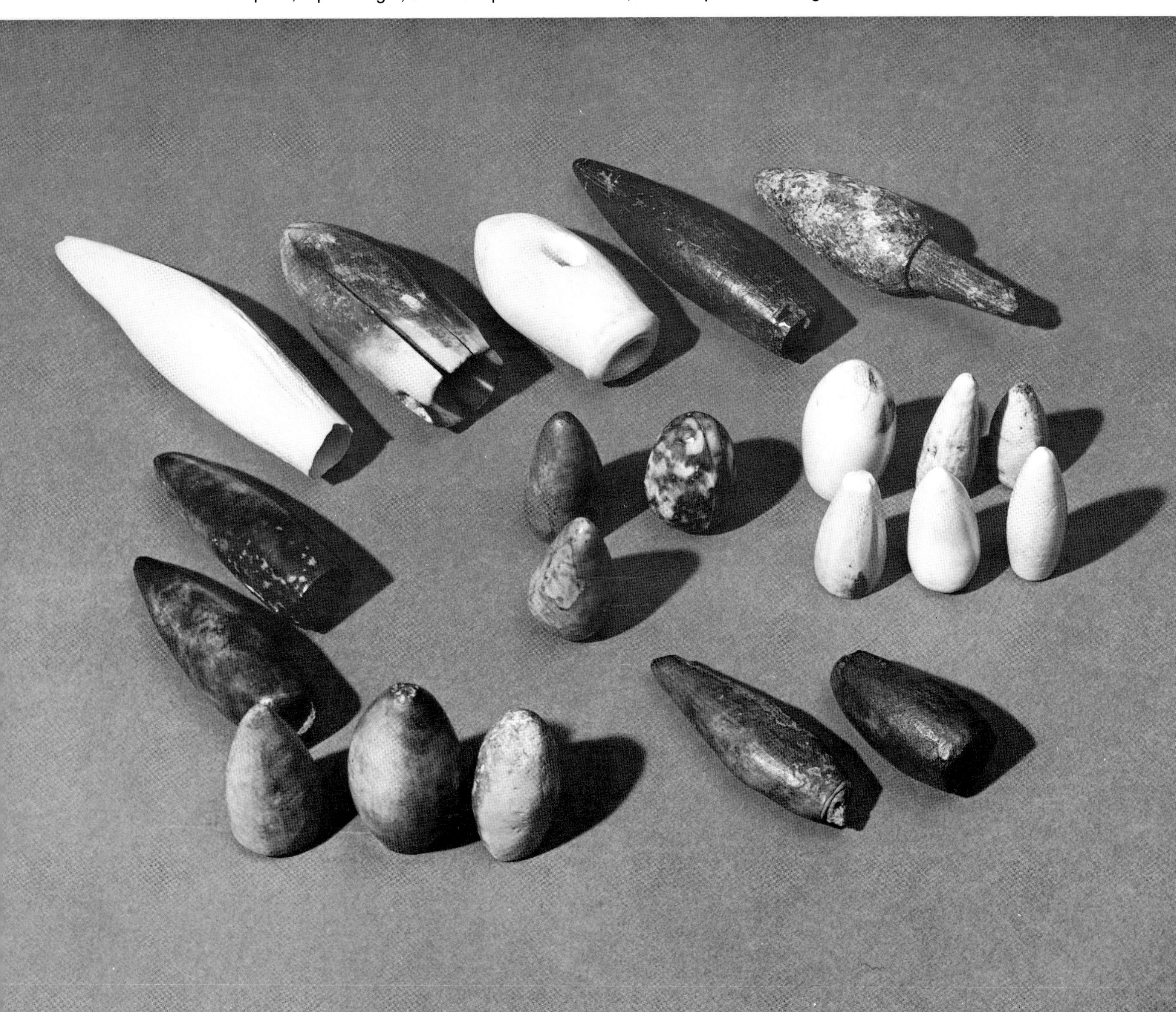

HARPOON HEADS

Rigged to foreshafts. The blade in the top spear head is metal, the middle is slate.

HARPOON HEADS

The upper and second spear heads are for large game such as reindeer. Three has a metal head. Four is brass with a metal blade.

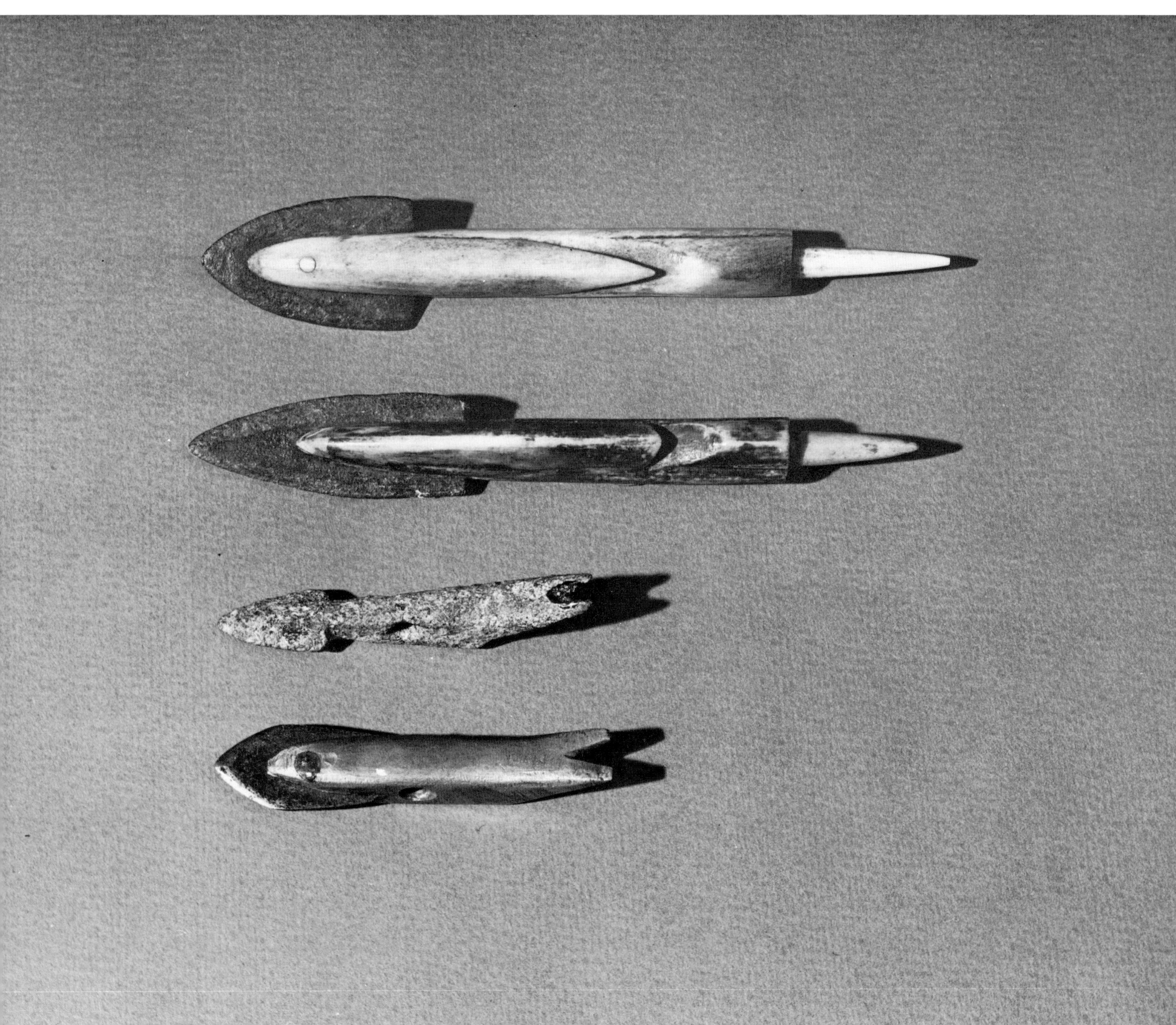

MISCELLANEOUS HARPOON HEADS

Early harpoon heads contrast with a later design head with a metal point (lower left). The head at the top left side has a slate point.

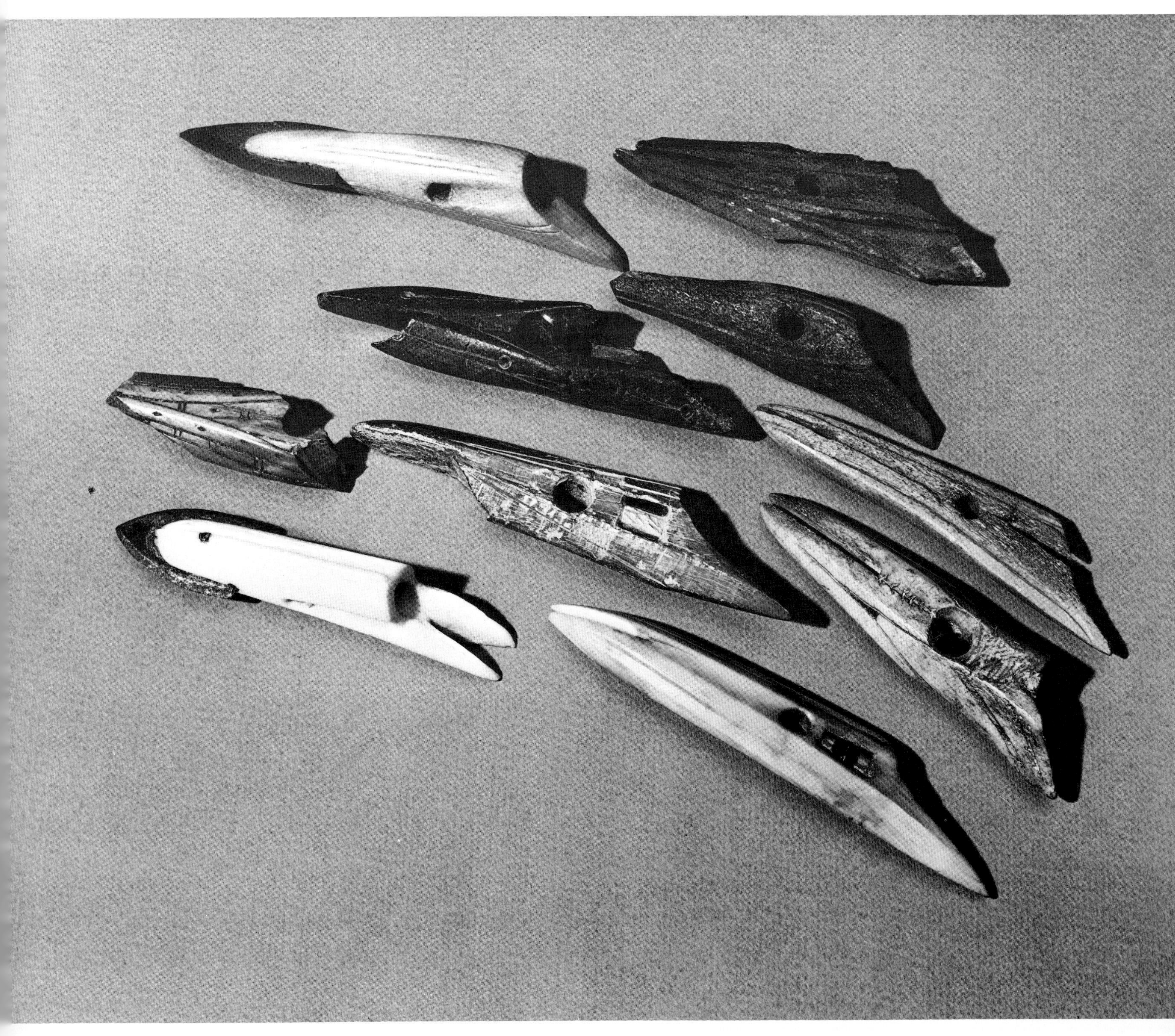

THREE ANCIENT HARPOON HEADS

Many of the earliest examples are heavily carved rather than etched. The center head is a good example.

Upper: An etched ivory head.
Middle: A deeply carved ivory head.
Lower: A carved ivory head in a simpler style.

DECORATED HARPOON HEADS

The first and fourth having a notch carved into the body.

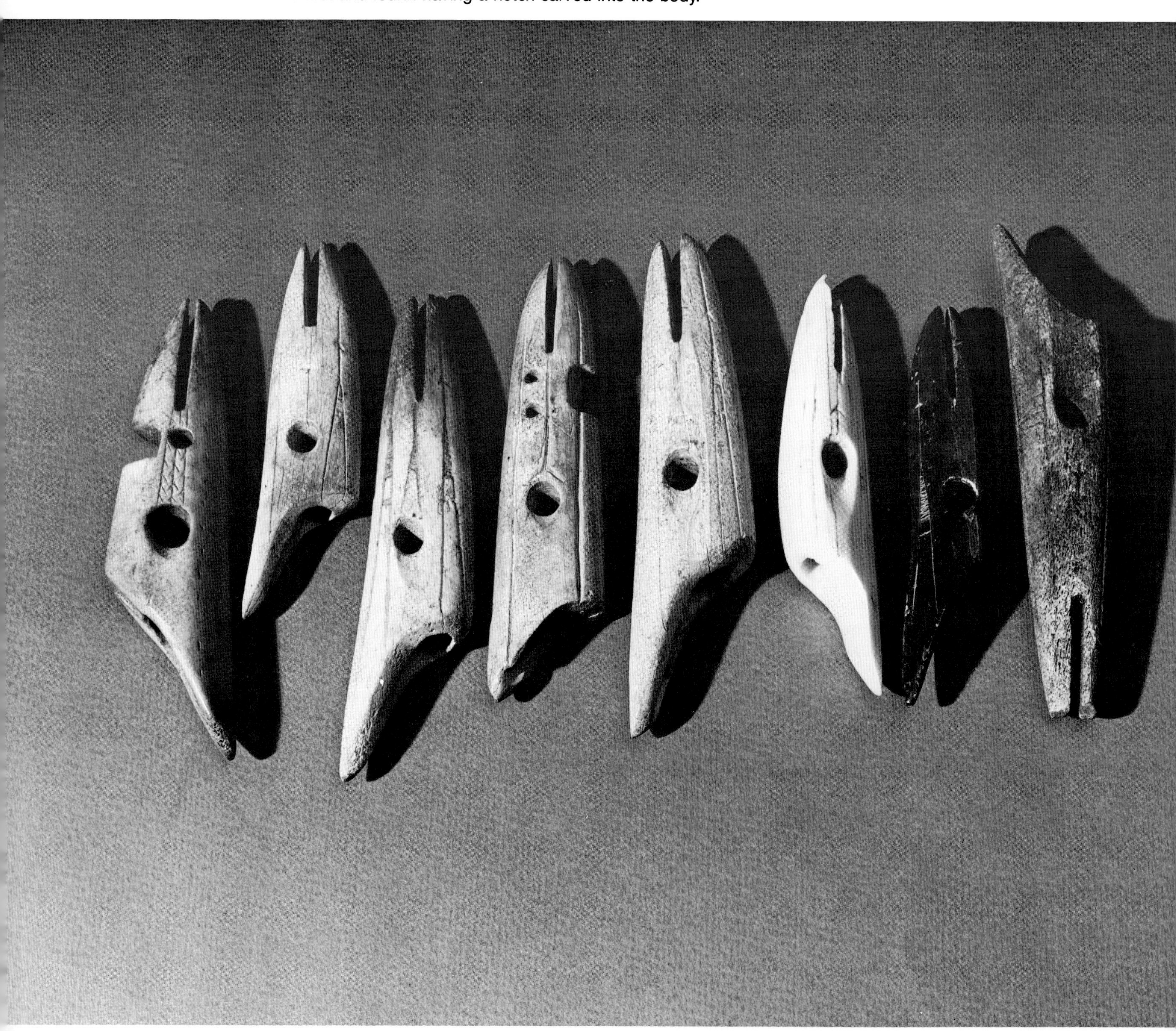

HARPOON HEADS

Three harpoon heads showing a similarity yet a great difference in design. The decoration does not detract from the efficiency of the projectile but rather suggests flight. The middle head has raven totem marks in the center.

BARBED HARPOON HEADS

The heads are slotted to receive blades.

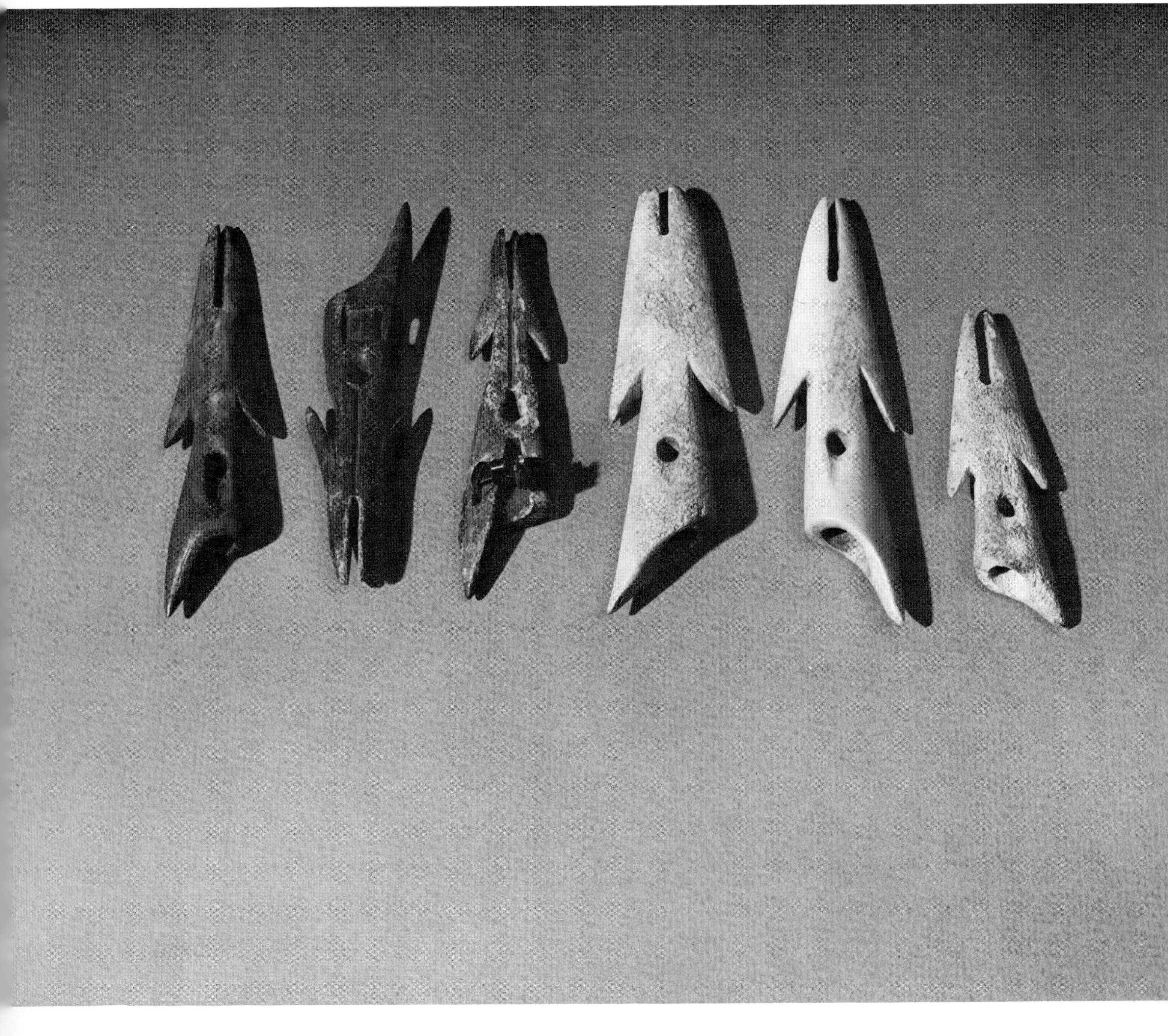

LARGER HARPOON HEADS

With barbs to hold them more firmly in the animal. Only the first specimen was made for a blade.

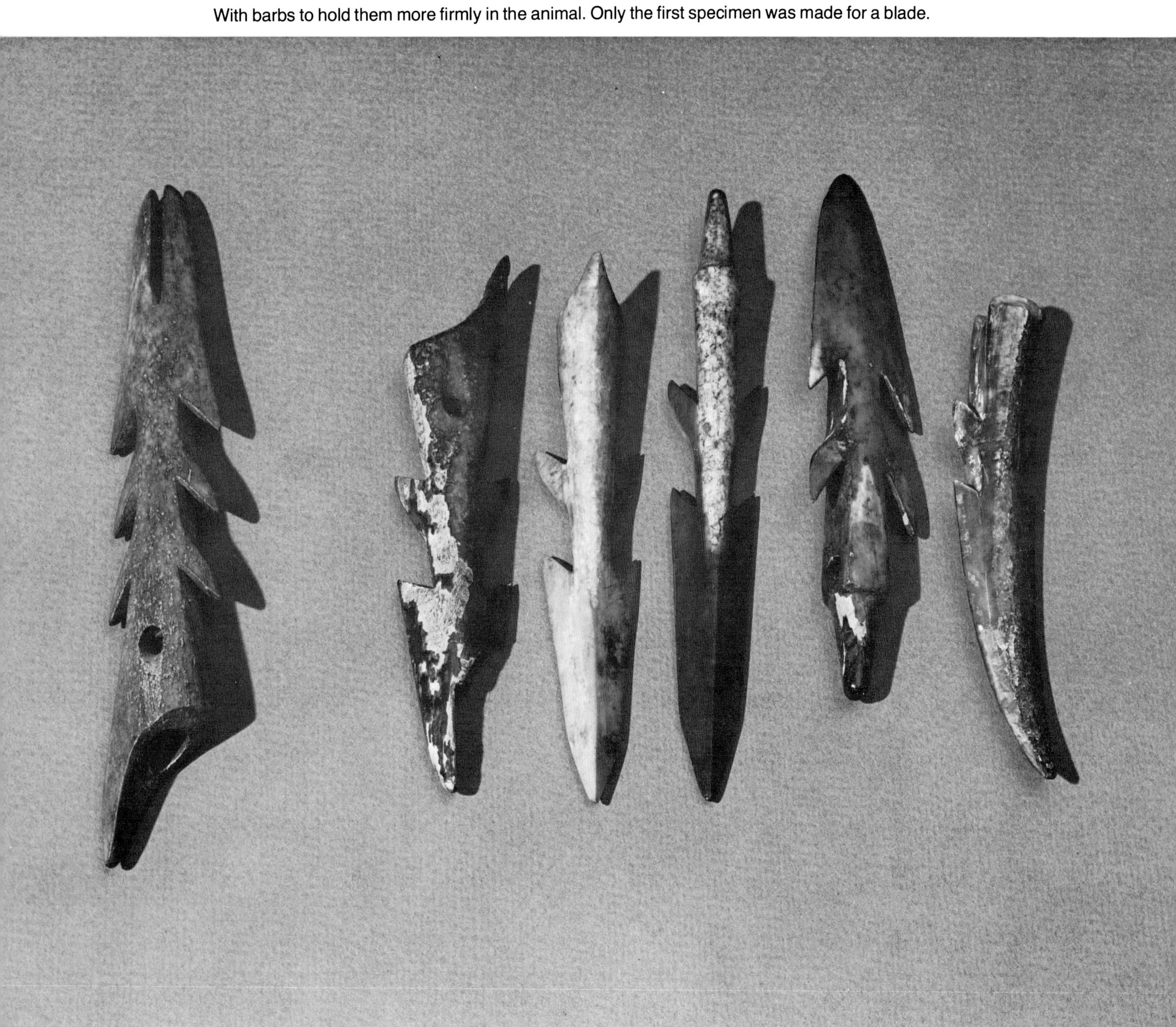

HARPOON HEADS

Showing the diversity of their fastening designs. The sharp ends are similar but the holes and grooves on the fastening end are all different.

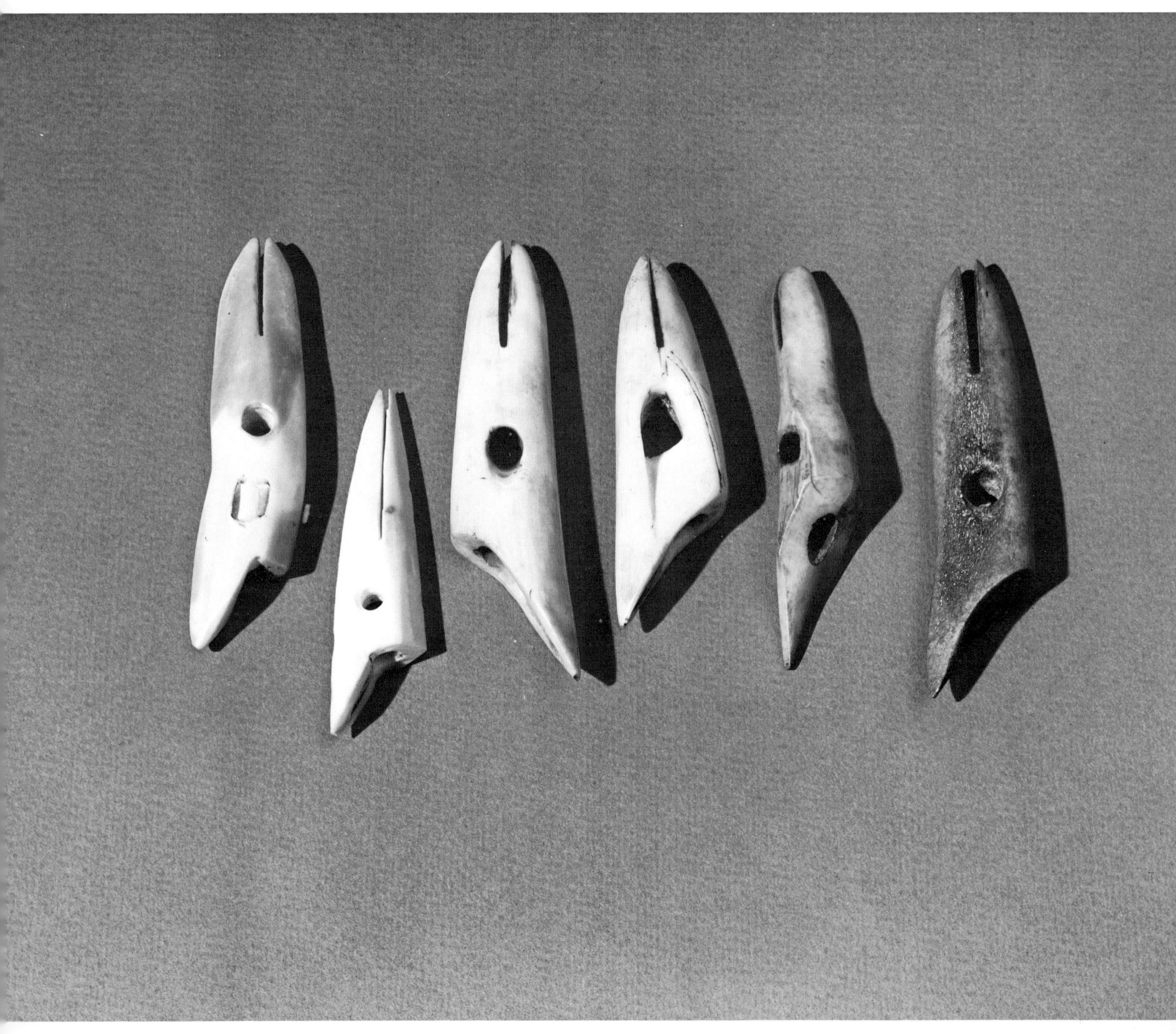

LARGE HARPOON HEADS

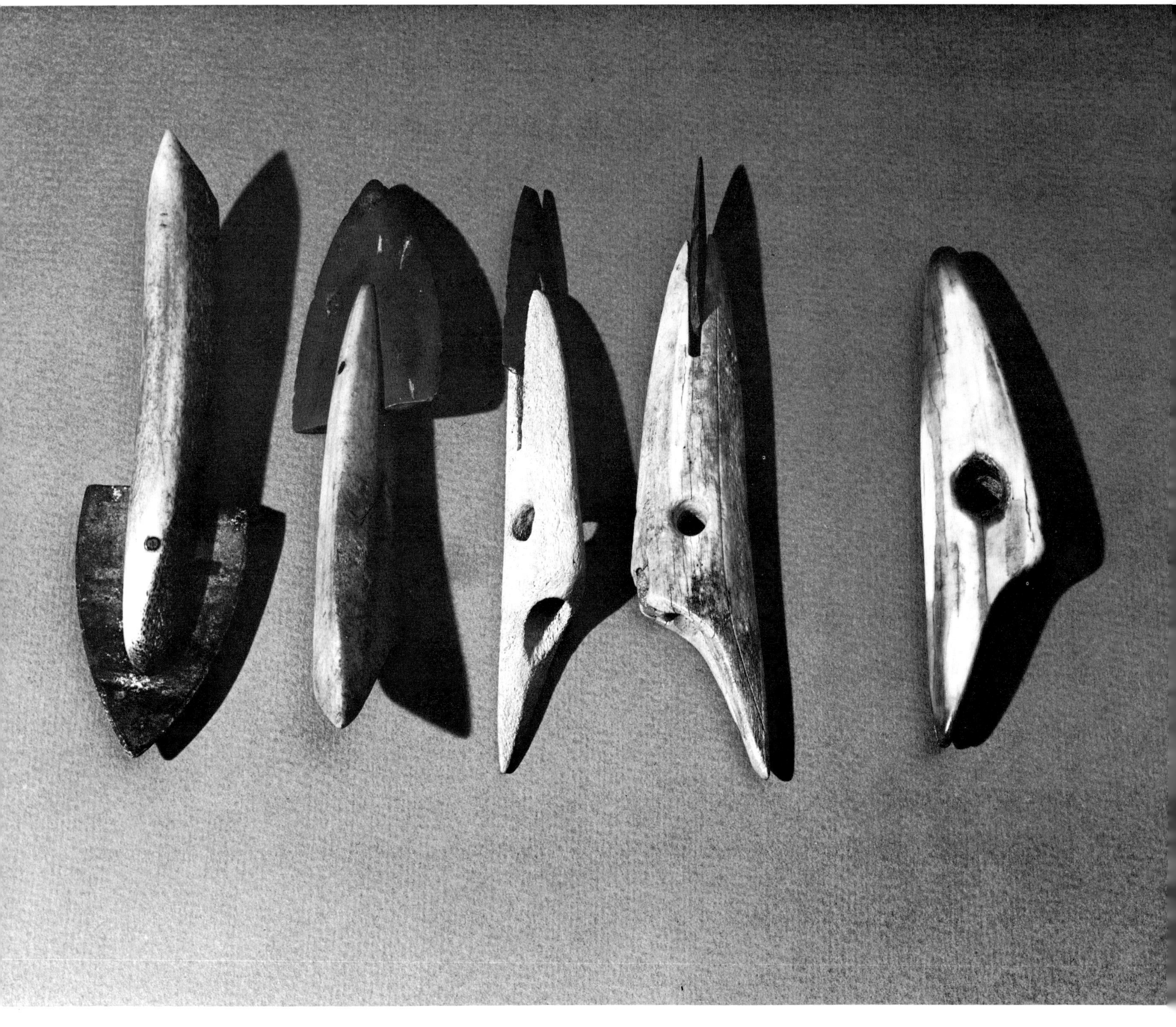

HARPOON HEADS

Showing different designs. Some have simple lines decorating them.

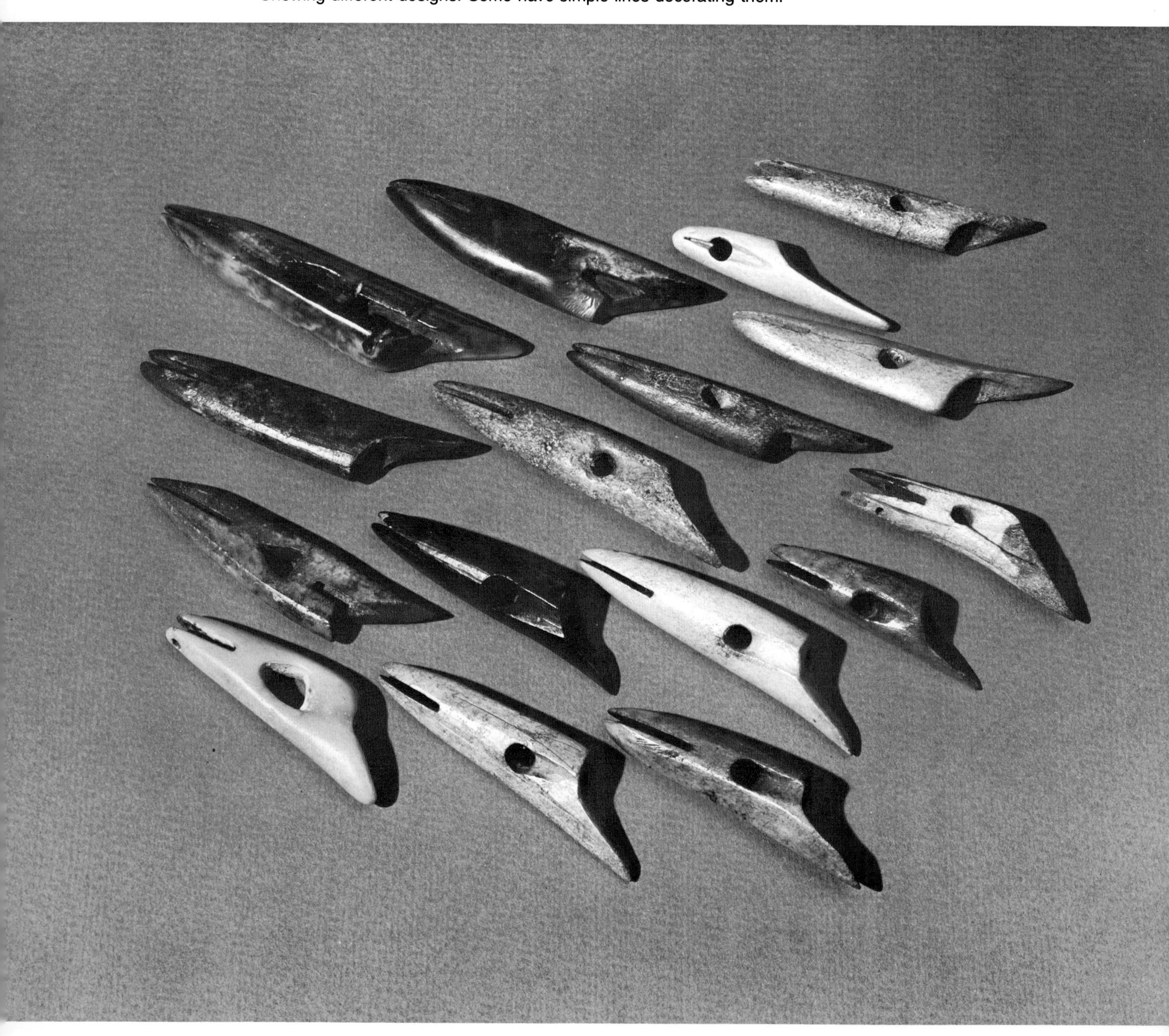

HARPOON HEADS

Spears with detachable heads were used in hunting various marine animals such as seals, walrus, and whales. The weapons were either thrown or thrust and differed in size and pattern according to the animal being hunted. The heads were usually ivory. A collection of harpoon heads is shown here, three with slate blades. These heads came clear of the spear remaining in the animal while attached to a line held by the hunter.

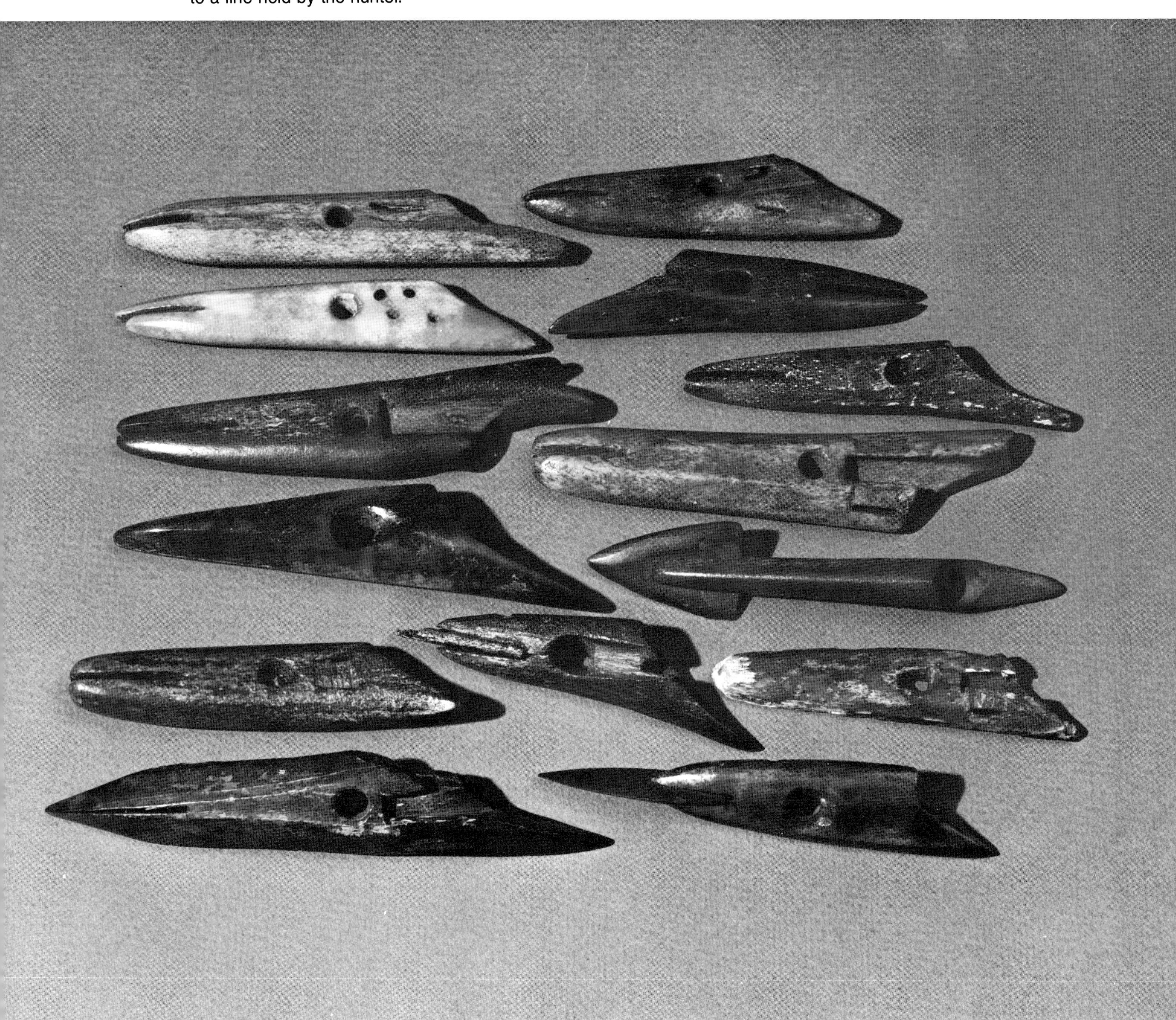

HARPOON HEADS

The dark ivory head has a slate point while the head above has an ivory point.

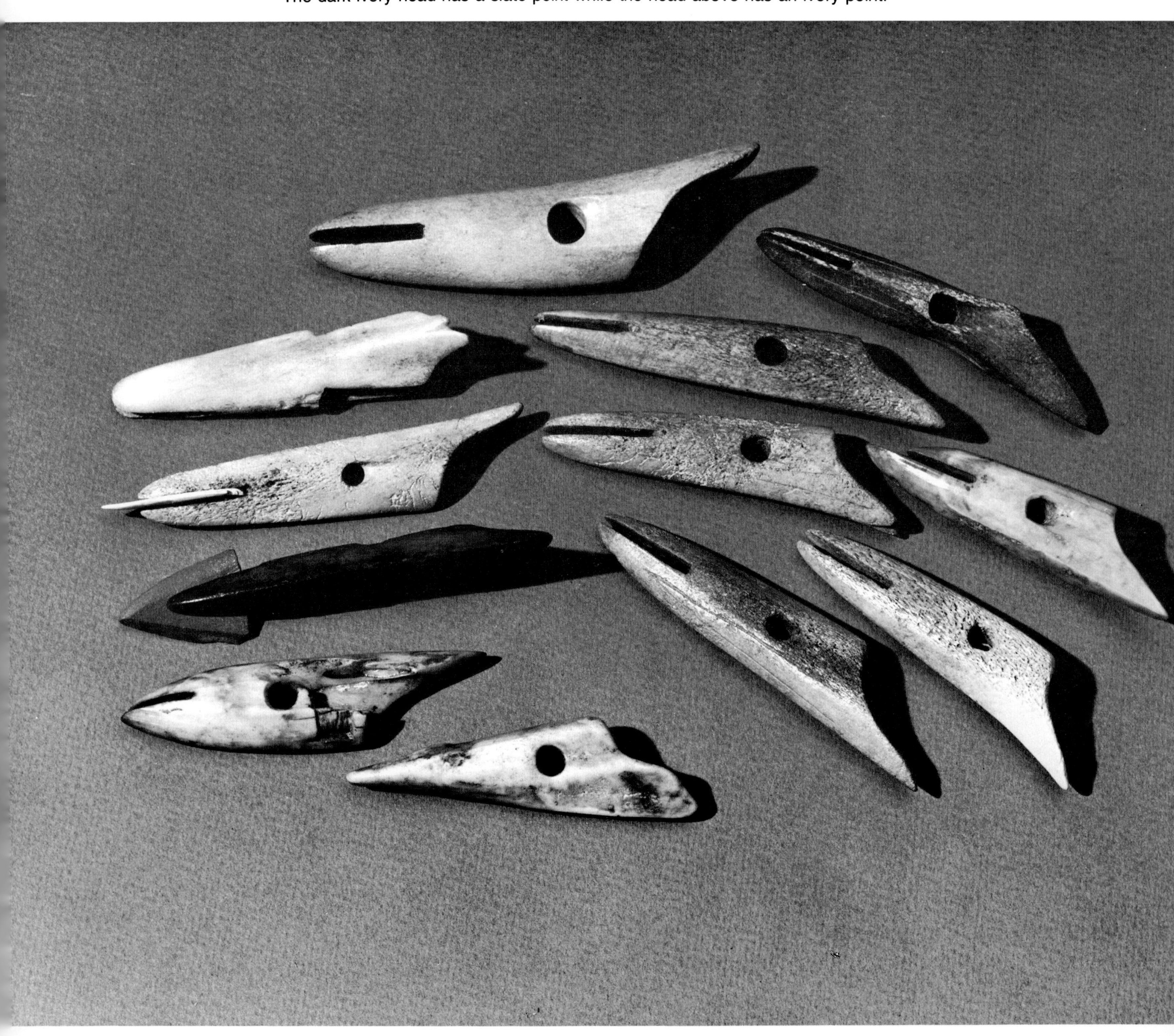

BONE AND IVORY HARPOON HEADS

Two have barbs to hold the point more firmly in the animal. These heads differ from others since they are not made to have stone or metal blades inserted in the head.

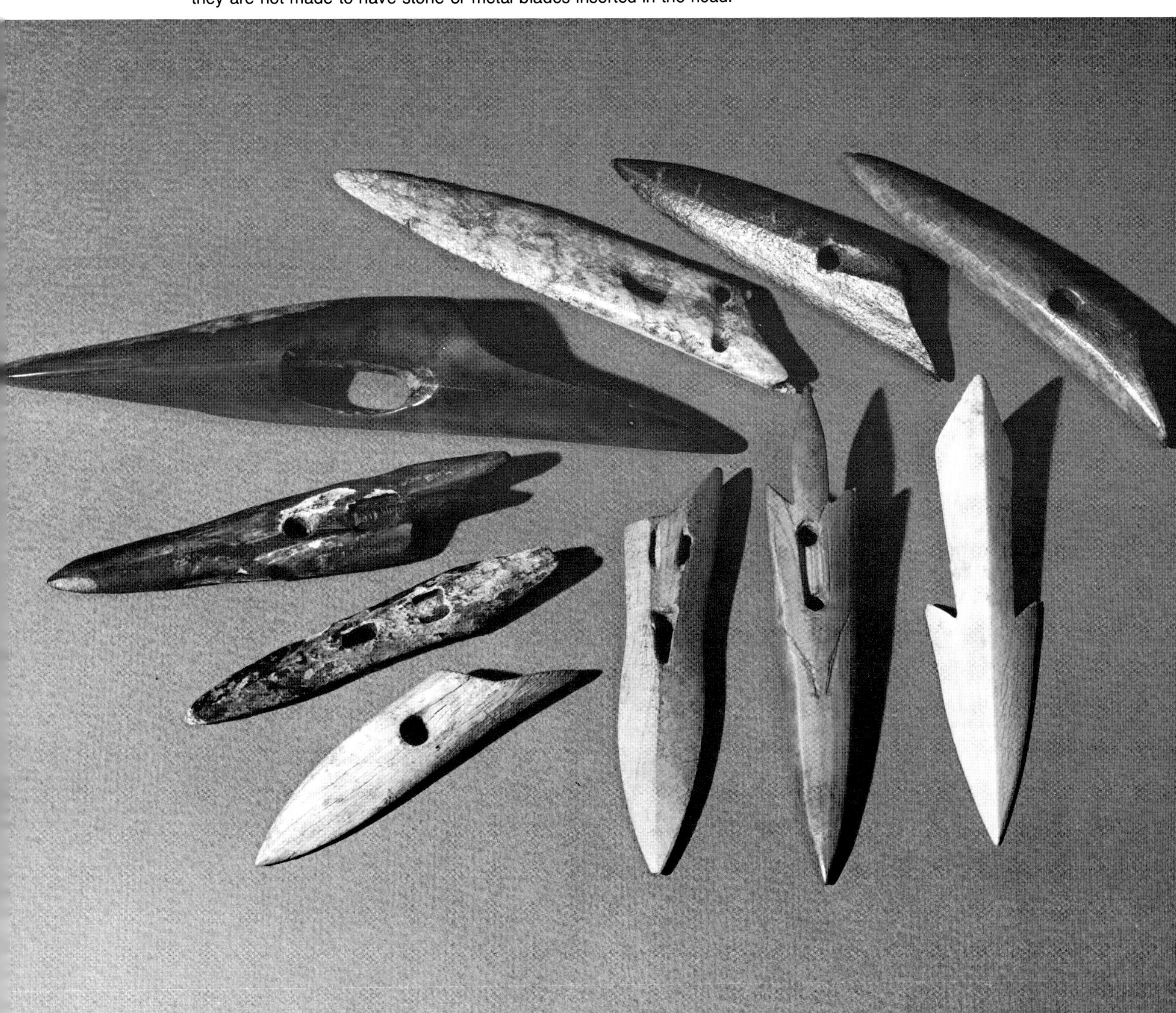

HARPOON HEADS

Designs of harpoon heads contrasting the ivory specimens on the left and on the far right to the heads which are made for blades.

IVORY HARPOON HEADS

Showing different designs. Three do not take blades.

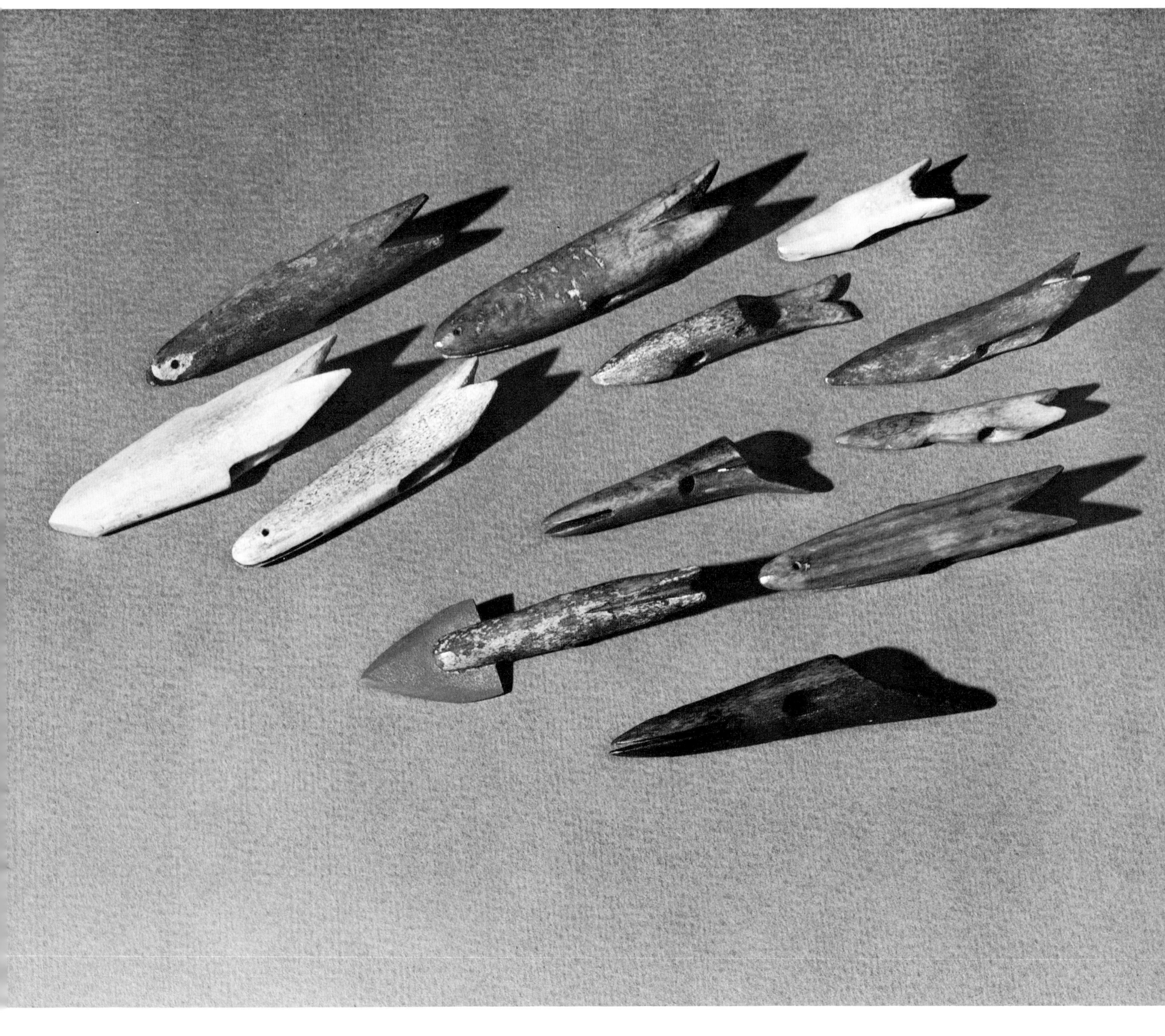

HARPOON HEADS

Bone walrus harpoon heads, the two center examples having metal blades, the other two, slate blades. These are very strong heads.

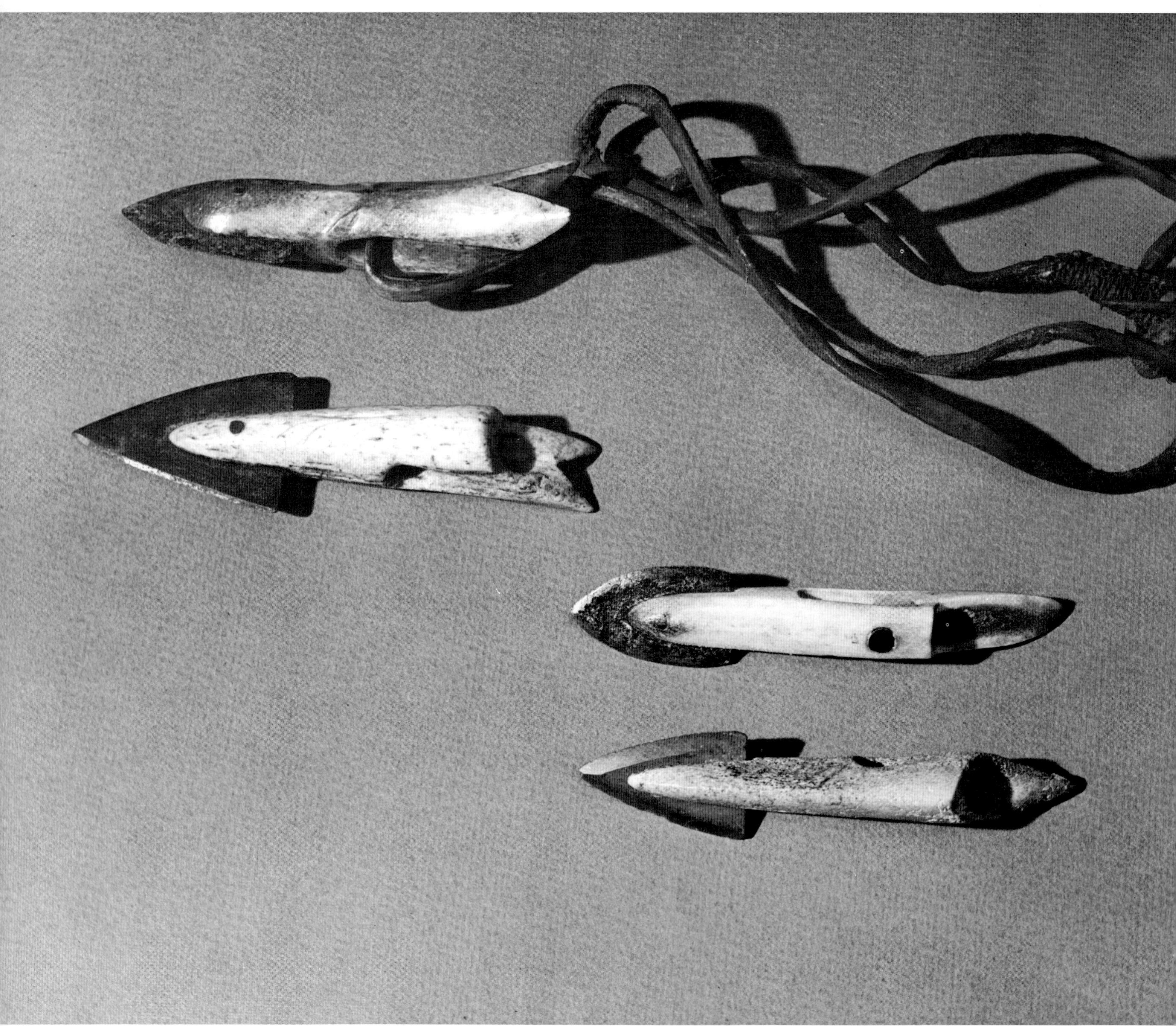

BONE AND IVORY HARPOON HEADS

For walrus and large seals. The heads, though the same general design, differ in length and width.

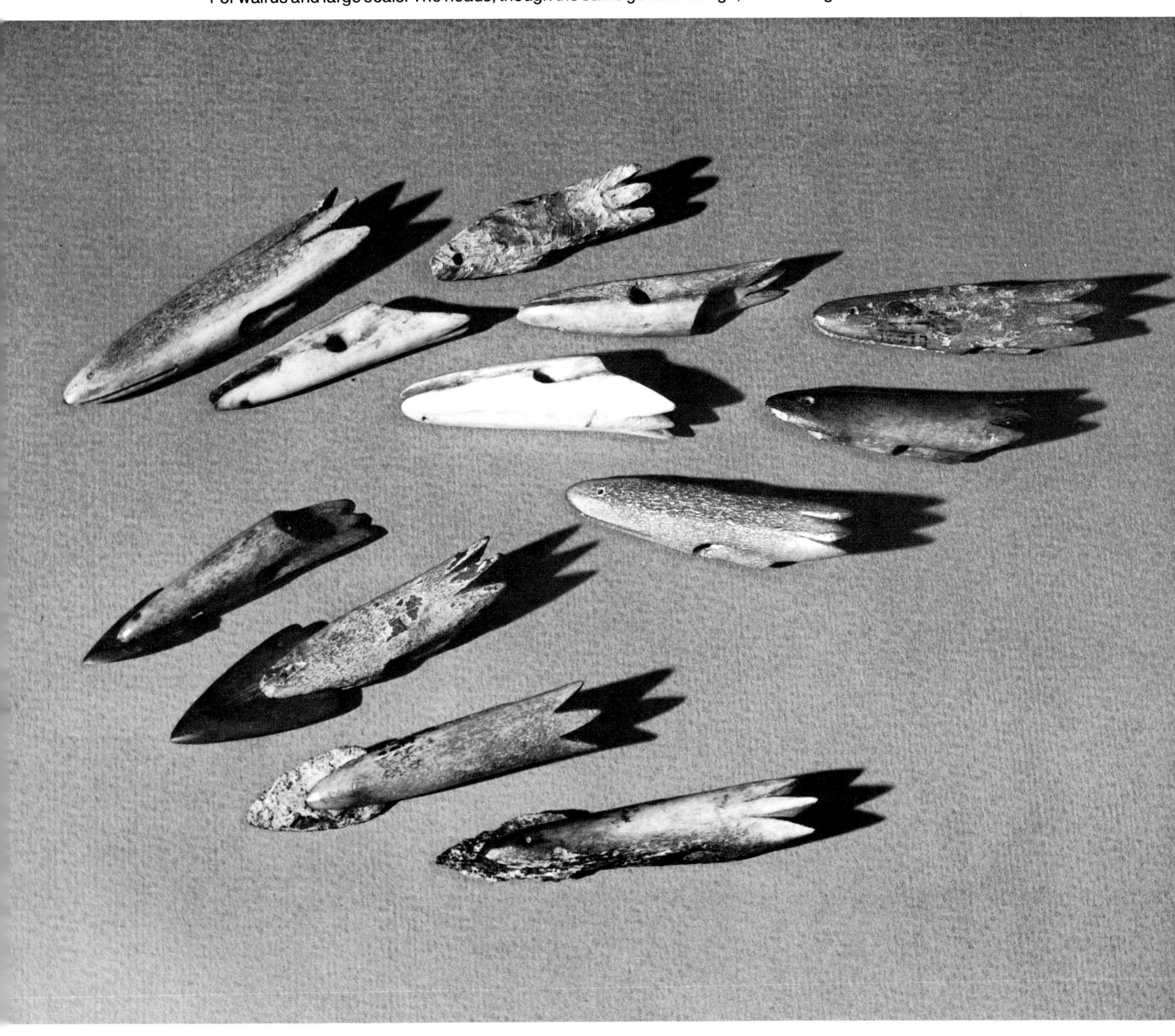

HARPOON HEAD

A complex harpoon head which resembles a bird of prey.

TWO WHALE HARPOON HEADS

Note the shaping of number one (upper) and the design on number two.

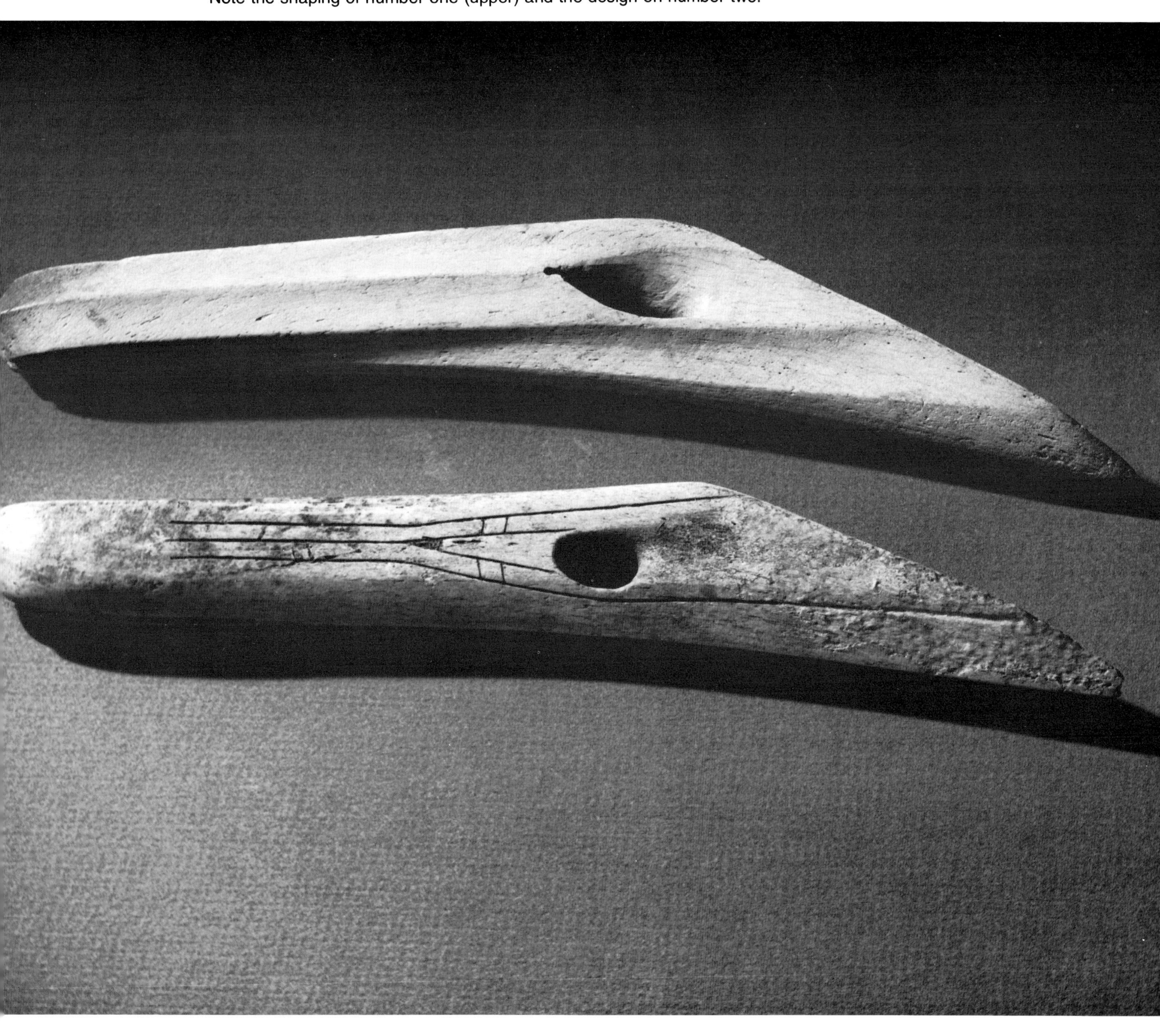

WHALE HARPOON FORESHAFTS

These are beautifully shaped and carved to fit the shaft. The harpoon head fits into the foreshaft on the right end separating from the spear when embedded in the animal. A line from the harpoon head is held by the hunter so the quarry does not escape.

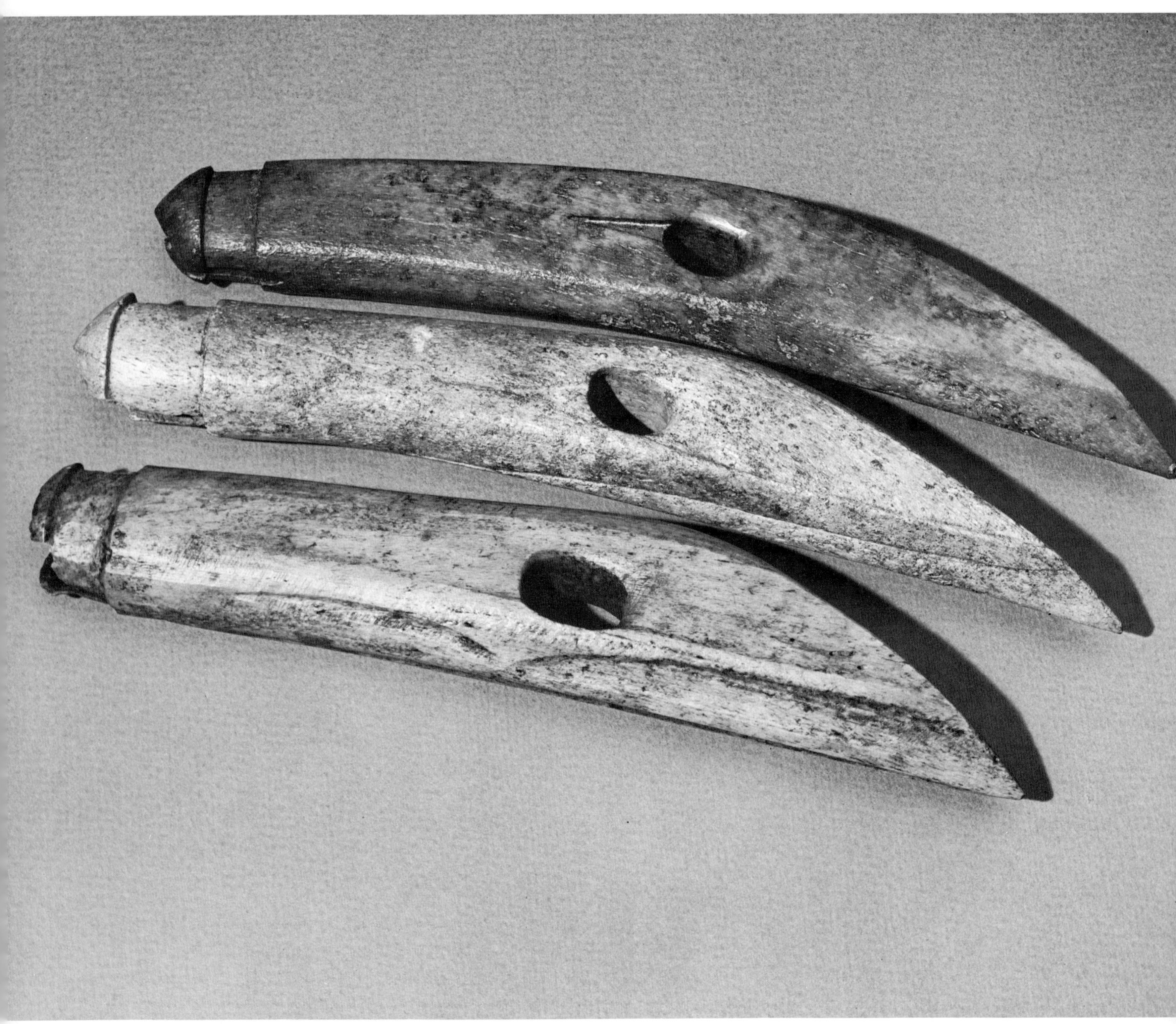

WHALE HARPOON HEADS

Showing the slots for the blades.

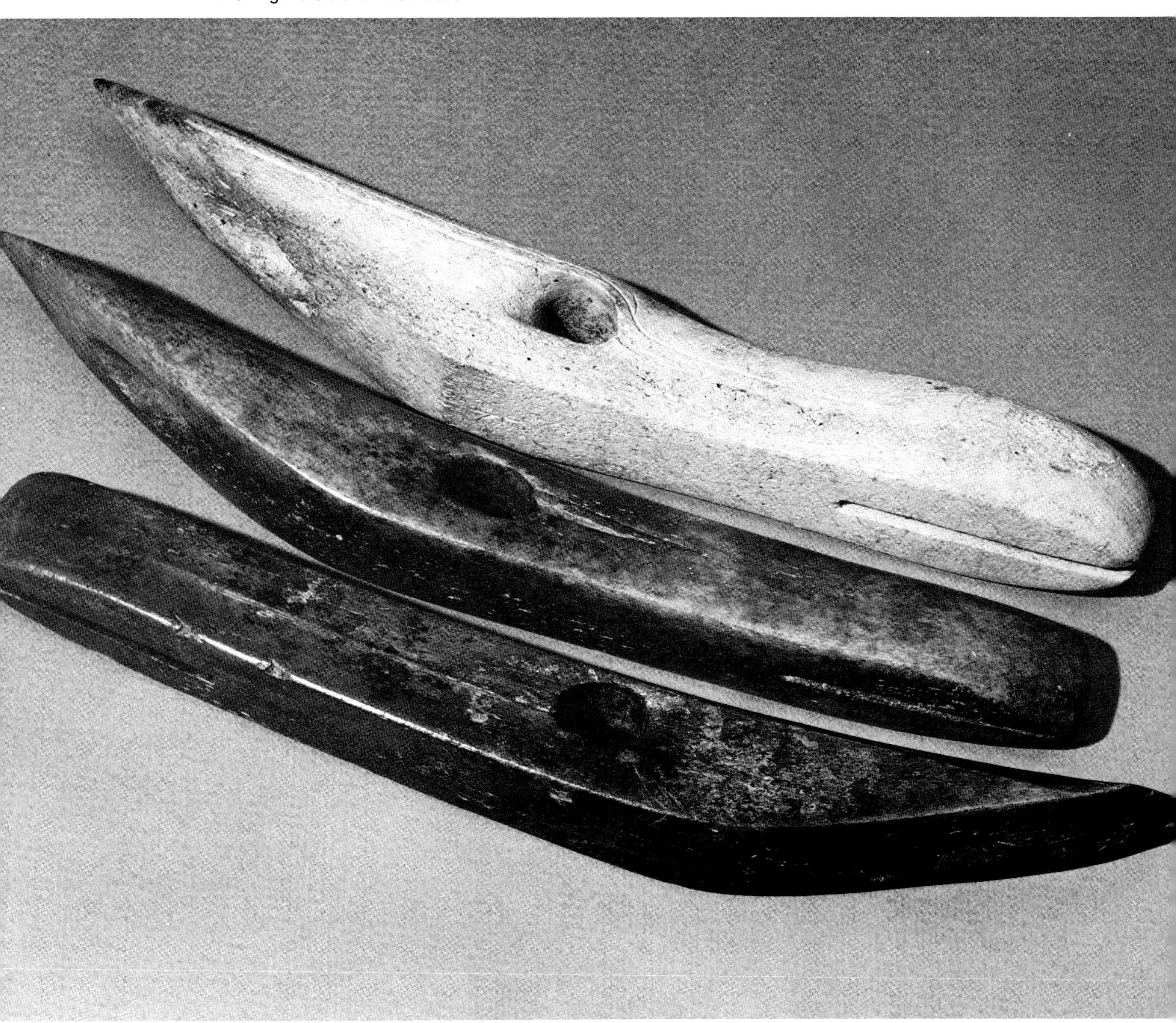

MISCELLANEOUS THROWING STICKS

Throwing sticks were used with spears to obtain greater distance. They had the effect of a second arm and enabled the hunter to throw with great accuracy.

These sticks are shown on the face side. The pegs are finger rests. The finger slots make the stick comfortable and secure to grasp.

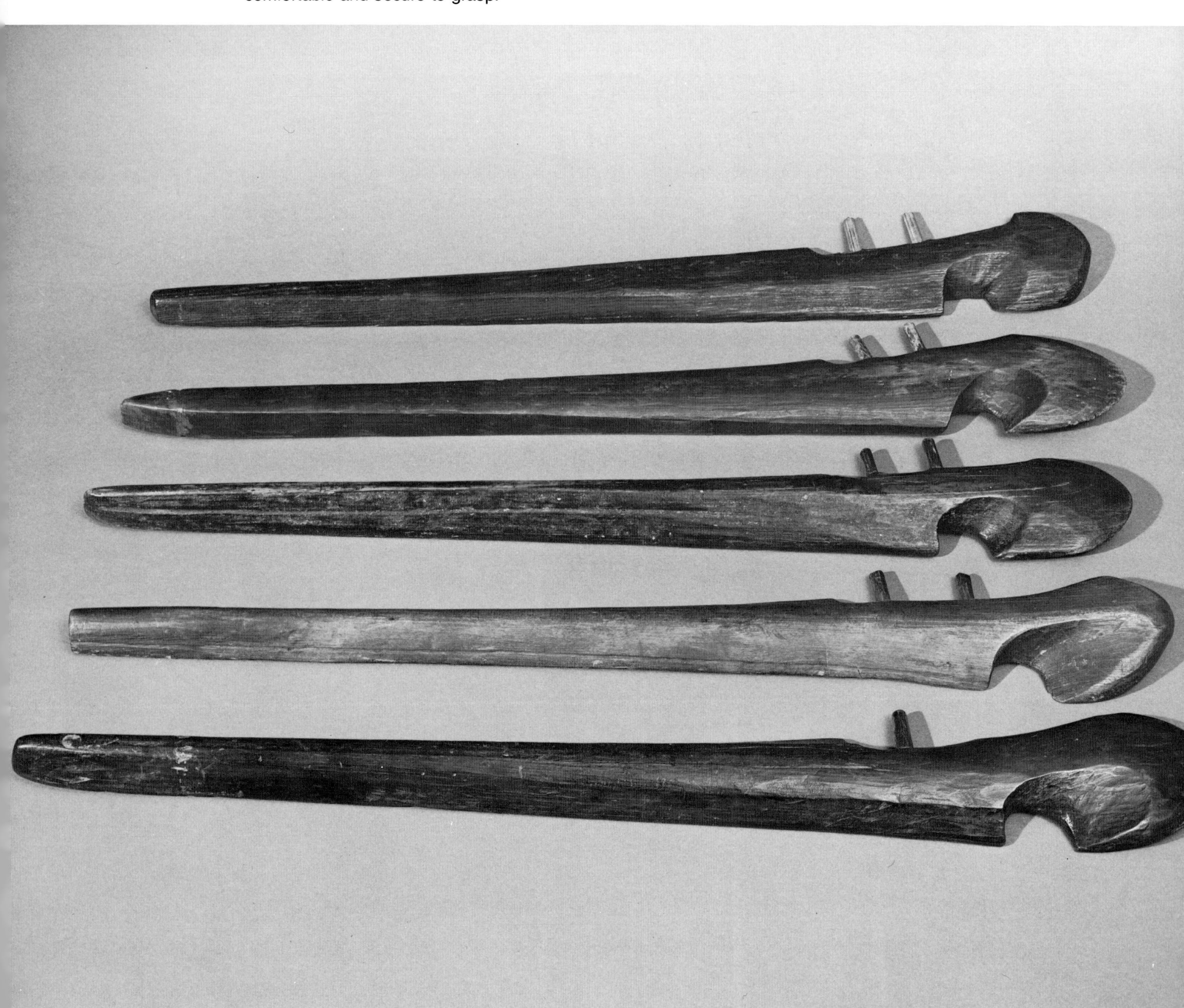

ACTUAL SIZE OF THROWING STICKS SHOWN ON OPPOSITE PAGE

The face view. Number three is grooved along the edge, a slight embellishment.

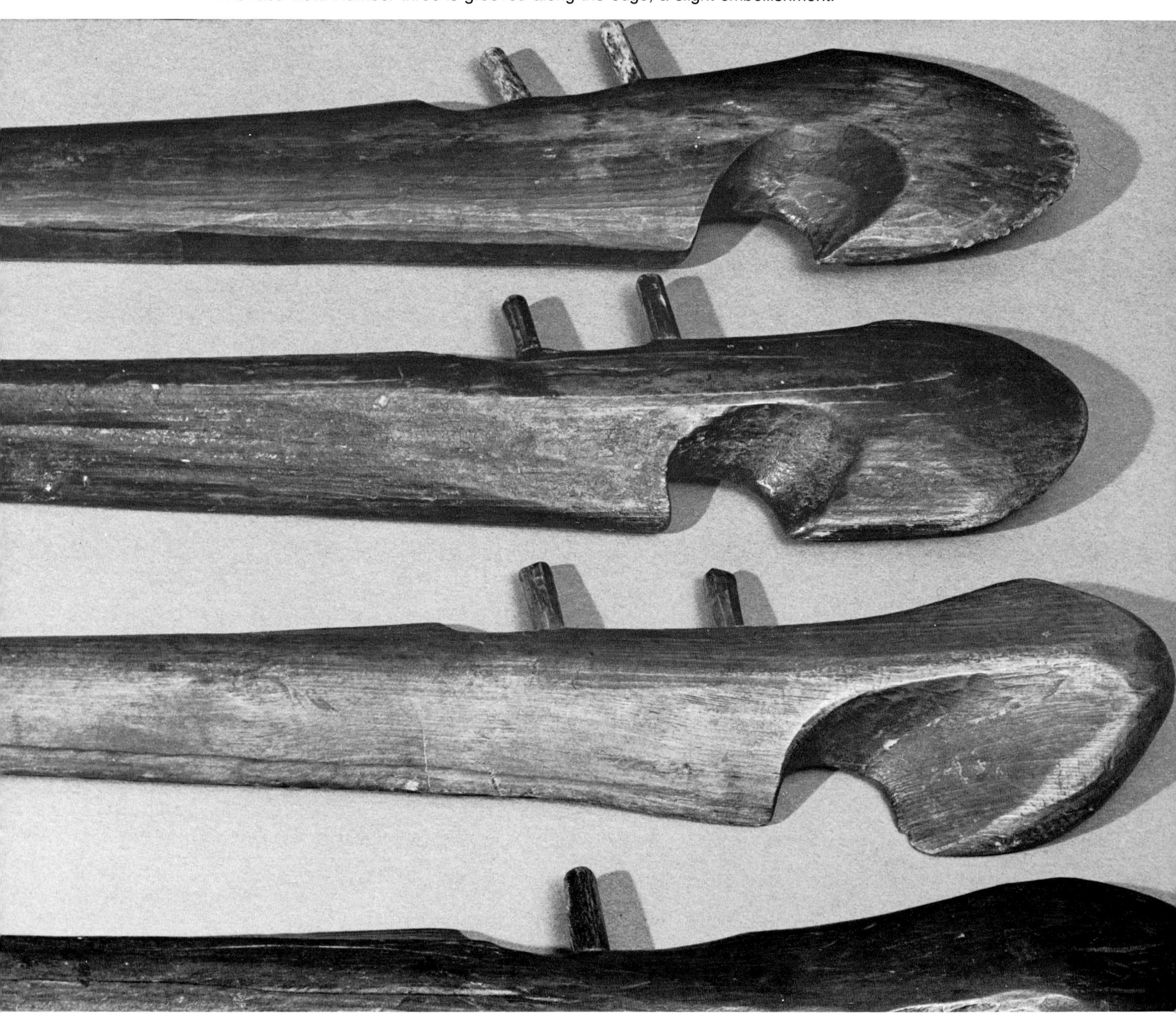

THROWING STICKS

The under side of the same throwing sticks showing the groove where the spear rests against the ivory pin at the base of the stick. The first four sticks have two finger rests each, the fifth had three rests, two of which are missing. Finger grooves can be seen in the first and fourth stick.

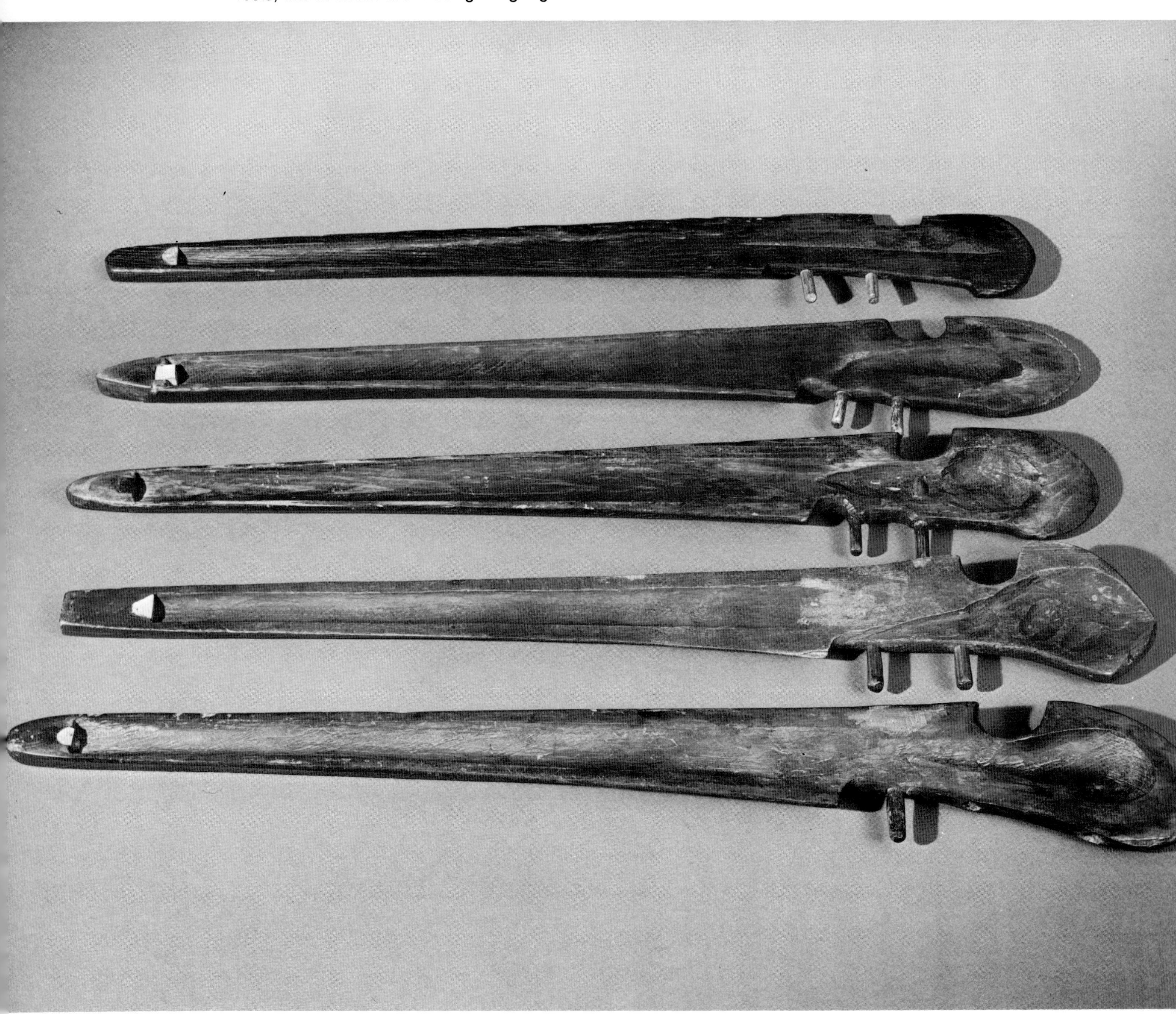

ACTUAL SIZE OF THE THROWING STICKS SHOWN ON OPPOSITE PAGE

View of the under side of the sticks. Note the shaping of the wood to accommodate the hand.

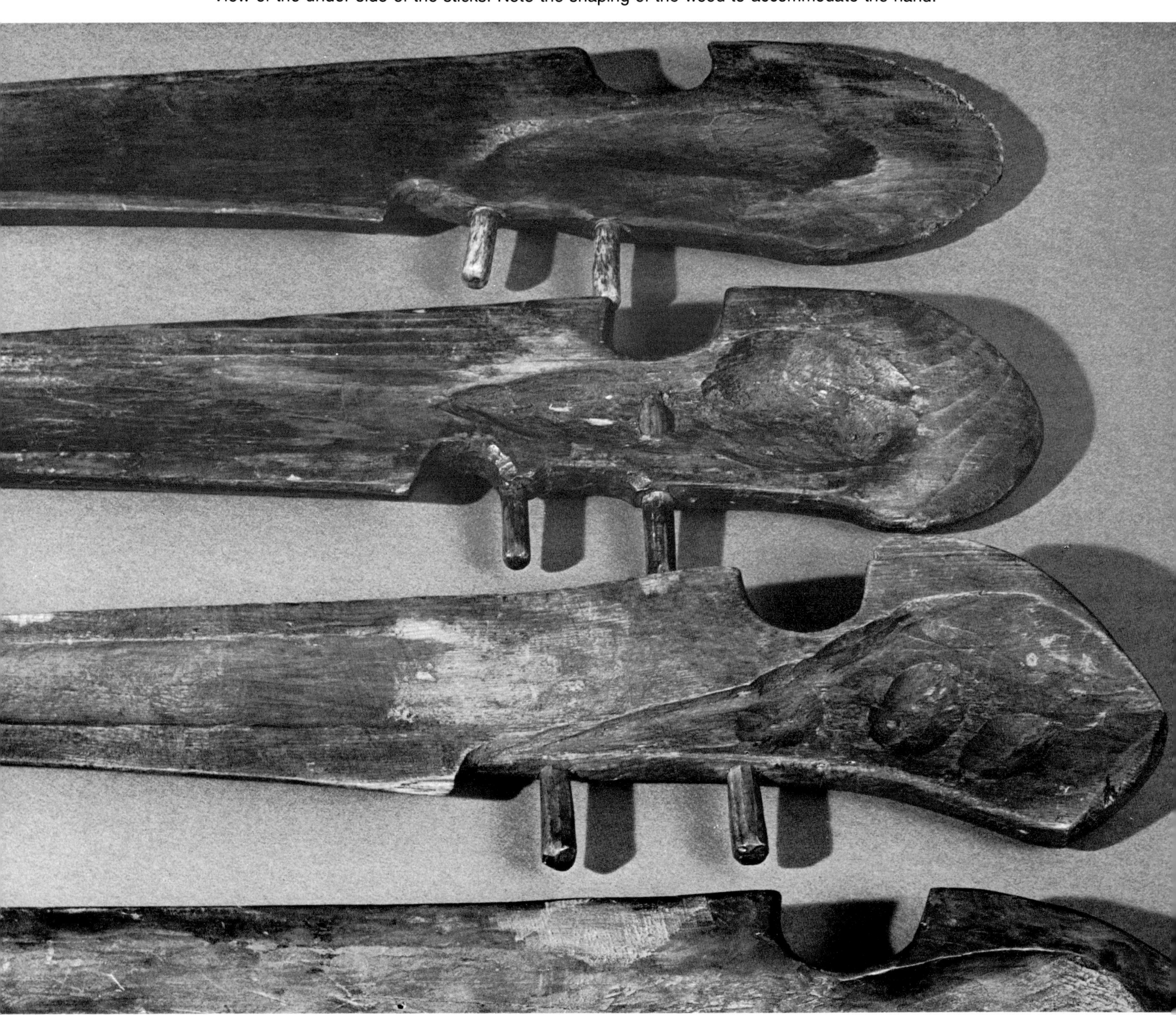

MISCELLANEOUS THROWING STICKS

Numbered top to bottom:

1-2. Flat throwing sticks from the vicinity of Nome have finger slots instead of pegs and are made to accommodate the spear in a slightly different position than other types of sticks. There are ivory pins at the lower end of the stick against which the spear rests.

Throwing sticks were held pointing backward for casting a spear in a curve through the air but if the spear was to be cast along the water surface, the throwing stick groove faced outward. The holding of the throwing stick was a studied procedure and depended upon how the spear was to be cast.

3. A small thrower with raised finger rests. There is a piece of ivory encircling the bottom of the stick as well as the ivory pin.
4. A throwing stick with three ivory finger pegs showing the bevel on the stick's side. The hand position was different for three pegged sticks than for sticks having no pegs or one or two.
5. A stick of similar design as others but having a different cut for the hand to grasp it and no pegs. The groove for the spear is clearly shown on this stick.

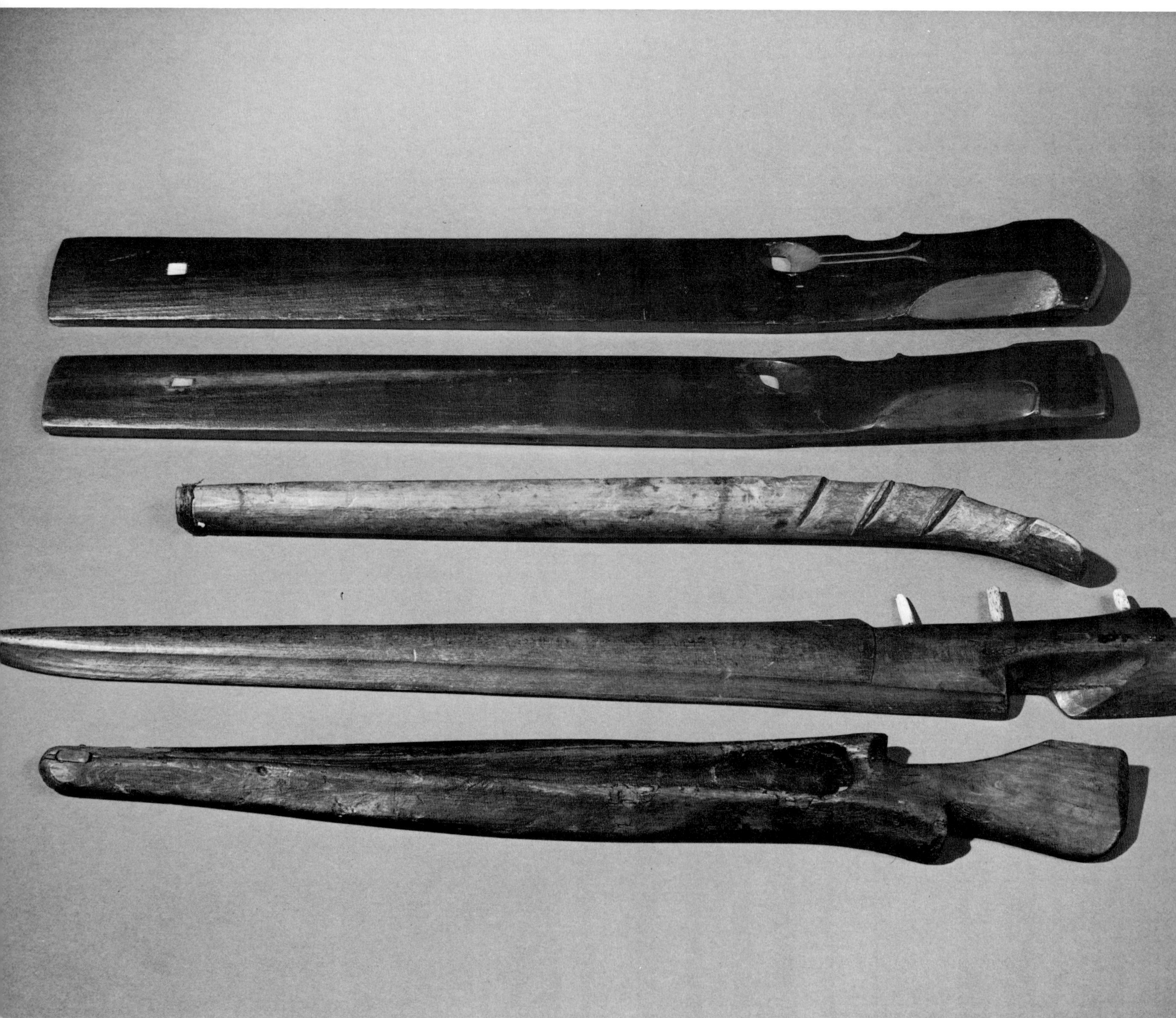

ACTUAL SIZE OF THROWING STICKS SHOWN ON OPPOSITE PAGE

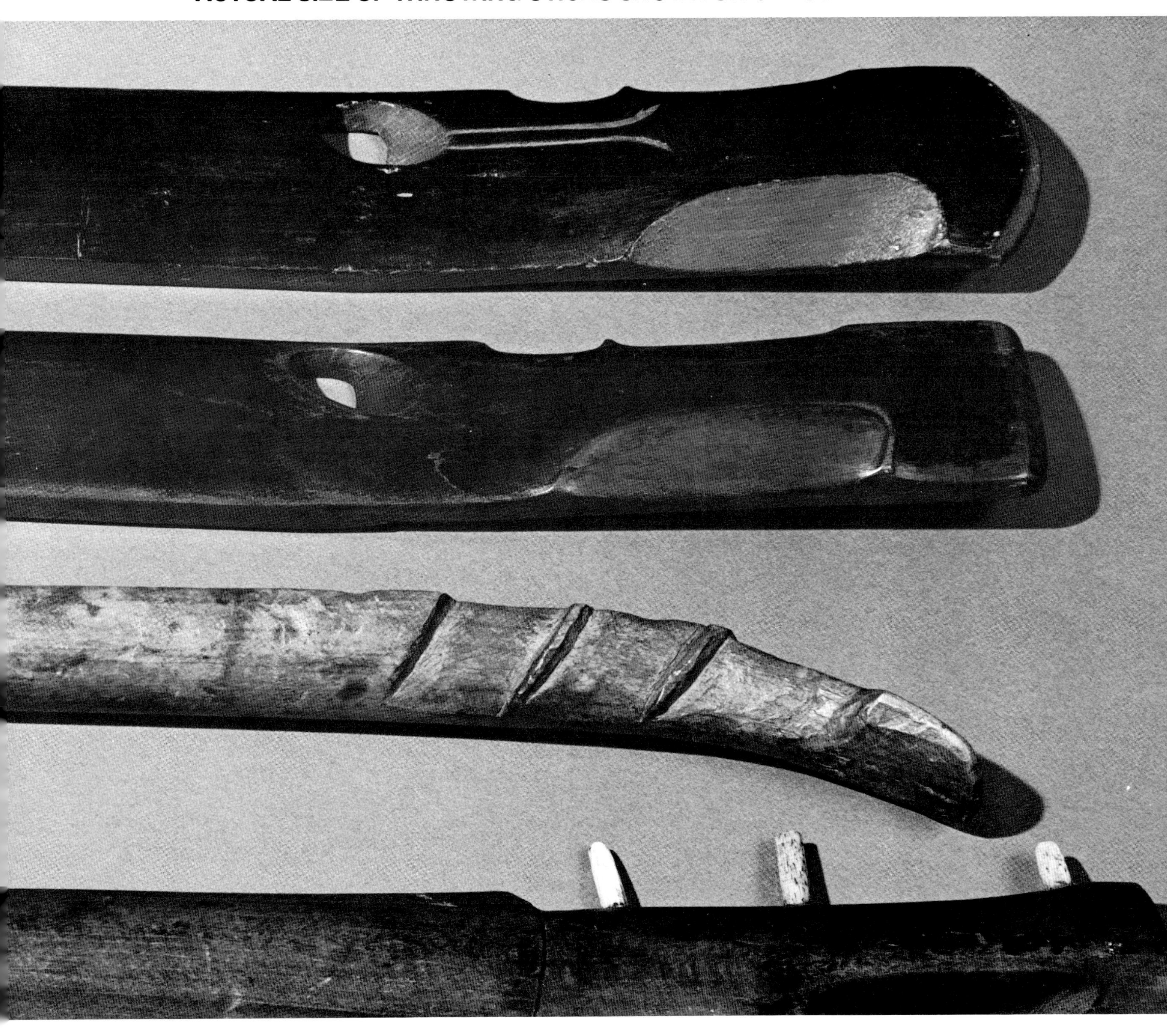

A BOLA

Used for killing birds. The feathers at the closed end aid in guiding the throw. This bola is made from a walrus' penis, cut and shaped into egg shaped missiles.

A BOLA

Ivory and deer horn odds and ends strung on sinew. The face, lower row, is probably the owner's own work. The material is haphazard but the design of each missile is not. Some are blunt, some pointed, others chipped to have sharp sides and smooth faces. The far left oval is a tooth formed like a seal's head. Ivory eyes have been plugged in.

A BOLA

Shaped ivory pieces strung on corded sinew. The "handle" at the closed end is grass.

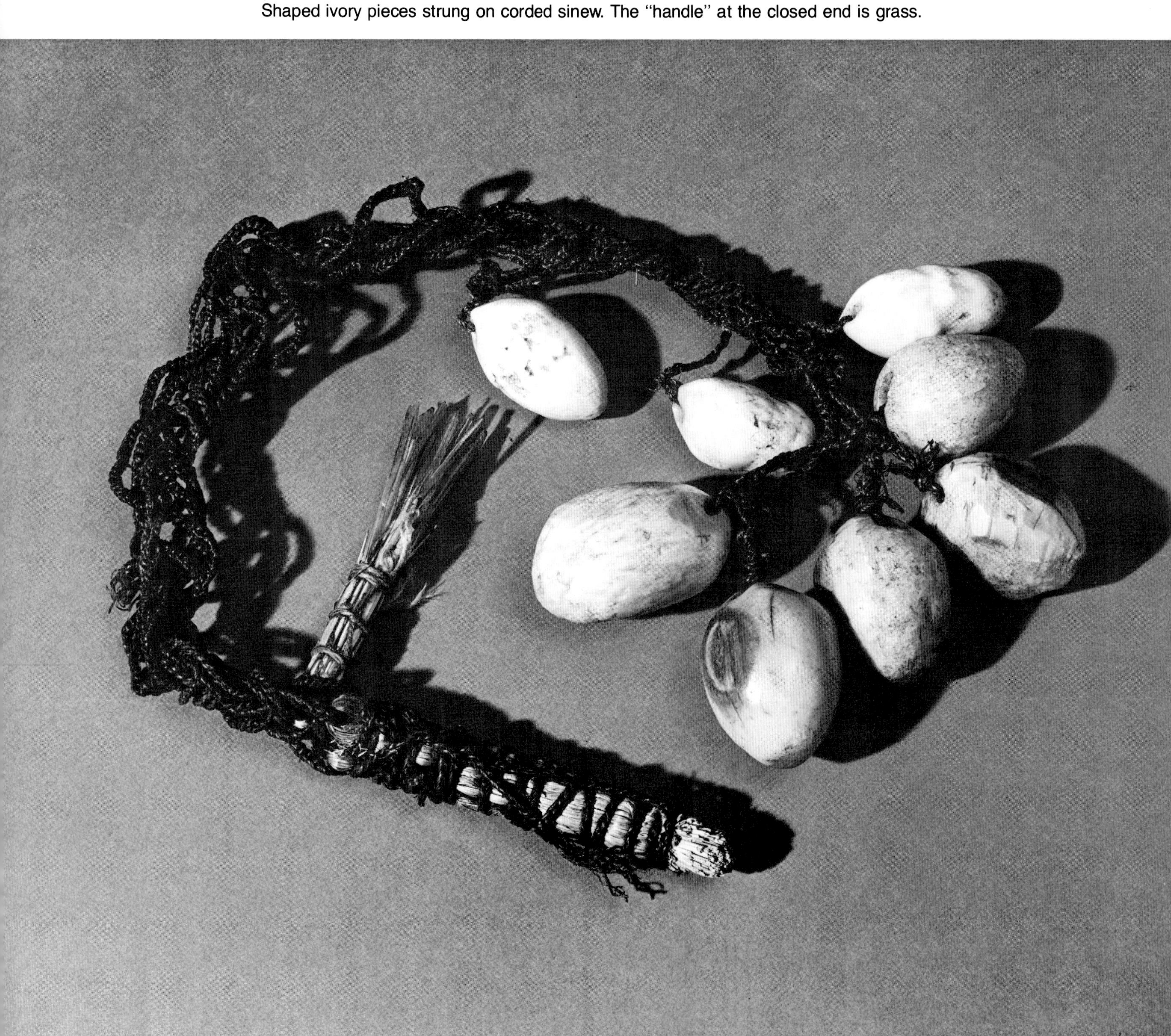

SNARES

Used for trapping marmots and other small burrowing animals. The cylinders are made of bone and hollow bird wing bones. The lines are whale bone or sinew. The two upper cylinders are tension type traps requiring a lever.

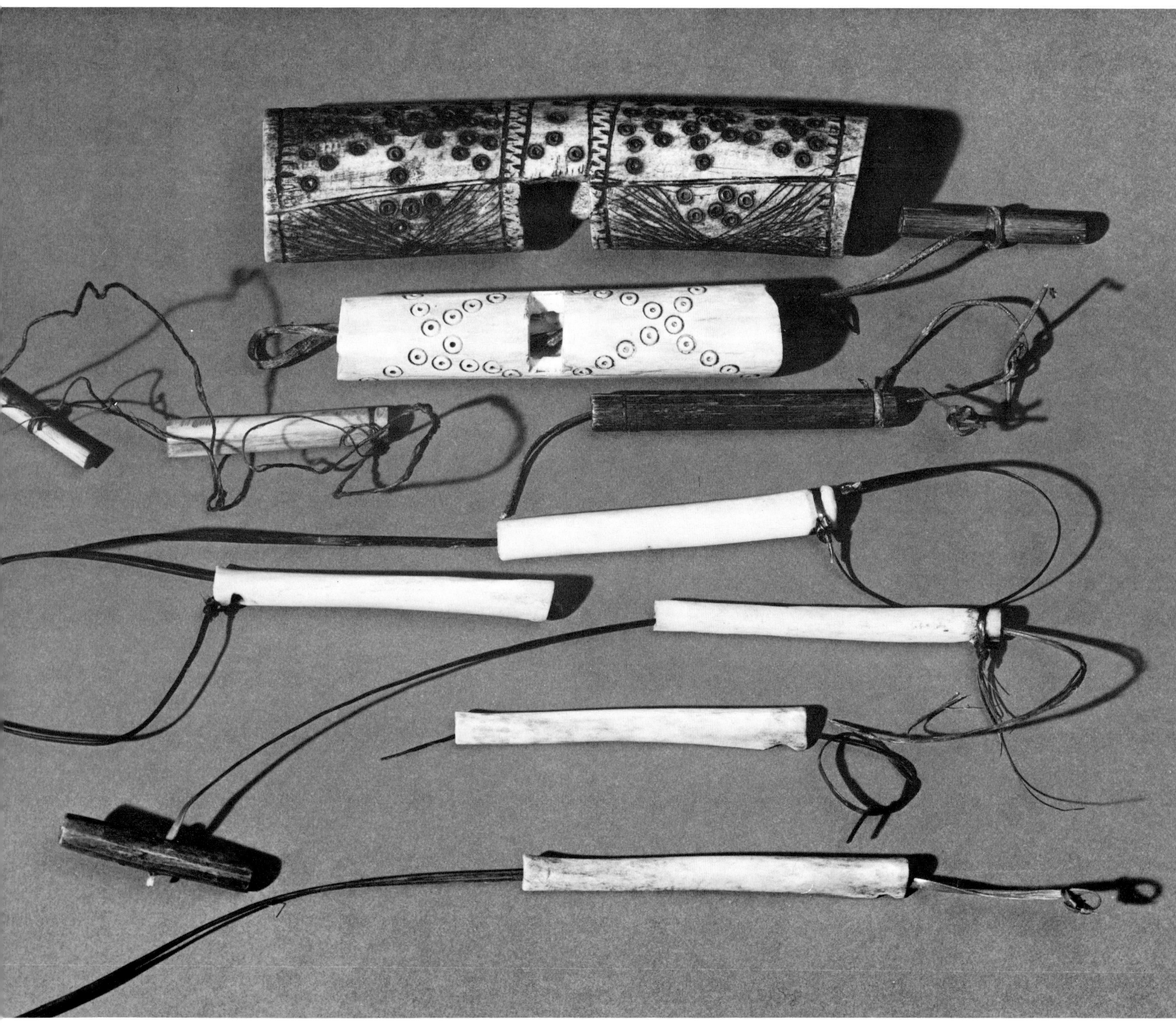

FLOATS FOR NETS

Carved in the shape of seals and a bird. The center seal still has ivory pegs for eyes. The bird has small black pebbles for eyes.

A FLOAT

A bird carved either for a decoy or as a toy. The spots and white body color is the same chalky wash as on other "painted" objects. The black is an oily residue like lamp black. There is a semicircular piece of wood fitted on the bottom which keeps the bird floating in an upright position, allowing the entire body to sit on the water looking very realistic. There are slits on each side for feathers.

WHALE CARVINGS

These two bone whale carvings may have been intended as fetishes since there are no holes for attachment as there are for instance in flipper toggles. The hole in the tail of the upper carving would allow it to be used as a sinker. The second carving has a deep cut which probably held a piece of ivory intended as a tail similar to the flippers on the sides.

IVORY NET SINKERS

With eyelet side openings carved from one piece of tusk.

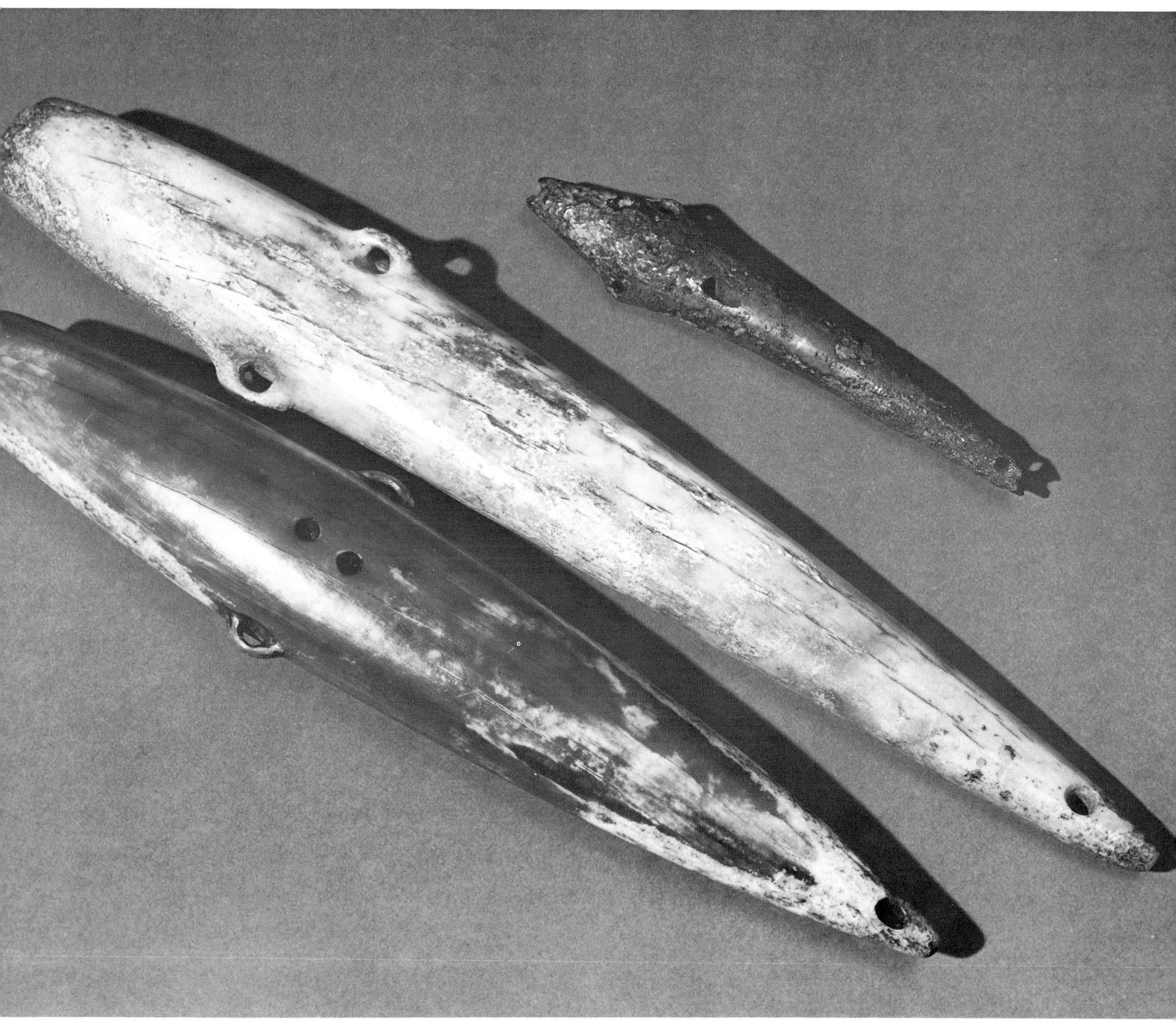

BONE SINKERS

The first sinker has a whale's head delineated on the right end.

IVORY SINKERS

Three ivory sinkers each of slightly different design.
Numbered top to bottom:

1. Number one has two eyelets one on either side as well as the hole in one end and two in the center. The eyelets are in the single piece of ivory and show great carving skill.
2. This sinker may have been another artifact at one time such as a sled runner judging from the channel in the center.
3. A small sinker having carved out guides on either end. These were to guide the line fastened through two holes on the underside.

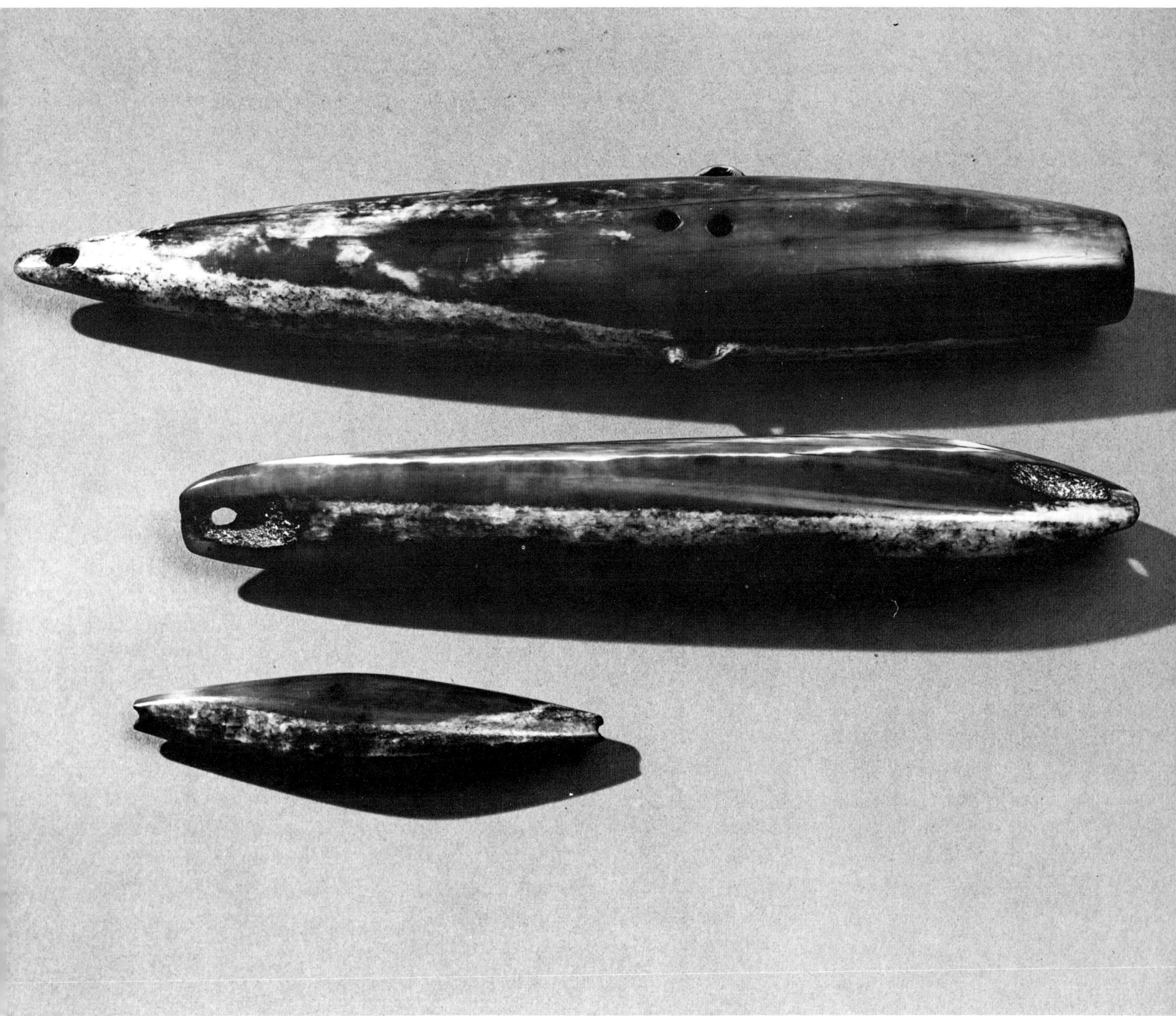

OBJECTS USED WITH GUNS

Guns supplied by traders and Russians took over primitive weapons, but did not entirely supplant them.

The Eskimos devised many of their own implements to be used with these primitive firearms. 1. A wood powder box with a brass tamptube. The ends of the box are stopped with metal ends placed into the wood permanently. There are circular metal pieces placed on the other two sides probably for decoration. The top secures tightly into the box and a rawhide pull tab extends to hold the tamp. There are similar boxes for caps made of wood. These are flattened and have a sliding cover over the entire top. 2. A cylindrical box made to hold a few caps. This box is in two pieces each hollowed out, fitted together and stoppered with a stemmed knob which fits down into the box. A rawhide cord ties around the lower part, and fastens around a peg which pierces the box through one side to the other. The unstoppered end has metal pieces fitted into the wood which makes a smooth and secure closure when the two parts are tied together. 3. An ivory powder box with a wood top formed into a funnel secured by a small wood stopper. The bottom is a well fitted piece of wood fastened, as is the top, with pegs. 4. A powder flask made from an antler tip with a wood bottom fitted in. There is an eyelet carved out for a tie cord.

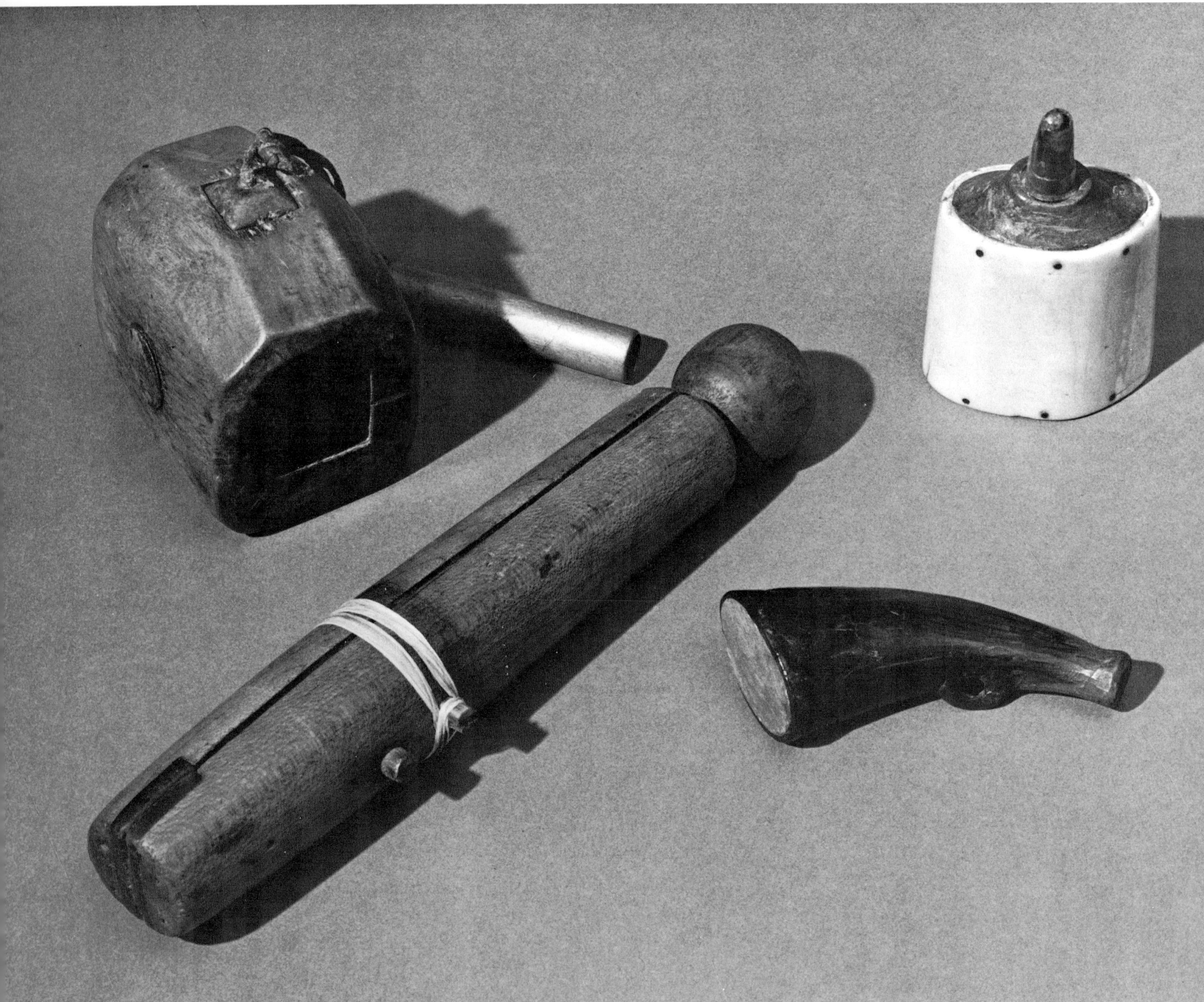

BONE ARMOR

One generally thinks of the Eskimos as being placid and genial but they have had bloody wars among the various tribes.

Plate armor was used by the people living on the coasts and islands around Bering Strait. Armor was fashioned from ivory or bone plates fastened together with seal skin cord. This is a section of such armor made from rib bones. The seal skin cord is not original.

SMALL BOXES

Numbered top to bottom:

1. This example is made of wood both sides hollowed out and the two held together with cord routed in channels on the outside of the box. A small ivory peg on the right of the box may indicate the top since both sides are identical.
2. A long slender box. This box is hollowed out but has a lip to receive the top which fits tightly when set into place like a stopper. A thumb piece for raising the top has been broken off.
3. A small wood box similar in construction to the first example but far more primitive. There is a groove only around the middle of the box for tying. This may have been a fetish box since it has numerous small bones, feathers and animal teeth still inside.

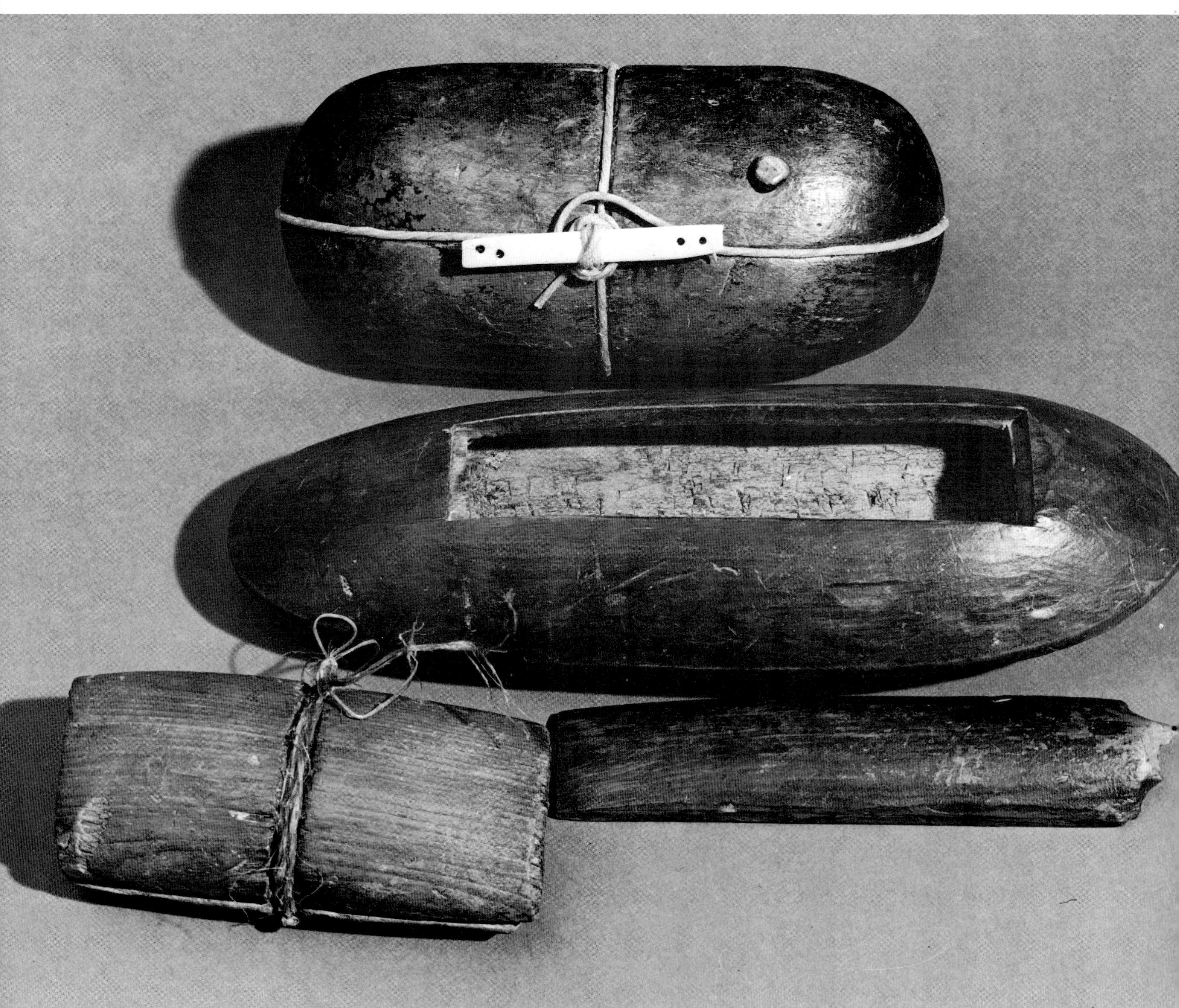

SMALL BOXES

Numbered top to bottom:

1. A box in the form of a seal. The lower surface of the body is hollowed out and is closed by a stopper like cover which rests on a lip. The eyes are ivory peg insets.
2. This small seal box is similar to the above, opening in the same way. The eyes at one time had insets.
3. A box of a single piece of wood hollowed out, the removed top piece replaced again and held with an ivory peg which acts like a hinge.

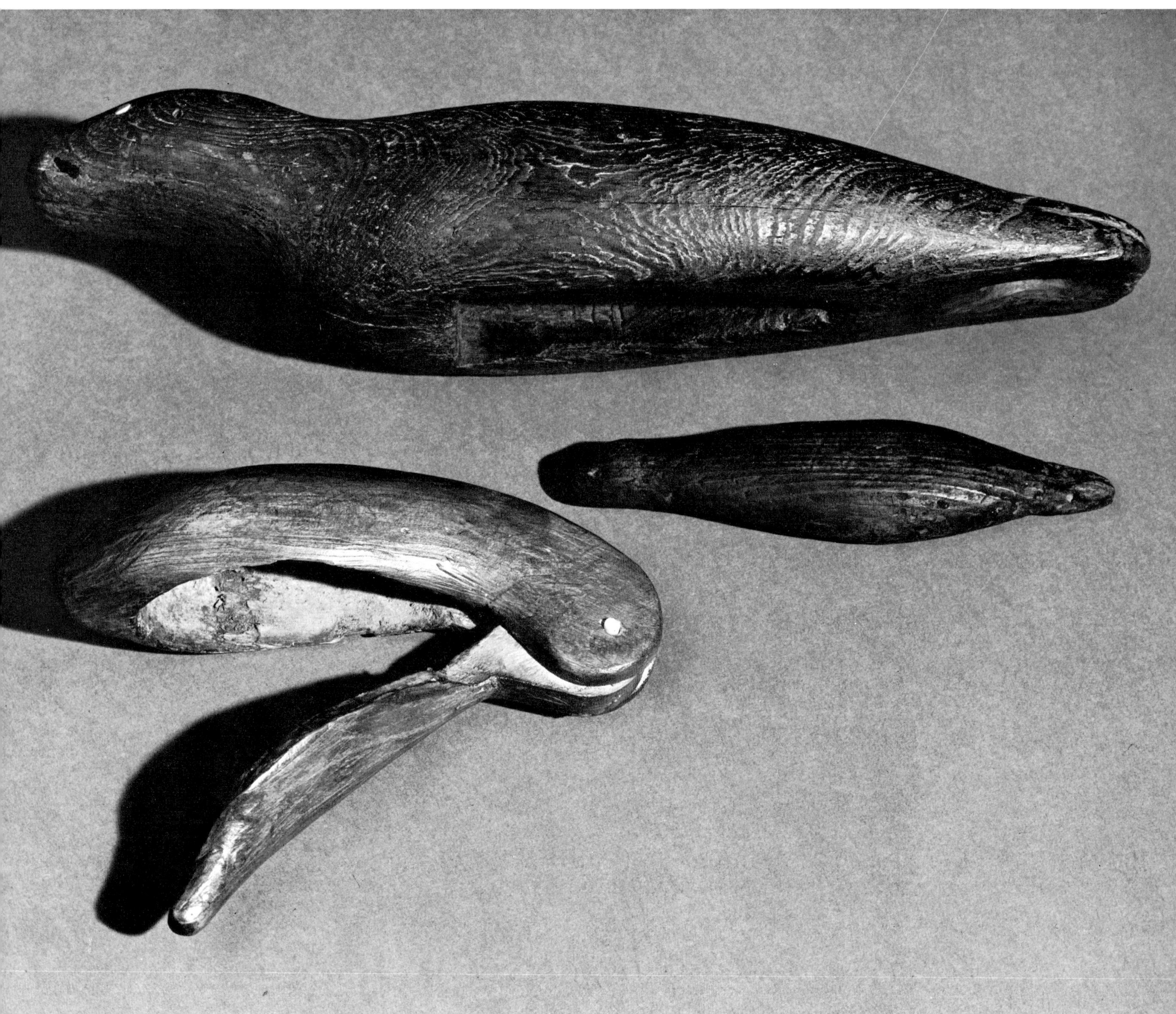

A BOW CASE AND QUIVER

Made of tanned fish skin. The bow case has a seal skin tip sewn at the bottom to reinforce the bag and the quiver has a creased bottom of white seal skin. A wood quiver rod remains in the bag to strengthen the side especially when there are no arrows. The rod is carved at the end with a bear head and has holes in it to fasten it to the quiver. Rods were also made of ivory or bone.

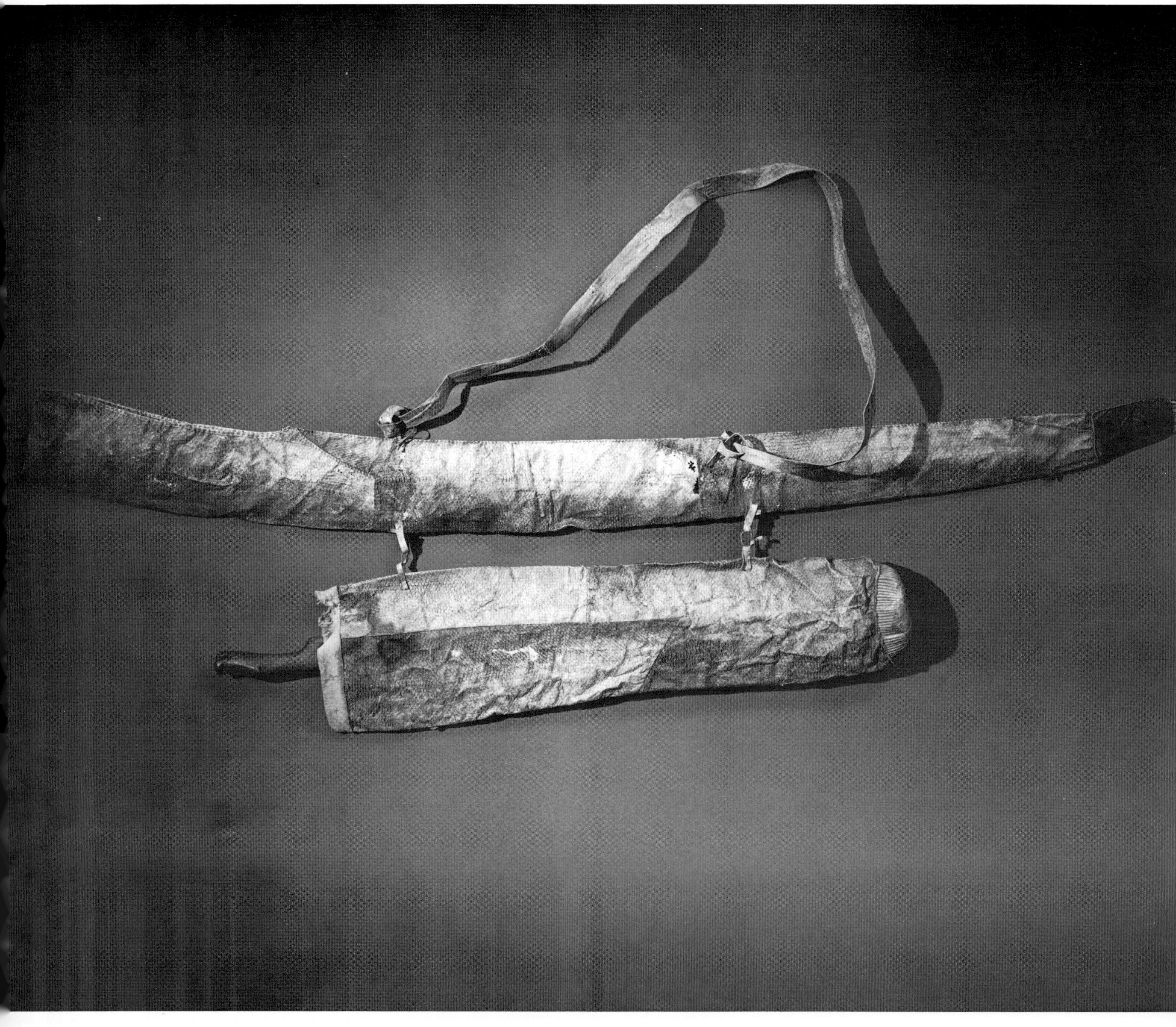

ACTUAL SIZE OF BOW CASE AND QUIVER SHOWN ON OPPOSITE PAGE

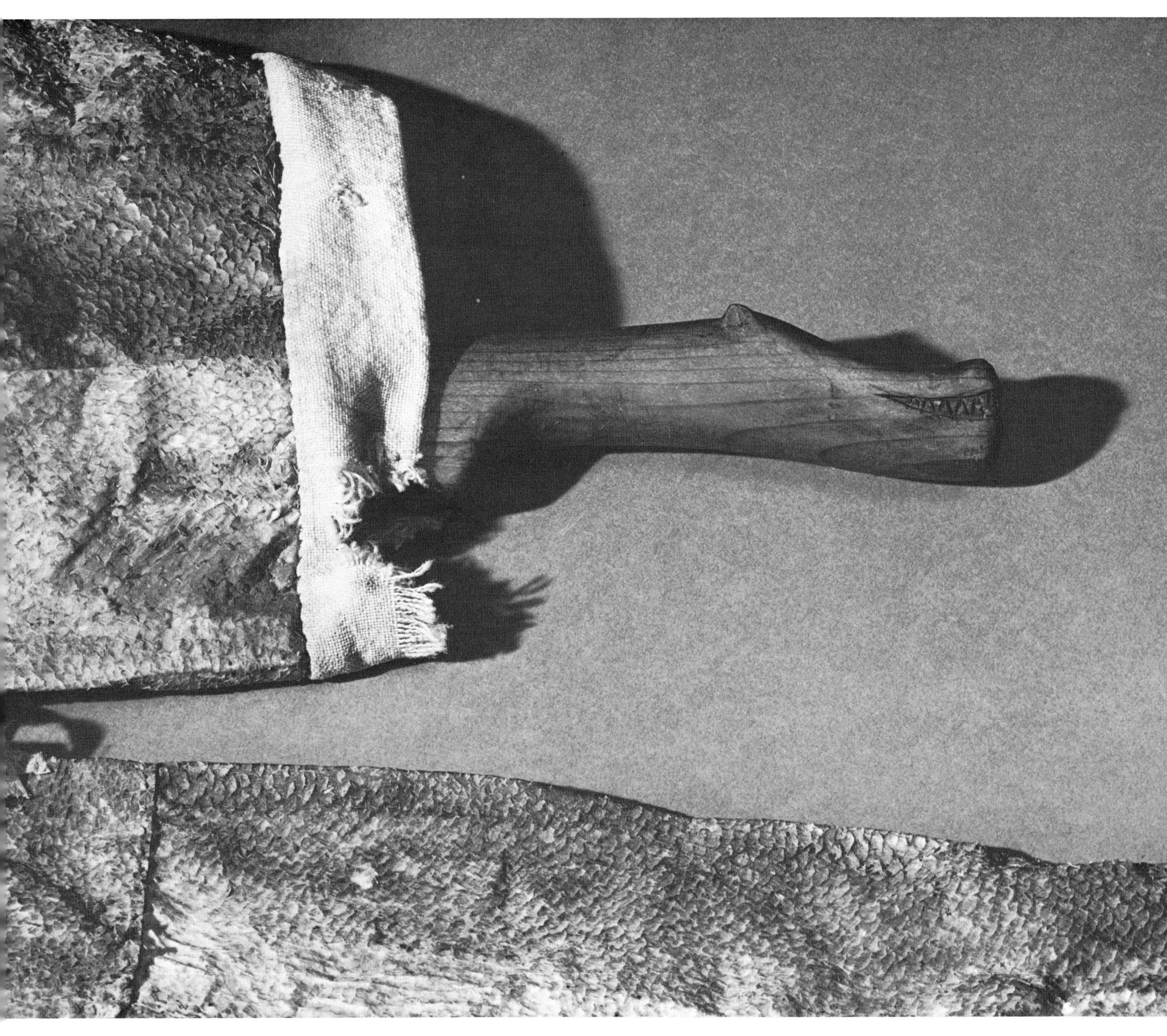

A SEAL SKIN BOW CASE

With fastenings and a wrist guard attached. There is a pouch for additional storage sewn onto the case side.

WRIST GUARDS OR BRACERS

Protected the wrist of the bow hand from injury or chafing. These were held in place by being strapped on with a thong.

Numbered left to right: 1. An old ivory wrist guard with an etched decoration around the outside edge. The thong slits on either side are beautifully made. 2. A bone bracer having not only thong holes but two elongated openings on the convex face. These two long slits may have been only for decoration. 3. An ivory guard with elongated thong holes. 4. An ivory wrist guard which either was not finished or was intended to be tied on the wrist. 5. Most wrist bracers are convex on the one side and concave on the other to fit the wearer well. However some hunters used flat bracers. This one of ivory is flat and larger than others. The brace was tied to the wrist the thong passing over the top of the bracer and around the wrist several times in a wrapping method.

Lower: 6. A bracer of antler beveled around the edges to make it fit tightly. The antler is thicker where the holes are made two on either side instead of just one insuring a very well personalized brace. 7. A similarly made ivory guard as #6 beveled on the edge to insure a close fit. 8. A narrow bone brace. This has well made slits for the thong for tying tight to the skin.

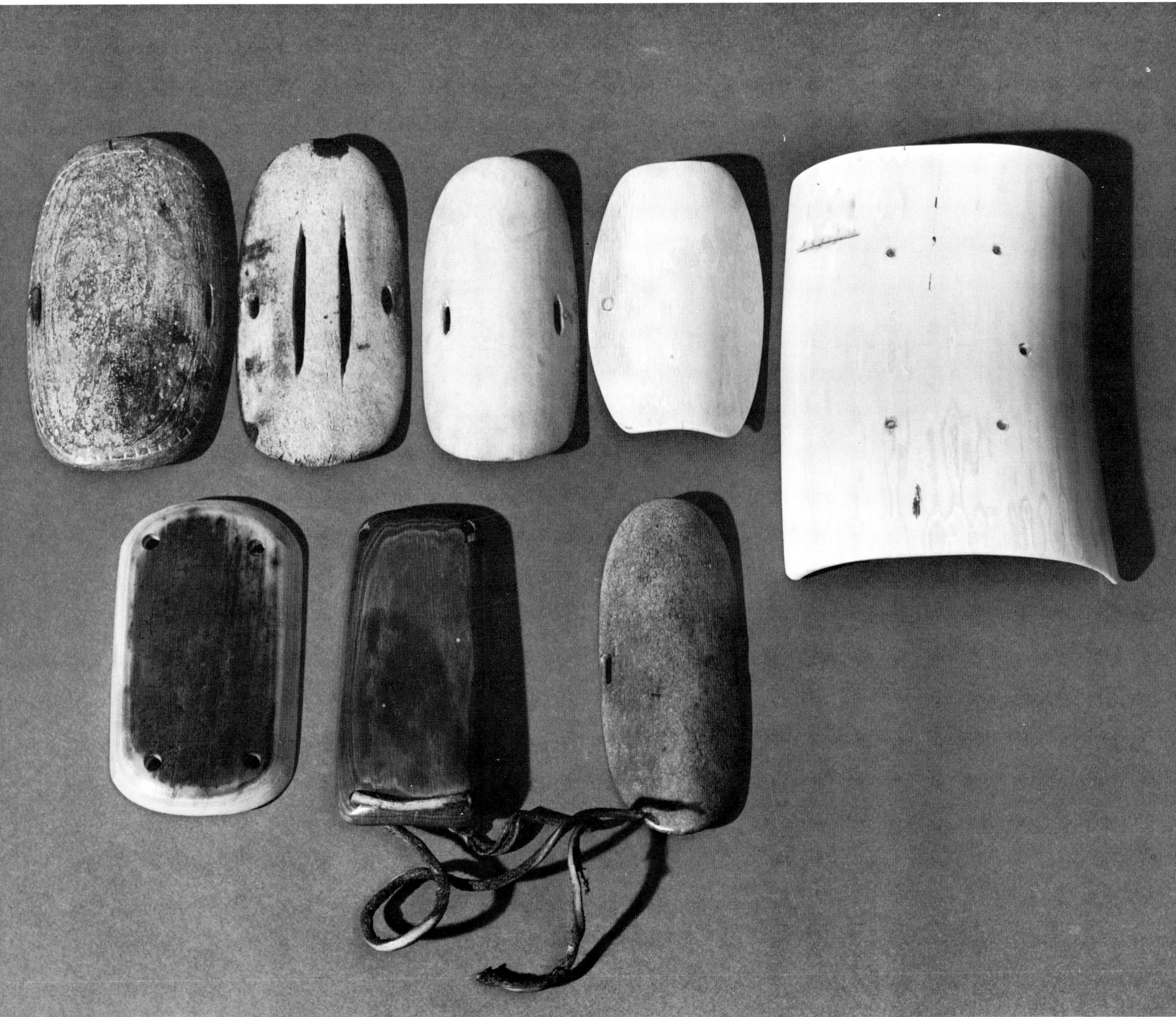

MARKERS FOR BLADDER FLOATS USED IN FISHING

These markers are carved of bone.

The hand shaped implements have the floats tied to them through holes similar to those in the first example.

ARROW SHAFT STRAIGHTENER

This is a very old ivory artifact. The animal's identity is not clear.

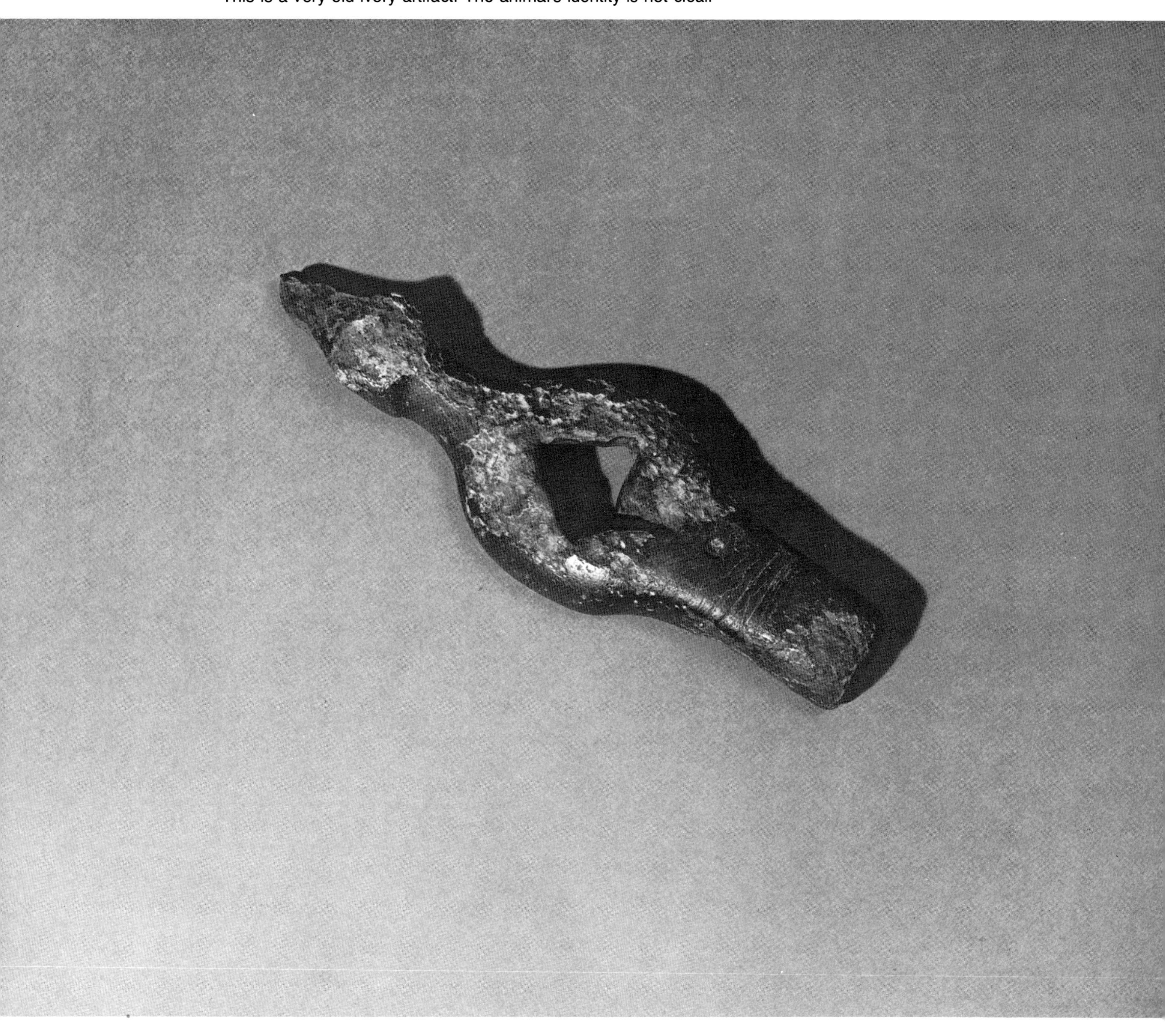

A SEAL HIDE FLOAT

Used when hunting large animals at sea. These floats are inflated using a mouthpiece as the one at left top. Holes in the float are mended and stopped by plugs such as the wood one in the foreground. Floats were not only used for buoyancy but as markers so the quarry would not be lost after being harpooned. Floats were also used on the sides of umiaks to give them greater buoyancy in heavy seas.

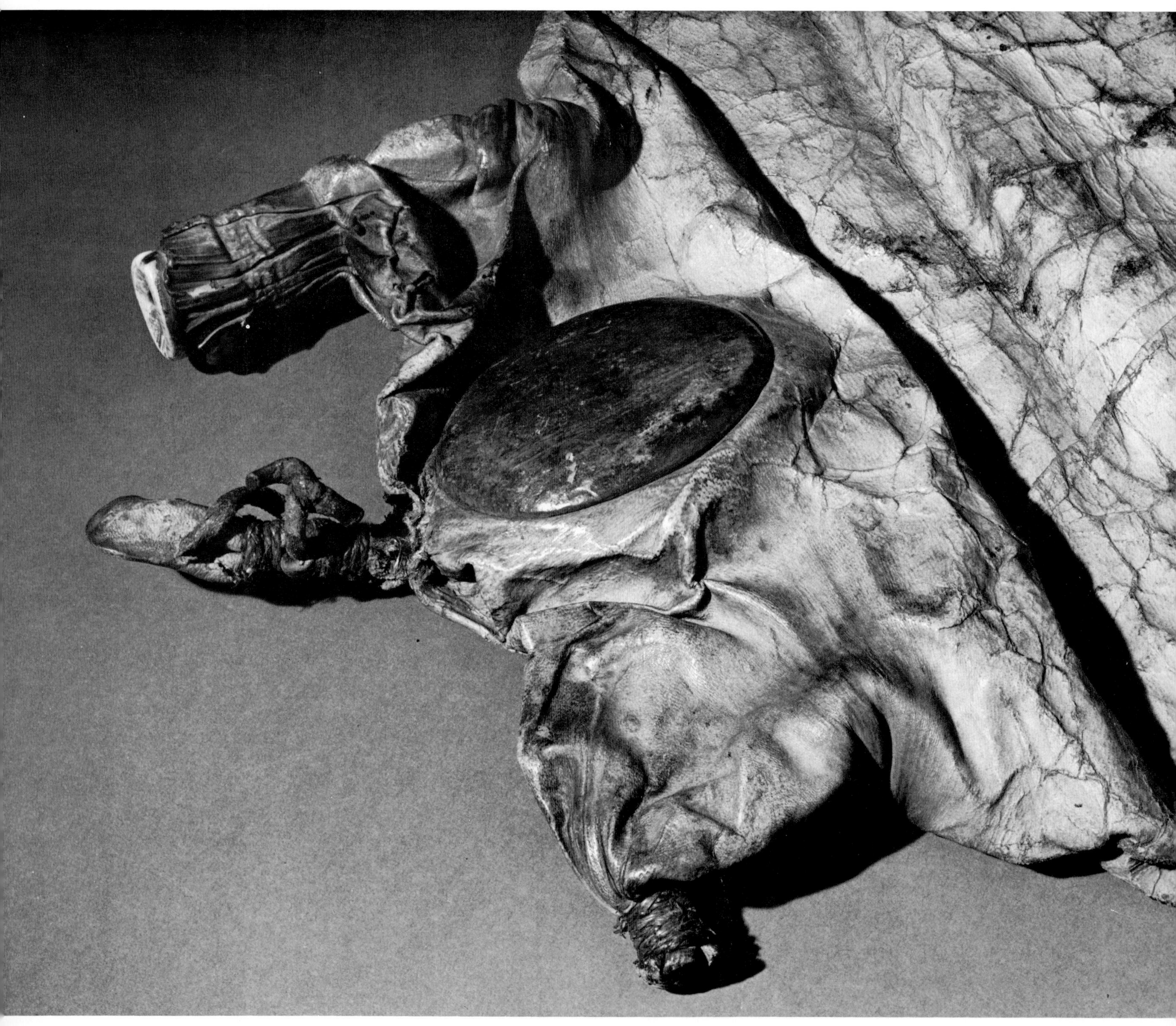

THE END SECTION OF THE FLOAT SHOWN ON THE OPPOSITE PAGE

The handle is for dragging or tying to a line. Example of an ivory plug is shown.

MOUTH PIECES

Used for inflating floats and oil and water bags.

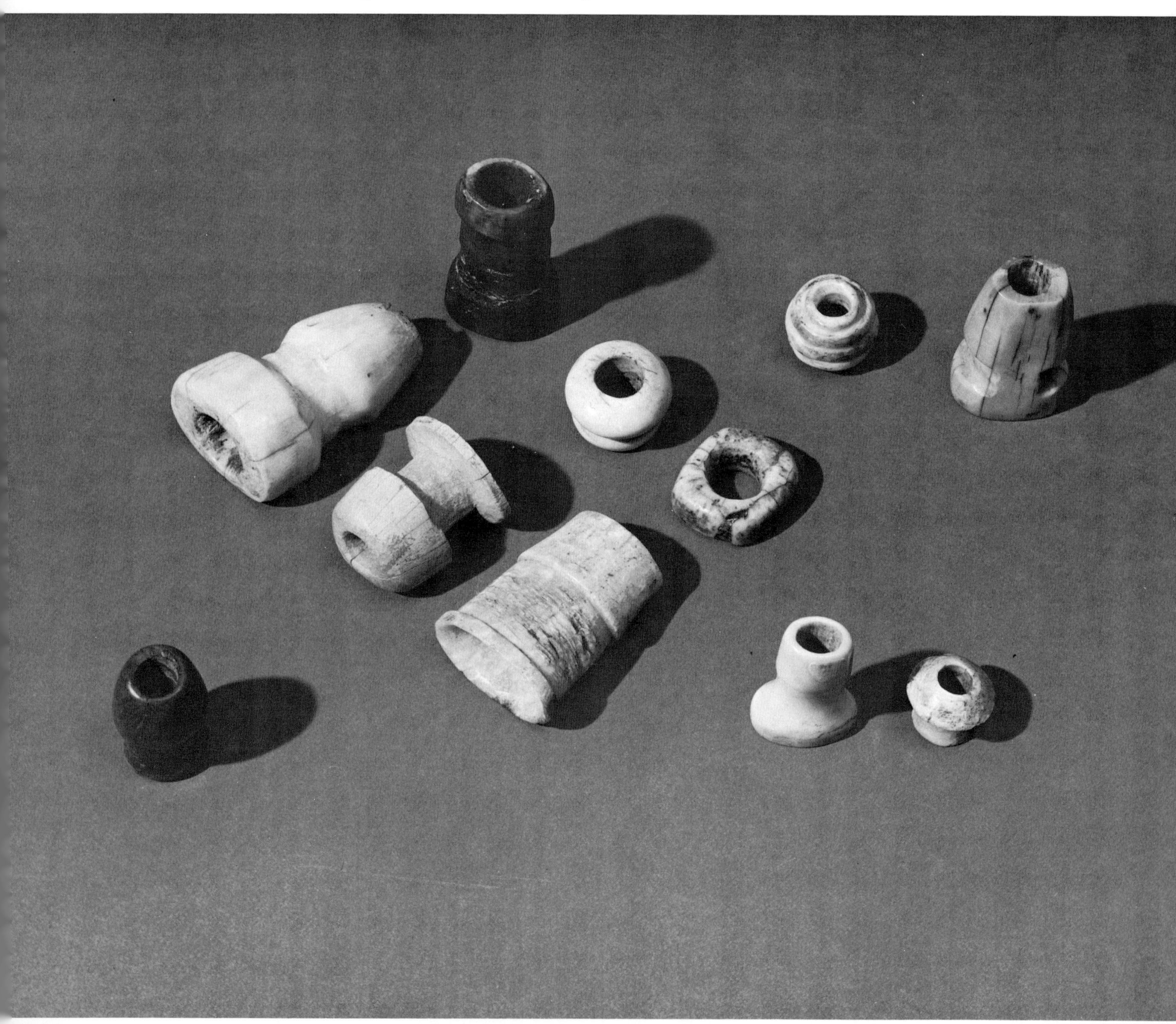

PLUGS REQUIRING STOPPERS

1.-2. Plugs requiring stoppers.
3. Is grooved around the top for a design.
4. This plug has had a bead or stone inlay at one time.
5. This plug is grooved in two places to receive a tie which probably went through the stopper.
7. Three swimming seals are carved on the float top.
8. This plug has a totem or owner's sign.
9. This plug has an indentation for a bead and is notched around the edge.
10. Is grooved around the top.

STOPPERS FOR WATER BAGS AND FLOATS

STOPPERS FOR FLOATS

Three bone stoppers shaped as whale tails for floats. The middle and lower stoppers have identical marks on them which may signify ownership of the float or serve as a fetish symbol.

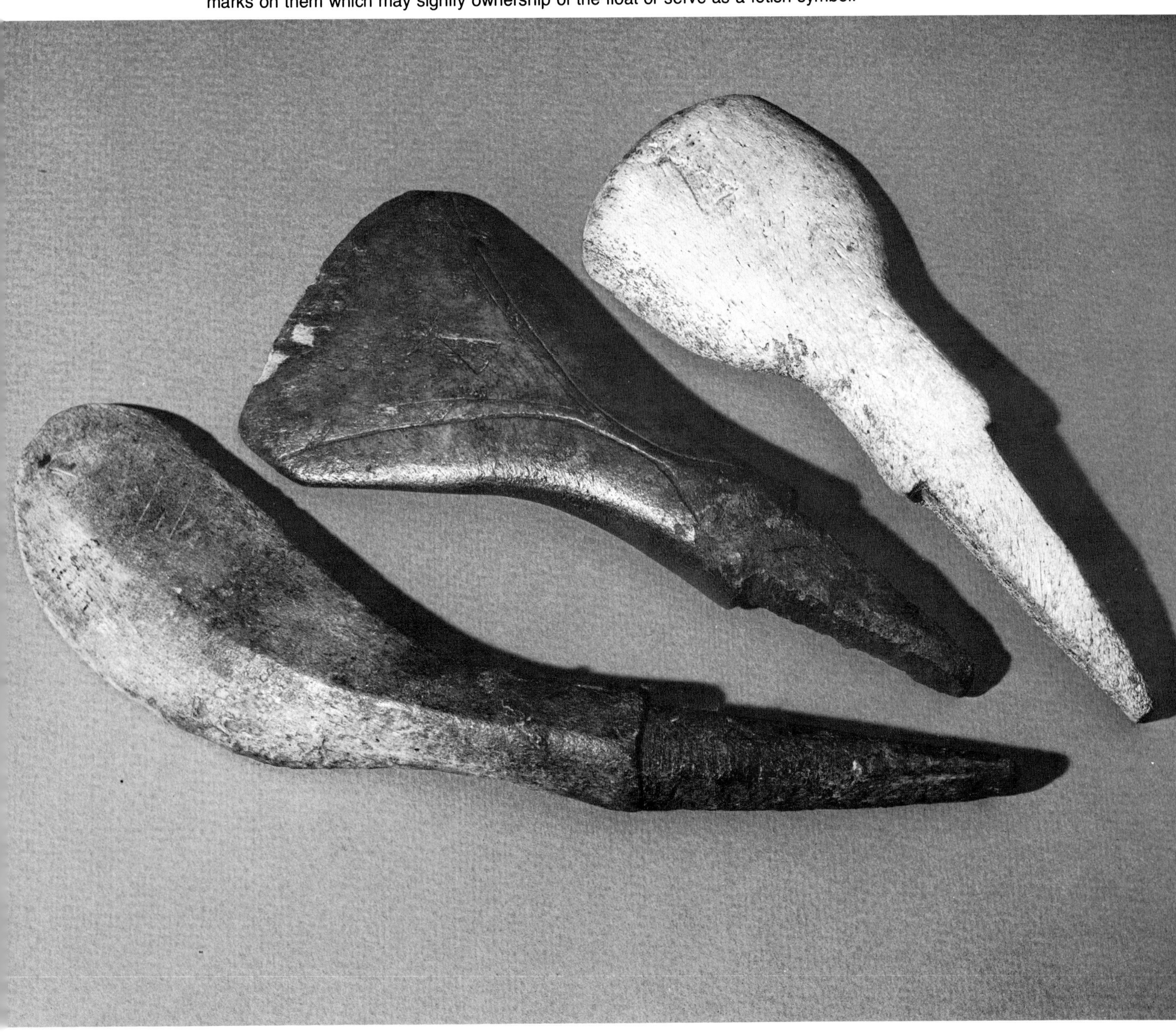

RATTLE

It is not certain whether this rattle was used by a shamen or was for another purpose. Puffin beaks threaded on twined reindeer cord are hung in clusters of four or five the full length of this long flat stick. The ends of the beak cords are concealed under a wrapping around the stick of the same kind of cord. This wrapping is measured off with white deer sinew in an over and under pattern on the edge opposite the beaks and in the centers of the stick on both sides except in the middle where the rattle is held. Some beaks showing signs of breaking have been mended with baleen.

RATTLE

A seal rattle made of very tough seal skin. A plain bag like receptacle contains small pebbles. A similar bag is pulled over the first and gathered in tightly to keep the rocks from falling out. The rattle was shaken gently to interest the seals who becoming curious usually moved closer to the hunter.

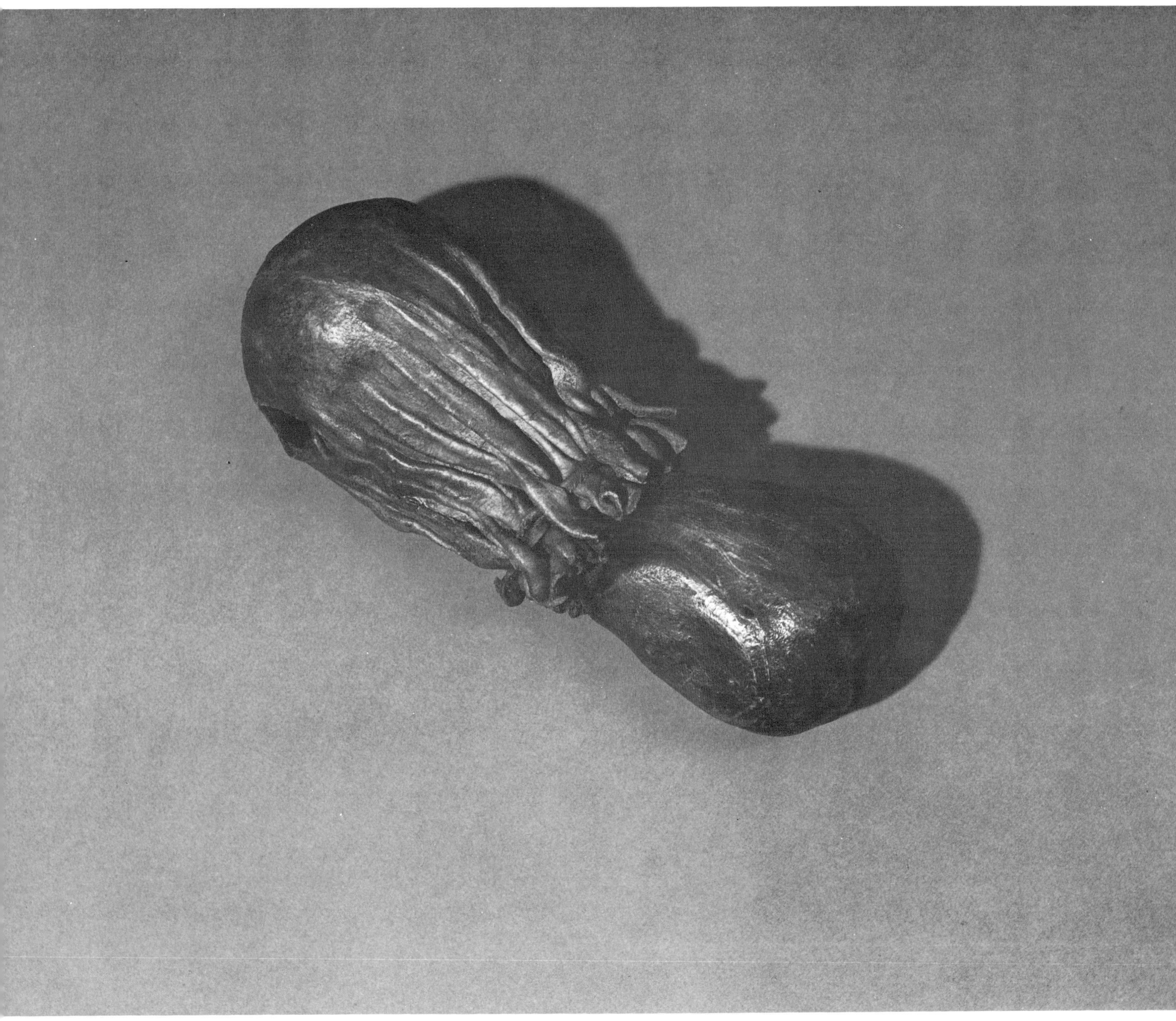

SCRATCHERS

Seal hunting implements made of wood, the carved "fingers" capped with claws secured by sinew wrappings. These scratchers were used by the hunters to enable them to come close enough to a seal to spear it. When the seal would become wary, the hunter would stop and scratch the snow gently. The sound, resembling animal noises, would reassure the seal and he would go back to sleep.

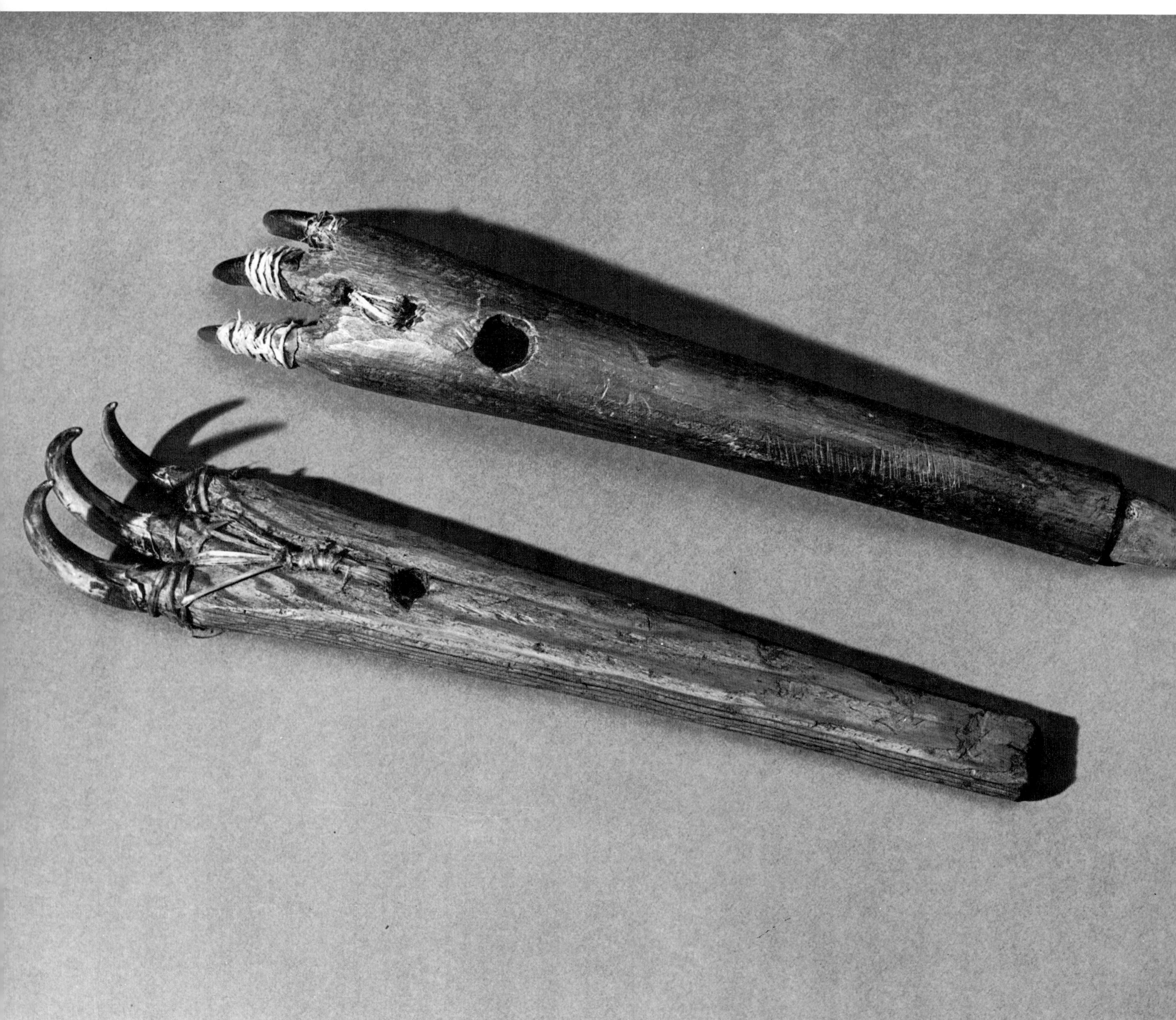

CLUBS

The upper example has a grip on the handle making it easy to hold firmly.
Below is an ivory tusk club for stunning fish or animals. The wrapping is seal skin.

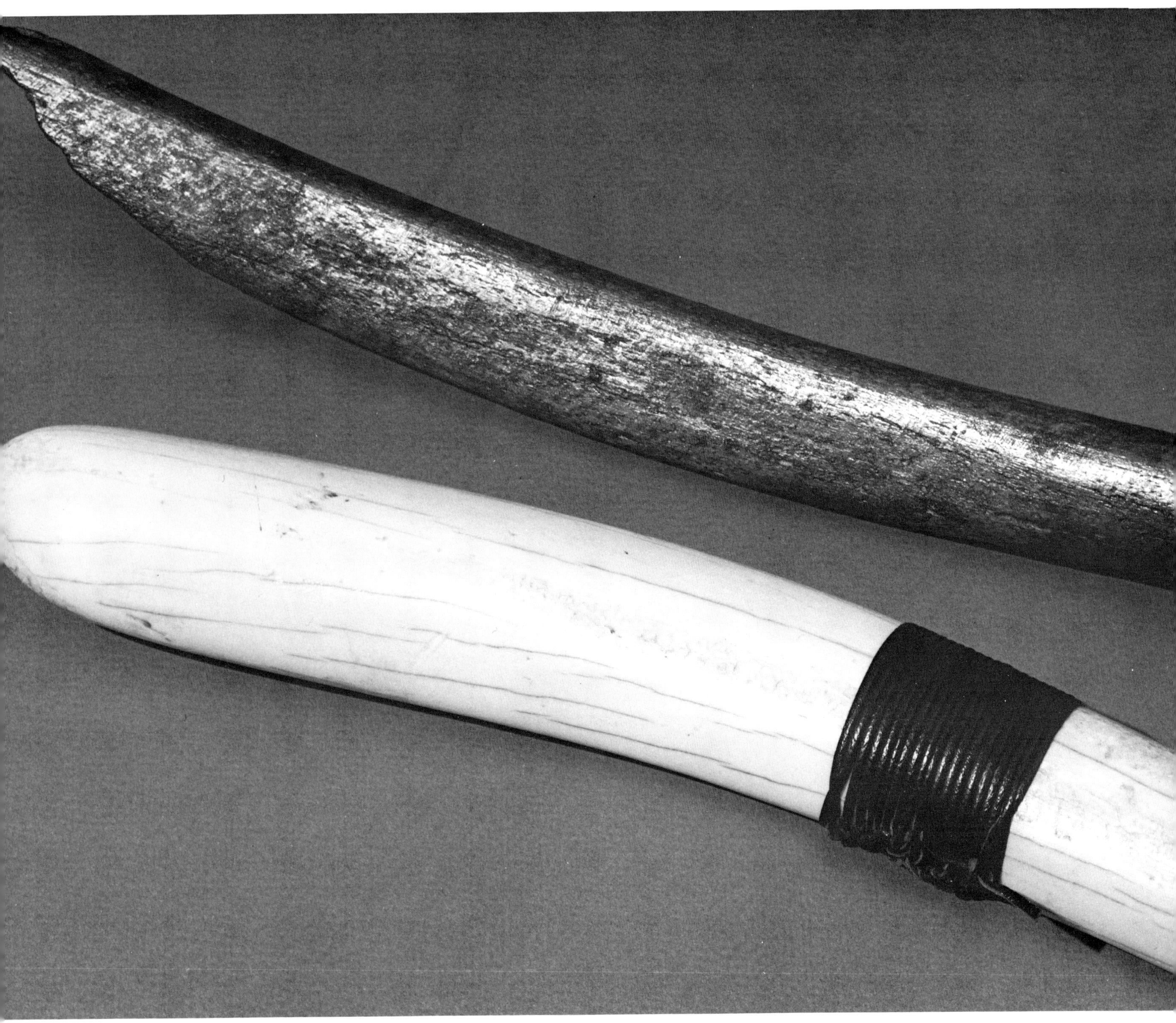

IVORY DRAG HANDLES

With lines for hauling heavy loads such as dead animals over ice.

1. This drag handle is in the form of a seal. The line is braided sinew.
2. This drag handle has a swivel to keep the lines from twisting.
3. A handle for a drag cord.
4. A kayak paddle handle cross piece.

5.-8. Cord fasteners.

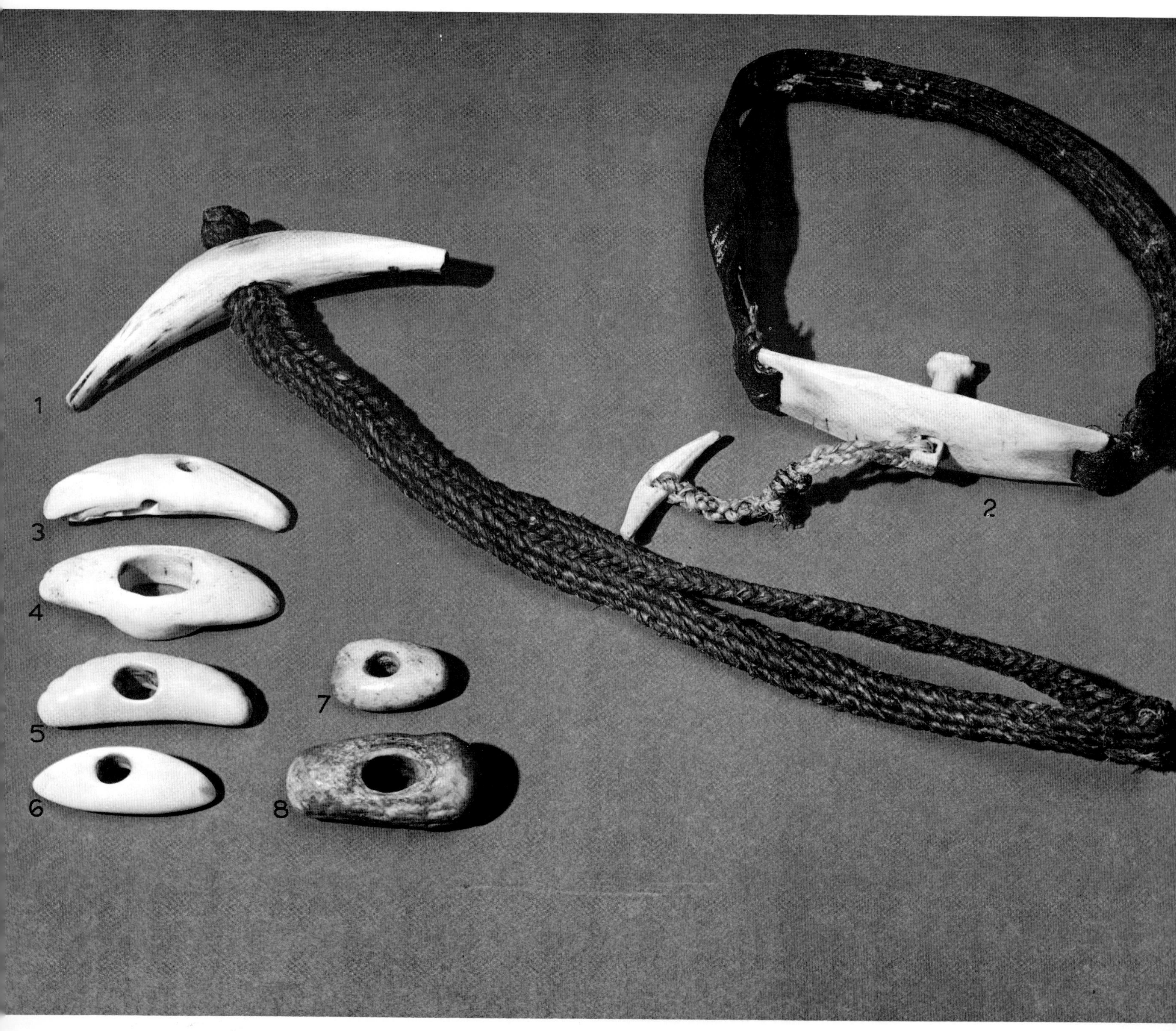

IVORY CORD ATTACHERS

These blocks were used to join lines together to give them greater strength.

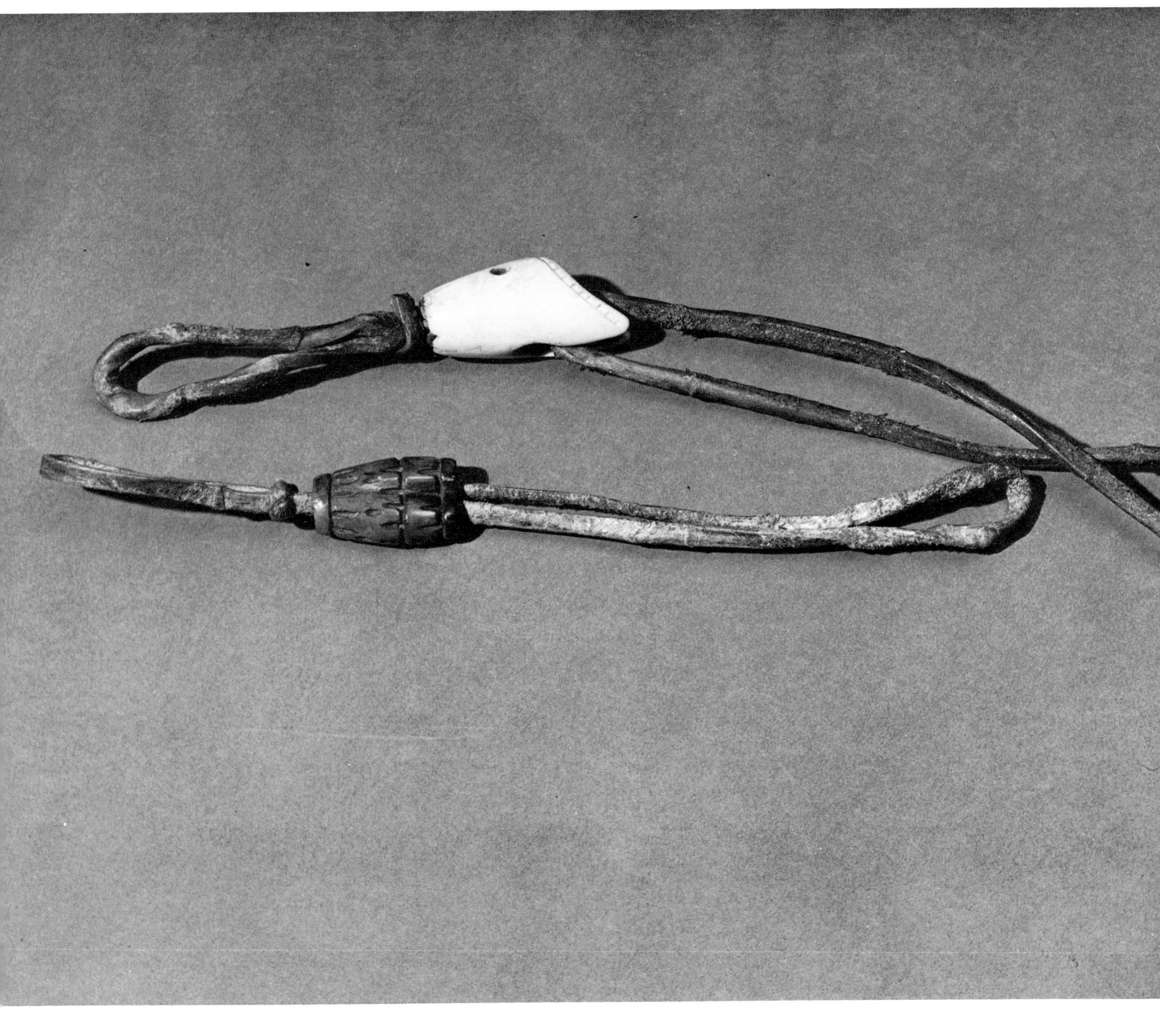

DRILL SET

Drills were used for making holes in ivory, bone, and other materials. The implements consisted of a drill bow, the cap and the drill. Cords used to twirl the drill were held on either side by grasp handles. Bows were straight, very curved or slightly curved depending on the preference of the user. In cross section they could be square, triangular or slightly oval. They were generally twelve to eighteen inches in length.

These are three ivory drill bows, a cap with a stone socket an ivory drill, cord handle and the drill.

Drill caps for smaller work usually had mouthpieces to hold the cap by the teeth. Large projects required larger drills which were rotated by a man at either end of the cord twirling the drill pulling the cord back and forth between them.

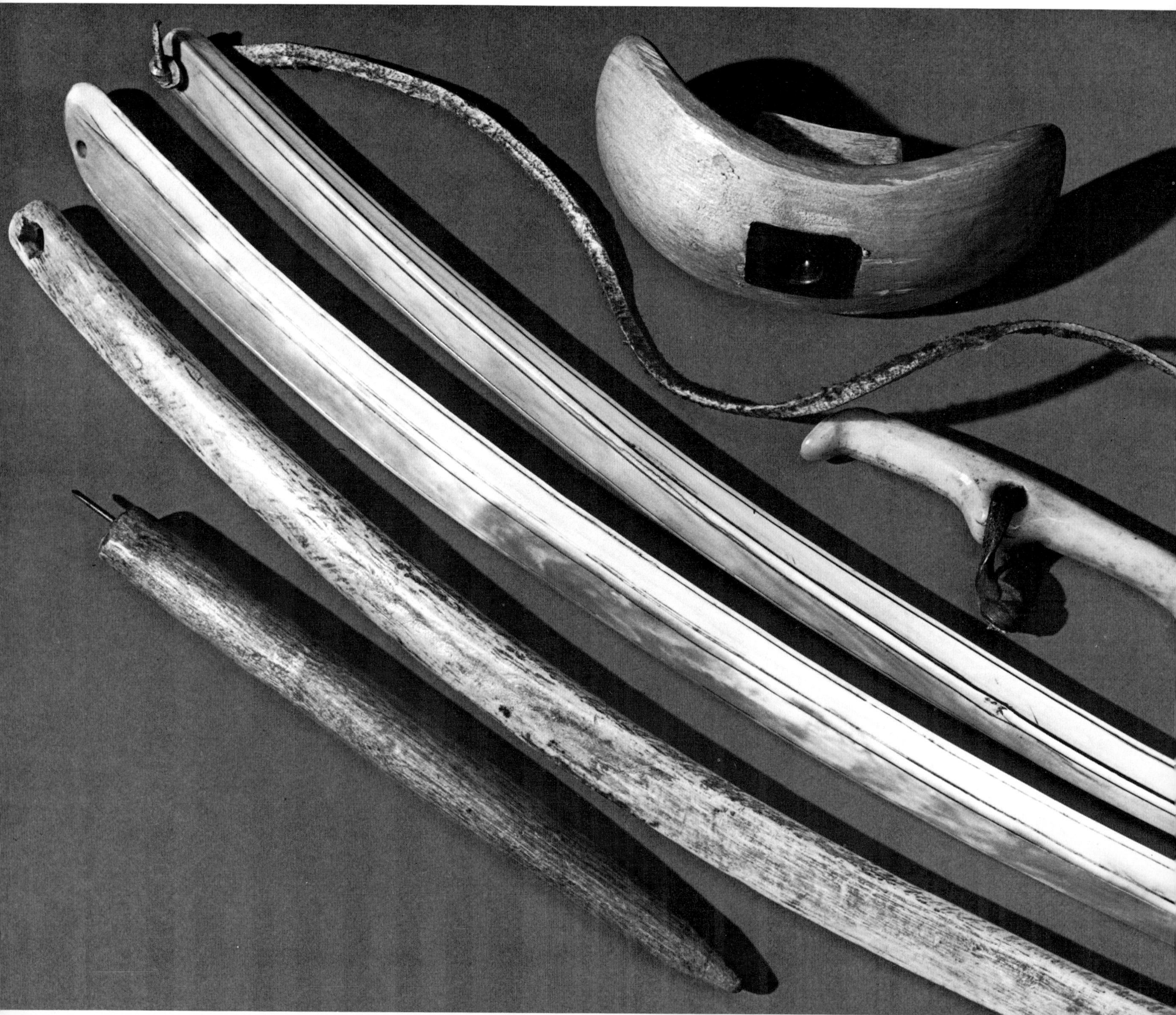

DRILL CAP WITH MOUTH PIECES

Each are a different design and have a different socket material uniquely shaped. The upper cap's socket is mottled black stone. The left, is green stone and the third, metal probably from a bullet casing. The stone socket was set into an existing cap since it has been shimmed on three sides.

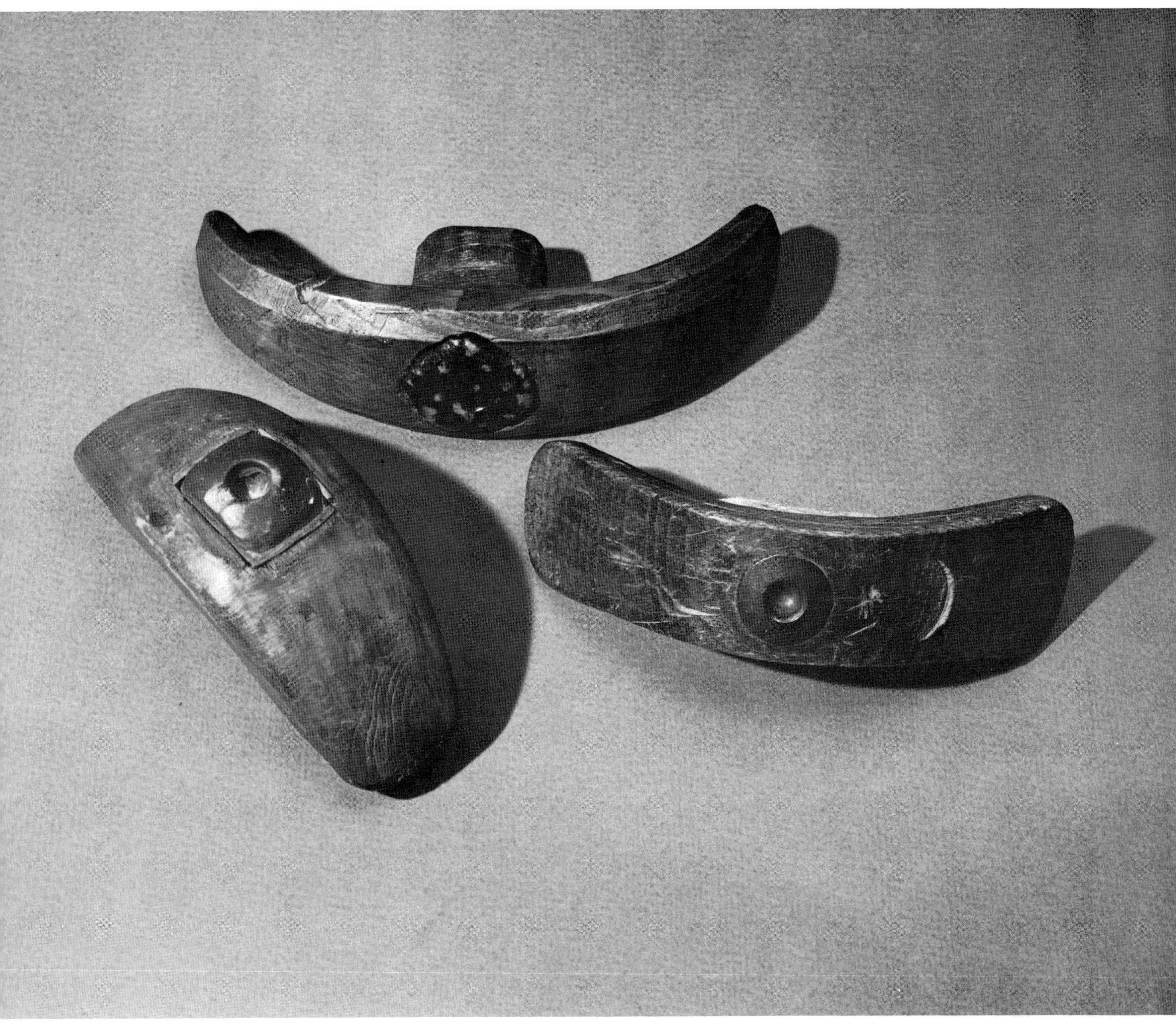

DRILL CAPS CARVED WITH ANIMALS

The upper cap is carved on one end with a whale having a white diamond shaped eye.
The lower cap has a bear carved on either end with blue stone eyes. The socket is black stone.

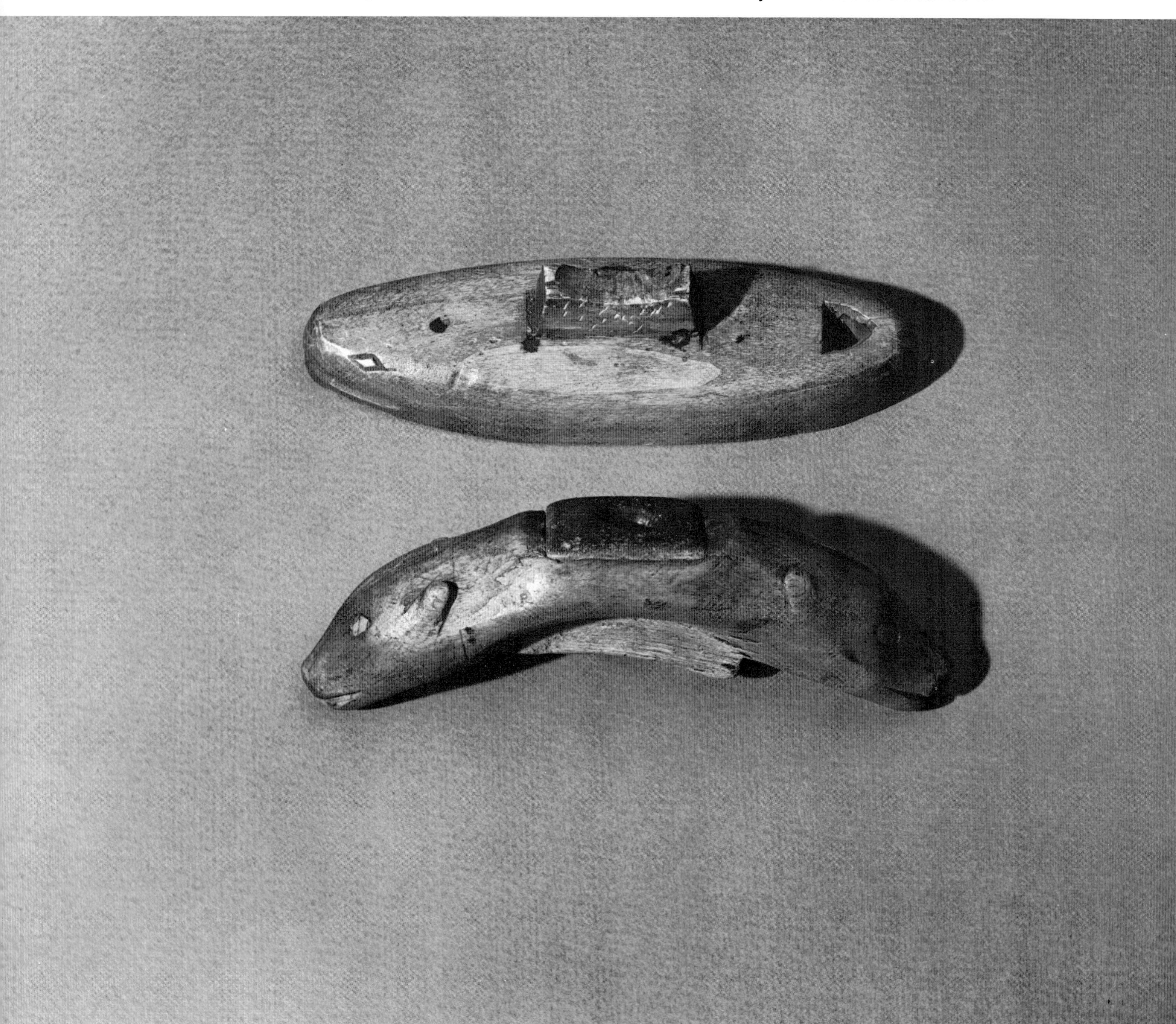

DRILL CAPS WITH CARVED ENDS

The upper depicts seals with white pebble eyes. The lower cap has the shape of seals only. The socket in the lower cap is iron.

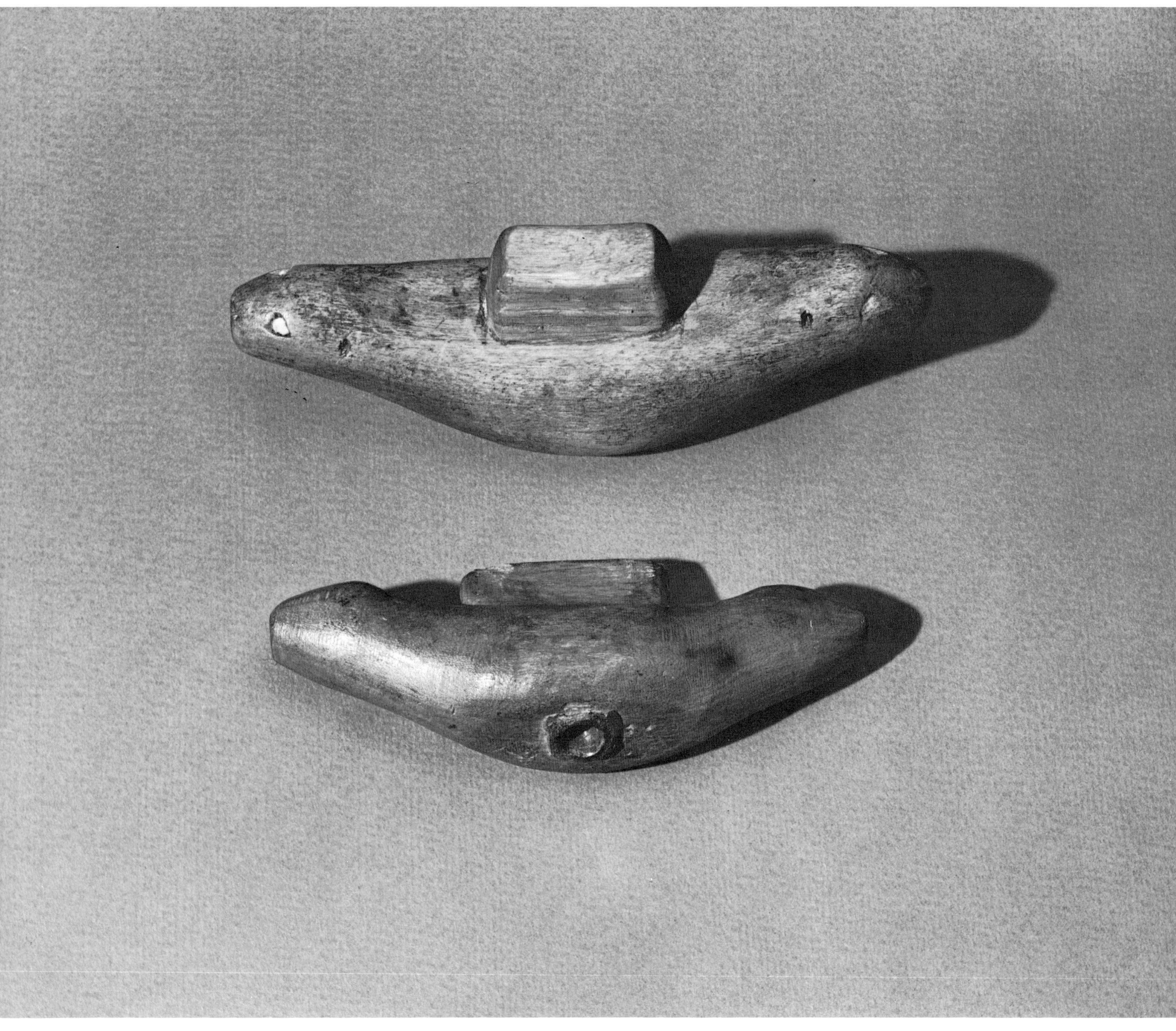

A CAP AND SOCKET FOR A DRILL BOW

The socket is a green jade-like stone, very hard, smooth, and exceptionally well made. The mouth piece is set similarly to the socket.

MISCELLANEOUS ITEMS

Objects similar in appearance but having different uses.

Top row:
1. Part of a flat fishing lure.
2. A cord attacher.
3. A ferrule for a dog whip.
4. A small rigging block used on a dog harness.
5. An ornament, a pendant or earring.
6. A dog whip ferrule.

Middle row:
7. A spear rest or guard.
8. Part of a drag line.

9-10. A complete and a broken block for rigging lines.
11-12. Parts of swivels.

Bottom row:
13-17. Cord or belt fasteners.

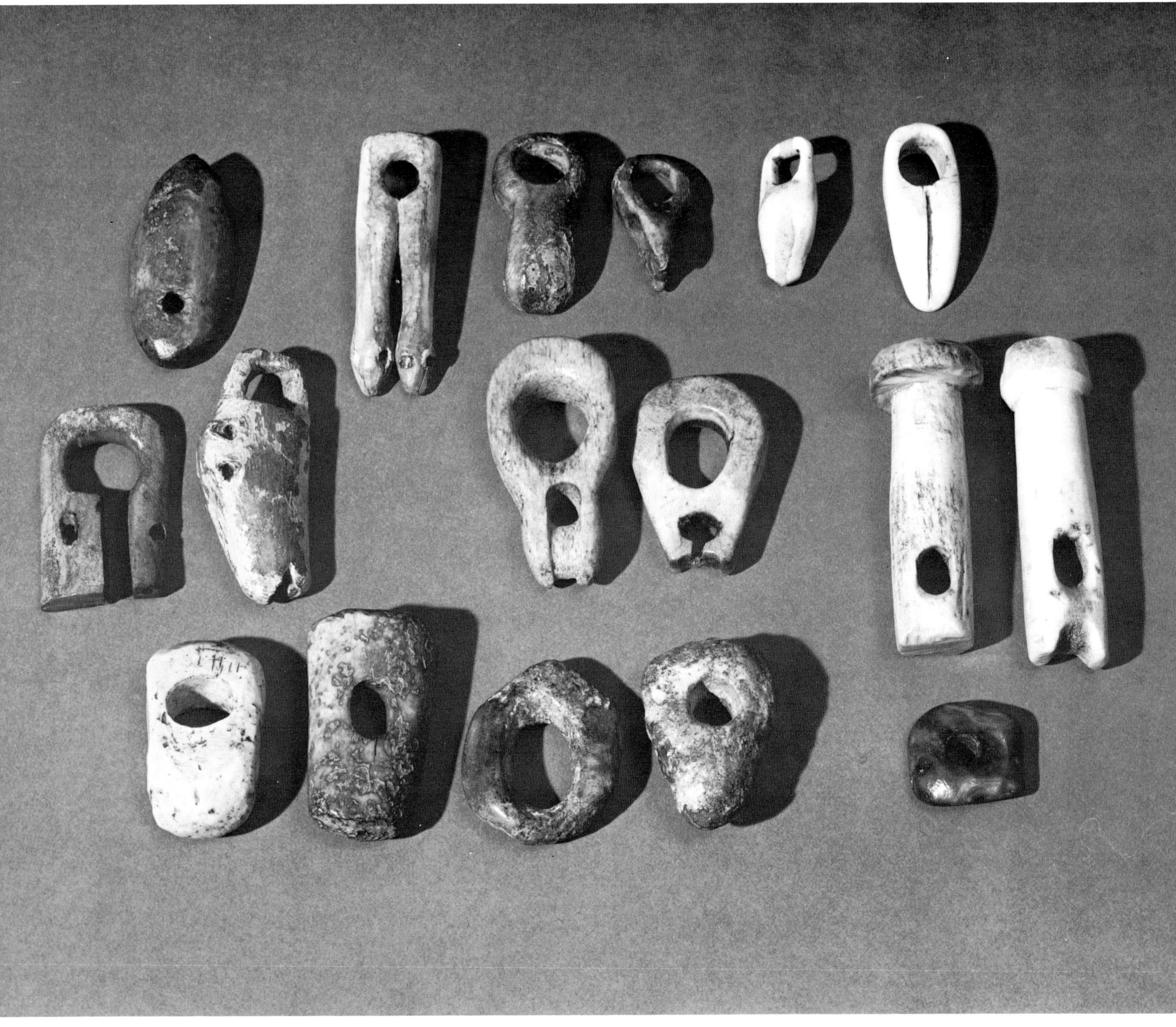

MISCELLANEOUS DEVICES

First row:
1. An ivory piece used to attach a gun to a tripod.
2. An ivory finger rest for use on a spear shaft.

Second row:
3. A root pick to be attached to a short handle.

Third row:
4.-5. These bone spurs were secured to a kayak by rawhide cords and projected upwards for rests for spear or paddles.
6. A rigging hook.
7. A bone rigging hook. Part of the wood frame is still attached held with a bone peg.
8. A bone kayak spear rest.

Fourth row:
9. A bone gun rest for attaching to a tripod.
10. A rigging hook.

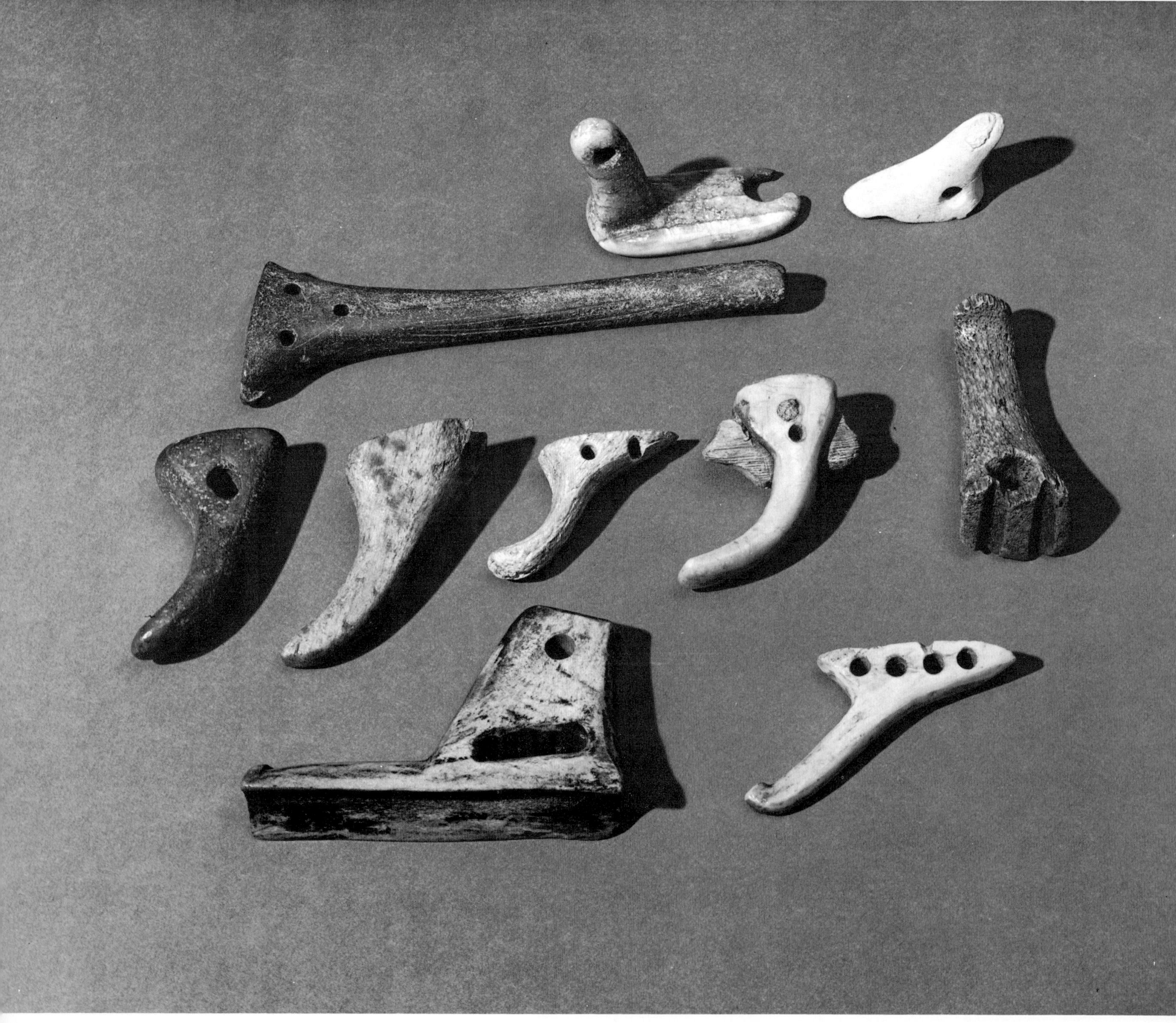

MISCELLANEOUS DEVICES

1. An ivory handle for a dog whip.
2. A bone gun rest for attaching to a tripod.
3. A root picker.
4. A bone boat rigging hook.
5. A bone kayak spear or paddle rest.
6. A bone kayak spear or paddle rest.
7. A gun tripod attachment.
8. A boat rigging hook.
9. An ivory rigging hook.
10. An ivory finger rest.
11. A whale bone spear rest which fastens to the inside of an umiak between the front rails to hold spears and lances.
12. A bone kayak spear or paddle rest.

MISCELLANEOUS ITEMS

1. An ivory ferrule for a dog whip.
2.-3. Ivory spouts for water or oil bags. The flat rim fits inside the bag with the small opening left outside to receive the stopper.
4. A frame for fishing hooks.
5. A deer horn line guide from a tom cod fishing pole.
6. This ivory implement was broken. It is a very old artifact the use of which is not known. The seal like animal is decorated with small dots.
7.-13. Ivory frames for fish hooks. The top eyelet for fastening has been broken off several frames.
14. An exceptionally beautiful finger rest for a spear.
15. A stopper made of rawhide with an attaching hole cut in the top.
16. A fishing hook frame.
17. A seal handle for a scraper.
18. A belt fastener.

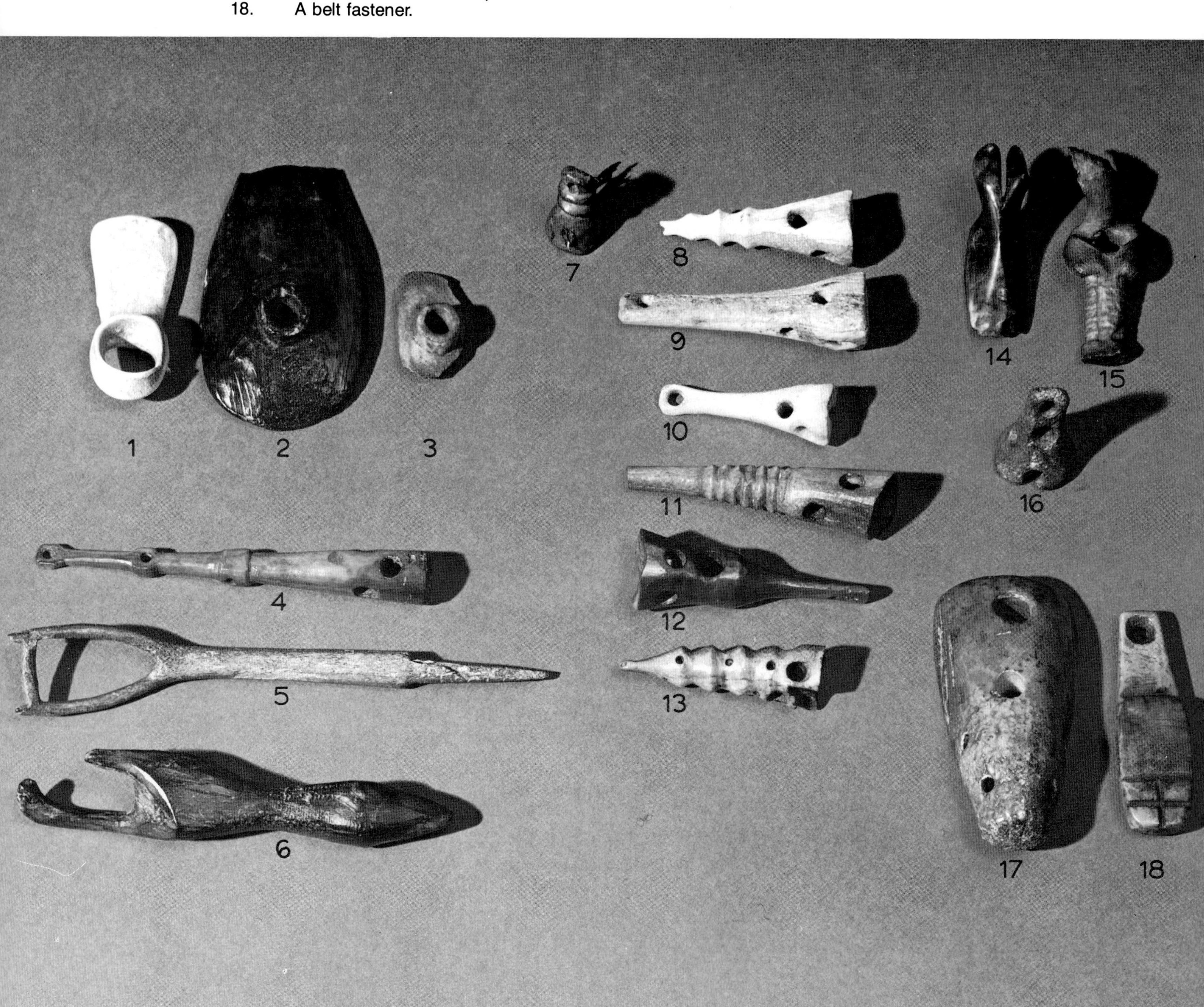

HOOKS

Eskimos employed a variety of hooks in their daily occupations and though generally alike in shape, their uses were quite different. There is evidence however, that interchanging these hooks and using them for other than the original intent was not uncommon. Here is a group of several kinds of devices undoubtedly interchangeable.

1. A crudely made hook grooved for tying. 2. An ivory hook used in the rigging of an umiak. 3. An ivory umiak rigging hook. 4. A thimble guard. 5. Hook used with an umiak. 6. An ivory belt fastener. 7. A hook used especially for a Kayak. 8. An ivory belt fastener. 9. An ivory boat hook. It size suggests it was used on a kyak. 10. A bone rigging hook. 11. This hook had a hand grab but its exact use is not known. The broken point resembles a thimble guard and the knob could have been used to soften skins.

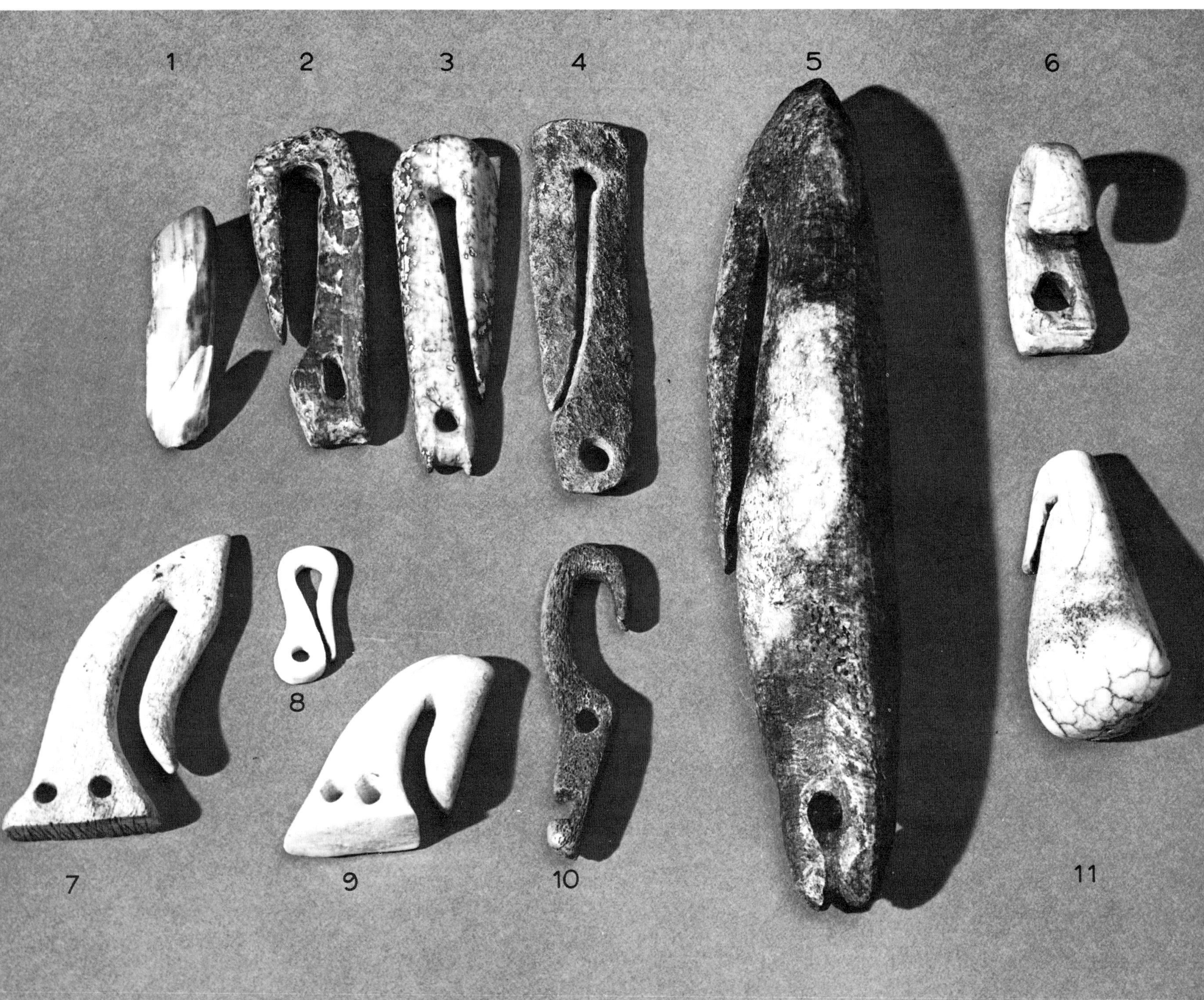

DRAG HANDLES

Parts of drag handles used for hauling dead animals over snow or ice. These handles were attached to a strong permanent loop of seal skin or walrus hide.

The whale effigy was attached to a similar chain.

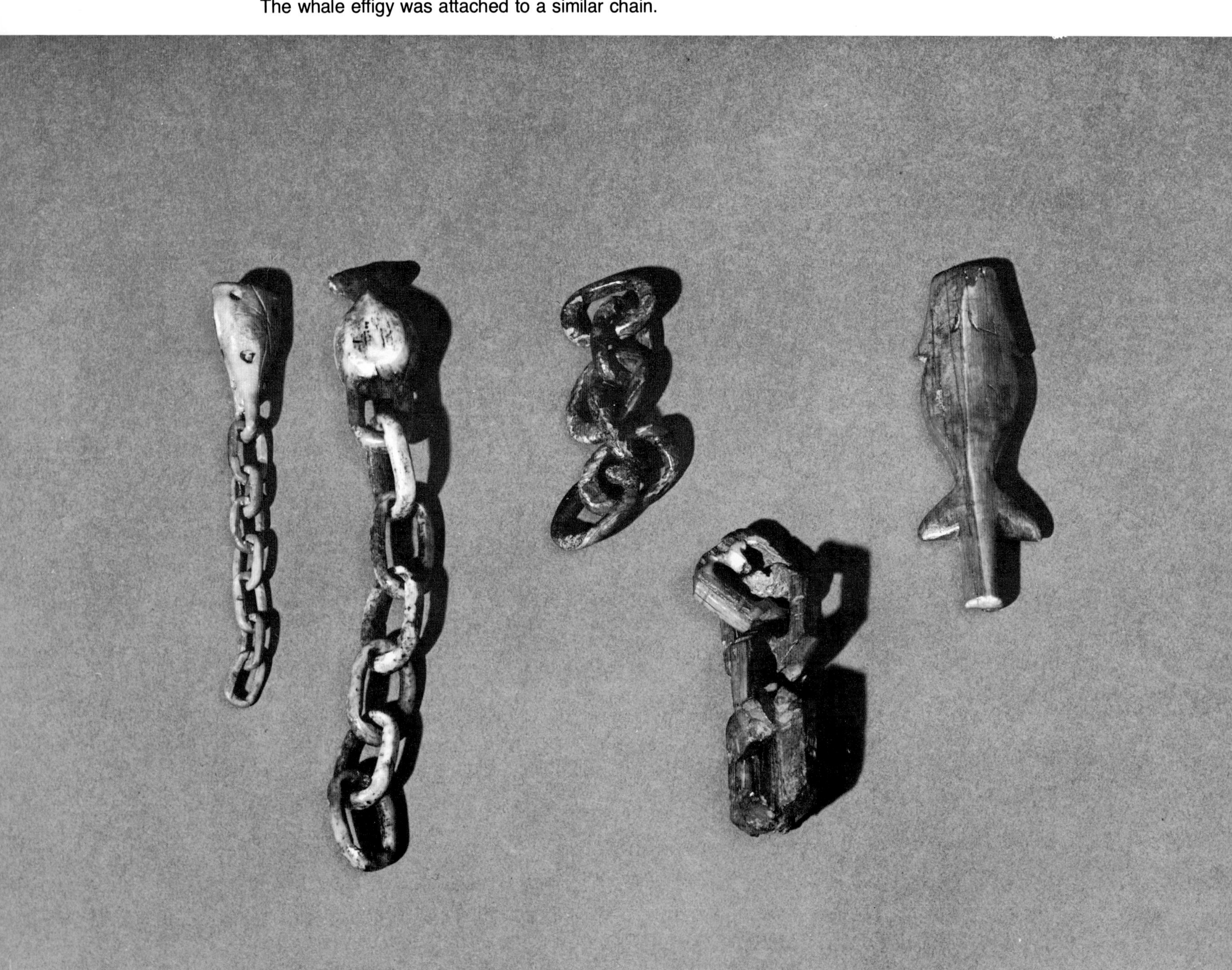

MISCELLANEOUS ITEMS

Upper: 1-2. Swivels were used in a number of tasks such as for staking out dogs while not working, dragging loads or dog harnesses. They were used to keep lines from twisting.

Left: 3-4. Are etched bone hand adz heads for working bone, ivory and antler. Splinters of a green hard stone point are embedded in the first example.

5-6. Are bone heads to be fitted to a wood handled adz. Pointed hard stone was fitted into these heads and used to work ivory, bone, or antler.

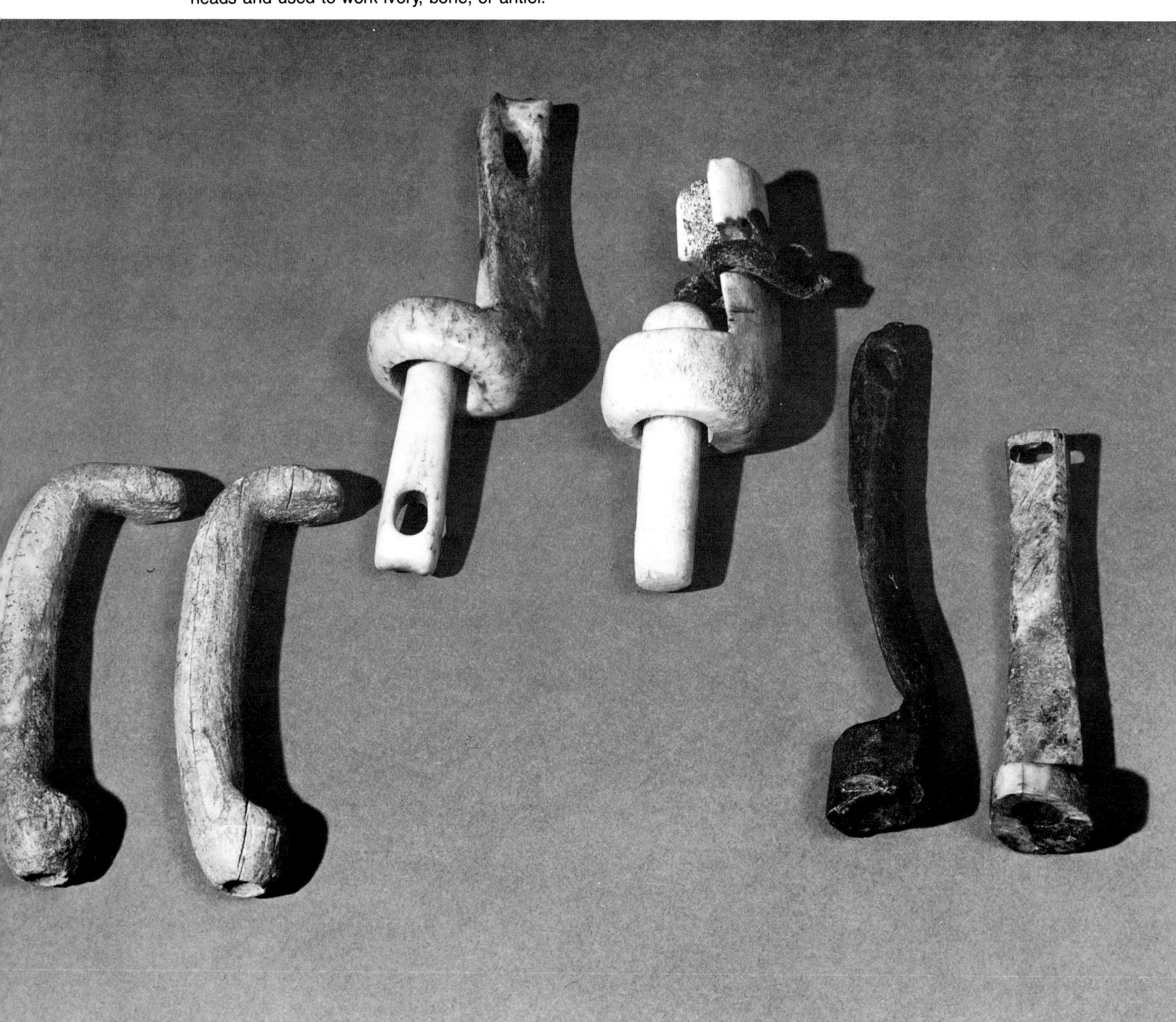

ANCIENT SKIN DRESSERS OR KNIVES WITH BONE HANDLES AND SLATE BLADES

SKIN SCRAPERS

Used to clean the fat and flesh from fresh pelts and prepare them for use. Stiff and dry skins also had to be renewed if they were damaged by water or exposure.

The scraper blades were usually stone set in wood holders made to fit the hand of the user.

Here are four holders made for their owners with the finger hollows and form made to fit the hand precisely.

Left to right:

1. A wood holder with a raised section well forward.
2. A wood holder with finger slots but no raised palm rest. The blade is flaked dark green jade like stone.
3. A wood holder with the palm rest considerably set back from the center with a groove through the handle.
4. A bone holder crudely shaped with a hard black stone blade.

ANCIENT IVORY MAULS

The first and third examples were attached to handles by rawhide and were used much as a hammer would be used to drive wedges or stakes.

The center specimen may have been used without being attached to a handle since there are finger spaces for a firm grip and may have been used for digging as in preparation for a dwelling. There are indications on the ivory that the implement had also been used as a hammer.

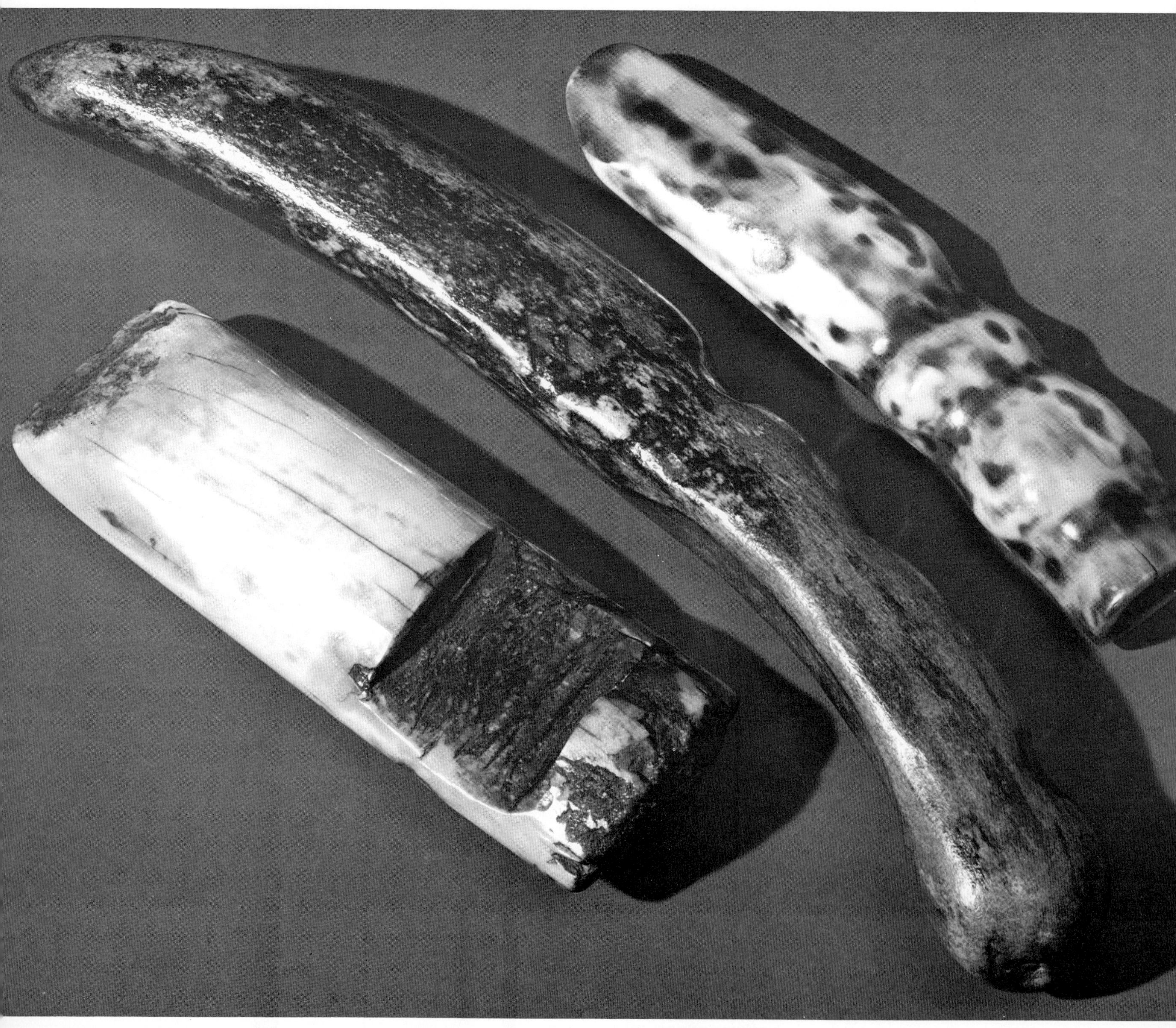

A STONE MALLET

Fastened to a bone haft with rawhide. The head shows considerable design, grooves for fastening cord, and signs of having been chipped to achieve a shape. The broken edge shows the type of stone used for this artifact a kind of less valuable jade. The wedge is made of similar material.

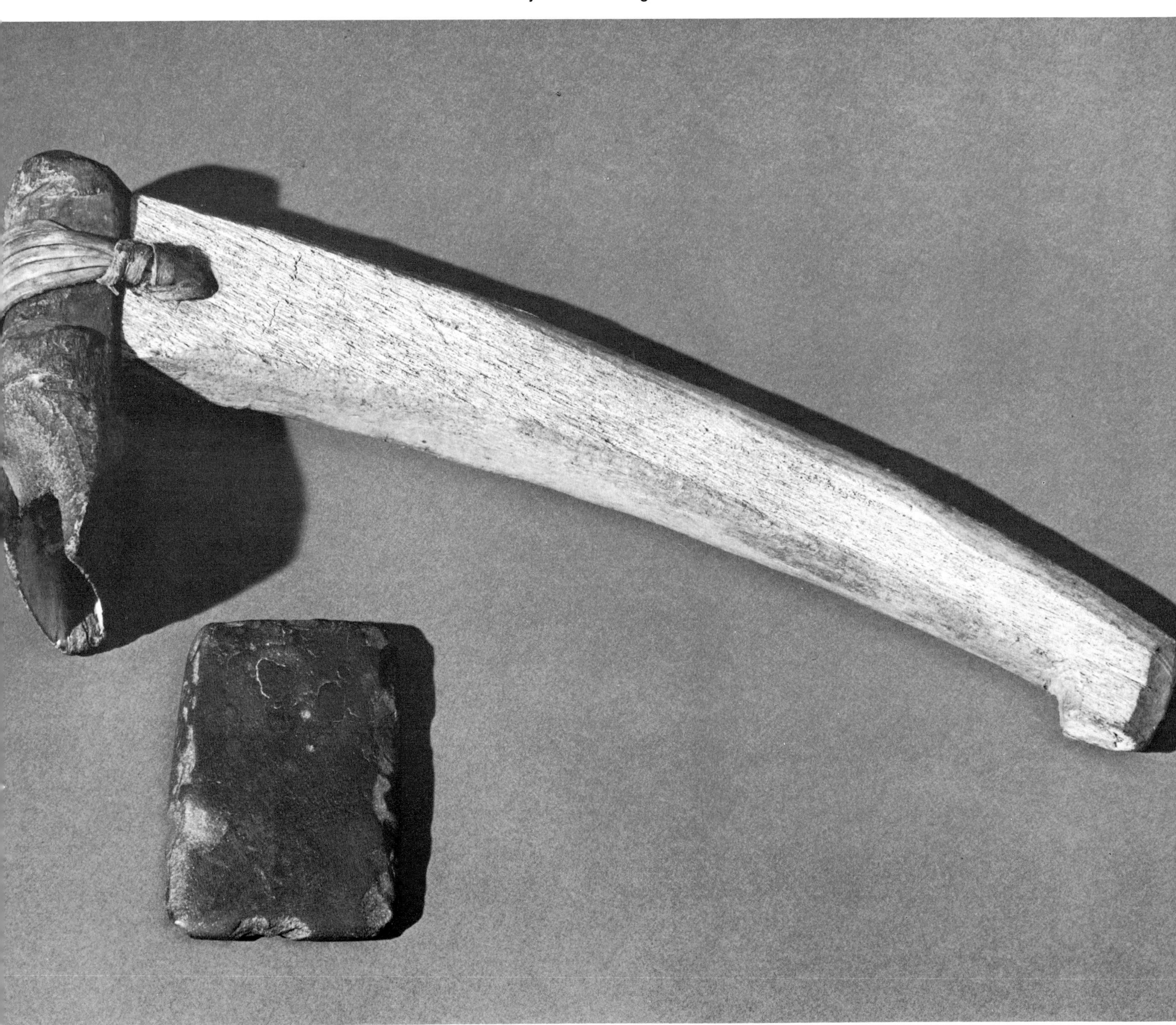

WEDGES AND ADZES

Upper: A black stone adz grooved around the end in two places for attaching a cord to a handle.

Middle: A dark green stone wedge probably used for preparing wood or logs.

Lower: A large piece of mastadon ivory formed into a wedge like maul. This example has one slightly beveled side and the attaching points are clearly defined. This maul is as hard as stone and surprisingly heavy.

Upper right: A sharp wedge of black stone may have been set into a handle.

MISCELLANEOUS STONE IMPLEMENTS

Stone was fashioned into many shapes in the manufacture of various implements such as hunting points and work tools. While the designs were somewhat standard for various locales, the individual had his preference which influenced the ultimate design.

BLADES

Harpoon and spear head blades of slate like stone.

MISCELLANEOUS KNIVES

Knife and skin dresser blades. The two blades with the serrated edges were for cleaning fat and other matter from the skins and for softening hard spots on the skins.

BLADES AND SHARPENING STONE

Numbered top to bottom:
1. A bone blade sharpened for a lance head.
2. A slate knife which was probably wrapped for a better grasp.
3. A slate blade which probably fitted into a handle.
4. A sharpening stone for points and knives.

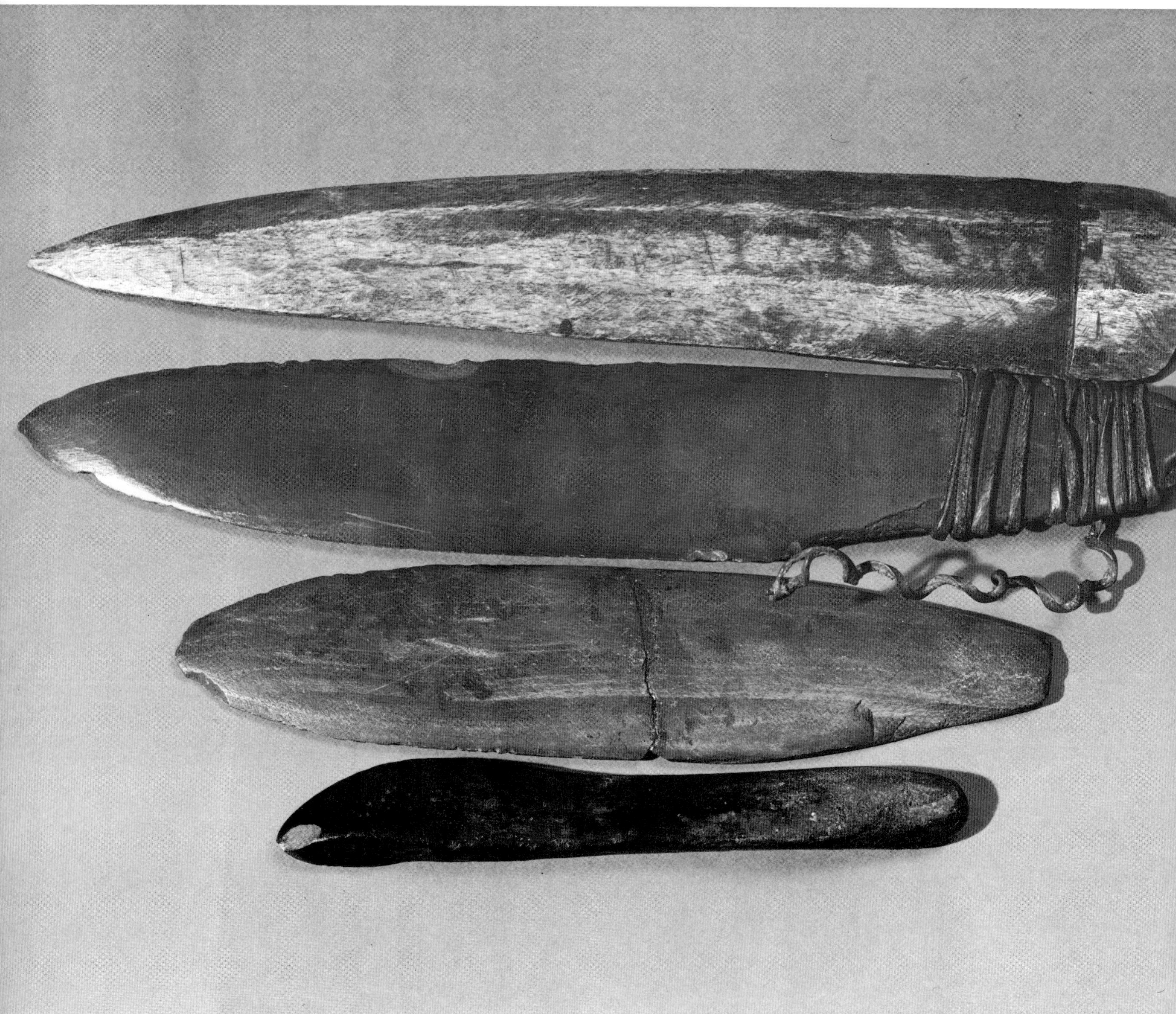

STONE BLADES

Numbered left to right:

1. The first example is a jade like stone and has a longer shank which probably fitted into a handle.
2. The second blade may have had a handle at one time.
3. The third blade has been flaked out for finger spaces.

FLAKED POINTS

Harpoon heads, one of which was set into a handle made of deer horn, this implement was possibly used as a dagger.

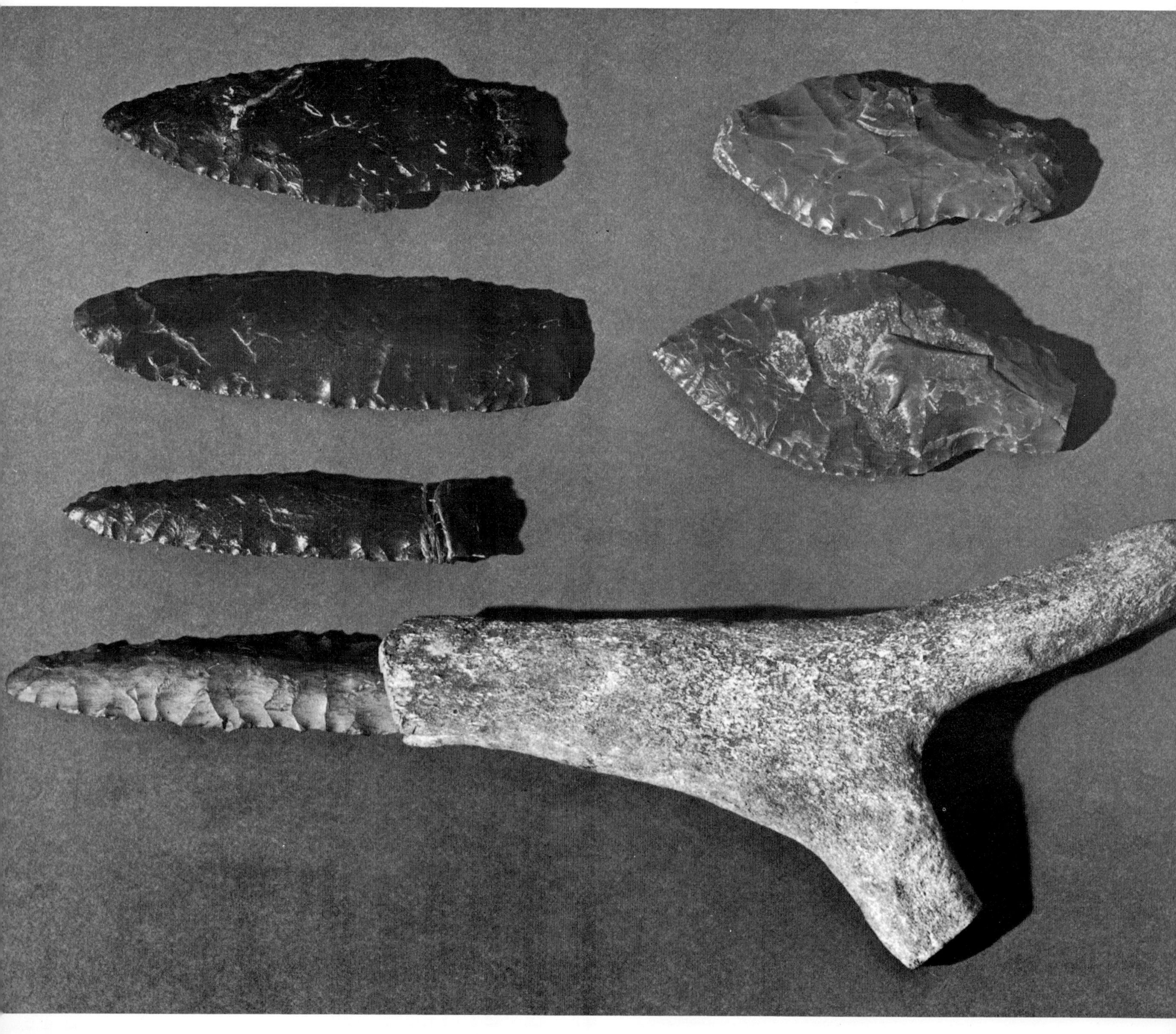

FLINT MAKERS

The design of flint makers is rather universal but the material from which they are made and their size differ. The shaft is generally ivory or bone with a channel the full length holding the rod of some hard material sturdy enough to fracture stone and chip it into the desired shape.
Numbered left to right:

1. An ivory shaft and a rod of antler bone. The rod points down and is secured by a tying cord.
2. A bone shaft with a tying groove around the bottom.
3. A bone shaft with a tying groove.
4. An old bone shaft wider than usual. The rod is a piece of antler horn.
5. An old ivory shaft etched on the top which has a long curve.
6. An ivory point to use in a shaft.
7. An ivory shaft with a long curve on the top. The ivory is flattened then ridged for a firmer grip.

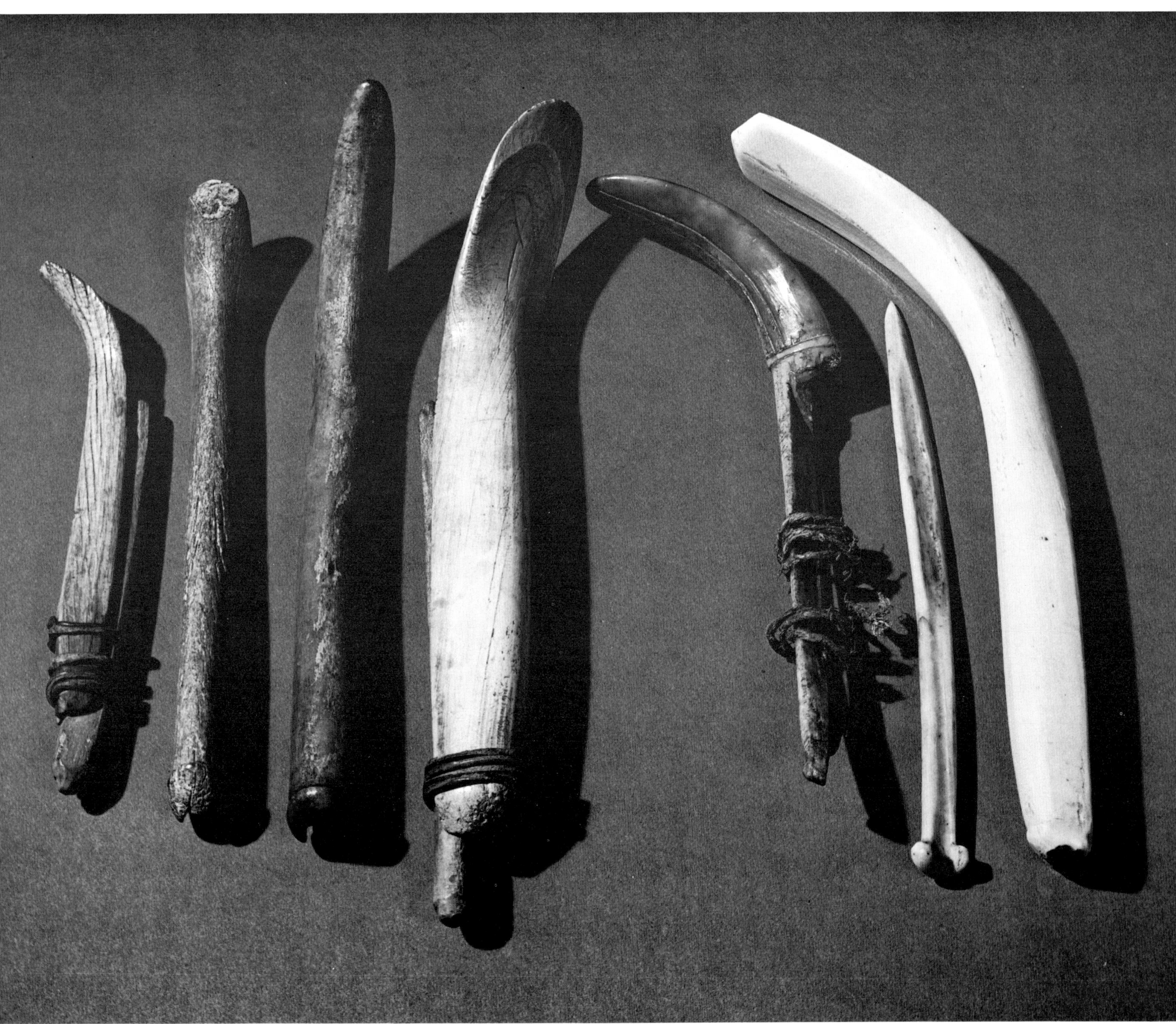

BONE SHAFTS FOR FLINT MAKERS

Used to make spear points, skin scrapers and other stone implements. The shafts are held with the spoon shape at the top, the heel of the hand resting against the curve.

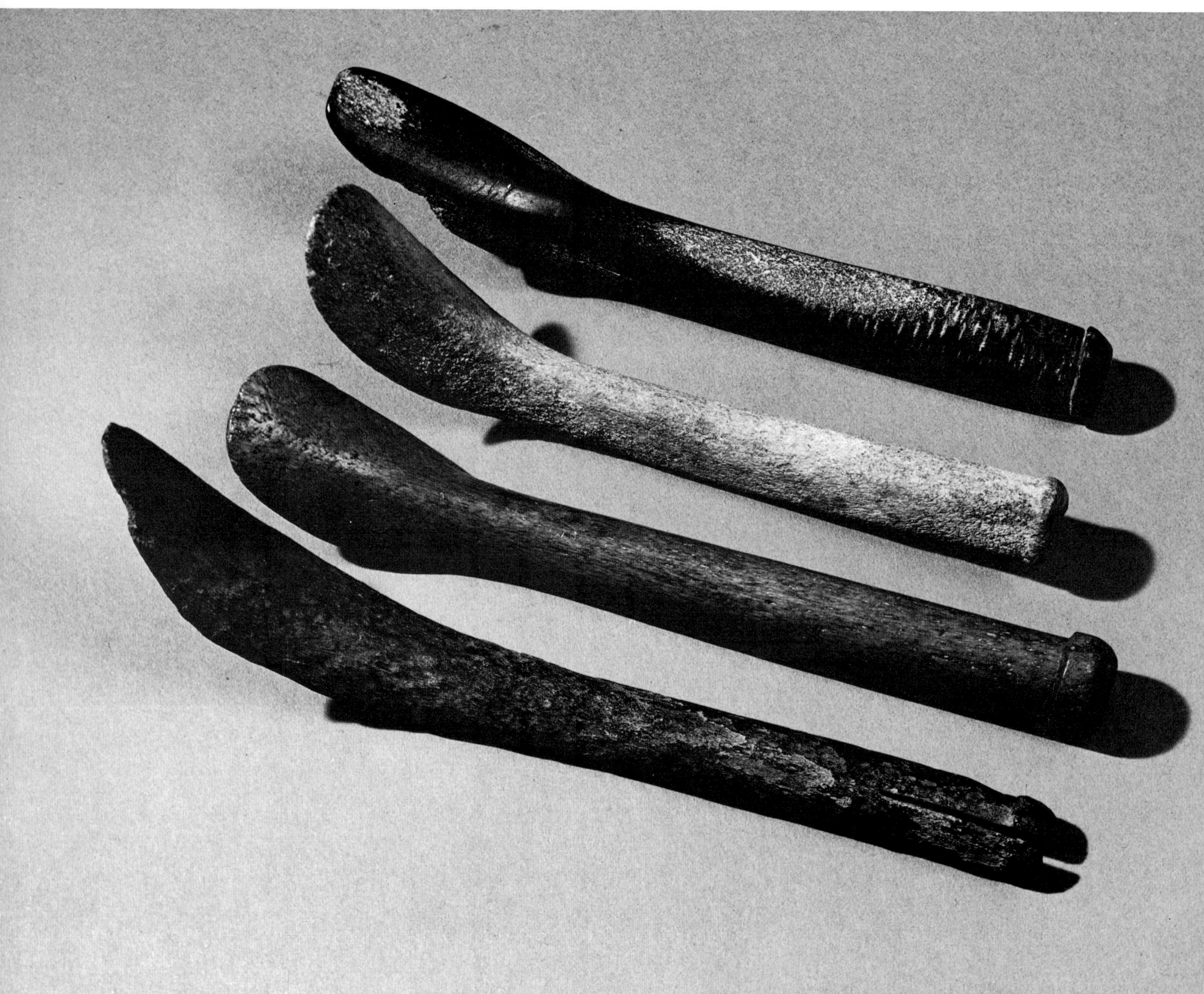

FLINT FLAKERS

Ivory and bone flint flakers with rods. The rods may be carried in the hollow for storage.

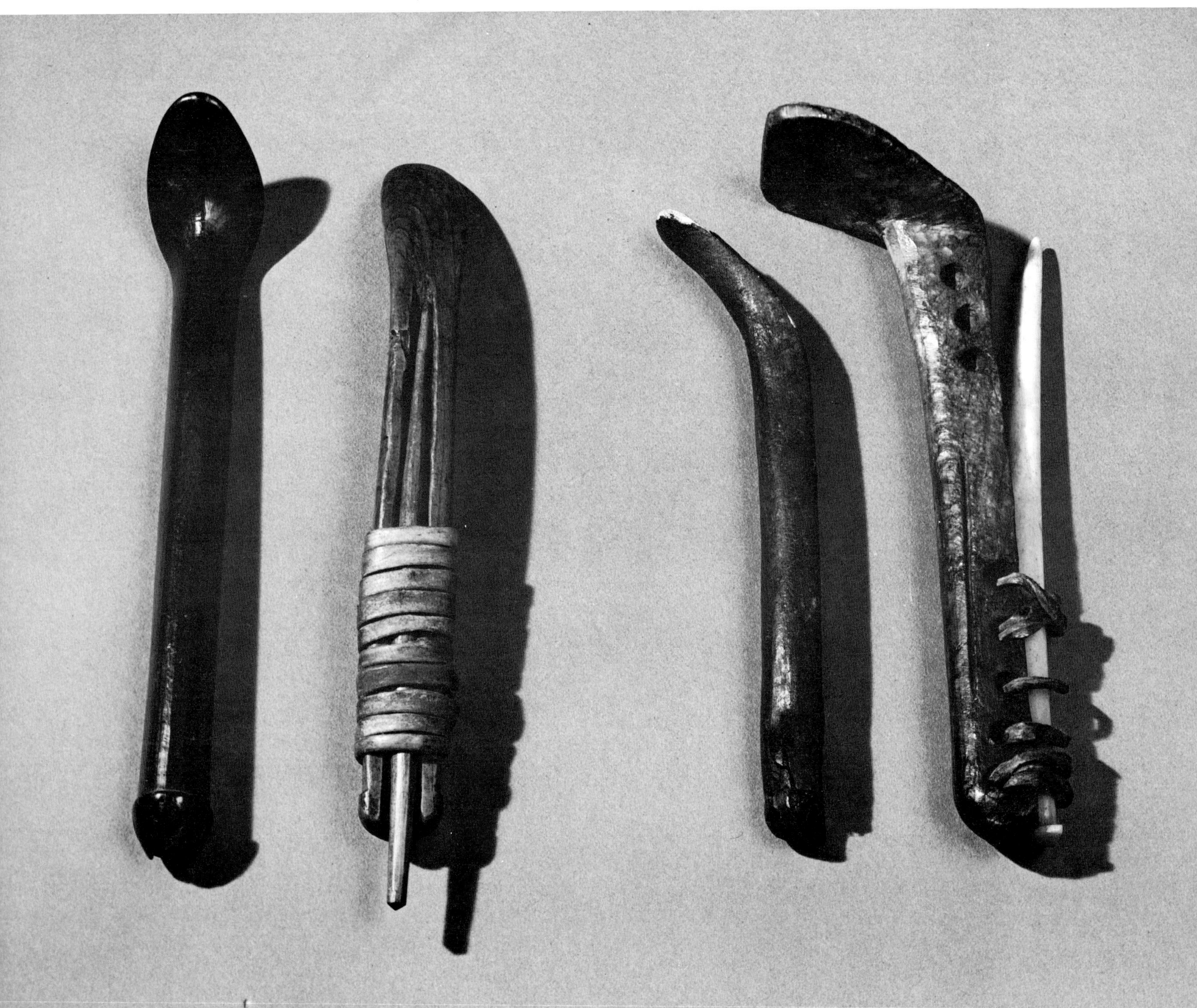

KNIVES

Slate knives with bone handles.

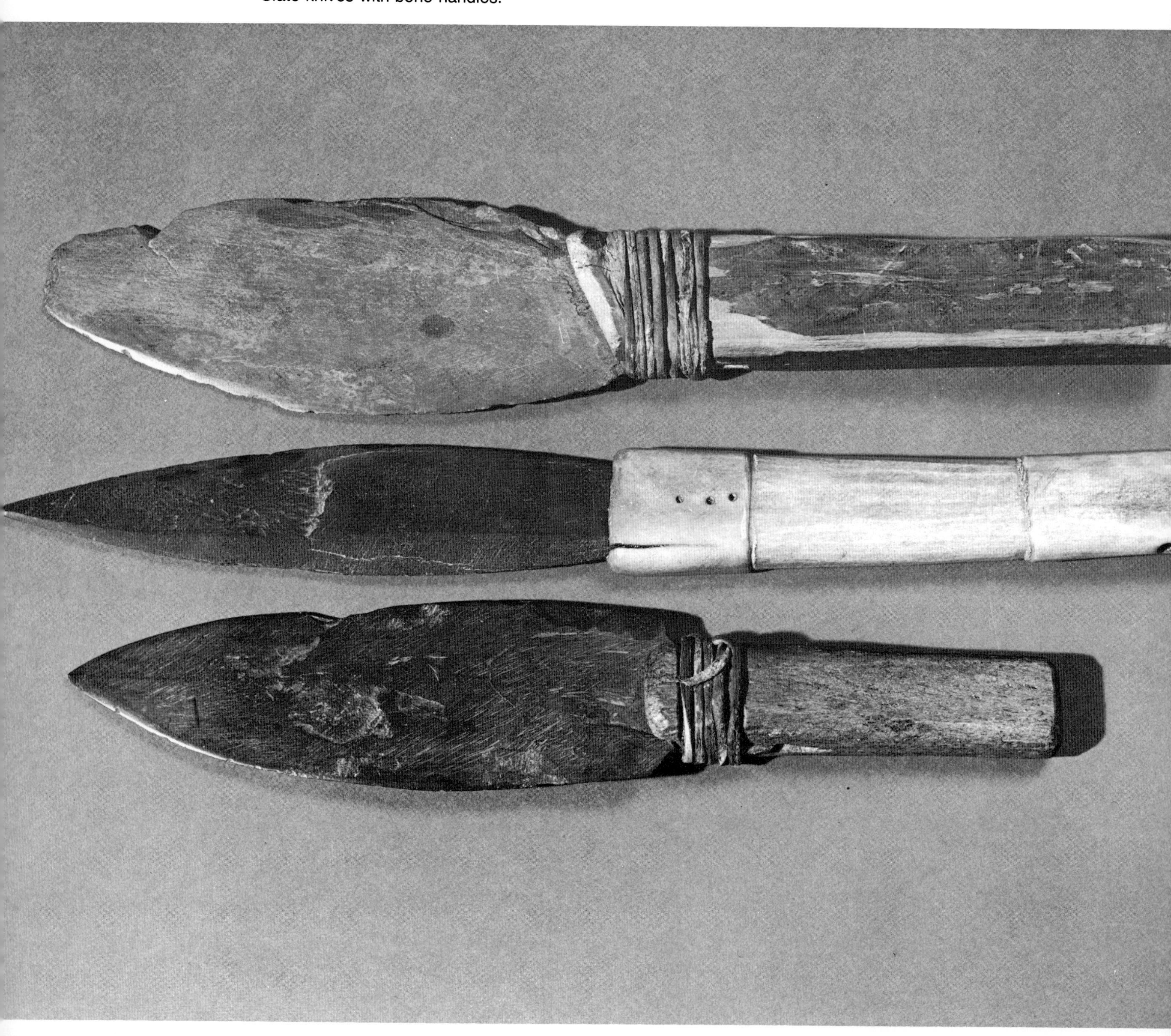

KNIVES

Slate knives with decorative bone handles. The holes in the handles indicate there was sinew lacing at one time to keep the hand from slipping.

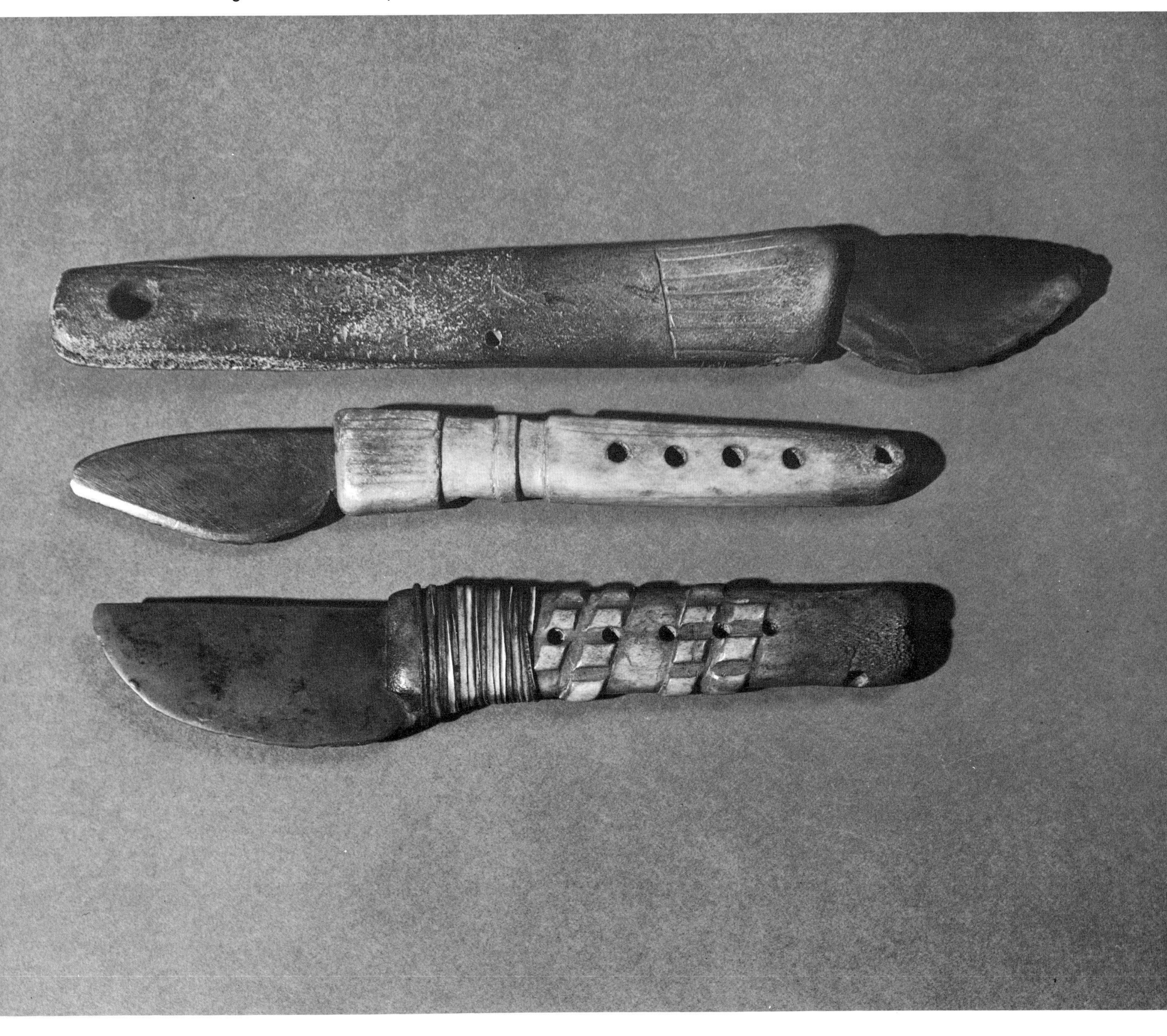

KNIVES

Numbered top to bottom:

1. This bone handle has a flaked stone blade. Blades such as this were generally used as spear points or on lances.

2, 3, & 4. Three slate knives with bone handles. The second handle has lacing holes and etching near the end. The third knife has finger spaces and a serrated blade still noticeable on the bottom of the blade.

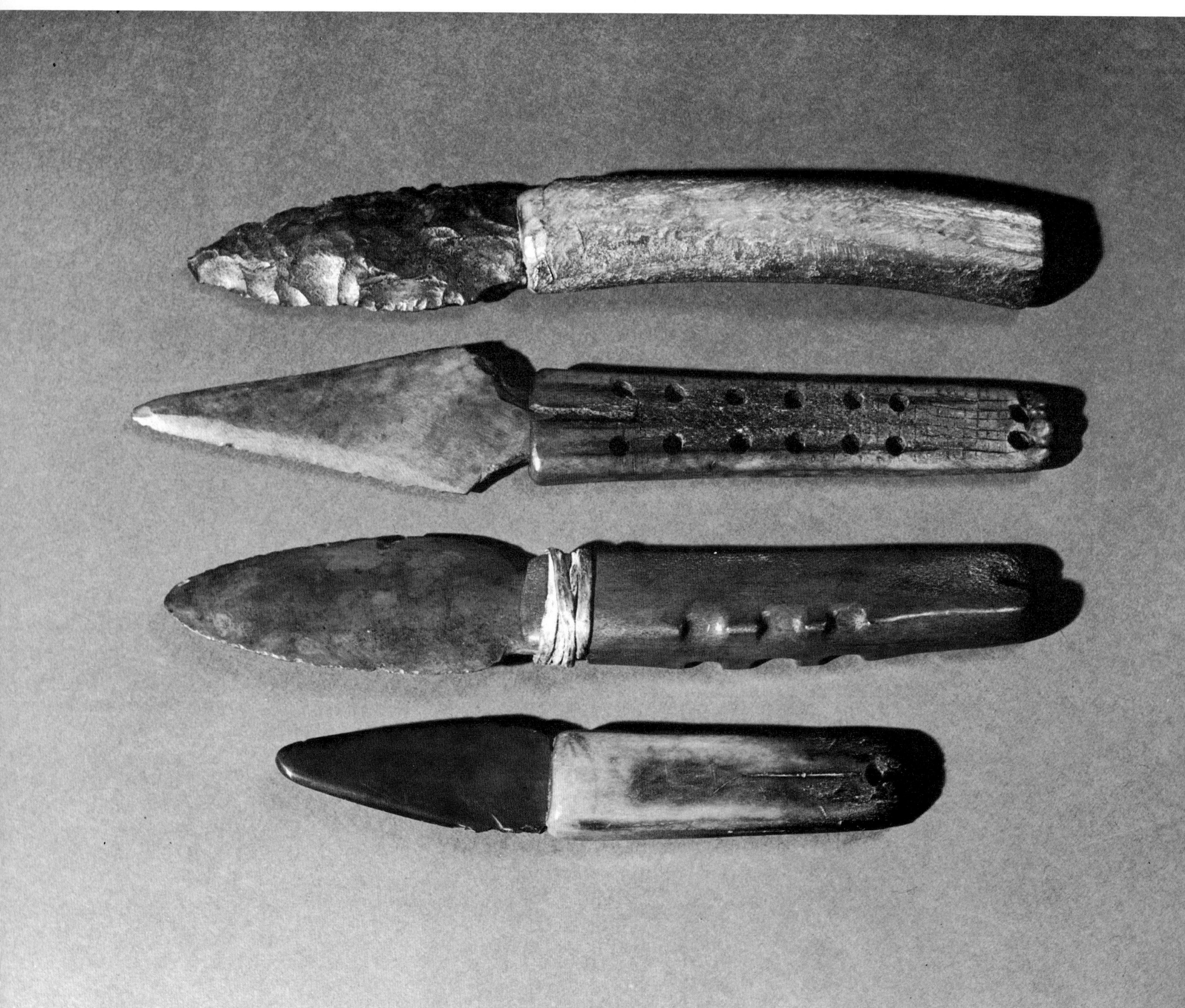

KNIVES

Knives with one beveled side to the blade were known sometimes as crooked knives.
Numbered top to bottom:

1. An ivory handle with a black slate blade. The handle has finger spaces which have three small barbs in each space.
2. An etched ivory handle with finger spaces for a side blade.
3. A bone handle for a side blade.
4. An etched ivory handle with a slate blade fitted into the bone and secured with a cord.

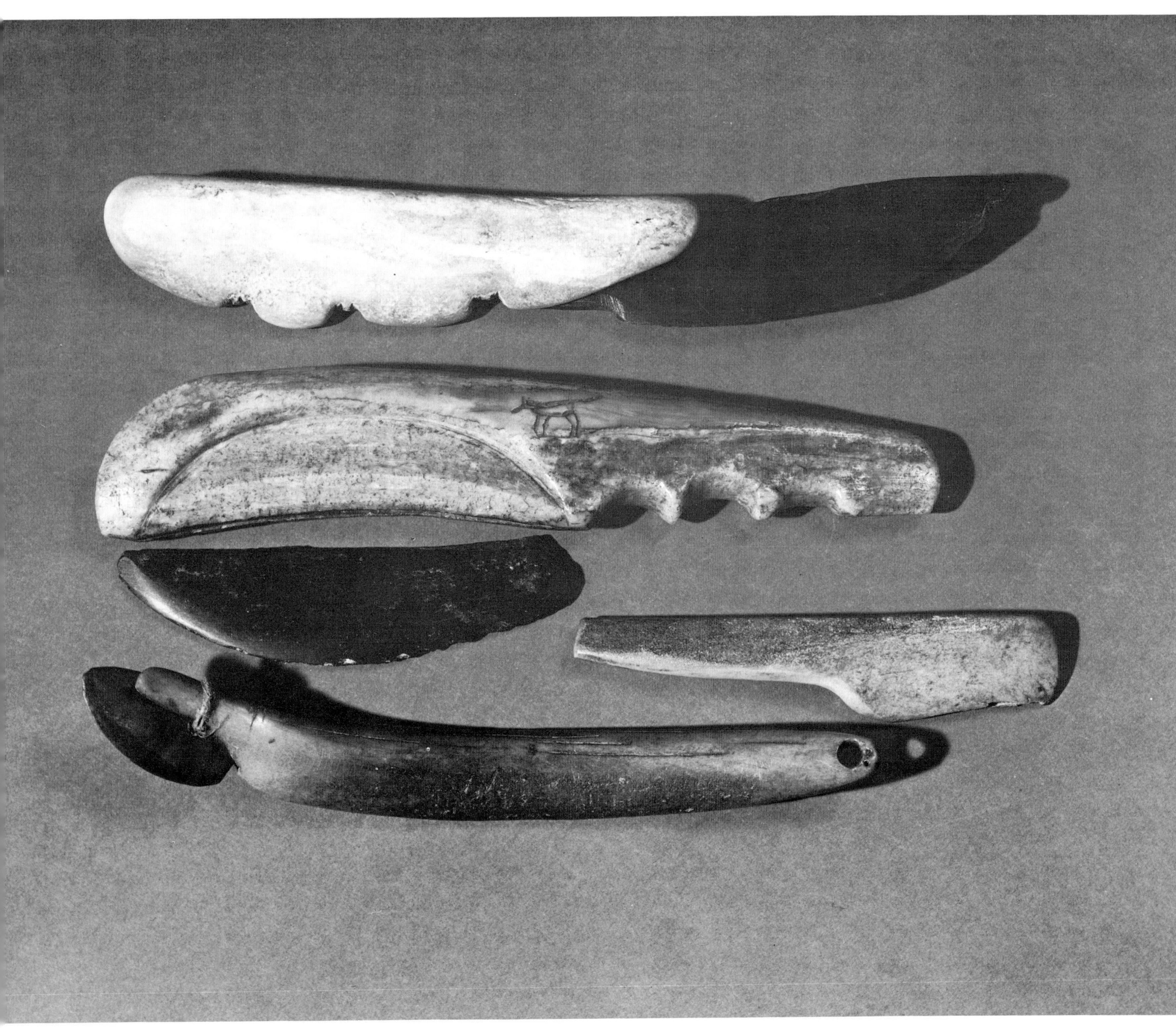

KNIVES

Crudely made small slate knives. The handles are bone except for the one farthest right which is wood, and secured at the point with gut cord. The third knife from the left had a serrated blade.

HANDLES FOR KNIVES

Four are carved for a firm hold the others have holes for lacing to insure a firm grasp.

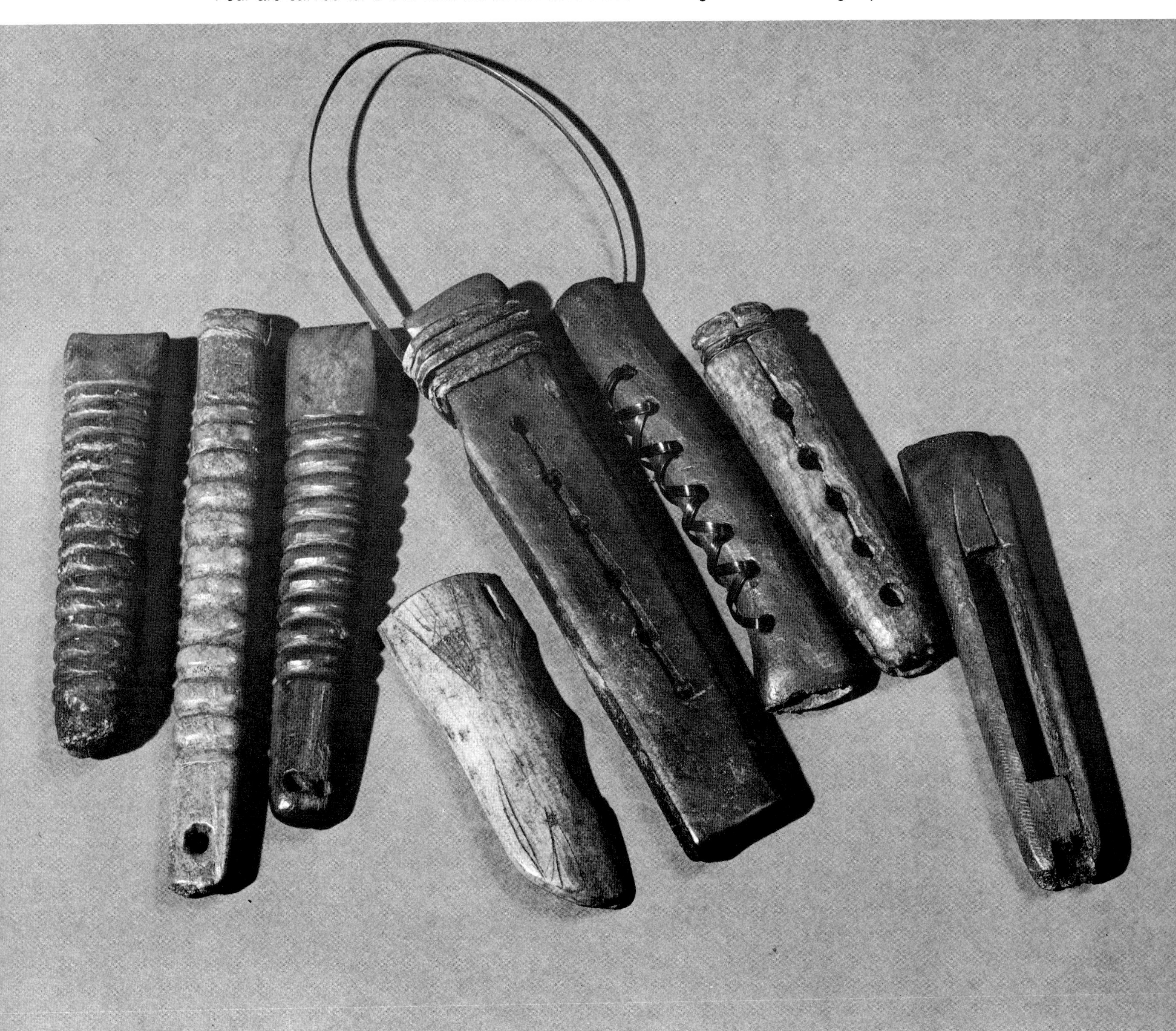

KNIVES

Long handled crooked knives, the first having an antler haft secured to a metal blade by bone pegs and the second, an antler haft secured to a bone blade by metal pegs.

A sharpening tool which has an ivory piece firmly embedded in an antler tip. There are parallel grooves on the ivory running lengthwise. The tying cord is strands of reindeer leg muscle.

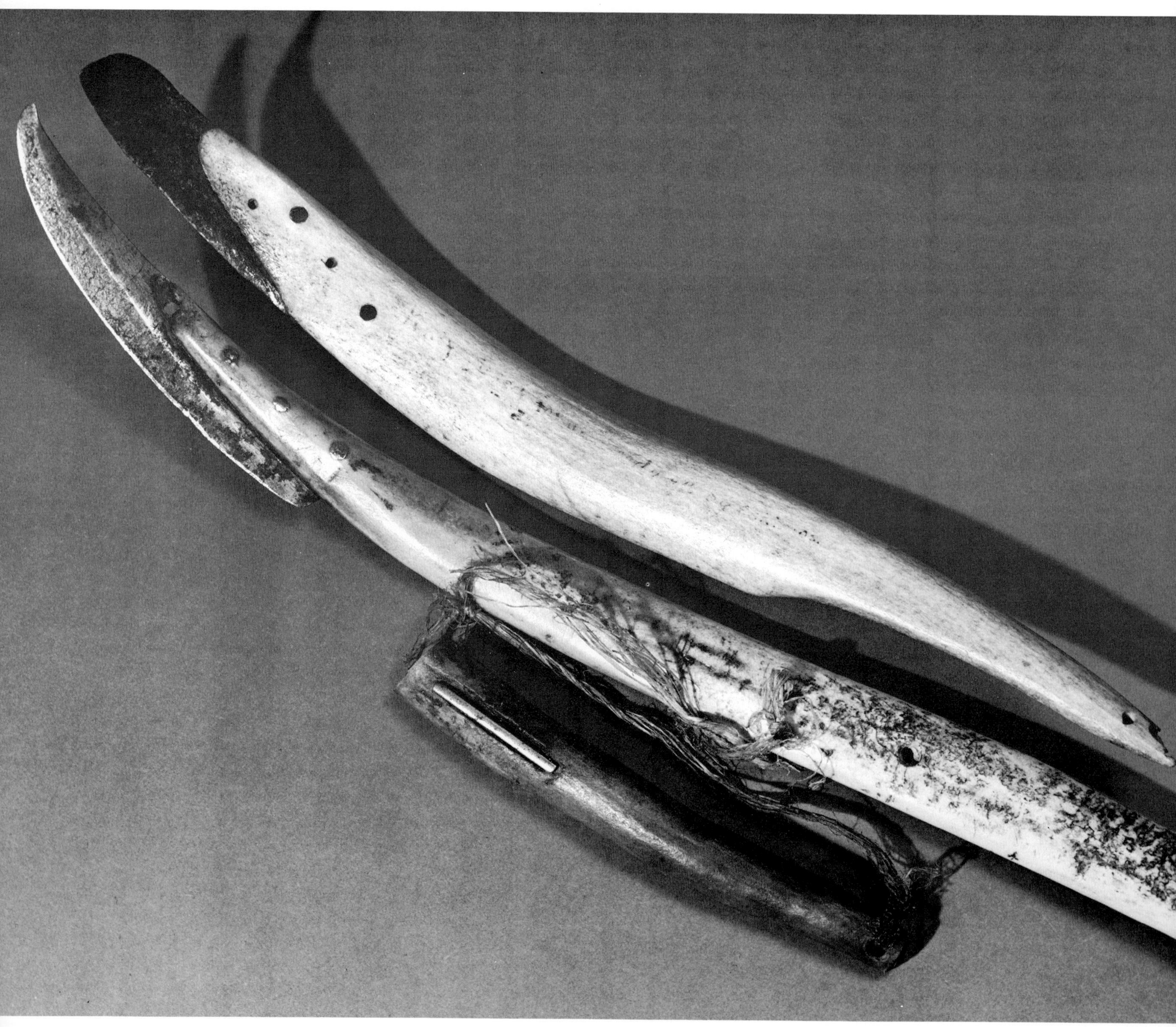

KNIVES

Numbered top to bottom:

1. A broken ivory haft with three bone pegs. The thong is laced through holes in the handle.
2. A bone blade secured to a bone handle with seal thong.
3. A crooked knife with seal thong wrapping. This example shows the characteristic way ends of wrapping were woven through to keep the wrapping intact. The broken blade is stone.
4. A rib bone handle with a metal blade. The wrapping is seal skin.

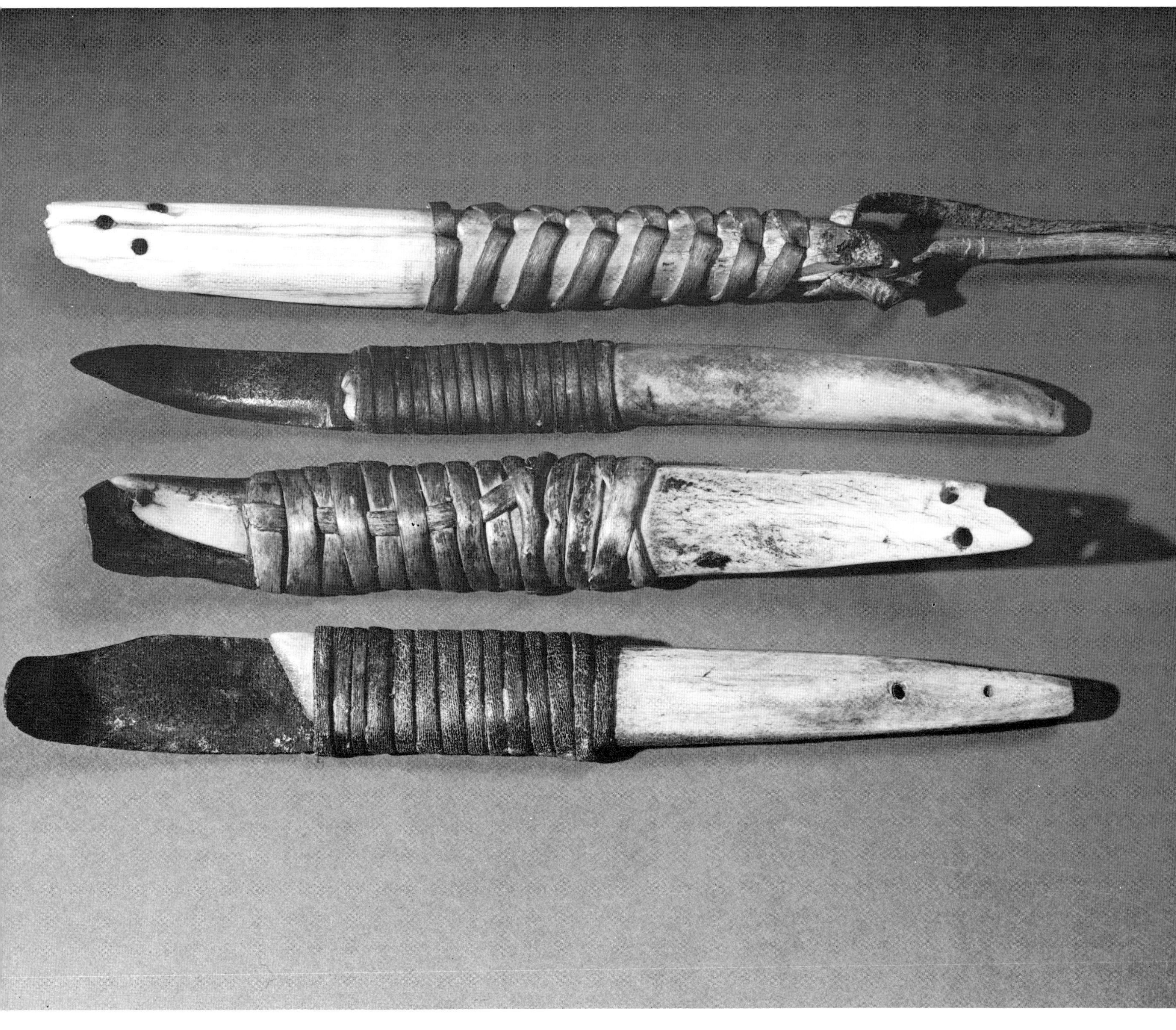

KNIVES

Numbered top to bottom:

Crooked knives were used mainly for whittling and similar work on ivory and bone objects. They were for finer carving.

1. An antler handle for a side blade. The holes were for lacing.
2. A bone handle with a curved metal blade fitted tightly into the bone and secured by a copper peg. Metal blades came much later than the stone.
3. An antler haft holds a metal knife with a considerably long blade turned up slightly at the point. The handle is reinforced with a bone peg inserted above the blade. This knife may also have been used as a saw since there are teeth cut into the edge of the blade on the sharp side.
4. A handle of bone is secured to a metal upward pointed blade by two bone pegs.

LANCE BLADES

The first is bone, the second ivory. These were attached to one end of a spear.

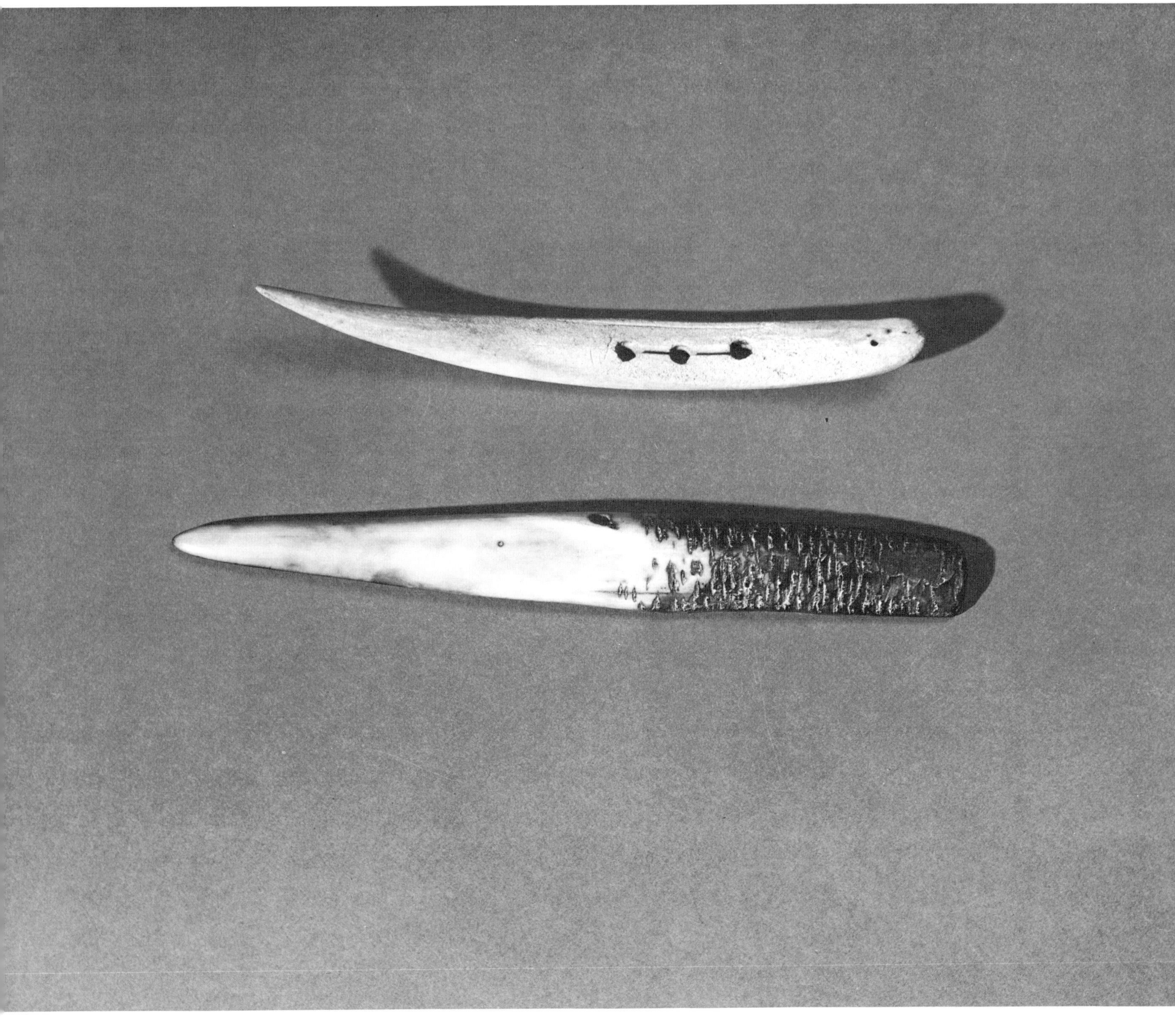

IVORY NET GAUGES

Mesh sticks were used in the manufacture of nets for gauging the size of the mesh. They were used with netting needles and range in size from large to small. They were usually made of bone.

Upper: A walrus tusk gauge. The head has an ivory peg inserted near the point to reinforce the ivory and two holes in the handle for wood inserts to keep it from splitting.

Lower: A decorated ivory head is fastened to a wood handle with seal skin. The handle is two hollowed out pieces of wood fitted together enclosing the long flat handle.

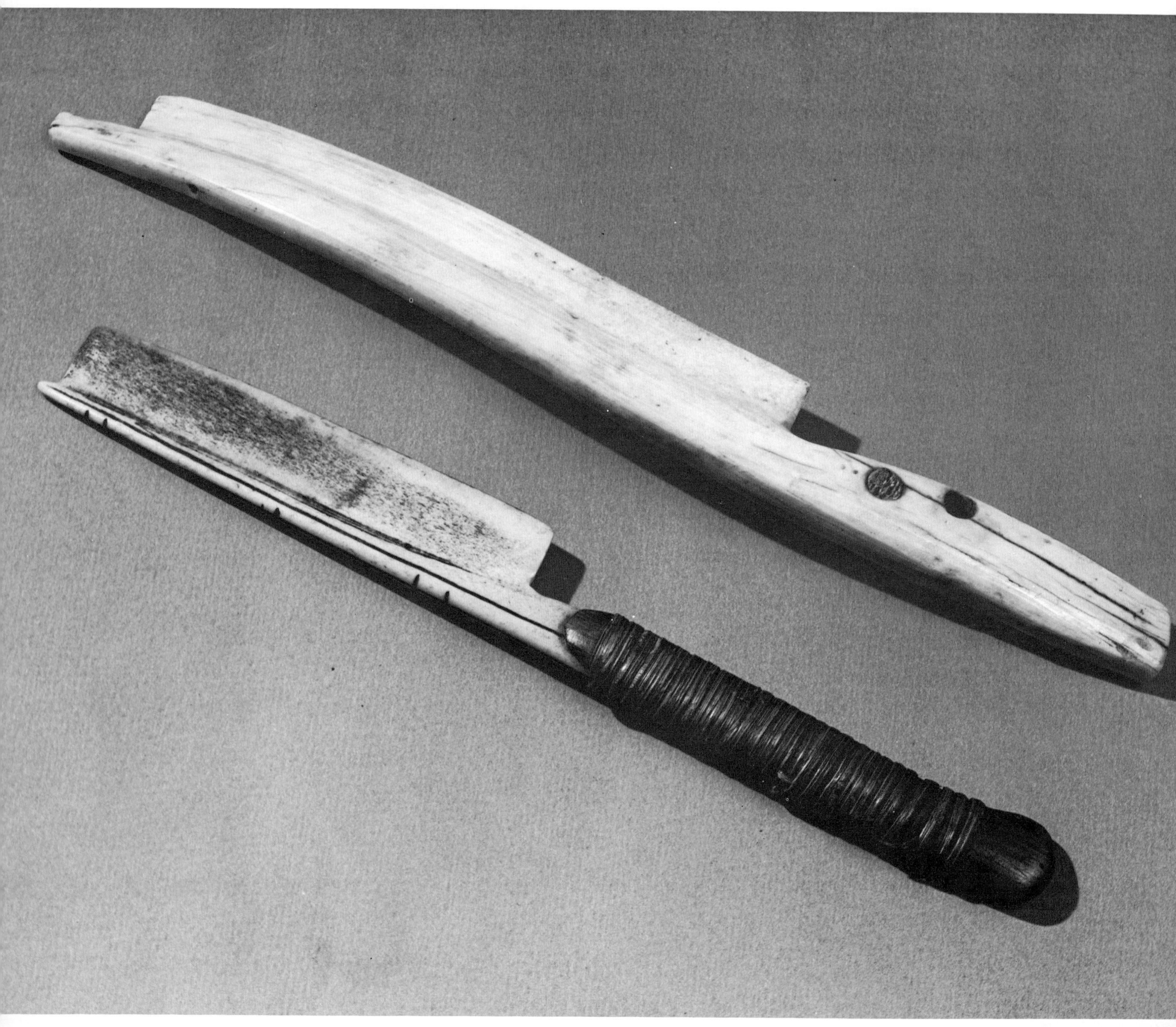

NET GAUGE

A large net gauge made from a walrus tusk. There has been an effort to beautify the handle by grooving it. There are shallow finger spaces on the inside of the handle.

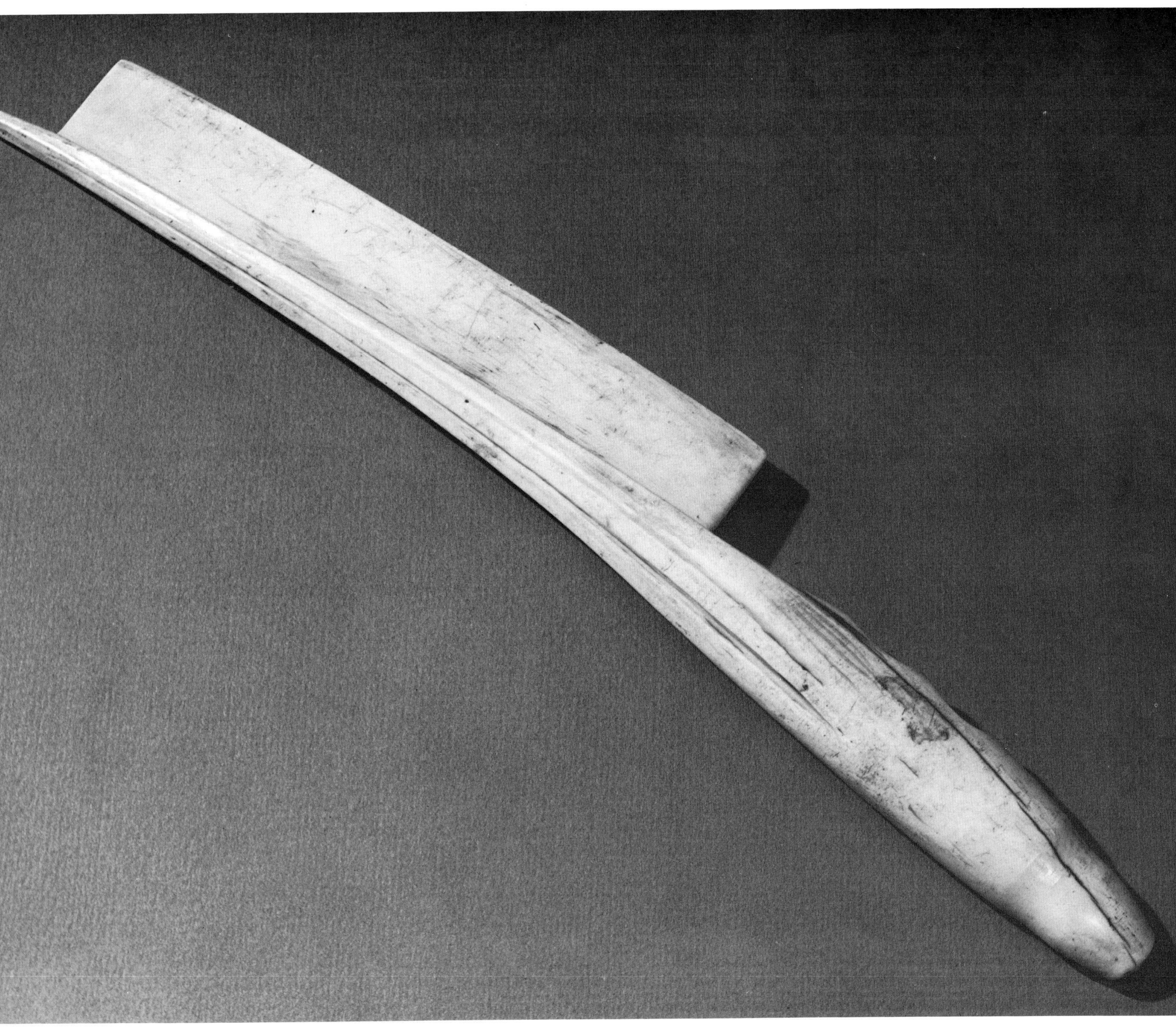

NET GAUGES

Numbered left to right:
1. A bone net gauge. The line on the face probably marks where the twine was to be drawn when making the mesh.
2. A bone gauge head fixed to a wood handle with seal skin.
3. A bone gauge, the head notched at the handle. The head is lashed to the wood with baleen and gut cord.
4. The haft of this gauge was broken and neatly mended by adding a wood replacement securing it with bone pegs and skin wrapping.
5. This bone gauge was mended by pegging it to a wood addition.
6. A neatly made mesh stick with finger spaces carved into the bone handle.

NET GAUGES

Numbered left to right:

1. A net gauge for a large mesh having an ample rounded handle.
2. A whale bone mesh stick with a finger space in the handle.
3. A very neatly made bone gauge with a measuring line on the head, and small grooves in the handle. The handle is etched and whether the grooves are for decoration or to hold wrapping is unknown.
4. A double headed bone gauge with a small and larger head. The larger head has been reinforced and leveled with an ivory peg.
5. A whale bone gauge with grooves on the handle either for decoration or wrapping. There is a seal etched on the handle and several totem signs.

NET GAUGES OF VARIOUS DIMENSIONS

Numbered from left to right:

1. A small bone gauge.
2. A bone gauge probably made from another implement.
3. An ivory gauge mended on either side of the handle by small ivory pegs being inserted into the broken pieces and replaced on the handle.
4. A well made bone gauge with a narrowed haft.
5. A small bone mesh stick with the handle narrowed toward the head.
6. A well worn antler gauge.
7. A bone gauge haft extremely narrowed at the head.

SHUTTLES

Used for making nets; large shuttles for coarse mesh and small shuttles for fine mesh nets. Numbered top to bottom:

1. A long narrow wood shuttle.
2. A wood shuttle.
3. An ivory shuttle similar in design to those found in Japan and Siberia with a rounded top rather than the Eskimo pointed version. The ivory has been carved out to form the sharp tongue.

4 & 6. These two shuttles could almost have been made by the same person they are so similar even to the location of the hole in the center. Number four is ivory and number six is bone.

5. Is a crudely finished shuttle of oak probably part of a foreign box or plank.

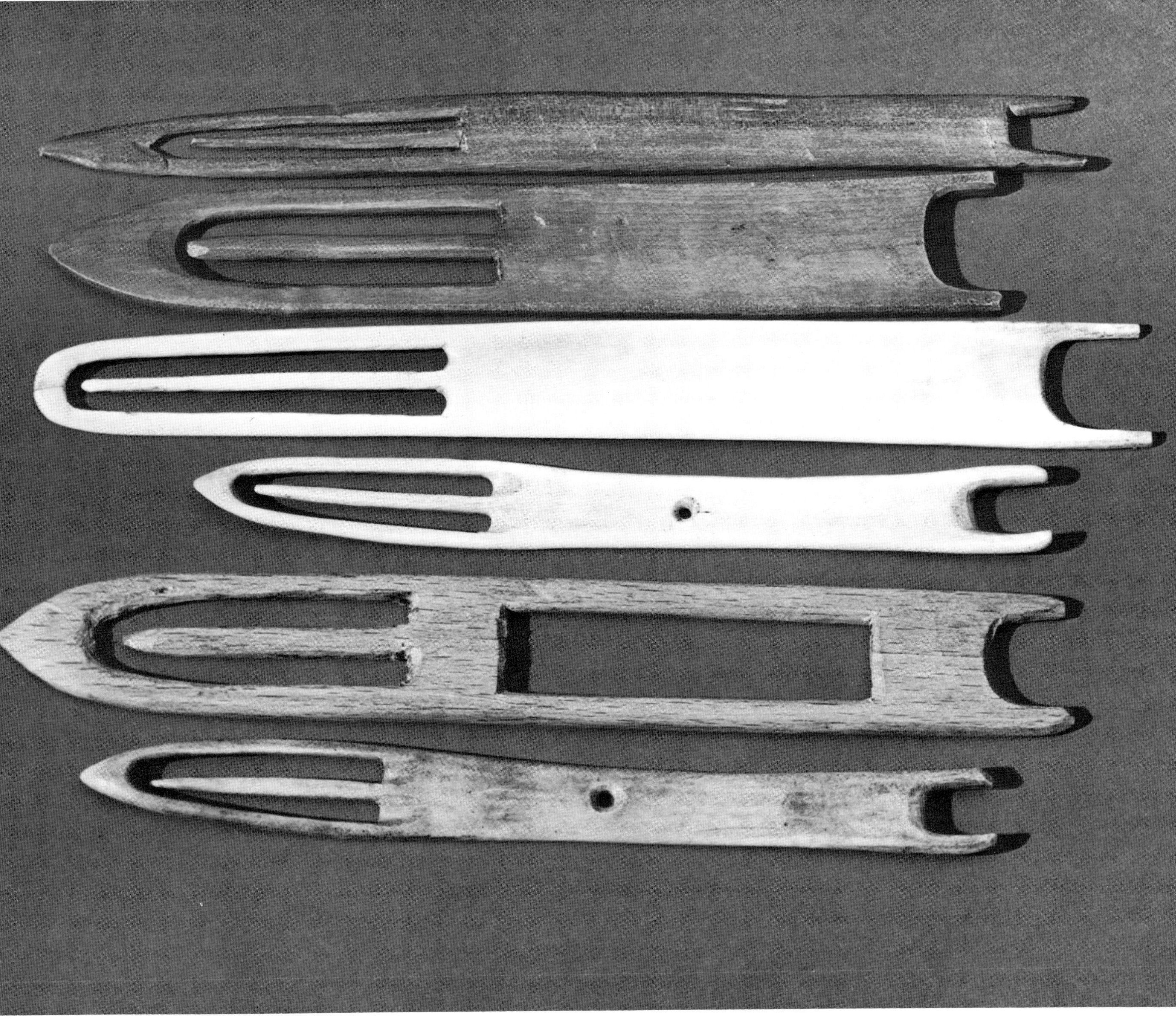

SHUTTLES

Four shuttles used for making nets. These implements differ in shape and size according to the gauge of net being manufactured. The first three shuttles are bone the fourth is antler.

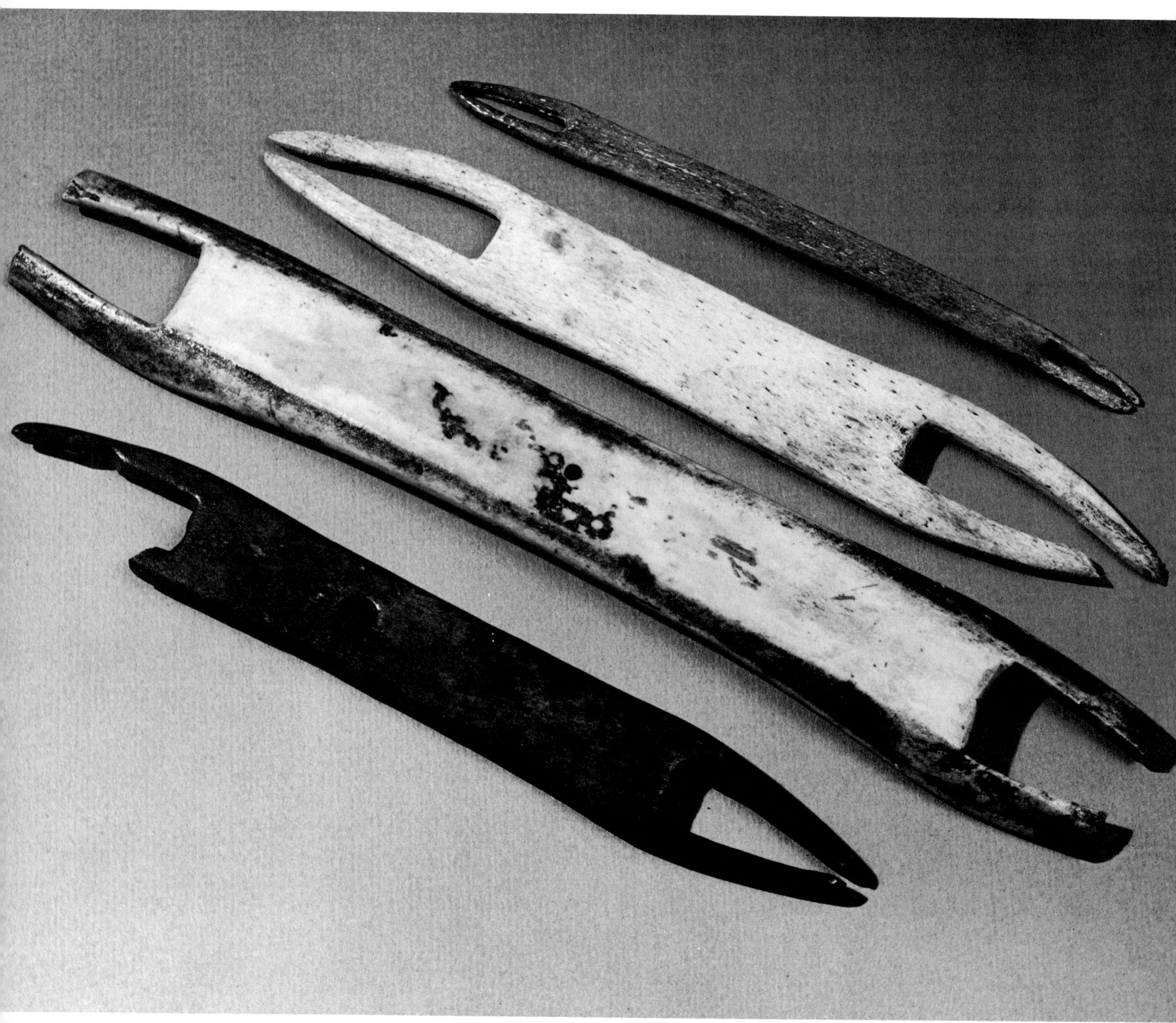

MISCELLANEOUS ITEMS

Numbered top to bottom:

Implements used in net making.

The first three are ivory the fourth is wood with a seal's head on the right side with bead eyes. The figure on the left resembles a fish head with an ivory peg for the eye.

5. Is a bone skin cleaning tool with sharp edges.
6. A bone boot creaser.
7. A bone shuttle for small cord.

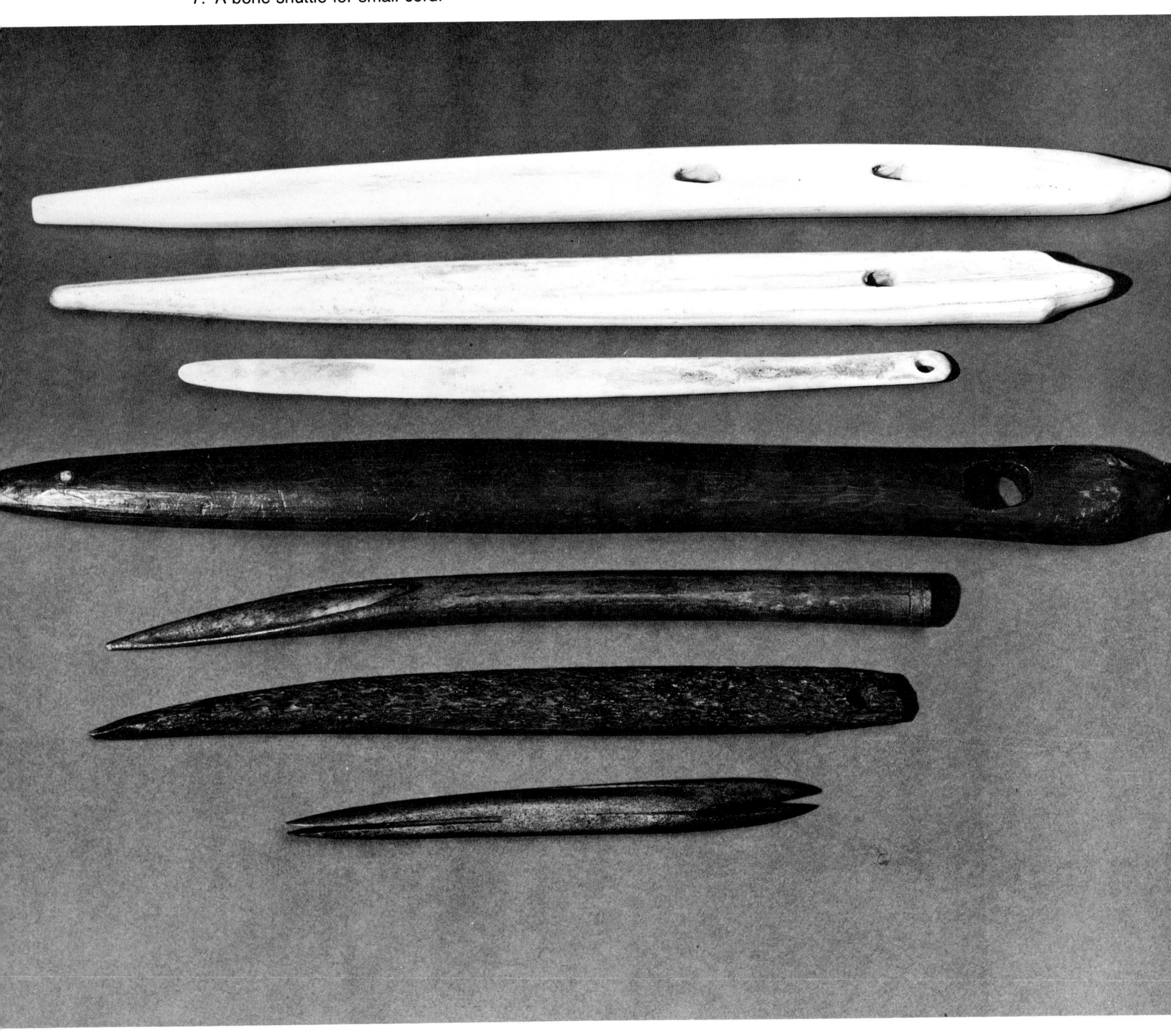

NETTING IMPLEMENTS

Two broken implements which may have been marlin-spikes. The first has two seals on the handle. The second has a bear's head and the handle has been flattened to make the grasp easier.

Marlin spikes were used for tying and slipping meshes when making nets. They were also used when one wished to revise the size of a net when used for another purpose such as reducing a seal net to a fishing net.

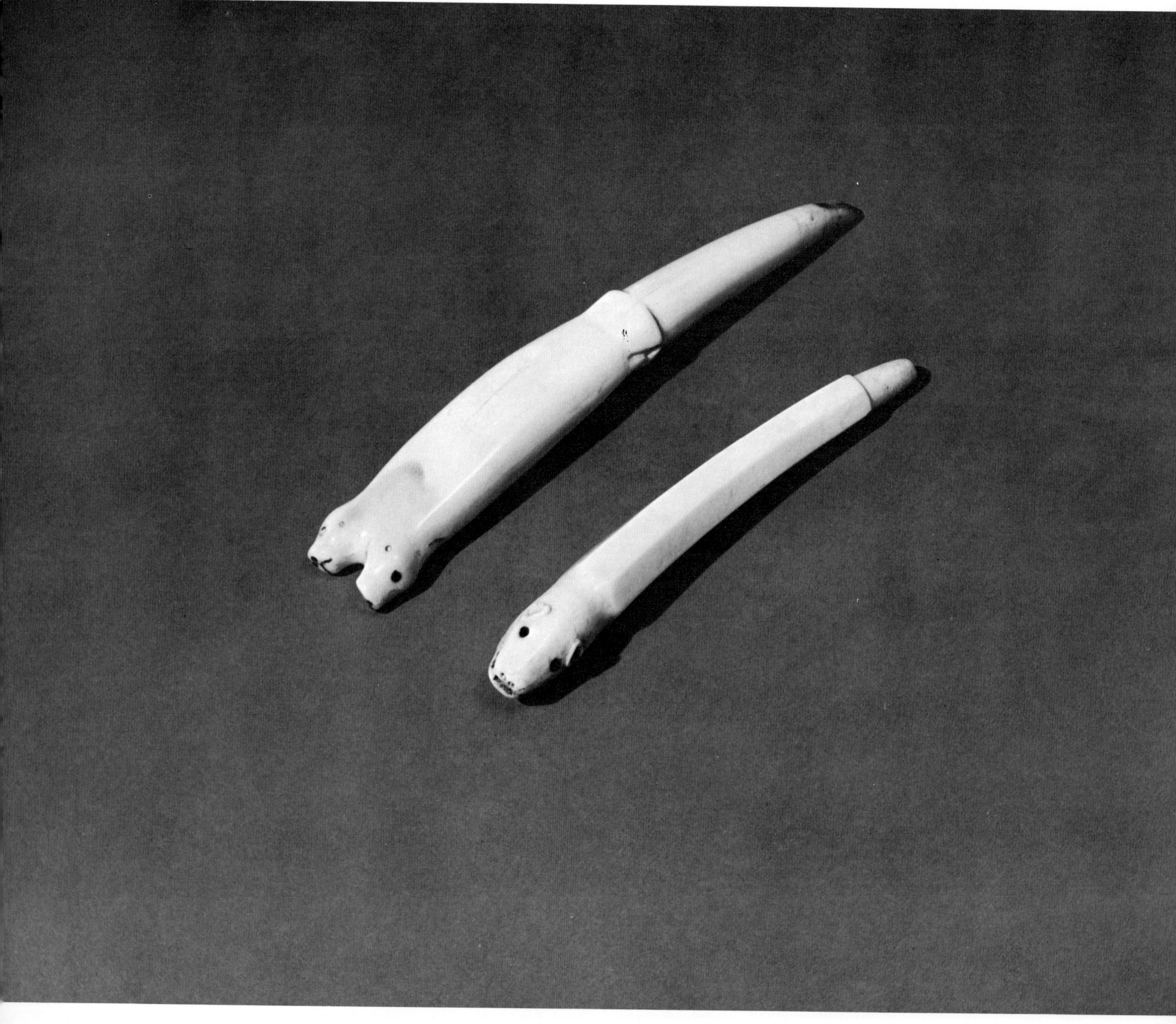

NETTING IMPLEMENTS

This pointed object appears to be a marlin-spike although its use is not certain. The walrus head was part of the handle of another artifact. The two examples are bone.

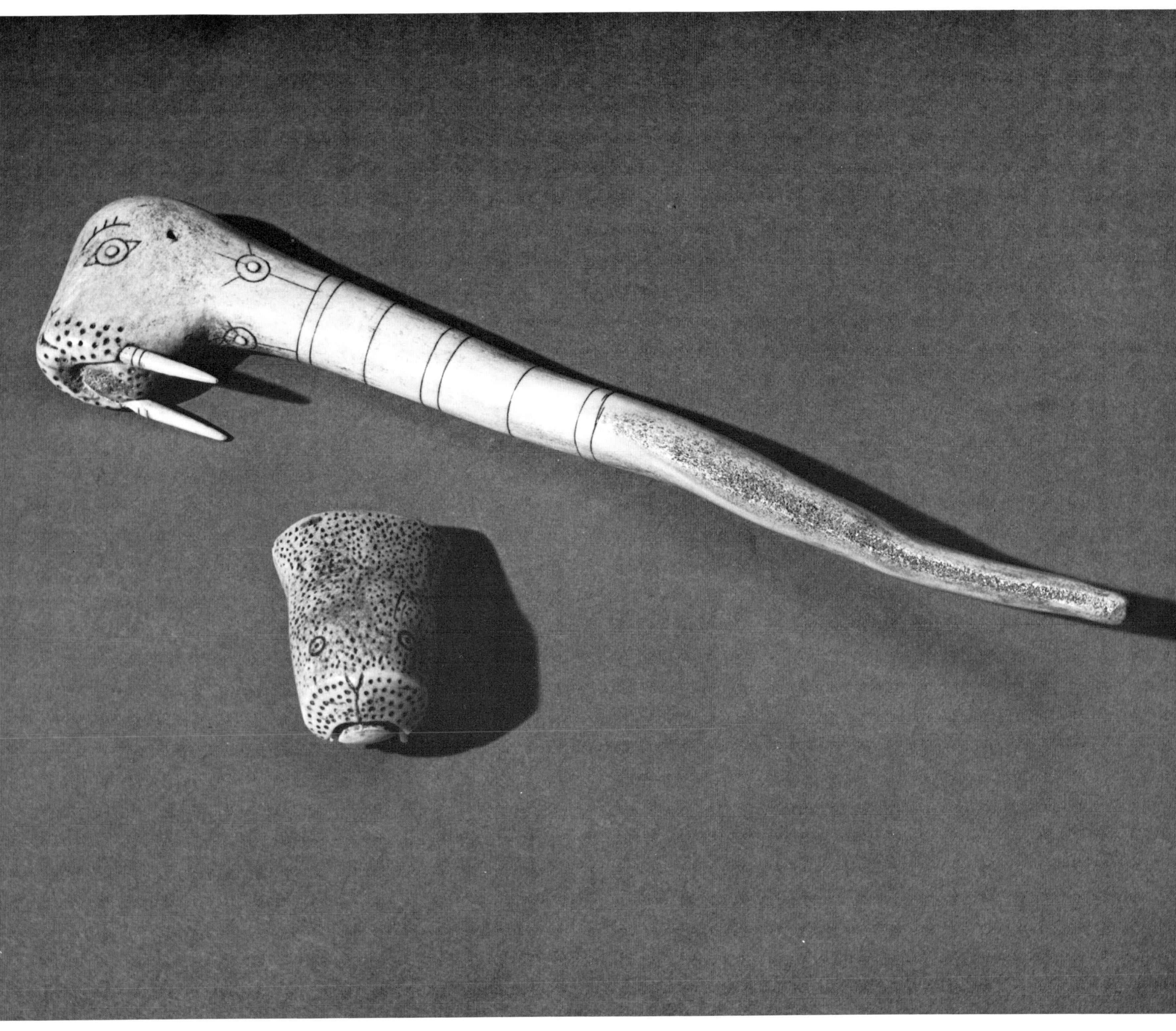

WORK BOX

A large bent wood tool box constructed with a set-in bottom which became secure when the sides were sewn together. The box is a continuous piece of wood, sewn in the back through three ivory bands, with rawhide. The handle is part of an old harpoon head, tied on through holes in the cover. An ivory spur is the catch. The box is grooved on the cover and around the bottom for decoration. The harpoon head used as the handle is a very old style and may have been a fetish belonging to the owner.

ACTUAL SIZE OF BOX SHOWN ON OPPOSITE PAGE

The catch device on the large work box. Note the grooving on the top and bottom of the box for decoration.

WORK BOX

The back of the work box, shown on the preceding page, shows the chamfered edges of the wood, joined together secured with ivory rods and stitching.

ACTUAL SIZE OF THE WORK BOX SHOWN ON THE OPPOSITE PAGE

WORK BOX

A tool box of bent wood in two pieces joined in front and back. The two pieces are sewn together through ivory reinforcements. The bottom was fitted into a groove becoming fixed when the box ends were secured. The cover is held on by rawhide ties in the back and a tie caught by an ivory barb in the front. The ivory handle is tied through two holes in the cover. Decoration consists of grooving around the top and lower part of the box. The stitching is rawhide.

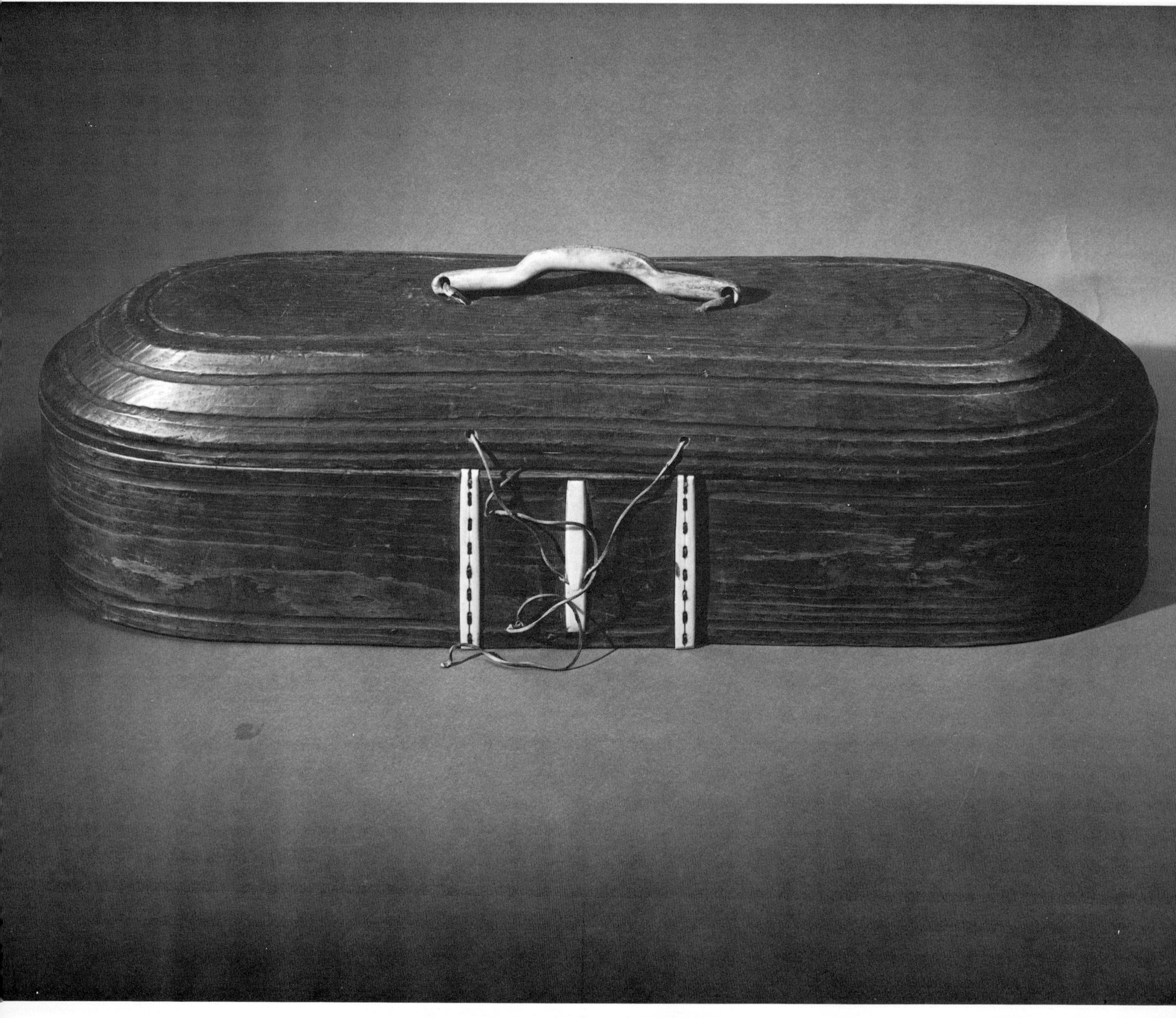

ACTUAL SIZE OF WORK BOX SHOWN ON OPPOSITE PAGE

A detail of the reinforcing bands, the stitching and the barbed fastener. The fastener is not stitched into the wood but attached on the inside of the box with pegs through eyelets.

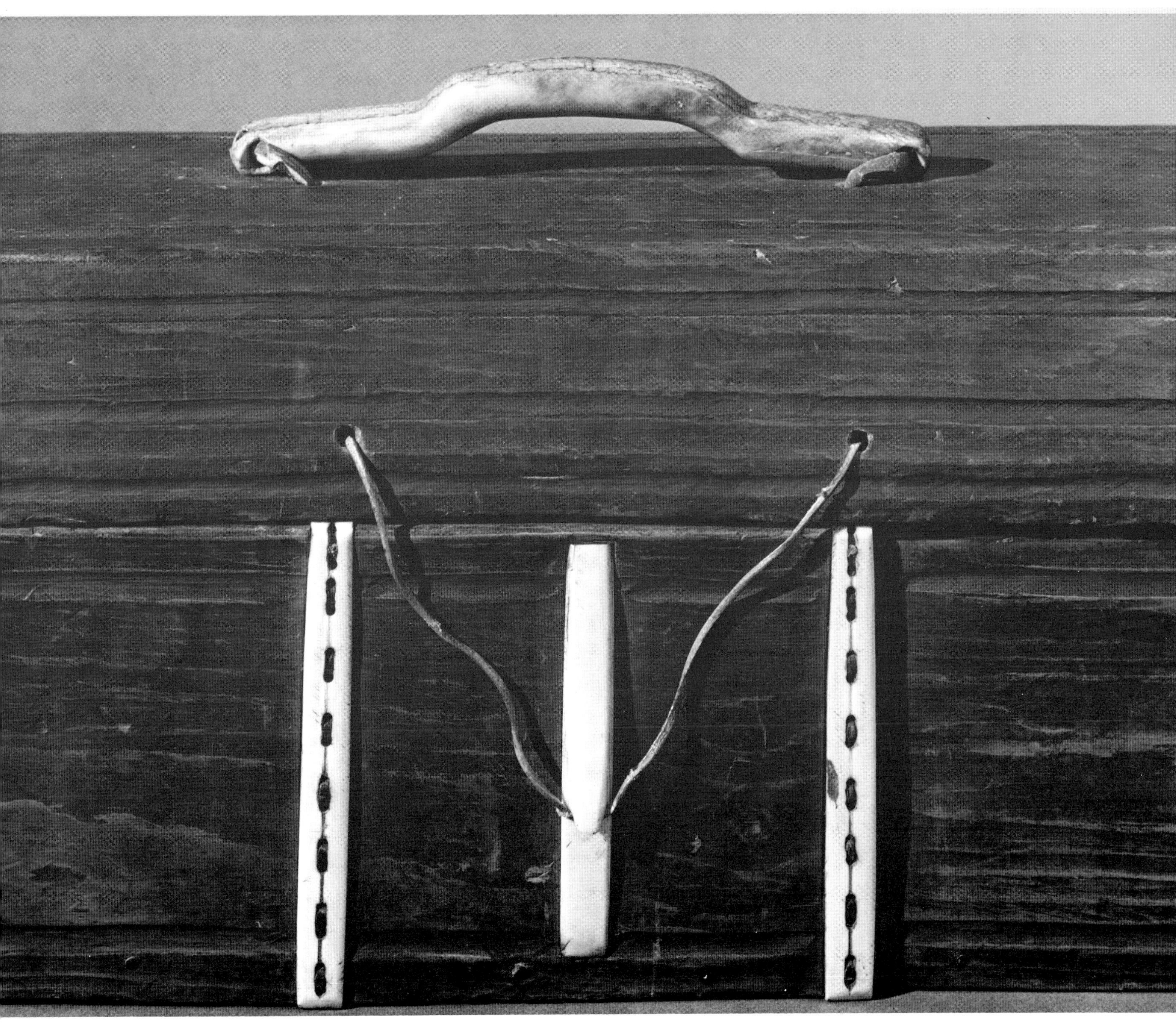

WORK BOX

An old tool box showing extensive repair with baleen strips. The handle is part of the repair material knotted in the middle.

ACTUAL SIZE OF WORK BOX SHOWN ON THE OPPOSITE PAGE

A detail showing extensive repair to an old tool box. The bottom is set into a groove and the sides drawn tight and sewn with baleen. The bottom of this box is slightly rounded. The catch is an ivory barb sewn onto the box with rawhide. The cover having been splintered or worn out was repaired with baleen sewn through joining the parts together.

TABLE OF CONTENTS BOOK I

PERSONAL AND DOMESTIC APPURTENANCES

A.

B.

C.

D.

P.

Q.

R.

S.

T.

U.

V.

W.

X.

Y.

Z.

TABLE OF CONTENTS BOOK II

SURVIVAL, HUNTING AND FISHING IMPLEMENTS

A.

B.

C.

D.

E.

F.

G.

H.

I.

J.

K.

L.

M.

N.

O.

P.

Q.

R.

S.

T.

U.

V.

W.

X.

Y.

Z.

Thiry, Paul, 1904-
Eskimo artifacts : designed for use / Paul and Mary Thiry -- 1st ed. -- Seattle : Superior Pub. Co., c1977.
337 p. : ill. (some col.) ; 32 cm.
"A Salisbury Press book."
Includes indexes.
ISBN 0-87564-016-8

1. Eskimos--Art--Pictorial works. 2. Eskimos--Implements--Pictorial works. I. Thiry, Mary, joint author. II. Title.